THE NEW (AB)NORMAL

Reshaping Business and Supply Chain Strategy Beyond Covid-19

Yossi Sheffi

MIT CTL MEDIA

Cambridge, Mass.

MIT CTL Media, 77 Massachusetts Avenue,
Building E40, Cambridge, MA 02139

This book was set in FreightText Pro and Montserrat by
MIT CTL Media. Produced in the United States of America.
Front cover image by Alex Stemmer.

Published 2020
ISBN-13: 978-1-7357661-1-9

Library of Congress Cataloging-in-Publication Data

Sheffi, Yossi, 1948-
The new (ab)normal : reshaping business and supply chain
strategy beyond Covid-19 / Yossi Sheffi.
Includes bibliographic references.

Contents

PREFACE

In early 2020, I was working on my fifth book (on the history of innovation in supply chain management) when Covid-19 struck. As the infection spread and the lockdowns started, it became increasingly apparent that Covid-19 was not going to miraculously disappear. Instead, it was going to have a tremendous impact on people's lives, livelihoods, and the global economy. My book on the history of innovation would have to wait—one of the biggest revolutions in supply chain history was raging before my eyes.

Much has been written about the personal stories of Covid-19 victims, how scientists raced to understand and treat the disease, and how governments did (or did not) take steps to protect their citizens. Less has been written about the impact of Covid-19 on the fabric of the global economy and how companies had to rapidly and radically change their operations in the face of disrupted supply, hoarding, government mandates, and the desperate need for medical supplies. This book looks at what businesses have done during the chaos of the pandemic, and what they are likely to do in the coming months and years to ensure they survive the virus and thrive afterwards.

Before the pandemic, when people asked my wife what I did, her reply about my work on supply chains confused them. The average person was simply unaware of the vast global web of manufacturing, warehousing, and transportation companies that bring a wealth of consumer products to the nearest store shelf or front doorstep. At some level, that lack of awareness is a testament to how well these supply chains usually function: The fact that the goods people wanted were almost always sitting on the store shelf when they wanted them made it easy to take for granted all the hard work it took to put them there. When the virus simultaneously disrupted suppliers, operations, and consumer demand, everyone became acutely aware of the existence of supply chains and how they were straining to cope with the challenge. My wife did not have to explain anymore.

From Pandemic to Potential

The book begins with a look at how companies fought to mend the global economic fabric even as the virus ripped more holes in it. Although Part 1, "What Happened," focuses on how supply chains handled the pandemic in the spring of 2020, this book is not a history of the pandemic itself. The other five parts of the book examine both the near-term effects of the ongoing pandemic and the likely impacts of the pandemic on supply chains and businesses in the coming years. As with the 1918 flu pandemic, Covid-19 is already creating further waves of infections and impacts in different regions of the world, creating a whack-a-mole challenge for business leaders and, especially, supply chain executives. Ultimately, some companies will die, some will survive, and others will thrive.

Although, as the Danish physicist Niels Bohr purportedly quipped, "Forecasting is difficult, especially about the future," this book attempts to ground its predictions in science, history, and the timeless structural elements of how businesses must function. The book incorporates interviews with company executives to show how diverse industries are thinking about the pandemic and the future. Many ideas and recommendations flow from analysis of the changes already wrought by the virus, the value propositions of various available technologies, how companies have managed previous disruptions, and many frameworks in risk management and supply chain management.

Accelerating the Demise of the Unhealthy

At some level, Covid-19 did to businesses what it did to people—primarily harming or killing those who had pre-existing health conditions. The virus accelerated the demise of people and companies that were in poor health but might have lived much longer had times been better. This sad fact began motivating people and companies to improve their health. For example, record numbers of people quit smoking.

Sustaining the health of a company means fighting the disruptive effects of the pandemic on suppliers, operations, and customers. Part 2, "Living with Uncertainty," uses a supply chain risk management lens—derived from two of my previous books, *The Resilient Enterprise* (2005) and *The Power of Resilience* (2015)—to show how companies create a corporate immune system that can quickly recognize and manage disruptions associated with pandemics, natural disasters, and other threats.

The New (Ab)Normal

Whereas standard disruption mitigation efforts focus on getting back to normal, the ongoing pandemic is creating a new normal in life, work, and education—covered in Part 3, "Adjustment Required." Ongoing consumer fear about contagion (and government mandates to curtail the spread of the virus) mean that the health of businesses in many industries such as retail, hospitality, entertainment, sports, and education all depend on creating "safe zones" for workers and customers. Another new normal is working from home, which will enable workers to live anywhere and enable companies to recruit talent from anywhere. Education, especially higher education, faces a major disruption (and major opportunity) that upends the high-cost model of in-person education in favor of online or hybrid education. Regrettably, one trend accentuated by Covid-19 is the growing gap between rich and poor—the new normal will be more stratified.

Accelerating the Adoption of Advancements

Many elements of the book (especially in Part 4, "Supply Chains for the Future") show how the virus accelerated preexisting trends in technology adoption by creating the need for distancing between people, avoiding infected surfaces, working from home, and not traveling. Technologies such as the Internet of Things (IoT), artificial intelligence (AI), real-time data analytics, cutting edge optimization, data visualization, and digitization provide visibility into remote portions of supply chains as well as into inventory on the move, and they also enable contactless, paperless operations. Automation and robotics help companies handle surges in demand and maintain productivity in sparsely populated offices and factories. Adoption of technologies for doing more from home (e.g., e-commerce, telecommuting, and online education) surged on fears of infection and government stay-at-home mandates. Although all these technologies were used to deal with the immediate impacts of Covid-19, the technologies also have long-term benefits for the performance of supply chains and businesses.

But the Digital Cannot Exist Without the Physical

Despite the push to make everything digital, much of the world and daily life remains physical. The food we eat, the clothes we wear, the medicines we take, the home appliances we use, the vehicles we drive, and so on all depend on physical products made from physical materials that are physically moved and delivered, often over long distances. There's no app that could ever replace toilet paper, but there are apps to help us find scarce supplies of it.

Covid-19 made clear we cannot simply turn off the economy and all shelter in place. Someone somewhere must still make and deliver the daily necessities (and luxuries) of life. Someone somewhere must still make and deliver the huge volumes of healthcare-related supplies required to treat the sick and prevent the uncontrolled spread of the disease. Civilization depends on supply chains to convert the bounty of the planet into the products we need and then deliver those products to 7.8 billion human beings at a price they can afford. When a virus, a government edict, or a recession hits hard, it tests the people and processes that keep the physical side of civilization running.

One of the biggest "somewheres" in physical supply chains was China, which was the epicenter of the pandemic: The first to be disrupted and the first to recover. Part 5, "Of Politics and Pandemics," talks about the potentially growing trend of companies leaving China (or other offshore supplier locations) and why it may not be as extensive or as beneficial as it seems from media conjectures or political rhetoric. As billions join the middle class around the world, companies will find they need suppliers, operations, and sales outlets around the world.

The Future: A New Roaring '20s?

Fundamentally, this book is about businesses trying to create a better future despite the very uncertain times, a point which is emphasized in Part 6, "The Next Opportunities." Although much has been said of the surge in profits for giant companies (e.g., Amazon, Walmart, and Target) and the damage done to small businesses by the virus, the accelerating trends in technology can actually level the playing field between small and large companies. Nimble small businesses are using a growing array of off-the-shelf cloud computing and mobile apps to deploy sophisticated technologies in their supply chains and customer interfaces.

What was clear in the research and interviews for this book was the core role of flexibility and agility in managing both the chaos of early 2020 and the pivot toward the changed future (Chapters 3, 4, and 25). Supply chains may have been strained to the breaking point by both the contagion of the virus and the contagion of breathless media messages that fomented consumer panic. However, many companies and their supply chains really did rise to the occasion to make masks, sanitizer, ventilators, and a host of sought-after and hoarded consumer products. Despite an unprecedented upheaval in the structure and quantities of the demand for food, the food supply chain held.

Covid-19 proved that we are all dependent on each other. That revelation scared some toward trying to retreat into a fantasy world of national self-sufficiency. In contrast, those familiar with supply chains knew the potential power of all the interconnecting pieces to do almost anything if one connected the right pieces and synchronized their activities. Thus, all those interdependencies provide an unparalleled opportunity to serve the needs of humanity even when those needs shift dramatically. Ultimately, this book focuses on how companies can improve the ways they create, nurture, and manage these interdependencies (i.e., supply chains) in order to thrive.

Thanks

Unlike any of my previous books, this book was written while the events on which it focuses were unfolding. Despite the compressed timeframe and the constantly changing environment, the book came to fruition. This was only possible owing to the help of an incredibly dedicated team. First and foremost, my thanks to Andrea and Dana Meyer, the team behind Working Knowledge®. They were responsible for researching and organizing the information, writing and editing drafts, and—most importantly—served as a tough sounding board for ideas and approaches to the coverage.

The marketing and communications team at the MIT Center for Transportation & Logistics helped in multiple ways. Dan McCool was a tough editor who made valuable suggestions, as did Ken Cottrill. Dan was also responsible for designing the look of the pages, redoing my PowerPoint figures as EPS files, and for typesetting the text into an ePub. Samantha Varney made sure that all the references were formatted correctly and, together with Emily Fagan, researched and organized the process of self-publishing. Arthur Grau handled production management and cover design. Many people gave the book a last going-over. They include Andrea and Dana Meyer; Samantha Varney, who also recruited her sister, Mackenzie, for the job; Bonnie Borthwick; and, as always, Dan McCool. They are all first-rate, dedicated professionals and it has been a delight to work with them all.

Finally, my deepest thanks to Anat, my wife of 51 years, who supported me throughout the grueling five months that it took to research, organize, write, and edit the book. Incredibly, on a last read-through, after five separate experienced writers and editors read and proofread the manuscript, she still found errors.

The book benefited from interviews with several executives who were generous with their time when they all had many other burning issues to worry about:

Daniel Biran, Vice President, Security, Biogen

Ralf Busche, Senior Vice President, Global Supply Chain Strategy & Management, BASF Group

Mike Duffy, CEO, C&S Wholesale Grocers

Lorne Darnell, Founder and Chairman, FreightVerify

Jeff Fleck, Senior Vice President – Chief Supply Chain Officer for the Consumer Products Group, Georgia-Pacific

Dennis Flynn, Senior Director, Supply Chain and Inventory Management, Walmart eCommerce

Elyssa Kotzen, Co-Founder and COO, New England Country Mart

Jeff Kotzen, Co-Founder and CEO, New England Country Mart

Stefan Lazarevic, General Manager, NCR Serbia & EMEA External Affairs Director

Nicole Murphy, Senior Vice President, Global Manufacturing & Technical Operations, Biogen

Peter Puype, Vice President of Global Supply Chain, Biogen

Heather Ostis, Vice President of Supply Chain, Delta Air Lines

Rich Pirrotta, Chief Revenue Officer, FreightVerify

Karl Siebrecht, Co-Founder & CEO, Flexe

Meri Stevens, Worldwide Vice President, Consumer Health Supply Chain and Deliver, Johnson & Johnson

Lynn Torrel, Chief Procurement and Supply Chain Officer, Flex

Bindiya Vakil, CEO, Resilinc

Dave Wheeler, Chief Operating Officer, New Balance

Marija Zivanovic-Smith, Senior Vice President, Corporate Marketing, Communications, and External Affairs, NCR

My deepest thanks to them all. Naturally, all errors, misquotes, and mistakes are my responsibility.

Yossi Sheffi
September 2020

PART 1
WHAT HAPPENED

"Es ist ernst." ("This is serious.")

—Angela Merkel, Chancellor of Germany
and PhD in quantum chemistry, in a (rare)
TV address to the German nation,
March 18, 2020[1]

The dawn of 2020 saw the arrival of one of the darkest black swans in modern history: a disease infectious enough to spread rapidly around the world but benign enough to make some think, "It's just the flu," and "It will just disappear." If Covid-19 had caused victims to erupt in the glowing green pustules favored by Hollywood apocalypse movies, then leaders would have quickly detected it and halted it in its tracks. Instead, the disease gave some people no obvious symptoms and others only mild symptoms. However, it also hospitalized and killed enough people to make the disease extremely dangerous.

1. The Virus Goes Viral

Sometime in the fall of 2019, a new virus made the leap from animals to humans in a wet market in Wuhan, China, a city of 11 million people (one-third larger than New York City). With that jump, the virus joined the more than 200 different kinds of viruses that cause respiratory infections such as rhinoviruses, coronaviruses, influenza viruses, measles, enteroviruses, adenoviruses, and parainfluenza viruses. Like many respiratory diseases, the virus spread by human contact and proximity: through respiratory excretions in droplets, aerosols, and residues on surfaces.

Yet, even after Chinese health officials detected the virus in December, they had no way of knowing if the virus could spread from person to person (versus just animal-to-person transmission from exposure to sick animals at the market). Chinese health officials also faced strong political pressure not to alarm the public—an ongoing self-destructive penchant of dysfunctional leaders of many countries around the world, who ignored and even punished the very people who knew the most about the virus.[1]

For example, Dr. Li Wenliang, the Wuhan physician who first alerted the public about the illness, was forced to confess to spreading "an unfounded and illegal rumor."[2] His warning went unheeded, and by February 2020, he was dead from the virus. Similarly, dozens of Iranians were arrested for "spreading rumors"[3] as the pandemic was spreading.[4] Russia did not fare any better while the Kremlin insisted that the outbreak was only happening elsewhere. In the United States, President Donald Trump insisted on February 17, "It's going to disappear. One day it's like a miracle, it will disappear."[5] Politicians, however, can be excused for downplaying the danger. Not so public health professionals.

Missing the Signs

In early January 2020, scientists determined that the disease was a coronavirus related to SARS (severe acute respiratory syndrome), which had caused a short-lived epidemic starting in 2002 that killed 11 percent of its known

8,422 cases. The new virus was dubbed SARS-CoV-2, and the disease it caused became known as Covid-19. Scientists also developed a sensitive test for detecting the genetic material of the virus in samples such as nose and throat swabs collected from people. The test could reveal people who had the virus replicating inside them.

However, Covid-19 had one insidious aspect that made it much worse than almost any other previous pandemic: Many infected people showed no symptoms yet were still infectious. In fact, some infected people *never* got any symptoms but could still spread the disease. Such asymptomatic transmissions make the virus much harder to fight, because a simple test with immediate results (such as checking body temperature or asking about symptoms) cannot detect such disease spreaders. In addition, health care officials dismissed this grave risk for months, despite data-supported evidence. Consequently, mitigation measures were delayed by months, and authorities missed most of the cases spreading throughout their communities, which contributed to untold numbers of preventable deaths.

On January 27, Dr. Camilla Rothe, an infectious disease researcher at University Hospital LMU Munich, identified the first German case of the new coronavirus: an employee of Webasto, an auto part company. Tracking contacts, Dr. Rothe verified that the infection could only have come from a colleague traveling from China, *who showed no symptoms while in Germany*. She alerted a few dozen doctors and public health officials in a short email: "Infections can actually be transmitted during the incubation period."[6] Despite the prevailing wisdom (based on SARS) that only symptomatic people could infect others, Dr. Rothe and her colleague in Munich sounded the alarm.

Rothe's team sent an email and then a paper to the *New England Journal of Medicine* detailing their findings.[7] The journal published the paper immediately on January 30. Rather than garner praise for this new and important finding, the Munich team came under attack from rival academics, politicians, public health officials, and—following them—the media. The attacks occurred even as more asymptomatic infections were taking place in French churches,[8] the Diamond Princess cruise ship (where more than 700 people were sickened),[9] the aircraft carrier USS *Theodore Roosevelt* (where 60 percent of the 4,800 sailors on board were infected)[10] and many other locations. Despite the growing evidence, on April 2, 2020, the World Health Organization (WHO) stated in its daily *Covid-19 Situation Report,* "To date, there has been no documented asymptomatic transmission."[11]

For two crucial months, health agencies, including the WHO and the European Center for Disease Prevention and Control, quibbled about the finding of the Munich team rather calling for immediate action. A crucial public health discussion devolved into a semantic debate over what to call infected people without clear symptoms.[12] The Public Health Agency of Sweden was not as forgiving: "The sources that claimed that the coronavirus would infect during the incubation period lack scientific support for this analysis."[13] French health officials were adamant in their public communications: "No symptoms = no risk of being contagious," proclaimed a government poster. Even as late as June, the WHO did not acknowledge the role of asymptomatic transmissions, only to be called out for giving "incorrect information" by the top US expert, Dr. Anthony Fauci.[14]

Only in late March did European health officials finally acknowledge that asymptomatic transmissions play a big part in the disease progression. Later studies found that between 40 and 55 percent of transmissions took place before any symptoms appeared.[15] Moreover, symptoms take an average of six days to appear. That length of time gives an infected individual almost a full week to come into contact with and infect other people. (Note, however, that it does take some time for the virus to replicate, and so individuals may be the most infectious a few days after contracting the virus). These infectious but asymptomatic people weren't the only serious cause for alarm with the Covid-19 pandemic.

Here Come the Superspreaders

By March 6, 2020, the news had reported 58 cases of Covid-19 in King County, Washington, where Seattle is located, and one death.[16] Skagit County, about an hour's drive north of Seattle, had only one reported case.[17] When Adam Burdick, conductor of the Skagit Valley Chorale, contemplated holding the choir's weekly rehearsal scheduled for March 10, he was not too worried. Life in Skagit County was normal. Schools and businesses were open, and there were no prohibitions on large gatherings. Burdick sent an email to the singers; the rehearsal was on. It would proceed as planned at the Mount Vernon Presbyterian Church.

Sixty-one members showed up. Some precautions were taken: Hand sanitizer was distributed at the door, and members did not shake hands or hug. Burdick recalled to a *Los Angeles Times* reporter, "It seemed like a normal rehearsal, except that choirs are huggy places."[18] Several members arrived early to set up chairs in a large multipurpose room. They arranged six rows of 20 chairs each, spaced 6–10 inches apart, with a center aisle dividing left and right stages. Most choir members sat in their usual rehearsal seats. Sitting in close proximity to each other, the members sang for two-and-a-half hours.

Within three weeks of the March 10 rehearsal, 52 of the singers (85 percent) were diagnosed with Covid-19, three were hospitalized, and two died.[19] A subsequent investigation by the Centers for Disease Control and Prevention (CDC) revealed that while no member showed any symptoms at the previous rehearsal on March 3, one person exhibited signs of a mild cold during the March 10 rehearsal.[20] Seemingly, a single person had infected dozens of people.[21]

It later became clear that such "superspreader events" play an outsized role in the spread of the disease. Such events include biotechnology company Biogen's leadership conference in Boston, involving 175 executives from around the world.[22] A funeral in Albany, Georgia, touched off an outbreak that soon led to the surrounding rural county posting one of the nation's highest cumulative incidences of the disease.[23] In the southeastern city of Daegu, South Korea, more than half of infected individuals were members of the Shincheonji Church of Jesus[24] and their contacts.[25] "If we could stop the superspreading from happening, we'd benefit the most people," said Ben Cowling, professor of epidemiology at the University of Hong Kong.[26]

Superspreader events are characterized by an infected person being among people, usually in large gatherings, indoors, in poorly ventilated venues, with minimal physical distancing and mask-wearing. Recent research suggests that 70 percent of infected individuals did not infect anyone; instead, super-spreader events account for most transmissions.[27] When an infected person attends large-scale gatherings, socializes extensively, or visits packed indoor locations such as bars and restaurants, that one individual can infect many others.[28]

Many superspreader clusters do not involve events but rather conditions, in facilities such as nursing homes and meatpacking plants as well as cruise ships and navy vessels. While an aircraft seems like an ideal place for spread-ing—having hundreds of people confined in an enclosed aluminum tube for many hours—statistics do not support this notion. Professor Arnold Barnett of the Massachusetts Institute of Technology, an expert in statistics and avia-tion, estimates that the probability of being infected by Covid-19 from a nearby passenger on a two-hour flight is about 1 in 4,300. For flights in which the middle seat is kept empty, the probability drops by almost half to 1 in 7,700.[29]

Even if a contagious person on an aircraft presents minimal risk to fellow passengers, they do present a more important community risk. In ordinary times, some 5 million people fly internationally every day.[30] Among those mil-lions of seemingly healthy tourists, returning citizens, or peripatetic business travelers, unwanted virus stowaways could easily be hiding. Thus, at the start of the pandemic, the virus literally flew under the radar and around the world, establishing undetected clusters of cases.

Early Spread

Analysis of old medical samples found that a man in France had Covid-19 in late December 2019, which he probably caught from his asymptomatic wife who worked at a grocery store frequented by travelers from Charles de Gaulle Airport in Paris. Thus, the disease may have arrived in France two or three weeks before China alerted the world on New Year's Eve and nearly two months before France knew that Covid-19 was in the country.[31] Also, Covid-19 was spreading in northern Italy by December 18, 2019.[32] Similarly, while authorities thought that the first US Covid-19 death took place in Seattle on February 26, 2020, postmortem analysis revealed a Covid-19 death in California on February 6.[33] In fact, a *CDC Morbidity and Mortality Weekly Report* in June concluded, "Diverse data sources suggest that limited community transmission of SARS-CoV-2 in the United States occurred between the latter half of January and the beginning of February."[34]

The *Boston Globe* identified the February 26 leadership conference of the Cambridge-based biotechnology company Biogen as the epicenter of the outbreak in Massachusetts, with 70 out of the 92 infections in the state linked to the conference.[35] The *Globe* gave a relatively even description, noting that most conference attendees who wanted to get tested were told that they did not meet the criteria for testing.

A more scientific and thorough study by the Broad Institute of MIT and Harvard, in collaboration with the Massachusetts General Hospital and the Massachusetts Department of Public Health, provided a less opinionated description regarding the entry of Covid-19 to the Boston area. As it turns out, the first confirmed case of the virus in Massachusetts dated back to early February, weeks before the Biogen conference. The researchers reported, "It is clear from the data that no single event or importation alone is responsible for the ongoing spread of the virus in the Boston area; rather, there were multiple entries within a few weeks, from both domestic and international sources."[36] Analyzing the genetic signatures of 331 Massachusetts cases, researchers found evidence that the virus entered the region through at least 30 unique introductions (mainly from Europe)—in many cases leading to further community transmissions.

Several factors contributed to the exponential international spread of Covid-19: the prevalence of air travel, asymptomatic transmission, and super-spreading events. Of course, lack of preparation and lack of acceptance of expert medical judgment by politicians in many counties did nothing to help.

Unlike natural disasters like earthquakes, tsunamis, or tornadoes, pandemics can spread around the world. Most natural disasters strike quickly, locally, and have instantly visible impacts. They then subside, letting people immediately start picking up the pieces. In contrast, pandemics grow, linger, or reappear everywhere over periods of months and years. Pandemics spread in fits and starts and explode in different places at different times. And the most striking difference between pandemics and other disasters is that the economic damage is not done by the pandemic itself, but by the response.

And so the multinational effort to contain the virus and halt the disease began.

Lights Out for the Economy

As the number of Covid-19 cases ballooned, epidemiologists soon realized that the virus was highly infectious and, of those infected, it sickened a high percentage enough to require hospitalization, intensive care, and the use of ventilators to keep oxygen flowing into patients' severely damaged lungs. The virus proved that it could double the number of sick people every three or four days in many locations. That meant that one case could become a thousand cases in a month, a million cases in two months, and a billion cases in three months. If not halted, the virus would quickly move around the world, killing millions. But the outlook was even worse than it first appeared.

With proper medical care, Covid-19 was not as fatal as SARS (although it was about 10 times more fatal than typical influenza viruses). The operative phrase, however, was "with proper medical care," which would soon prove impossible in places like Wuhan, northern Italy, and New York City as cases overwhelmed hospitals. Most countries—even the rich ones of the developed world—have fewer than five hospital beds per 1,000 citizens,[37] with most of those beds already occupied by people with other health conditions. Were authorities to allow the virus to spread unimpeded, it would have quickly overwhelmed the hospitals and resulted in even greater numbers of deaths.

With no vaccine, no cure, and a high rate of hospitalization, the only way to avoid a catastrophe of deaths was to bend the exponential growth curve of the infection. That required reducing the rate at which infected people spread the disease to others, calling for drastically curtailing human interactions.

The Chinese were the first to implement what became a familiar strategy employed around the world: Close all places where people gathered, limit people's movements to "essential" activities, and require people to stay at home and away from others. Neighborhood authorities and the police enforced the shutdowns. By mid-February, analysis by the *New York Times* concluded that residential lockdowns of varying strictness—from checkpoints at building entrances to hard limits on going outdoors—covered at least 760 million people in China, or more than half the country's population.[38] To stop the spread of the virus beyond its epicenter in Hubei Province (home to more than 60 million people, including Wuhan), Chinese authorities suspended flights and train services and blocked roads in and out of the province.[39]

After 10 weeks under lockdown, Wuhan reopened. But it opened as a profoundly damaged place. Not only was the economy in shambles, but the fear, sickness, and death had traumatized millions of people. Neighborhood authorities continued to regulate people's comings and goings, with no return to normalcy in sight.[40]

In the US, a patchwork of closures and shelter-in-place orders in March 2020 had a devastating impact on business and employment. In less than two months, more than 36 million Americans filed for unemployment,[41] and the official unemployment rate surged to 14.7 percent in late April 2020.[42] The speed of the economic shock was unlike any prior economic crisis. Whereas the global financial meltdown of 2008 required 18 months to slowly increase the US unemployment rate from 5 to 10 percent, the Covid-19 crisis instantly boosted unemployment from 4.4 to 14.7 percent in only one month.

Kevin Clark, the president and CEO of Aptiv, a $14 billion supplier of automotive electronics, described the effects in the company's Q1 2020 earnings call on May 5: "The impact of Covid-19 on global vehicle production has been more sudden and severe than any recession scenario we've previously planned for. What started as extended production downtime in China after January's Lunar New Year evolved into complete shutdowns in Europe and the Americas beginning in mid-March."[43] Companies were just not prepared for the speed of the economic downturn. Jim Hackett, CEO of Ford at the time, said incredulously, "We didn't realize there was an off switch. We knew it might go into a recession, more like a dimmer switch, but off?"[44]

The effects of the virus weren't just biological and economic; they were also psychological. In the beginning, the percentage of the population actually infected was minuscule. At the time of the shutdowns in the US in mid-March, known cases in the US were 0.001 percent of the population. However, the infection was growing so quickly that the impact on the 99.999 percent who were not infected was profound. This impact arose from a different kind of viral phenomenon—one created by people.

"If It Bleeds, It Leads"

What began as rumor of a shortage of toilet paper in Hong Kong morphed into a strange global obsession—toilet paper hoarding.[45] Leaders tried to debunk the stream of rumors concerning toilet paper. "This is totally false.... The raw materials for toilet paper and face masks are different. Please do not believe rumors," wrote President Tsai Ing-wen of Taiwan on her Facebook page.[46]

Respected media outlets such as the BBC used headlines like "Coronavirus panic: why are people buying toilet paper?"[47] Images of barren grocery store shelves and throngs clutching huge stacks of toilet paper made for riveting TV, internet, and newspaper headlines. Such headlines and images drove people to buy more, forcing retailers to put a limit on purchases, which only increased the panic. In Sydney, Australia, supermarket shelves were cleared as soon as supplies arrived. One newspaper report claimed that police were even called to a dispute involving a knife that was pulled out in an argument over toilet paper between panicked shoppers.[48]

The media soon found a new and better target for attracting anxious eyeballs. "Panicked Shoppers Empty Shelves as Coronavirus Anxiety Rises," claimed the *New York Times* on March 13, 2020, adding to the warning a picture of frustrated shoppers gazing at empty supermarket shelves.[49] Bill Morrissey, vice president of environmental sustainability at Clorox, noted that consumers might attach different importance to products whether the product goes "in me," "on me," or "around me." Consumers are more sensitive to food ("in me") than to toilet paper ("on me").[50] Indeed, the food shortage scare gave media outlets, both traditional and social, an opportunity to reap dollars and clicks, milking the old adage, "If it bleeds, it leads," contributing to widespread panic.

At times, the warnings were more focused. "Egg prices are skyrocketing because of coronavirus panic shopping," claimed CNN Business on March 25, along with a much-repeated video of empty store shelves.[51] And *U.S. News & World Report* announced on April 6, "Coronavirus-fueled panic buying cleared the shelves of eggs. What's next for egg markets?"[52]—again, creating a wave of panic buying. No systemic egg shortage materialized. Yet the media continued.

These stories were followed by another wave of scary headlines about meat shortages caused by the closure of several beef and pork processing plants. For example, on April 29, the *Boston Globe* warned its readers: "Coming to a grocery store near you: meat shortages."[53]

The Truth Behind a Flood of Sensationalism

What the media never told its readers and viewers was that the pictures of empty shelves were typically taken at the end of the day. Anyone visiting in the morning as supermarkets opened would have found well-stocked shelves. The reason, which most newspaper reports did not bother to cover, is the way the last leg of grocery supply chains work. Warehouse workers prepare shipments during the day. The shipments leave in the evening and hit the stores at night. There, workers offload the trucks, unpack the boxes, and replenish the shelves. Stores replenish at night because it allows workers to stock the shelves without congestion in the aisles from shoppers, something that is even more important—critically so—during the pandemic.

The pandemic did have some impact on toilet paper supply. Because offices, factories, universities, restaurants were all closed, the demand for the low-grade toilet paper used in these institutions disappeared, and the demand for the high-grade toilet paper used in homes went up. The retail toilet-paper supply chain could have handled the 40 percent increase in consumers' use of toilet paper with ease, but not the more than 200 percent surge in hoarding-related sales caused by alarming media headlines.

Some headlines—such as those referring to farmers plowing under unharvested crops, dumping milk, and euthanizing animals—were heartachingly correct but, again, without context, created the wrong impression. Each one of these phenomena had a different underlying cause. The demand for fresh produce collapsed following the closures of restaurants, corporate campuses, and universities. By and large, it was replaced with demand for comfort food, canned goods, and other nonperishable foods. This shift resulted in the destruction of fresh produce.

The spilled milk was the result of the disappearance of demand from schools and restaurants, which was not replaced to any large degree by demand at home. It also hit during dairy farms' "flush" period when cows naturally produce more milk. Finally, while the *New York Times* bemoaned the dumping of 3.7 million gallons of milk per day,[54] it neglected to put this number in context: This waste was a puny 5 percent of the milk supply, and 30–40 percent of the food in the US is wasted anyway (mostly by consumers), as estimated by the US Department of Agriculture.[55]

The meat scare arose from the temporary closure of several large meat processing plants, but the shortage eased within days. News articles and TV reports neglected to mention that the US exports 27 percent of its pork production,[56] 18 percent of its poultry,[57] 13 percent of its beef,[58] and 11 percent of its turkey.[59] It is the fourth-largest exporter of meat in the world after Brazil, India, and Australia. In short, the US produces more than enough food to feed its population.

Furthermore, the media failed to provide adequate context for retailers' practice of limiting purchases. On April 21, a headline on Bloomberg News claimed, "Food Rationing Confronts Shoppers Once Spoiled for Choice."[60] In fact, retailers instituted limits on purchases in order to prevent shortages caused by hoarding; they did not do it because they faced supply shortages. Instead of calmly explaining what stores are doing in order to dampen panic buying and hoarding, to make sure that all customers can be served, such headlines only exacerbated the panic buying.

However, either because fear sells, financial pressures, the quest for clicks, or personal aggrandizement, journalists seem to cherry-pick sensational stories—whether accurate, with full context, or not. The fact is that there was never a true shortage of food. At some places and at some times, shoppers could not find their favorite cuts of meat or their preferred choice of granola bar. While some buyers may have genuinely panicked over the prospect of food shortages, the apocalyptic headlines that contributed to the panic buying and hoarding were not justified.

Panic buying went beyond toilet paper and nonperishable foods. Some consumers became convinced that the end of civilization was imminent, or that calamity was around the corner. Disaster supplies like bottled water flew off the shelves, too. In March 2020, online sales of batteries doubled and sales of generators tripled[61] as if people expected the electricity to go out.

Thus, the media became the superspreader of panic and proved that bad information can be even more viral than a bad virus. A single misleading image, video, or tweet can infect millions of minds in an instant. The Germans called the resulting panicked consumer behavior *Hamsterkauf*,[62] evoking images of hamsters stuffing their cheeks to the point of bursting in preparation for bleak northern European winters. The end was nigh, so time to buy. Only later did the media tone down its feverish coverage with more balanced reporting.[63]

The Perils of False Confidence

From the beginning, Covid-19 came with many uncertainties: How infectious was it? Who was infectious, and when did they become so? How was the virus transmitted? And how should those sick with the virus be treated? Even after some eight months of the pandemic, scientists were still not sure how infectious children might be, how long someone who has had the virus might be immune to it, and whether vaccines will work as expected. Not only did these uncertainties pose increased risks, but so too did early false answers and overconfidence by experts, journalists, and public officials.

Citizens, journalists, and decision makers naturally demanded immediate answers to important questions about the virus. Many experts and would-be experts were only too happy to supply answers—happy to help out and have their 15 minutes of fame. Alas, many of those answers were based on opinion, supposition, anecdotal evidence, or data tainted by bias or methodological errors. Some false answers were even driven by conspiracy theories (5G cell towers cause Covid-19)[64] or alleged financial gains by promoters (repackaged industrial bleach can prevent Covid-19).[65]

Even if the experts carefully qualified their answers with all the uncertainties and limitations of the prevailing scientific knowledge at the time, the media tended to condense a nuanced answer into an unequivocal sound bite. Finally, the decision makers and authorities around the world had to act, which meant picking a specific interpretation that, in theory, weighed the evidence and the consequences. The result was that erroneous ideas were presented as absolute facts and enshrined in policies. When later evidence contradicted an earlier notion and finally convinced the vigorous believers in the initial falsehood, the public felt whipsawed and lost confidence in the experts and officials.

Many leaders, media commentators, and even scientists often forgot the fact that absence of evidence about how Covid-19 behaved was not actually evidence of absence. For example, just because no cases were known to have been spread by an asymptomatic person did not mean that no such cases happened (*see* "Missing the Signs," p. 2). The logic that "we have not seen it happen, therefore it cannot happen" is only true if people have carefully tried to look for evidence that whatever "it" is does not happen. Paradoxically, the way to confirm that something is not happening (e.g., asymptomatic infections or asymptomatic transmission) is to diligently search for evidence that it *does* happen (e.g., testing asymptomatic people).

The essence of good scientific reasoning centers on falsification, not verification. This is the moral of the "black swan" concept. The source of the adage is probably the second-century Roman poet Juvenal, who characterized nonexistent events as "very much like a black swan." At the time and for centuries later, Europeans did not believe that black swans existed, since the only swans they had ever seen were white. Yet each sighting of a white swan was not proof that all swans are white; this belief was proven wrong in 1697, when Dutch explorers became the first Europeans to see black swans in western Australia. Thus, if one wants to prove that black swans do not exist, one has to look for them—and only after examining all the world's swans can one conclude there are no black swans.

Because of flawed absence-of-evidence reasoning, authorities around the world consistently missed the entry into and early spread of the pandemic through their communities, because they only tested people with a strong connection to travel from China. They then thought that the low numbers of positive test results proved a lack of community infections. Instead, all that those low early case counts proved was the ineptitude of the officials running the testing programs. Later analysis of old samples proved that the pandemic arrived much earlier than the "first known" cases in many locations, and serological data suggested that for every case known to authorities, many more unknown cases were wandering around the community, spreading the disease.

Naturally, Covid-19 was by no means unique in having such uncertainties and falsely confident answers. Every disruption comes with fundamental unknowns that frustrate decision makers. Hurricane forecasters can plot the possible paths of a hurricane, but the forecasts change day by day as new data comes in. The rapidly changing 2008 financial crisis created uncertainties about which companies, banks, and even countries were on the verge of financial ruin. With every disruption, decision makers may not know if the other shoe is about to drop or even how many shoes are in the event's shoebox of despair.

2. Eruptions of Supply Chain Disruptions

Supply chains are the economic networks that use natural-resource production, product manufacturing, transportation, and retailing to deliver all the products needed for human life. Covid-19 triggered three categories of ongoing disruptions to supply chains. First, the pandemic disrupted supply as facilities closed under outbreaks of infection and government lockdown. Second, the pandemic disrupted demand as people stopped or reduced consumption of some items as a result of unemployment, lockdown orders, or changes in needs and wants. Third, it significantly boosted demand for other items, such as medical supplies (PPE, ventilators, cures du jour), cleaning supplies, certain foods, and many other products suitable for shelter-in-place lifestyles (bread making machines, flour, yeast, jigsaw puzzles, exercise equipment, hair dye, etc.). For modern economies and modern supply chains accustomed to humming along like well-oiled machines, Covid-19 threw a box full of wrenches into the works.

Those Demanding (Panicked) Customers

"We experienced unprecedented demand in categories like paper goods, surface cleaners, and grocery staples," said Doug McMillon, CEO of Walmart.[1] Walmart's nearly 5,000 outlets were on the front lines of consumers' abrupt surges in demand. "For many of these items, we were selling in two or three hours what we normally sell in two or three days," McMillon added. Sales of packaged foods more than quadrupled, and sales of soups nearly quintupled.[2] "Not only have products and categories like hand sanitizer, disinfecting wipes and sprays, toilet paper, beef, and pork been hard to find, but items such as laptops, office chairs, and fabric have been cleared out in some of our stores and online," McMillon said.[3]

Whether caused by *Hamsterkauf* panic to hoard toilet paper, health officials' appropriate advice to use more disinfecting products, or a significant increase in eating all meals at home, demand for many products surged as the pandemic reshaped the economy and psychology of consumers. Although an accountant or Walmart shareholder might cheer the surge in revenues, the store's inventory managers responsible for keeping the store shelves and fulfillment centers stocked faced a serious challenge. Moreover, their pain would be amplified upstream in the supply chain.

In the typical retail supply chain, the retail store gets product from the retailer's warehouse, which gets its products directly from a manufacturer or from a distributor, who aggregates products from many manufacturers and supplies many retailers' warehouses. The manufacturers' factories get their component parts and materials from various suppliers, and, somewhere far up the chain from the retailer, the suppliers get their raw materials from farms, mines, and other harvesters of natural resources wherever those resources are found naturally or grown. Thus, orders for products go "up the links of the supply chain" to request delivery of more of a product such as toilet paper. The product then flows "downstream" (down the supply chain). Forests become logs, logs become pulp, and pulp becomes toilet paper. The final product is then shipped through various distribution centers until it reaches the retailer's physical or e-commerce shelf, where it is quickly snatched up by a panicked shopper.

In order to provide customers with what they want, retailers carry many items—a typical grocery store might carry 40,000–75,000 kinds of products and product variations referred to as stock keeping units (SKUs). Stores keep inventory in the form of both cycle stock (to account for the fact that many processes, such as transportation, are done in bulk while sales take place over time) and safety stock (to compensate for the randomness of demand during the replenishment lead time). While inventory ensures that consumers will find what they want when they visit the store or order online, it also costs the retailer money. This includes the cost of money tied up in inventory, storage and space expenses, obsolescence risk, taxes, and the costs of servicing the inventory. Furthermore, the more SKUs a retailer carries, the lower the average amount carried and sold of each SKU, and the higher the impacts of demand variability. Store managers have to balance the breadth of assortment of products on the shelves, making sure that they do not spend too much in inventory carrying costs and yet do not find themselves in stockout situations in which sales are lost.

In order to hit a Goldilocks inventory of goods—not too much, not too little—of every product, stores forecast demand for each SKU. A typical grocer maintains about a month's worth of inventory in its networks (including both in its stores and its distribution centers). Of course, retailers can't maintain very large inventories of perishable items—fresh fruits, vegetables, diary, bread, and fresh fish—without a lot of waste from spoilage if consumers buy less fresh food than forecasted.

Then Covid-19 hit the scene.

When consumers everywhere suddenly rushed to every retail outlet to buy much greater volumes of paper goods, surface cleaners, and grocery staples than they ever had before, the massive spike in sales denuded the shelves and emptied retailers' warehouses. Sales volumes equivalent to two to three days of sales every two or three hours, as Walmart experienced, meant that consumers bought the retailers' entire one-month supply of those products in just a few days. "The three-month period we are going through is going to equate to three years of consumer changes wrapped up in one quarter," declared David Gibbs, CEO of Yum Brands Inc.[4]

Retailers increased their orders, but the replenishment process from deep in the supply chain can take days, weeks, or months, depending on where the supplies are coming from. Up the supply chain, manufacturers had to ramp up their production, but the need to boost manufacturing highlighted another major effect of Covid-19. At the same time that the pandemic was affecting demand, it was also disrupting supply.

Supply Disruptions

When Covid-19 infected communities, it prompted shutdowns starting in Wuhan and spreading around the world. Wuhan, for example, is one of China's "Detroits," with car factories for General Motors, Honda, Nissan, PSA Group, and Renault, as well as hundreds of auto part manufacturers. Overall, Chinese automakers and parts producers exported $53 billion worth of automotive components to the US, Europe, Japan, South Korea, and elsewhere in 2019.[5] "In some cities, one worker gets infected, the whole factory where he works needs to be shut down," said a Honda official with a manufacturing hub and more than 100 suppliers in Wuhan area.[6] Even "essential" factories such as meatpacking plants in the US and elsewhere were forced to shut down for a time when the virus entered the plants and found easy pickings among people working in close proximity.

When it comes to supply disruptions, complex products contain a ticking BOM (bill of materials). The BOM for a product lists all the parts and quantities required to make that product—like a recipe in a cookbook. If a car maker can't get every last part on the BOM, then it can't make any cars. A car without the little one-dollar, made-in-China electric motor that opens and closes the window cannot be sold. Similarly, if a drug maker cannot get all of the ingredients for a medication, it cannot make any of that medication. As Benjamin Franklin warned (using an old adage), "For want of a nail…the kingdom was lost."[7] In the US, shutdowns in China and India provoked fears that the US would run out of certain crucial medical supplies. As it turned out, these fears were unfounded. While the US and Europe did run short on protective personal equipment (PPE) such as masks and gowns (as well as ventilators), the US never ran out of important pharmaceuticals.

Whereas the effects of a surge in demand might be immediate and highly visible on store shelves, the effects of supply disruptions can take time to be felt. During the 2011 Tōhoku earthquake in Japan, it took General Motors about a month just to realize which parts were missing from its inventory. Many parts were still on their way to the assembly plant, because even if the supplier's factory where they came from may have been hit, parts were still in transit on trucks, rail, or ships. These in-transit inventories, in conjunction with parts inventories at the customer's end help delay or buffer the impact of a supplier shutdown on its customers.

In contrast, car makers closer to the point of an infectious outbreak face a more immediate impact. Wuhan car makers were immediately impacted by the shutdown, followed by car makers in nearby South Korea[8] and Japan.[9] Thus, the effects of a supply disruption spread out from the initial point of impact and move at the speed of freight and inventory toward the consumers.

Transportation Disruptions

The pandemic halted the movement of people through shelter-in-place, travel ban, and quarantine orders. Halting the movement of people had unintended consequences on the movement of goods, because the movement of goods requires people: truck drivers, railroad engineers, aircraft pilots, and ship crews. In interviews for this book, both Heather Ostis, vice president of supply chain management at Delta Air Lines[10] and Mike Duffy, CEO of C&S Wholesale Grocers,[11] the $27 billion food wholesaler, spoke of the disruptive impact of local rules requiring 14-day quarantines for outsiders. Aircrew and truck drivers were reluctant to go to locations with quarantine rules (such as China or New York City) for fear they might get stuck there. Local shutdown rules created another challenge for long-haul truck drivers: the closure of highway rest areas and limited hours of truck stops deprived truckers of restrooms, places to eat, and places to park their trucks for the night.

Covid-19 is only the latest in a long line of pandemics that have disrupted trade and freight transportation. In fact, the word "quarantine" originates from the time of the bubonic plague, which ripped through Europe from 1345 through 1350, wiping out about a third of its population. Officials in the Venetian-controlled port city of Ragusa (now Dubrovnik, Croatia) issued edicts that ships and caravans from plague-infested regions could not enter the harbor or city until they sat at anchor or spent time in an outlying camp for disinfection. In the beginning, ships and caravans had to isolate for 30 (*trentino* in Italian) days.[12] As other locations in Europe adopted the idea, they expanded the duration of isolation to 40 days and the term changed to *quarantino*. The reason for the change may have been that the 40-day period had a religious significance, as the biblical flood "was on the earth for forty days" (Genesis 7:17), Moses "stayed on the mountain forty days and forty nights" (Exodus 24:18), and Jesus fasted in the wilderness for forty days (Matthew 4:2).[13]

The miracle of modern freight transportation is that, by and large, it works quietly and efficiently. In normal times, thousands of ships, thousands of aircraft, millions of rail cars, and millions of trucks carry billions of shipments from origin to destination. "The cost structure, the ability to get products, your capacity for shipping and delivering, those are usually things that you can take for granted," Amazon CFO Brian Olsavsky told investors at the end of Q1 2020. "And in this quarter, you can't. That's really where the uncertainty is driven."[14]

Stung by the Bullwhip

Hidden in all the patterns of sales and replenishment activities is another source of disruptive dynamics for all supply chains: the *bullwhip effect*. When consumers stripped the shelves bare, retailers such as Walmart, Target, and Amazon had to order replenishments. In fact, they had to order enough to both refill the empty shelves and anticipate future sales (which seemed to be extremely high). Tracing the effects of a change in consumer demand on all the participants in the supply chain reveals that changes at the end-consumer level are amplified going up the chain as they force changes upstream in the supply chain.

For a simplified explanation of this phenomenon, assume that during ordinary times a retailer sells 100 packages of toilet paper each day and has four days' worth of inventory (400 units). Say the retailer experiences a surge in which it sells 200 packages of toilet paper in one day, leaving it with an inventory of only 200 packages. At the end of the day, the retailer will order at least 200 packages just to replace what it sold, but if the retailer expects the sales surge to last, it will order another 400 packages—a total of 600 packages—to make sure that it will have four days' worth of inventory at the new 200 package-per-day sales rate. The distributor then sees a jump in orders from 100 to 600 packages from the retailer. The distributor will then follow similar logic of replacing what was sold *and* boosting inventory to handle future higher sales when it orders substantially more from the factory, and so it goes upstream in the supply chain as the factory orders even more from its suppliers. Thus, a change in consumer demand amplifies as orders travel up the supply chain—hence the term "bullwhip."

This amplification effect also happens when customer demand falls. Say, for example, consumer demand for party supplies during the pandemic drops by 50 percent. Retailers will order even less, and the same logic travels up the supply chain again. Upstream at a factory, orders may plummet to zero for a long time while all the downstream distributors and retailers slowly sell off what is now a lot of excess inventory. For both increases and decreases in consumer demand, the result is a bullwhip effect in the supply chain that is especially hard on companies at the upstream end of the supply chain.

Macroeconomic data during the 2008 financial crisis shows that the bullwhip effect operates at global scale. For example, US retail sales (representing consumer demand) declined by 12 percent; yet US manufacturers pulled down inventories by 15 percent and manufacturing sales declined almost 30 percent, while imports plunged by more than 30 percent.[15] A survey of 125 Dutch companies found that those closer to end consumers saw a 25 percent drop in revenues, while those further from consumers saw a 39–43 percent drop.[16]

During the onset of the Covid-19 pandemic, the Chinese leadership immediately understood the potential effects of the bullwhip on the many small and medium Chinese suppliers that operate deep in global supply chains. The bullwhip could inflict a death blow on them. Therefore, the Chinese government told state banks to start loaning money at very low rates, sometimes zero, to small businesses; it also called for significant reductions in the taxes on all small manufacturers.[17]

The bullwhip effect also takes place when demand recovers after a recession or a pandemic-induced shutdown. It can take weeks or months for suppliers to gear back up and send parts downstream to manufacturers who have to produce the products and supply them to retailers. If retailers don't order from manufacturers and manufacturers don't order from their suppliers well before the demand materializes, potential sales will be lost throughout the channel. Thus, timing the orders before they materialize can separate winners from losers when the economy wakes up.[18] Yet, ordering too soon can leave an overeager retailer holding lots of unsold merchandise. The bullwhip effect was only one source of volatility that supply chain managers had to contend with during the pandemic and in preparation for the future.

3. Their Finest Hour

As people hunkered down in their homes to isolate themselves from the pandemic, an army of dedicated professionals kept the country's food supply chains humming under trying conditions. That army consisted of distributors' employees, fulfillment center personnel, logistics planners, pallet manufacturing crews, procurement professionals, transportation brokers, truck drivers, truck stop attendants, warehouse workers, wholesalers, and countless other specialists. They ensured that food flowed to supermarkets and other retail outlets as well as to e-commerce fulfillment centers, even though media images of empty shelves tried to tell a different story.

The incredibly fast catch-up of supply is a testament to the great people who run and operate US supply chains. Behind the grocery delivery person or the supermarket clerk who serves customers is a complex supply chain involving millions of men and women who make sure that vital supplies reach consumers. During the pandemic, they often carry out this taxing work in the face of unprecedented demand. These supply chain professionals and operators who continue to accomplish the impossible every day are some of the unknown and unsung heroes of the Covid-19 crisis.

Food for Thought on What Really Happened

Contrary to the media's apocalyptic assessment, the Covid-19 pandemic did not break America's or Europe's food supply chains. The retail shortages experienced by consumers were only temporary. As is often the case, looking behind the headlines can reveal the real situation—a tectonic shift in where people got all their food and a shift in what people wanted to purchase. The sudden shutdown of the US economy delivered two straight-to-the-gut blows to the country's supply chains for consumer goods and food. Consumers rapidly changed both *where* and *what* they bought in terms of foodstuff and household goods.

The first blow happened when states suddenly shut down public gathering places such as restaurants, bars, offices, schools, sports venues, and big catered events. All of these places stopped ordering much of the food and other products they purveyed. Suddenly, the manufacturers and distributors that specialize in products for these public places were stuck with excess inventories and excess capacity for products, such as 15-quart cases of liquid eggs, 50-pound bags of onions, 10-pound boxes of 30 beef patties, and those giant rolls of one-ply toilet paper found in public restrooms. Meanwhile, consumers started buying more food and products from supermarkets because they were spending more time at home. At the same time, the manufacturers and distributors that specialize in products for retail outlets saw growing demand for cartons of a dozen eggs, two-pound bags of onions, one-pound packages of ground beef, and normal-sized rolls of ultra-soft toilet paper.

The second blow came from a change in what people bought and ate at home. People did not just shop for more at the grocery store; they shopped differently. Food durability and ease of storage became key factors in consumers' purchasing decisions.[1] To cope with anxiety, they bought more comfort food (bread, pasta, etc.), and to cope with fears of future shortages, they bought more nonperishable goods (canned food, grains, rice, dried food, frozen food, etc.). Some bought less fresh produce when ordering for delivery or pickup, because they were not confident that harried order-fulfillment staff would carefully select the best produce.

These two blows revealed a deep division in the economic machinery that provides much of the food and other supplies that people need and use every day. Many everyday products, such as food and cleaning supplies, come from two distinct manufacturing and distribution supply chain channels. The retail channel makes consumer-sized packages of these goods for sale in ordinary stores. The institutional, commercial, and professional channels serve restaurants, offices, schools, hotels, catering firms, sports venues, and the like by making and distributing bulk-sized packages of these kinds of goods.

Although both supply chains might start with the same types of agricultural raw materials (eggs, vegetables, milk, beef, etc.), they create different products, use different packaging, have different labels, and sometimes even buy from different farmers who may specialize in particular crops or livestock favored by either retail or food service outlets. For example, a sour cream manufacturer might offer 8-ounce or 16-ounce containers for retailers and either 5-pound tubs or boxes filled with 100 tiny 1-ounce single-serving cups for restaurants and other food service outlets. Commercial products often lack the serving-level nutrition information required by the Food and Drug Administration (FDA), and they also lack a UPC bar code required for grocery store checkout scanners. The food service products might even bear the warning "this unit not labeled for retail sale."

The differences in products for retail and commercial channels makes them noninterchangeable. The equipment used to fill these jumbo tubs and tiny cups typically can't be used to fill more 8-ounce or 16-ounce containers needed for the surge of retail sales.

Government regulations also limited agility. For example, the US Department of Agriculture (USDA) regulates the egg-laying chicken, the FDA regulates the egg, but the USDA takes over again if the egg is cracked open for use as an ingredient in another product.[2] Other US government regulations prevented small- and medium-sized meat processing plants from selling their meat across state lines or into retail and food service channels. Issues with the availability of meat inspectors and questions over who covers inspection costs also created problems for expanding production at some facilities. The FDA did relax some nutrition labeling requirements so that restaurants could sell packaged food.[3]

Lela Nargi, a reporter for nonprofit food journalism publication The Counter, interviewed several agricultural experts about the problem of farmers plowing their crops under, dumping milk, or euthanizing livestock. Hope Sippola, co-owner of Fiery Ginger, a one-acre urban produce farm in California, bemoaned, "60 percent of our business is the 350 pounds a week of lettuce mix and baby romaine we produce for four school districts. They were our only wholesale customers and in the first weeks they were shut down, we had 4,500 heads of romaine that bolted that we had to mow down." Lacy Stephens, senior program manager for the National Farm to School Network, added, "Some milk goes to K-12 schools in bulk, but grab-and-go meals require small cartons; the missing link is flexibility in packaging." Dr. Gail Feenstra, deputy director of the Sustainable Agriculture Research and Education Program at the University of California, Davis, explained further: "Our food system generally is built for global distribution. Now that's suddenly cracked, people are going back to more local food systems, where [important middle-tier components] like storage facilities [for meat and grain] aren't available."[4]

Coronavirus-induced closures did reduce meat processing capacity for the short time that each plant was closed. Many plants quickly reopened after adding new safety measures, such as spacing workers farther apart, putting up dividers between workers, mandatory mask wearing, disinfection, and staggered shifts to enable distancing in entryways, locker rooms, and break rooms. However, the countermeasures came with a cost. The lines could not have as many workers or process as many animals per hour as before, increasing the cost of meat.

Some of the resultant price increases for meat came from the use of more expensive cuts of surplus restaurant-quality meat in ground-meat products.[5] The closure of steakhouses and other high-end restaurants meant filet mignon prices plummeted 40 percent to 10-year lows.[6] Covid-19 upended the economic model of beef production, by which the high prices on the best cuts of meat helped subsidize lower prices on other cuts of meat and ground beef. This pattern—in which some customers pay far more than the "cost" of the product to get the best parts, which then lowers the potential price for lower-grade items—occurs in many supply chains such as computer chips, fruits and vegetables, automobiles, airlines, etc. If the high end stops buying, the low end pays the price.

The added inefficiency of working under pandemic rules affected many supply chains. Manufacturing plants, warehouses, and terminal operations all had to institute physical distancing among workers as well as extra shifts, each with a smaller number of workers. All of these changes increased manufacturing and logistics costs. The changes even affected food distribution to the poor and recently unemployed, because not only did the demand for food aid increase substantially, but shelter-at-home rules also created a shortage of volunteers. Physical distancing rules, disinfection protocols, and PPE requirements added more costs and took more labor away from food banks' central mission.

The Food Supply Chain Kept Going

Although temporary spot shortages did occur and the media made hay, most people in the developed world still had access to the safest, most plentiful, and most affordable food supply in the history of humanity. During the second half of the 20th century, agricultural yields soared—for example, the wheat yields in the United Kingdom increased fourfold, and corn yields in the United States increased more than fivefold, as did oat yields in Chile.[7]

During the pandemic, a morning visitor to any supermarket in the developed world still found a cornucopia of fresh fruits and vegetables. As presenter James Wong described in the BBC's *Follow the Food* series, "Standing amid aisle after aisle of food, my biggest concern was that my normal brand of loo roll was temporarily out of stock. A privilege my ancestors would barely have been able to imagine." He added, "The ability of the food system to keep offering up such plenty in the face of unprecedented challenges is testament to its spectacular resilience."[8]

How could the food supply chains keep humming in the face of such obstacles? The incredibly fast catch-up of supply is a testament to the ingenuity and commitment of the people and the organizations who run and operate the food supply chains. For example, the Food Marketing Institute and the International Foodservice Distributors Association in Virginia formed a partnership that provides excess capacity (products, transportation services, and warehousing services) to food retailers and wholesalers that require additional resources to fulfill needs at grocery stores.[9] While front-line healthcare workers were deservingly lauded for their heroic efforts to help pandemic victims, food manufacturing, logistics, and retail workers kept the country fed under difficult and sometimes dangerous conditions.

On farms across the US, seasonal workers kept harvesting crops.[10] Food processing plants implemented the required safety measures, including extra shifts to keep the supplies coming. "Now is a time when people are depending on us more than ever," said Jeff Harmening, CEO of General Mills.[11] Mark Allen, CEO of the International Foodservice Distributors Association, said, "You're seeing heroic efforts across the board to make sure product gets to where it needs to go so it can make it to the consumers who are looking to buy. It doesn't matter if it's grocery or food service. I think carriers are doing an amazing job in a very difficult situation."[12]

4. Finding the Agility to Defeat Fragility

In addition to the herculean efforts of workers, many organizations changed the way they work to contribute to fighting the pandemic and staying in business. A survey of senior supply chain executives found that 38 percent of companies had redeployed assets and capabilities to supply urgently needed goods, especially medical equipment.[1] Some of these changes were short-term measures focused strictly on the pandemic, while others made changes that offered new business opportunities for the future (*see* Chapter 25, p. 219).

These changes fell roughly into three categories of agility. First, some companies showed *scale agility* by finding ways to make more of their existing products to meet surging demand. A second group showed *asset agility* in finding uses for their underutilized assets to provide products or services closely related to the company's preexisting business. Finally, some demonstrated *scope agility* by pivoting their production to entirely new types of products.

Making More, More, More

"Moving fast and being agile is probably not one of our strengths normally," said Jeff Harmening, CEO of General Mills at the end of April 2020. "I have seen us move faster than we ever have before."[2] General Mills's office staff volunteered to work in factories, and the company's frozen pizza factory ran 24-7 to meet demand.[3] Meanwhile, the company also had to implement distancing and disinfection protocols that reduced the capacity of some plants. Overall, the company boosted capacity by 10–20 percent. Sales for the March–May quarter increased by 21 percent compared to the same quarter a year earlier, and operating profits increased by 16 percent.[4]

3M is a Minnesota-based multinational conglomerate producing over 60,000 products under multiple brands. Importantly, it is a major supplier of

N95 masks which are the "gold standard" of protective equipment since they can filter at least 95 percent of airborne particulates. Healthcare workers wear N95 masks when treating contagious patients as well as workers in environments that include airborne contaminants. From January 2020 through the summer of 2020, the company doubled its production rate in its global manufacturing plants to 1.1 billion masks per year, with a plan to grow it to 2 billion per year by the first quarter of 2021.[5] At the same time, the company increased its effort to fight fraud and counterfeiting of 3M products around the world, problems that concerned healthcare professionals and equipment suppliers.

Similarly, Unilever surprised analysts during its July 23, 2020, earnings report by revealing the degree to which it was able to ramp up its production of sanitizers. "We've stepped up capacity across multiple brands by a factor of, believe it or not, 600 times in just five months and we've launched sanitizers in 65 new markets," said CEO Alan Jope. The company was able to repurpose factories previously devoted to making products for which demand was now reduced (such as ice cream) to making sanitizers. Despite a slight decrease in revenue for the first six months of 2020 compared to 2019, overall profits were up by more than 9 percent.[6]

In an example of maximum effort, a group of more than 40 workers at a Braskem America plant locked themselves into their polypropylene factory (polypropylene is a crucial ingredient in N95 masks). For 28 days straight, they worked 12 hours on, 12 hours off to crank out resin needed for N95 mask manufacturing. By isolating themselves, they ensured they could work with no chance of catching the virus from the community, infecting their coworkers, and forcing the plant to shut down.[7]

Paper goods saw huge changes in both the volume of demand and sales. Toilet paper saw hoarding and a marked shift from professional to consumer sales as more people stayed home and stocked up for the calamity. Paper towel demand, both professional and retail, increased as both consumers and businesses that remained open intensified their cleaning activities. Sales of paper plates boomed as more consumers ate at home and as restaurants shifted to selling takeout food. On the other hand, hot-beverage cup sales dropped as people stopped commuting and stayed indoors, abandoning the habit of picking up a morning cup of coffee.

Jeff Fleck, senior vice president and chief supply chain officer for the consumer products group of Georgia-Pacific, a major American pulp and paper company, described both the extreme changes in demand and the company's response. He explained, "It started to really hit in February as people started panic buying. By the time February ended, we were definitely seeing orders spike across the board in the marketplace. During that same timeframe, retailers' shelves became empty and the stock they held in their stores' backrooms and distribution centers was steadily diminishing to zero."

Georgia-Pacific took several steps to boost production and accelerate deliveries to retailers. On the production side, Fleck described two tactics they used to meet heightened consumer demand: "One was to sell some of the professional products into retailers, which is the easiest thing to do, because we already had those products made and we did not have to change anything. The second was to increase output on current assets where we could and switch some of our professional products assets over to run what I call more consumer-centric retail products. These actions have enabled us to get more product into the marketplace than we historically supplied," Fleck said.

However, the larger problem was distribution, which Fleck described as like needing "a 17-lane highway during a rush hour that lasts from 9:00 in the morning until 5:00 at night." Making toilet paper was one thing, but getting it to retailers was another. Fleck took two key steps to support the logistics side of the business: "The first thing was ensuring that we had the carrier base to be able to deliver more. The second was ramping up and ability to increase shipping capacity out of the number of dock doors that we had existing."

One key change, Fleck said, was, "We did things like going directly from our mills, bypassing our distribution centers trying to get out product faster." Shipping direct to the store had two big benefits for retailers and Georgia-Pacific. First, the store got the product sooner and could put it on the shelf sooner. Second, it meant the distribution centers had fewer inbound products coming in that needed to be put away. Thus, Georgia-Pacific's distribution centers could focus more of their staff and dock door capacity for other outbound deliveries.[8]

On the retail side, retailers ramped up their workforces to handle the growing volume of products and customers. Walmart hired 235,000 additional employees to help clean stores, stock shelves, and fulfill online orders.[9] Amazon, likewise, hired 175,000 workers to handle the surge[10] and offered a $500 "thank-you" bonus to all front-line employees as well as a salary increase to attract workers to its online grocery operations.[11]

Successful retailers accelerated their digital transformations to becoming omnichannel providers in order to be able to do more with existing assets and serve the surges in demand, as described in Chapter 22 (p. 198).

Yet, for many needs—especially medical supplies and protective equipment—it was clear that increased production by existing suppliers of these items was not enough.

Repurposing Idled Assets

At the same time that demand surged for some things such as medical supplies, toilet paper, and groceries, it plummeted for others, such as passenger air travel and eating in restaurants. These ups and downs impacted all the deeply interconnected supply chains designed for normal levels of all these activities. The declines idled some assets and people while overstressing others. As the pandemic raged, companies found ways to repurpose underutilized assets to respond to surging demand.

Feeding the Belly of the Airfreight Beast

Faced with the threat of an airborne virus, governments, businesses, and individuals all took steps to limit air travel. Governments banned the admission of air passengers from infected countries or imposed mandatory 14-day quarantines; businesses banned employees' travel; tourist destinations closed, and many consumers canceled flight reservations and stopped flying for fear of being stuck for hours in a petri dish flying at 37,000 feet. These actions all contributed to the near-total decimation of passenger air travel. In addition, FedEx, UPS, and DHL all reduced their China services in the early months of the pandemic.

The grounding of passenger airline fleets tore out the soft underbelly of international supply chains for time-critical products such as medical supplies, emergency spare parts, perishable goods like seafood, and other high-value items. Unbeknownst to many airline passengers, their checked-in luggage typically shares the cargo hold with large volumes of airfreight. Shippers of time-critical packages depend on the world's normal schedule of more than 100,000 daily commercial flights. Overall, before Covid-19, passenger aircraft were providing just over half of the world's airfreight capacity, including 45 percent of Asian airfreight capacity and some 80 percent of transatlantic capacity.[12]

Meri Stevens, Johnson & Johnson's worldwide vice president of consumer health supply chain and deliver, explained, "Prior to the pandemic, about 70 percent of our J&J products were transported in the bellies of commercial aircraft. Further, many of our products are temperature sensitive, so we need to protect them even as we are managing inventories and protecting patients."[13]

The loss of all this capacity threatened the world's response to the pandemic and the operations of many essential and ordinary supply chains. "Air transport is key to moving critical pharmaceutical goods through the supply chain, particularly during this global pandemic," Anne McDonald Pritchett, an executive at Pharmaceutical Research and Manufacturers of America, wrote to the US Department of Transportation at the end of April 2020.[14] China–US air-freight rates tripled and then quadrupled between early March 2020 and mid-May, when they started leveling off.[15] Heather Ostis, vice president of supply chain at Delta Air Lines, commented, "Gouging is happening everywhere right now—on products, on flights, on health transportation. Delta, however, was careful not to play this game."[16]

Some airlines stepped up to the challenge (and opportunity) of both filling the need for more airfreight and filling their idled aircraft with revenue-pay-ing "customers," even if those customers were just plain brown boxes sitting quietly in the seats. Delta Air Lines's Ostis described the airline's approach. Delta did not remove seats or reconfigure its planes, because it wanted to pre-serve flexibility; it might use a plane for cargo one day and passengers the next.

Converting from passenger operations to cargo operations required more than just converting the aircraft. It also meant connecting to other freight transportation providers to get the cargo to and from Delta's planes. Ostis explained: "For example, there was an awful lot of stuff coming out of Shen-zhen, yet we didn't have landing rights there. But we had them in Shanghai, so we'd have to help transport the desired freight from one city in China to another or get it to our operations in Hong Kong."[17]

Some airlines opted to use "seat bags" that could be pre-filled with cargo and then dropped into the seats.[18] Like Delta, most airlines did not unbolt their seats or fully convert passenger planes to freighters. Removing the seats takes time and money. A skilled maintenance crew needs a few days to disconnect, unbolt, and remove an aircraft's coach-class seats and a similar duration to reinstall the seats when passenger volumes increase. (The more sophisticated seats in business class and first class are harder to remove and reinstall). One challenge with any kind of conversion is getting regulatory sign-off on the airworthiness certificate of the modified aircraft. Thus, in August, Delta was planning to take advantage of a special FAA exemption, and strip seats from its 767 jets, converting them to cargo haulers.[19]

Other airlines did convert their aircraft quickly. For example, Canada needed to ship medical supplies and industrial parts from Southeast Asia and, especially, from China. However, cargo airlines serving Southeast Asia and North America fly to the US but not to Canada (Canada had relied on belly freight before the pandemic). This left the Canadian market short on airfreight capacity. To solve this, Air Canada converted three of its flagship Boeing 777-300s into cargo jets by unbolting the seats from the plane.[20] Within six days, Air Canada developed the process, implemented it, and had it approved by national regulator Transport Canada.

Airbus also developed a cargo solution that includes both seat removal and installation of a reinforced floor with rollers on the passenger cabin deck, allowing for easy loading and unloading of heavy pallets and greater cargo capacity. As airlines retire older aircraft such as the venerable Boeing 747, many will probably be fully converted to freighters in the years to come.

Cargo was a bright spot for airlines. During Q2 2020, Korean Air Lines reported rare good news in the devastated airline industry in the form of quarterly profits. The profits came from cargo flights, mostly of South Korean tech products from the likes of Samsung and LG, to homebound consumers around the world.[21]

Lending a Hand (or 2,000 Hands)

In March 2020, C&S Wholesale Grocers needed more workers and trucks as soon as possible for distributing surging volumes of groceries to the more than 7,000 retail outlets that it serves. Normally, hiring takes a lot of time: advertising the job, interviewing candidates, evaluating them, vetting them, contacting the selected hirees, onboarding new employees, and training them. The whole process would take too long because Mike Duffy, C&S's CEO, needed them immediately.

Duffy recounted that he knew Pietro Satriano, CEO and chairman of US Foods, a $24 billion distributor of foods to restaurants and other institutions that were experiencing plummeting demand as consumers stayed home. Duffy called up Satriano and asked, "Do you have resources—both people and trucks—that we could use? Because we need 2,000 people." Satriano agreed, and the two companies worked out an arrangement whereby US Foods workers stayed with their company but were temporarily reassigned to work at nearby C&S facilities. "Within a week, [Satriano] had people in our facilities getting trained on our equipment and then, the next day, being productive," Duffy said.

Satriano remarked to *Supermarket News* in March, "This partnership is an excellent example of the ways in which we are leveraging our distribution capabilities in new ways to support our nation's retailers, and we value this important opportunity."[22] Duffy inked similar arrangements with other restaurant and institutional food distributors, such as Performance Food Group and Sysco. Other players in the retail food industries did the same to meet their burgeoning labor requirements. For example, grocery chain Albertsons secured partnerships with 17 companies in the restaurant and hospitality industry to help immediately bring in 30,000 part-time associates.[23] Duffy said of the group effort, "It's nice to see the cross-industry collaboration with everybody rallying to that single goal of just keeping our communities fed."[24]

(Parking) Lots to Fill

Mall and superstore parking lots were always considered an undesirable but necessary expense for retailers. Walmart, which always looks for ways to glean a little more revenue from every asset, tries to extract more income from the large parking lots in front of its stores. For example, long-time corporate policy permits RV travelers to spend a night in store parking lots.[25] Naturally, Walmart hopes that the travelers will shop at the store for supplies and indeed, these are some of the company's best customers. Beginning in August 2020, Walmart started converting 160 of its stores' parking lots to drive-in movie venues, with films curated by Robert De Niro's Tribeca Enterprises. The experience even includes movie premieres and concessions delivered right to customers' vehicles.[26]

Walmart, however, was not alone. Mall operator Brookfield Properties connected with entertainment company Kilburn Live to turn the parking lots at a number of its malls into drive-in theaters, hosting movies and virtual concerts. Such a new revenue source is likely a welcome reprieve for mall landlords coping with the new reality of a number of their tenants either closing for good, paying less in rent, or not paying rent altogether during the pandemic.[27]

Other examples of innovative uses of mall parking lots include holding music festivals, food festivals with food trucks, a chocolate festival with area restaurants, and a Legoland in the parking lot, among others.[28] In these cases, the parking lot owners either charge for use of the space or rely on increased store sales to create a much-needed revenue stream.

Pivoting to PPE and Other Products

As the pandemic hit, it became painfully apparent that no country was ready. Hospitals and countries did not have enough supplies of personal protective equipment for healthcare workers, including N95 masks, face shields, and gowns. There was also a glaring shortage of ventilators, the potentially life-saving devices that keep air flowing into a patient whose ability to breathe is failing.

Taking Up the Task of Masks

One of the most tragic crises of Covid-19 was caused by the lack of personal protective equipment to protect healthcare workers in many countries. About

600 of them died just in the United States during March, April, and May 2020.[29] Hoarding of masks in the US began in January 2020, when the US had only five known cases.[30]

Many manufacturers and retailers answered the call. Existing mask makers ramped up production—China alone increased its total production tenfold to 40 billion per year.[31] One of the many companies using its assets to make masks was Boston-based athletic apparel company New Balance (*see* Chapter 25, p. 219). At Walmart, CEO Doug McMillon said, "We've also asked some of our apparel suppliers to convert production to PPE for healthcare workers."[32] Many other retailers and manufacturers—including Eddie Bauer, Hanesbrands, Gap, Ralph Lauren, Canada Goose, L.L. Bean, and others—started making and distributing protective masks and gowns.

Getting into the Spirit of the Occasion

Hand sanitizer sales surged after reports that the virus could linger on surfaces, transfer to fingertips, and infect a person when they touched their face. Worried consumers and businesses stripped retail shelves bare of hand sanitizer, disinfectants, and other cleaning supplies. As mentioned earlier in this chapter, Unilever was able to show profit in Q2 2020 due to its increased production of hand sanitizers. But existing suppliers could not keep up with demand, so others in unrelated industries swung into action.

The experience of Swamp Fox Distilling in Buena Vista, Georgia, illustrates both the power and the challenges needed for pivoting to a new product. At one level, the small distillery made the switchover from whiskey to hand sanitizer quickly and easily. The company had all the key assets: alcohol distillery equipment, a bottling line, and storage facilities for bulk liquids and bottles— which could readily make and bottle alcohol-based products, whether they be whiskey or sanitizer. "When I left work on a Friday evening, I was in the whiskey business," said co-owner Britt Moon. "[Then I] woke up on Monday morning and I was making hand sanitizer."[33]

The change, however, was not without challenges for the company on both sides of the supply chain. On the supply side, the distillery needed a source of alcohol. Initially, it used its existing inventories of young whiskey to make sanitizer. When that supply was exhausted, the company used surplus wine from a nearby winery. Then demand outstripped supply. That led the distiller to source alcohol from a bulk ethanol producer, which enabled it to make up to 10,000 750-milliliter bottles a week.

The demand side posed a challenge, too. "Every morning, every day, our phones are ringing from large companies that need it," co-owner Angie Moon told Fox News. "UPS, FedEx, hospitals, VAs, Georgia Parks and Recreation, sheriff's departments from all over the state."[34] To handle orders and customer service, the company had to create its own call center.

More than 600 distilleries, big and small, went from making spirits like whiskey to bottling their raw alcohol as sanitizer. French luxury brand LVMH repurposed manufacturing lines for perfumes and cosmetics to make and distribute free sanitizing gel.[35]

Manufacturers Rushed to Help with Ventilators

In March 2020, estimates suggested that the world needed 880,000 more ventilators to handle the exponentially growing numbers of seriously ill Covid-19 victims.[36] In the US alone, the FDA expected the country was short by 75,000 units.[37] Many companies stepped in to help.

Ventilators, first invented in 1780, seem simple in principle but have evolved into complex, highly regulated medical devices to ensure they do not kill or injure the patient. They contain more than 650 advanced, high-reliability components such as precision sensors and high-performance motorized blowers, as well as a built-in computer with more than 1 million lines of code in its algorithms that ensure the patient receives the proper volumes, pressures, and cycle rate of air.[38]

Royal Philips, the Dutch healthcare technology company and second-largest maker of ventilators, typically manufactures 500 ventilators per week. The company was ramping this rate up to 4,000 per week by partnering with contract manufacturers Flex and Jabil.

Flex, a $24 billion multinational contract manufacturer and supply chain services provider, started working immediately to support customer requirements, setting a production target of 25,000–30,000 ventilators per month.[39] Lynn Torrel, the chief procurement and supply chain officer at Flex, described the company's ongoing efforts: "It's going very well. There have been quite a few challenges along the way—from design changes, industry allocations, and many critical shortages that we've had to address. Suppliers are working diligently. Everybody's prioritizing. There are going to be a few articles coming out about that, because going from nothing to ventilator production in six weeks, it's pretty amazing."[40]

While not the only company pivoting to make ventilators, Flex had two big advantages. First, it had an army of engineers who were adept at bringing anyone's idea of a product into mass production—what they call "sketch to scale." This breadth and depth of knowledge allowed it to manufacture parts in-house that were in short supply by using 3D printing. Second, Flex used its supply chain know-how and relationships with 16,000 suppliers to reduce lead times for critical parts and launch the product quickly.

Other companies also created partnerships to accelerate production. The largest ventilator maker in the world is Vyaire Medical of Mettawa, Illinois. Vyaire increased its own production, but in order to meet the exploding demand, it partnered with Spirit AeroSystems, one of the world's largest non-OEM (original equipment manufacturer) designers and manufacturers of aerostructures for commercial and defense aircraft.[41] The partnership added sophisticated manufacturing capacity to Vyaire.

Many automotive companies also stepped up to address the ventilator shortage.[42] Ford teamed up with GE Healthcare to make ventilators and the partnership expected to reach 50,000 ventilators by the end of August 2020, fulfilling its $336 million contract with the US Department of Health and Human Services. Similarly, General Motors used one of its mothballed plants in Indiana and teamed with Seattle-area medical-device maker Ventec Life Systems to complete 30,000 ventilators by the end of August, fulfilling its terms under a $490 million federal contract.[43] Tesla came up with its own design, using many parts from Tesla cars. Mercedes started making simpler continuous positive airway pressure (CPAP) ventilators. These efforts were not the first time that car makers made medical devices during a pandemic: In the 1940s, William Morris (of Morris Minor fame, an icon of the British car industry) used his factories to build iron lungs to help victims of the waves of polio pandemics at that time.[44]

Many other manufacturing and technology companies as well as technical universities, including MIT, have designed and licensed the manufacturing of simplified ventilators.[45] This was done in order to make sure that the sick have access to treatment that is not constrained by ventilator shortages, as a step on the way to the "new normal": Despite the virus, life must go on.

PART 2
LIVING WITH
UNCERTAINTY

"Let me conclude by reinforcing the enormity of
the task ahead. It will require a level of response
and depth of resilience that have yet to be fully
realized."

—Olivier Le Peuch, CEO and Director,
Schlumberger Limited[1]

The first eight months of the pandemic saw a mix of selfish hoarding
and selfless heroism amidst the challenge of everyone in the world trying to cope with fundamental uncertainties about the exact nature of
the threat. Everyone was hoping the pandemic would subside, but the
history and biology of human epidemics taught humanity not to count
on that. Unlike the one-and-done disruption of a fire, flood, or hurricane,
Covid-19 continues to percolate through society. As long as billions of
people remain susceptible to the disease, Covid-19 will live among us and
we will need ways to manage a "new normal."

This part of the book delves into the possible scenarios for the future of the Covid-19 pandemic in the coming years and how companies can manage what might be a rough period of uncertain infection rates, supply, demand, economic conditions, and government action (or inaction). Thus, although one can certainly hope for the best, the uncertain nature of the situation calls for preparing for the worst.

5. The Whack-a-Mole Recovery

Covid-19 prompted shutdowns of schools, businesses, and many daily activities around the world as governments attempted to slow the spread of infection by limiting human-to-human contact.

The result was a precipitous drop in consumer demand, interruptions in supply, and a spike in unemployment—particularly in countries that chose not to directly subsidize employers. The suddenness of the downturn caught many unprepared. This pain prompted immediate pressures to reopen the economy, with statements about the cure being "worse than the disease."

Each country, state, and locality followed its own trajectory of closures, mandates, countermeasures, levels of citizen compliance, and concomitant changes in the rates of infections. Each location made decisions about reopening—some based on science, some based on economics, some based on politics. However, hasty reopenings sparked resurgent infections in many locations, which forced more closures and quarantines. For example, the end of the summer travel season in Europe resulted in a surge in cases and growing concerns in Spain, France, and other EU member countries.[1] "The exact trajectory of our recovery is highly uncertain," said Chris Kempczinski, CEO of McDonald's.[2]

Overall, governments may have less control over the recovery and the pandemic than the public does; ultimately, citizens' behavior regarding masks, distancing, gathering, travel, and quarantining is what determines the spread of the virus and its patterns of infectiousness and virulence.

Johnson & Johnson's Meri Stevens described the impact on the company's supply chains: "The most challenging for us is the dynamic nature of what's going on. Transport is disrupted almost daily by new rules and regulations around the world. A border can close. A new regulation can come in for an aircraft. Every day, something is changing in the way the rules are being applied. And it's almost country by country, different states, different roads. In China, there were roadblocks in various places—and so a road that was open today may not be open tomorrow, and you wouldn't know until you got there."[3]

Scenarios of Sickness

"I think what people have to remember is that the virus isn't gone. The disease isn't gone. And it's going to be with us for a while," said Ashish Jha, director of Harvard's Global Health Institute.[4] Pandemics often create waves of infections spanning several years and flaring up in different regions at different times. Dr. Anthony Fauci, director of the National Institute of Allergy and Infectious Diseases, warned at the end of April that another wave is "inevitable" and that the severity depends on how the US prepares for it. "If by that time we have put into place all of the countermeasures that you need to address this, we should do reasonably well," Fauci said. "If we don't do that successfully, we could be in for a bad fall and a bad winter."[5] The resurgence of infections in southern US states in June–July 2020 proved his point.

Researchers at the University of Minnesota's Center for Infectious Disease Research and Policy analyzed the current Covid-19 pandemic and eight previous flu pandemics to create three likely scenarios for the future of the Covid-19 pandemic.[6] In the first scenario, the coronavirus spawns a series of peaks and valleys that reoccur consistently over a one- to two-year period but gradually diminish sometime in 2021. In the second scenario, the virus resurges violently in the fall or winter of 2020 with a larger wave of cases than have been seen to date, paralleling the 1918 flu pandemic.[7] In the third scenario, it continues a slow burn of ongoing community transmission and modest, fluctuating numbers of positive cases. Regardless of the scenario, the researchers concluded at the end of April 2020, "We must be prepared for at least another 18 to 24 months of significant Covid-19 activity, with hotspots popping up periodically in diverse geographic areas."[8] The researchers, however, did not include the possibility of an early vaccine or an effective therapeutic in their forecasts.

Just as humans have adapted their response to the virus—testing, isolating the infected, social distancing, etc.—the virus is changing, too. Each time the virus replicates, its molecular machinery sometimes makes mistakes in the copy of the genetic material; these changes are passed on if that mutant copy of the virus finds a host. As of August 2020, scientists have identified some 4,300 different genetic variants of the SARS-CoV-2 virus that causes Covid-19,[9] and many more will no doubt appear over time. For example, on August 14, a new strain of the virus was reported by Malaysian and Philippine authorities with the warning that it seemed to have higher infectiousness.[10] Usually, a mutation changes nothing. Sometimes, it makes that offspring nonviable, but sometimes it changes the character of the infection that significantly impacts humanity.

As the virus spreads to millions and then billions of people and replicates billions or trillions of times in each person, the potential for mutations that can spread and change the pandemic (for better or worse) increases. In some cases, a less deadly mutant may well arise that humanity essentially learns to live with, as is the case with four other coronaviruses that cause common colds. Or, a mutant might arise that can infect vaccinated people or evade detection by current tests for Covid-19 infections. This would restart the pandemic disease cycle by creating a new respiratory disease that is not detected by tests for Covid-19, flu, or other known pathogens. National healthcare systems would then somehow need to identify it as a new cause of illness. (This happens regularly with the flu, which is why people get a new flu shot each year to hopefully cope with that year's strains.) The point is that, in the coming years, the virus may be a recurring phenomenon with greater or lesser burdens of disease on the population and the economy.

While all eyes—and healthcare resources—are focused on Covid-19, other infectious diseases are taking advantage of the diverted focus.[11] In early 2020, the rise of Covid-19 caused countries to postpone immunization programs for other serious childhood diseases. They did this to reduce the spread of the virus, to redirect healthcare workers to fight Covid-19, and because of disruptions in vaccine logistics. But this later led to outbreaks of diphtheria, polio, and measles in more than 30 countries. Dr. Tedros Adhanom Ghebreyesus, director-general of the WHO, warned, "Disruption to immunization programs from the Covid-19 pandemic threatens to unwind decades of progress against vaccine-preventable diseases like measles."[12] In fact, in an online interview with the editors of *The Economist* on August 18, Bill Gates estimated that 90 percent of deaths from the coronavirus will not be caused by Covid-19 directly but by other diseases as well as poverty and food shortages in developing countries.[13]

Three Exits from the Pandemic's Not-So-Merry-Go-Round

"We do have a big problem in what the exit strategy is and how we get out of this," said Mark Woolhouse, a professor of infectious disease epidemiology at the University of Edinburgh. "It's not just the UK, no country has an exit strategy."[14] Epidemiologist Gabriel Leung of the University of Hong Kong added, "This pandemic is not going to settle down until there is sufficient population immunity."[15] That immunity can come from vaccination or controlled spreading: two of three possible strategies for exit from the pandemic.

"Long term, clearly a vaccine is one way out of this and we all hope that will happen as quickly as possible," said the UK's chief medical advisor, Prof. Chris Whitty.[16] Vaccination of about two-thirds of the population would ensure that any outbreaks would be small and local—confined to the unvaccinated and those with weak immune systems. The more people who are immune, the less chance the virus has to spread.

By mid-August 2020, 29 candidate vaccines were in clinical evaluation, while 138 more candidates were in pre-clinical evaluation[17] by dedicated scientific teams hunting for a vaccine in an intense and collaborative (among scientists) global race.[18] Governments, companies, and philanthropic NGOs dedicated billions of dollars for research and for securing mass production capacity. Vaccination, however, is a risky exit strategy that can't be guaranteed owing to two significant challenges. The first challenge is the risky and uncertain nature of vaccine development. Will the vaccine be safe, effective, easily mass-produced, and confer lasting immunity? The history of this issue shows that the road to vaccine development has been paved with disappointments and crashes.[19] "The fastest vaccine we previously developed was for mumps, and that took four years to develop. And typically, it takes 10 to 15 years to develop a vaccine. So, 12 to 18 months would be record-breaking," said Dr. Seema Yasmin, director of the Stanford Health Communication Initiative.[20]

Vaccination's second challenge is that it cannot work without widespread adoption, and adoption is far from guaranteed. A poll from the Associated Press–NORC Center for Public Affairs Research found that only about half of Americans say they would get a Covid-19 vaccine.[21] Many fear that "warp speed" development and a fast rollout will mean a higher risk of side effects. Others don't think Covid-19 is dangerous enough to warrant getting a shot. A 50 percent vaccination rate makes it more likely that Covid-19 becomes endemic, like measles. That is, it will continue to reappear, spreading here and there among unvaccinated populations as well as those who are vaccinated but whose immune systems don't respond well (e.g., the elderly, individuals with asthmatic disease, and those taking immunosuppressant medications).

A second exit strategy is to allow the virus to continue spreading throughout the community until enough people have been infected and recovered to create "herd immunity." If a vaccine really is a distant, uncertain hope and draconian lockdowns only delay the inevitable spread of the disease, then a managed spread may be the best option. This was a key element of Sweden's strategy.[22] Unfortunately, this strategy requires that most people get the disease (with all the disruptions, costs, and long-term health effects of millions of Covid-19 cases) and that some—potentially many—die. This strategy may also require maintaining some level of physical distancing (which may be voluntary) for months or years to ensure the disease only spreads slowly and avoids overwhelming local hospitals. The Swedish model, which was widely supported in Sweden, came under increasing criticism when the resulting high death rate among (mainly elderly) Swedes became apparent.[23]

"The third option," Woolhouse said, is "permanent changes in our behavior that allow us to keep transmission rates low."[24] Some combination of masks in public places, distancing, disinfection, and avoidance of mass gatherings may become a way of life. Coming to work while sick may become grounds for dismissal rather than a sign of dedication. Movement-tracking apps or government test-and-trace programs may become embedded (or required) in public life. Proof of Covid-19 status could become like proof of age at a nightclub door, proof of identity at an airport screening point, or proof of identity when entering an office building.

With Covid-19 being an entirely new disease, scientists don't know what either the virus or scientific progress has in store. When might a viable vaccine pass clinical trials, make it into mass production, and be used widely enough to thwart the spread of the virus? Will vaccinated or previously infected people enjoy long-term immunity, such that once most of the population has had the disease (or gotten vaccinated), they will provide herd immunity to the remaining population? Or will people be susceptible to catching it again within a few months or years, as is the case with the four coronaviruses that cause common colds?[25] Might Covid-19 mutate into more or less virulent forms to become an annual misery of greater or lesser extent? Will drug makers finally find treatments that reduce fatality rates and reduce the fears of catching the disease?

As the pandemic grinds on, the citizens of the world have become the unwitting and often unwilling guinea pigs for hundreds of uncoordinated natural experiments. As each jurisdiction makes its own decisions about testing, contact tracing, physical distancing, business closures, reopening schedules, and financial support for those affected, it is experimenting with its citizens' lives and livelihoods. Time will tell which places suffered the highest death tolls and which suffered the worst economic effects. If the experiences of the 1918 flu pandemic are repeated today, we will see those jurisdictions with the longest, harshest lockdowns exhibit both lower death tolls and better economic recoveries compared to places that rushed to reopen.[26]

The Threat of Financial Contagion

More than half a year before the virus invaded the global economy, Federal Reserve Chairman Jerome Powell warned, "Business debt has clearly reached a level that should give businesses and investors reason to pause and reflect. If a downturn were to arrive unexpectedly, some firms would face challenges."[27] He further noted that "a highly leveraged business sector could amplify any economic downturn as companies are forced to lay off workers and cut back on investments." With Covid-19, an especially sharp downturn certainly did arrive unexpectedly, threatening repayment on some of the world's $74 trillion in corporate debt.[28]

Many households, companies, and even countries did not have the resources to absorb the financial shocks created by the disease, such as unemployment, slumping consumer spending, added costs, and declining tax revenues. Mortgage payment delinquencies in the US jumped to their highest level in 21 years (50 percent higher than during the worst of the housing-induced financial crisis in 2008).[29] Datex Property Solutions found that about 40 percent of retail rents went unpaid in April and May 2020.[30] Late mortgage payments, rents, and debt repayments by consumers, retailers, and companies, in turn, jeopardized landlords and banks. "Social distancing means financial Armageddon for commercial real estate and municipalities in coming months," wrote R. Christopher Whalen, head of Whalen Global Advisors, on his blog for investors.[31]

A similar problem afflicted the public sector with municipal, state, and many national governments being under severe financial stress. The economic collapse has devastated tax revenues, while the pandemic has added costs. Some countries entered the pandemic with already high debt loads that they will have trouble servicing.[32] Countries that depend on tourism have been hit particularly hard, as have countries where many of the jobs cannot be performed from home, or where the corporate sector is dominated by small firms. *The Economist* suggested a ranking of the countries most vulnerable to a lockdown.[33] In Europe, the most badly affected countries were Greece, Spain, and Italy. Similarly, cities dependent on tourism (Las Vegas, New York City), on direct state aid (Buffalo, Rochester), or on sales taxes (New Orleans) are the most vulnerable. Cities like Boston, which rely heavily on relatively stable sources of revenue such as property taxes, are in the strongest position.[34] This may force some jurisdictions—in particular those that cannot print their own currency—to go bankrupt (in "sovereign default"); levy draconian taxes, sacrificing future growth; or forgo crucial government services in the name of balancing their budgets. Others will have to restructure and reform their economies under the rules of the IMF.

As with the 2008 financial crisis, the inability of households, companies, or governments to repay their debts to others can create a domino effect. In many cases, lenders have important obligations to others too that they may be forced to default on if too many of their borrowers or renters fail to pay. For example, if too many mortgage holders cannot repay their local bank, the local bank cannot repay its depositors and bondholders. Ditto an insurance company that invested in commercial real estate investment trusts and needs to pay retirees their annuities from the stream of commercial rents. Defaults, forbearance, and debt forgiveness ripple through the financial fabric of the economy to bring about unintended consequences.

Long-Term Economic Effects

As the Covid-19 crisis continued around the world, it became clear that the economic impacts would linger for a long time.[35] In all of the serious financial crises since the mid-19th century, it took an average of eight years for per capita GDP to return to pre-crisis levels.[36] While the US, China, and Europe have the wherewithal to provide massive financial stimulus, most other countries do not have the capacity to overcome the economic damage.

The reduction in trade due to trade wars and the pandemic (*see* Chapter 18, p. 157) means that many trade links have been broken. Commodity prices have declined and tourism has collapsed. High unemployment means that many of the unemployed will lose skills and will find it harder to reenter the workforce. Finally, the pandemic is causing a massive number of small firms—where most people are employed—to go out of business.[37] It is likely to take a long time for new businesses to emerge and provide new employment opportunities.

The IMF predicted that the deficit-to-GDP ratio in advanced economies will swell from 3.9 percent in 2019 to 16.6 percent in 2020.[38] Dealing with this debt will hinder the rebuilding of the world's economies as well as put a dent in other grand plans to tackle social, infrastructure, environmental, and a host of other challenges (*see* Chapter 20, p. 180).

Social Unrest

If a rising tide lifts all boats, a receding tide reveals the rocks in the harbor. Just as the 2008 financial crisis contributed to the 2011 Arab Spring uprisings,[39] Covid-19 created knock-on effects on social stability and crime. Most big cities in the US saw an increase in crime. For example, the *Wall Street Journal* reported that, by June 2020, "murders soared 160 percent this year over last, while burglaries are up 56 percent and car-jackings have more than doubled." Only residential burglaries and larceny fell in many places—no doubt because people were at home."[40]

Festering racial and social inequality, stir-crazy citizens, and high unemployment provided the toxic ingredients for protest, civil unrest, violence, and looting. The alleged murder of George Floyd by police in Minneapolis may have triggered the waves of protests and violence that swept across the US and beyond, but Covid-19 likely created the bone-dry conditions that enabled the firestorm.

For retailers, restaurants, and other urban businesses already pushed to the cliff edge by coronavirus-related closures and plummeting sales, looting and vandalism may have been the final nudge into bankruptcy. In turn, this worsened unemployment and real estate values in cities most hurt by the riots.

Chaotic Reopenings, Closings, and Other Disruptions

Speculating on the shape of economic recovery, economists have proposed an alphabet soup of recovery shapes such as the speedy V shape, a slower U shape, a depressing L, or an oscillating W. Such simple shapes ignore both the complexities of the global economy and the potential for local disruptions caused by resurgent local clusters of infections or knock-on financial damage to countries and companies. "We need to be careful that we don't project straight lines—the moment the state opens, we are all free and the business will come back. I think there's going to be a lot of iterations," said PepsiCo CEO Ramon Laguarta.[41] An epidemiologist at the Johns Hopkins Center for Health Security, Dr. Caitlin Rivers, remarked, "The talk of a second wave as if we've exited the first doesn't capture what's really happening."[42]

Instead, the more likely scenario is a patchwork of local cycles of infections and related impacts that, in turn, create cycles of economic rebirth and relapse, which then plague businesses and their supply chains. With supply and demand cycling at different times and in different places, the bullwhip effect will be especially fierce as companies are whipsawed by the changes. That is, businesses face a global game of whack-a-mole as the virus rears its head or subsides in the different cities, states, and countries that house the far-flung supply chains on which companies rely.[43]

Unfortunately for companies, the conventional approaches of "demand forecasting" do not work when there are underlying structural changes in the demand patterns, such as during the pandemic. All of these forecasting models depend on future sales behaving, statistically, like historical sales, and that is not the case when consumers change their behavior markedly. Models based on artificial intelligence (AI) and machine learning (ML) tools are usually no better in such an environment because they are also based on past data that is used to train these models.[44] Supply may also not be assured because suppliers, the company's own facilities, and interconnecting transportation systems may not be available or may have limited capacity owing to facility infections, regional lockdowns, or various countries' changing regulations.

CEOs are wondering when (and whether) the trillions of dollars in economic stimulus will restart consumer sales, especially for big-ticket items like cars. "Is that going to get spent and going to go right back into new vehicle sales or not?" wondered James Kamsickas, chairman and CEO of automotive part manufacturer Dana. "Who knows what's going to happen there. Is it a recovery? Is it not? Who knows?"[45]

Another automotive industry chief executive, Kevin Clark of Aptiv, a maker of electronics and computer systems for vehicles, said, "As we sit here today [May 5, 2020], the situation is very fluid. Visibility [into] the timing and pace of restarts remains very low. We're also concerned about underlying consumer demand, taking into account the record unemployment levels, decreased personal income, and declining consumer sentiment."[46] Similarly, Randall Stephenson, CEO of AT&T, said in May 2020, "We bring in the smartest and the most genius economists in the world, and you can bring a dozen of them in, and the range of possible outcomes just for the second quarter of 2020 is unbelievably wide."[47]

Another trend that should add to CEOs' worries is the increasing savings glut in Western countries. Rather than spend their money, consumers in the US and Europe have shunted record amounts of money into savings.[48] Furthermore, a research paper published by the Federal Reserve Bank of San Francisco argued that unlike other crises, pandemics seem to cause interest rates to fall for decades and precautionary savings to rise rather than be spent.[49]

Given these challenges, the words of General Dwight D. Eisenhower ring true: "Plans are useless, but planning is indispensable." In the case of Covid-19, planning for the coming months and years should focus on preparing to react flexibly and quickly to changing circumstances in both supply and demand. Such planning includes not only detecting and mitigating disruptions, but also adapting to changing times and looking for business opportunities during the whack-a-mole recovery.

6. Managing for Ongoing Disruptions

In his novel *Anna Karenina*, Leo Tolstoy wrote, "Happy families are all alike; every unhappy family is unhappy in its own way." This observation has two analogous truths when it comes to disruptions such as Covid-19. The first is that every unhappy disruption comes with its own litany of unwanted causes and cascade of miserable effects. Covid-19 is certainly unlike any other recent disruption in its global scope, chaotic timescales, ongoing uncertainties, lingering aftereffects, and political ramifications. Covid-19 is many different disruptions rolled into one. The second truth, though, is that dealing with the challenges presented by the pandemic and preparing for return to economic growth involve many core principles of resilience that apply to Covid-19 as they apply to any other disruption.

"We cannot control the pandemic, but we can control how we're mitigating risk to our operations and supply chain, engaging with customers, managing costs and preserving liquidity," said Darius Adamczyk, chairman and CEO of Honeywell on a Q1 2020 earnings call with investors.[1] With Covid-19, companies may be managing disruptions for a long time. As of the summer of 2020, companies face immediate challenges of additional waves of infection, reactions to those outbreaks, and the impacts of the rapid deceleration of the economy. In the long term, companies face basic uncertainty about post-pandemic "normal" customer demand, employee working arrangements, and trade rules.

Ongoing health-related directives, personal anxieties, and risks, combined with a deep recession, mean that the nature of work, retail, education, and life may be different for quite some time. Thus, emergency management practices for dealing with the continuing crisis may become a new normal for many companies.

Overall, managing in a highly uncertain new normal calls for three main initiatives:

- preserving resources required for survival, response, and recovery
- focusing on agile decision-making processes that can navigate both anarchic and glacially slow bureaucracies in managing very complex organizations at speed
- attaining new levels of information sharing both inside and outside the organization to coordinate action and stabilize stakeholders.

Cash Is King

Remarking on the first quarter of 2020, Olivier Le Peuch, CEO of Schlumberger, said, "The actions we have taken so far have been focused on those things we can control in protecting our business—with a clear priority on cash and liquidity—in an uncertain industry and global environment."[2] In April 2020, the American Chamber of Commerce and Kearney conducted a survey of 80 top executives on the business impact of the coronavirus crisis. They found that almost 50 percent expected cash problems within six months. CFOs at many companies took financial steps to marshal cash. As of July 14, 2020, 773 public companies had cut or reduced their dividend payments to shareholders. By then, more S&P 500 companies had already decreased or suspended their dividend payments than they had in all of 2008.[3] Others also tapped lines of credit or raised debt to increase their levels of cash.

Cutting costs typically (and unfortunately) involves cutting workers' pay. At least 4 million private-sector employees had their pay cut during the pandemic.[4] White-collar jobs in finance, tech and law have experienced the most rapid pay cuts. In many organizations, highly paid senior managers cut their own pay voluntarily. For example, as thousands of Delta Air Lines employees were taking unpaid leave, Ed Bastian, the airline's CEO, announced in mid-March that he would forgo his salary for six months from April through September, as did board members. The company's officers were taking a 50 percent pay cut, and directors and managing directors were taking a 25 percent pay cut.[5] On top of this, their stock options, which are the bulk of their compensation, are worthless. In 2016, the company paid $1.6 billion in profit sharing to employees, something that is not likely to repeat any time soon.

"The way I think about the crisis is," said Ford's CEO at the time, Jim Hackett, on May 6, "you've got a priority first of stabilizing [so] you can operate and recover some of the costs that are just flying out the door."[6] That means tough decisions about delaying any capital investments and cutting discretionary spending. For example, car makers were curtailing spending on longer-range technology bets—such as electric vehicles, self-driving cars, and car-sharing services—that have been widely considered critical to car companies' future.[7] GM was the only Detroit automaker to report a quarterly profit, while it, as well as Ford and Fiat-Chrysler, sought to manage the cash crunch amid plunging demand and worker absenteeism.[8] Commenting on capital outflows, GM CEO Mary Barra told analysts, "When you really challenge them, you find opportunities to save."[9]

In addition to cost cutting, three operating parameters of supply chain management can help improve cash levels through what is known as the cash conversion cycle (CCC) or cash-to-cash time.[10] The cycle involves the timing of events related to suppliers, customers, and inventory.

First, companies can conserve cash by slowing the speed at which the company pays its suppliers. Days payable outstanding (DPO) is the average delay between when the company incurs an obligation to pay a supplier and when it makes payment to that supplier. Delaying payment where possible keeps that cash with the company. Although increasing the DPO can improve cash levels, it does risk damaging financially weak suppliers, leading to supply disruptions.[11]

Second, inventory is basically cash sitting in a warehouse or on a retail shelf. Days inventory outstanding (DIO) is the average number of days of sales held by the company in parts from suppliers, partially built products in manufacturing, finished products in warehouses and store shelves, and anything moving from supplier to factory to warehouse to shelf. Inventory ties up cash that can be released by selling off that inventory and reducing the time parts and products spend sitting or traveling in the supply chain. Even in today's just-in-time inventory management systems, most companies keep large amounts of inventory. Before Covid-19, the growing economy of the last decade encouraged companies to focus on customer service, which often meant using inventories to reduce the likelihood of out-of-stock situations and incomplete orders. Decreasing the amount of inventory to release cash can improve cash levels, though it does increase level-of-service risk if supplies are disrupted or if demand surges.

Finally, companies can boost cash levels by reducing the time lag of payments. Days sales outstanding (DSO) is the average delay between when the customer incurs an obligation to pay the company and when the company receives payment from that customer. If a company can reduce DSO below DPO, it will receive payment from its customers before having to pay its own suppliers, thus effectively being funded by its suppliers.

Tiger Teams

The pandemic may be global, but the effects of the virus in a whack-a-mole pattern are local, diverse, and ever-changing. To manage fluctuating supply and demand around the world and at speed, leading companies such as Flex and Johnson & Johnson have "tiger teams" to help manage crises in critical regions around the world or to focus on critical segments of their supply chains. These teams both collect data and take action.

First and foremost, these teams act as listening posts that communicate with local stakeholders in local languages. Although the teams and companies certainly maintain constant contact with local governments, the Covid-19 crisis proved that governments might downplay the problem to avoid panic rather than disseminate candid information. Getting an accurate sense of a situation requires information from nontraditional sources, such as contacts in hospitals and tracking social media postings around the world. These teams also report the implications of local news and local resources.

Tiger teams also act as quick reaction forces, providing "boots on the ground." They can help ensure the safety of local workers and help local suppliers or customers to recover. They can work with local governments to get permission to move crucial shipments or to reopen either company facilities or key supplier facilities. Such teams are coordinated by a central emergency management center managing the overall global response.

For example, Lynn Torrel, chief procurement and supply chain officer of Flex, explained that the company's management team in China quickly detected the seriousness of Covid-19. She described the first alerts: "When I think about Wuhan when it was first breaking out, it was before Chinese New Year. So, our employees were at home with their families. And about two days before the Chinese New Year, the gentleman who was responsible for operations in Asia heard about shutting down Wuhan. He called some people he knows in the government to confirm, because he said it was just shocking to hear that they would shut down the city. And when it was confirmed, he sprang into action. He called up our regional lead for GPSC [global procurement and supply chain] for indirect procurement and asked her to secure two months' worth of masks for our employees in China. He said, 'Hey—forget the normal processes for procurement and go get the masks.' So, we went from zero to 60 days of supply for our facility in Asia."[12] This quick action secured PPE for Flex's 60,000 workers in China.

Remarking on when the pandemic started to hit Europe, Torrel added: "We had sourced all of our personal protection equipment for our employees, and we had it staged in a hub in Hungary." Information coming from the field on our daily calls prompted another change. "We had a call where it was mentioned, 'It seems like the border crossings are getting a little longer. Wonder what will happen longer term.'" The information was immediately acted upon, Torrel explained: "We made the decision in advance [of] the border closures and the delays; we moved all of the equipment to the sites instead of going to the hub."[13]

A Virtual Room with a View (and a Mandate)

In disruptive times, companies depend on timely information, quick coordination, and fast decision making. Even in normal times, competition drives companies toward faster, better decision making processes. To this end, some companies have created supply chain control towers or network operations centers to manage their global networks and also manage disruptions. For example, Procter & Gamble has a supply chain control tower with a cloud-based platform to provide real-time information on production and external demand. The company used the visibility and analytics offered by this control tower to manage disruptions such as Hurricane Sandy (2012) and Hurricane Irma (2017).[14] Some large corporations, like Walmart, have emergency operations centers (EOCs): "war rooms" that help monitor dynamic situations and provide a central venue for coordinated decision making.

Centralizing the information helps organizations detect problems as quickly as possible, make fast decisions, and actively monitor the trajectories of events and activities against forecasts and mitigation efforts. During the pandemic, "the place" to manage crises became the cloud, with its growing functionality of internet video, document sharing, real-time dashboards, and analytics.

More important than the place is the people. Crisis management calls for a leadership team that has direct knowledge of affected areas and control of key resources. In manufacturing companies, this team is typically led by supply chain and engineering professionals. They consult daily with key leaders of marketing, sales, HR, legal, finance, facilities, and public relations.

Daniel Biran, vice president of security at Biogen, described the company's enterprise risk management team operations during the pandemic in an interview for this book: "Every function in Biogen is part of it, from supply chain to medical to legal to HR to IT. Everybody sits around the table. We also decided last year that the enterprise risk management community will serve as a crisis management team for Biogen."[15] Essential elements for an effective team were a clear roster of participants with clear decision-making rules and the power to act as needed when time is of the essence. At Flex, for its daily virtual war room meeting amid Covid-19, the company had about 40 to 45 people involved. Daily meetings continued for months until processes were in place to allow less frequent meetings.[16]

Similarly, Mike Duffy, CEO of C&S Wholesale Grocers, described the ramp-up and ramp-down of their response in the spring of 2020: "We didn't really see the spike in orders until that first week in March." He added, "But that's when it really started. And that's when we enacted our crisis management team, on that Thursday. We moved to twice-a-day meetings, 7:30 in the morning, 5:00 at night, through the weekend. Those [meetings] continued for probably a month before we started to eliminate Sundays, then we peeled back on the morning. Just did the night. So, we started to reduce the frequency probably in mid to late April. But March was a whirl. I mean, it was just hand-to-mouth, trying to get stuff through the door."[17]

The foci of crisis management efforts are threefold: the employees, the business, and the community. Best practice is to empower separate teams to deal with each area of focus to avoid neglecting any one. One team takes care of employees: ensuring their safety, continuity of medical insurance, acquiring PPE as needed, helping with mental health needs, and helping with family challenges. Another team can focus on the business: satisfying customers, working with suppliers, and getting the business back up and running. Finally, the community care team might arrange donations for community activities, contribute to safe reopening discussions, or help in the procurement and manufacturing of PPE for the community.

Stay in Your Swim Lane

People's natural inclination to help in any way possible can create unintended consequences in the frantic atmosphere of a disruption. During the 2011 Tōhoko earthquake, tsunami, and nuclear disaster, GM faced a shortage of the electronic modules used to control heated seats. To address the issue, a vice president decided GM should simply build vehicles without heated seats. But this solution would have created more problems than it solved, because heating is a standard feature of leather seats in luxury variants of car models.

Shifting production to cars without heated seats would create three major problems: shortages of unheated cloth seats; stranded piles of parts and partially built vehicles in the company's supply chain and factories associated with luxury-option vehicles; and disappointment for dealers and customers.

To prevent everyone in the company from making well-intentioned decisions that might cause bad unintended consequences, GM adopted a mantra of "Stay in Your Swim Lane," restricting people to decisions in their own parts of the complex system.[18] "Stay in Your Swim Lane" means creating clearly delineated and delegated roles to define all those swim lanes. It also implies that the people deployed to manage a crisis need to be steeped in the intricacies of how supply chain, manufacturing, distribution, and sales all connect together. Finally, part of the reason a company might need a 24-7 EOC during a disruption is to coordinate local decisions around the world that can have impacts elsewhere.

Less Bureaucracy

The need for urgent action puts a premium on accelerated decision making and removing hurdles to actions. Less bureaucracy enables more speed. Tiger teams as well as some form of EOC accomplishes this. Tiger teams empower fast, local decision making in contrast with traditional "up-the-chain" approvals processes. When crises are fast-moving, decision making at the lowest level of the organization, close to the problem, even without senior management approvals, can help avoid a small crisis turning into a big one by taking mitigation actions quickly.

As the 19th-century German Field Marshal Helmuth von Moltke is credited with saying, "No plan survives first contact with the enemy."[19] Thus, companies like Zara and organizations like the US Coast Guard empower line operators and local commanders to take corrective actions quickly when a problem is spotted.[20] When the crisis is global, however, central coordination is required. Thus, centralized EOCs bring data and decision makers together (virtually) to create quick-cadence decision making cycles. The center can create protocols and playbooks that guide fast, local action, while tiger teams can collect information and monitor events so that the EOC is continuously updated.

Crisis Communications to Calm the Nerves

"We don't feel like we have all the answers, but we're very clear on how we're acting and what's important to us," explained Jeff Harmening, CEO of General Mills.[21] Both anxiety and actual risk come from uncertainty. The more stakeholders know about a company's intentions, the better they can combine it with other information they have and improve their own recovery processes.

Thus, information sharing goes a long way toward reducing mutual risks in supply chains, economies, and communities. Companies should be prepared to communicate accurately and candidly with all stakeholders: employees, customers, suppliers, media, shareholders, analysts, and the community. It means communicating continuously about new developments and assurances of progress on the course of action.

Some of the rules of crisis communications are:

- It is better to communicate frequently rather than completely. A leader may communicate what is not known and what the organization is doing about it.
- During crises, communications need to be simple. While nuances may be part of the issue, simple messages are absorbed better by an anxious audience.
- Candor trumps charisma. People crave leadership that they can believe in; therefore, a leader should never hide problems but be transparent, honest, and emphatic.
- Information should be relevant, even if it is not consistent with prior messages. People understand that a crisis may change the situation and thus initiatives and instructions may change. That is why consistency is less important than relevance.
- Leaders should be inclusive whenever possible. While some instances may call for decisive unilateral action, consultation with all stakeholders helps mitigate the normal anxiety in crisis situations.

Of course, the best communication channel is action, because actions speak louder than words. When athletic equipment company New Balance decided to make masks, the company did not announce its plans. Instead, it waited until it had figured out the design, started making the product, and was delivering the masks. Only then did the company announce it with a simple ad, said Dave Wheeler, New Balance's COO.[22] The simple ad elicited 1.7 million likes on Instagram and 8 billion impressions. The ad did not convey plans, intentions, or future commitments—just action (*see* Chapter 25, p. 219).

Finally, it is important for management to speak with one voice. In contrast, the disappearance of Malaysia Airlines flight 370 in 2014 saw a confusing cacophony of conflicting communications from the Malaysian prime minister, the minister of transport, the airline, the military, and others.[23]

Summarizing several of these communications principles, General Mills's CEO Jeff Harmening said, "In a time of great uncertainty, it's more important to be clear than it is to be certain. For us, that clarity is the safety of employees, the safety of the food supply, and executing on the here and now."[24]

7. Managing for Whack-a-Mole Supply

In the ongoing pandemic and post-pandemic worlds, suppliers may fail to handle orders for many reasons. A new cluster of infections in a supplier's facility or community might force a closure. Financial damage to the supplier—especially if the supplier depends on heavily impacted industries such as tourism, hospitality, or commercial aircraft manufacturing—might cause bankruptcy. And, of course, the world's usual disruptions in the form of typhoons, earthquakes, floods, and other natural disasters continue whether there's a pandemic or not.

The economic crisis resulting from the response to Covid-19 meant that, with some exceptions, most of the world's companies have suffered a loss of sales. Companies also endured added business costs or productivity declines associated with worker safety measures. At the same time, they had to make their debt payments. Corporate debt was at record highs in the summer of 2020. By the end of June, for example, US companies owed $15.5 trillion (equal to 74 percent of US GDP) with almost one-third of it in the form of leveraged loans and below-investment-grade bonds.[1] Typically, this means that the US is heading into a recession. More money going out, less money coming in, and high debt translate into more bankruptcies.

"We experience new headwinds every day," said Darius Adamczyk, chairman and CEO of Honeywell. "But we continue to monitor our supply chain, work closely with our suppliers and respond swiftly when new challenges arise."[2] Managing the risk that supply won't meet demand depends on a combination of planning, monitoring, and reaction.

Preparations for Supply Disruptions

My books, *The Resilient Enterprise* (2005)[3] and *The Power of Resilience* (2015),[4] described many supply chain disruptions and how companies should prepare for them. With the exception of the 1997 Asian financial crisis and the 2008 global financial meltdown, the crises described there were a result of supply disruptions in a particular area (such as the 2011 Tōhoko earthquake, tsunami, and nuclear disaster)[5] or a specific supplier impacting a large company or even an entire industry (such as the Evonik plant explosion in 2012).[6]

Before companies can prepare effectively, they need to understand the risk landscape. That means classifying potential disruptions according to how likely they are to occur and, if they do occur, how damaging can they be. These dimensions help prioritize the risks. A third classification dimension is how quickly can risks be spotted, which helps the company think about monitoring systems and the required timelines for response to different threats. Companies can then prepare for supply disruptions in several ways, which can be classified as (1) building in redundancy, (2) building flexibility, and (3) developing early detection capabilities.

Supply chain redundancy mainly involves extra inventory and multi-sourcing, which aren't without their own downsides. Extra inventory is expensive as it incurs inventory holding costs. Worse, it may affect product quality in that workers may find it easy to "take one from the pile" when encountering a damaged part or product rather than fix any underlying cause. This insight was one of the roots of Toyota's original success in building affordable, high-quality cars. Multiple suppliers mean that the company is less of an important customer to any one supplier, and its volume with each is low, leading to higher costs. In addition, the greater the number of suppliers, the higher the risk that of one of them may become involved in a social justice or environmental breach, dragging down the company's reputation and sales.

Flexibility involves several elements, including (1) cross-training of employees so they can be moved around to places where they are needed; (2) standardizing of parts and products so that they are interchangeable; (3) postponement, or late customization, which involves delaying the time when products are committed to a certain product variant or customer; and (4) a flexibility culture. A corporate culture of flexibility has several distinguishing characteristics: a norm of speaking the truth to higher-ups freely; letting the people closest to the problem make decisions when there is no time for hierarchical approval processes; and allowing deference to expertise rather than corporate rank during a disruption. Companies that are good at responding to disruptions are typically organizations that are disrupted frequently and cognizant of risks, such as the military, airlines, and high-risk operations like nuclear or chemical plants.

Mapping the Supply Chain

One of the most effective ways to understand overall risk exposure and enable early warning is to know all the locations of suppliers' facilities that make all the parts that go into the company's products and which customers buy products that use these parts. Armed with such a map, a company can pinpoint where natural disasters or a Covid-19 outbreak is taking place, and decide which of its parts supply, product deliveries, and customers will be affected. However, creating supply mapping is not something that can be done in the heat of the moment.

In 2005, Bindiya Vakil got her master's degree in supply chain management from the MIT Center for Transportation & Logistics. She joined Cisco in Silicon Valley, where her experience with several supply chain disruptions over five years showed her that companies did not know where their suppliers' facilities were. In an interview, she explained, "The address we had was a corporate office or their 'ship from' location, not the plant where the items were made."[7]

Getting that supplier factory location data for every part from every supplier is laborious for both the company and its suppliers. For example, Cisco had more than 1,000 suppliers, including four large contract manufacturers, and purchased 50,000 types of parts going into more than 12,000 products in over 200 product families.[8] Many of Cisco's suppliers were also large companies such as Flex, which had more than 100 manufacturing locations around the world and 16,000 suppliers of its own. Staff at Cisco would need to contact each supplier and ask about where it made each part, while staff at all the suppliers would need to track down all that location data for all the parts they sold to Cisco. If many companies tried to map their supply chains, then suppliers would be inundated by requests for location data from all their customers.

Vakil understood that for cost-effective mapping of supply chains involving multiple companies and multiple suppliers, the information "needs to be flowing through a single platform."[9] A third-party service provider could get much of the data once from each supplier and amortize the information collection costs over multiple customer companies. Vakil left Cisco and founded Resilinc in 2010, with the goal of mapping and monitoring all of the facilities of a company and its suppliers.

For industries in which a mapping company such as Resilinc has documented the supply chains of a few OEMs, mapping a new OEM is relatively quick because companies in the same industry often use many of the same suppliers. Vakil explained the leverage a single platform offers: "So supplier A could sell five parts that are made at three sites to customer X and 25 parts made at all 80 sites to customer Y. Each customer will get that tailored view. But to the supplier, it's less work because they had to do this work once, and the system parses the data intelligently to 50 customers over time."

The next step in this exercise is to cross-reference the bills of materials (BOMs) of the company's products with the suppliers' locations that make each part to identify which products and how much revenue are at risk in the event of a disruption at a given supplier location. Finally, combining this product risk data with customer order data allows the company to determine which customers might be affected by a disruption at that supplier location. This data is then combined with a global alert system, so that when a supplier location experiences a disruption, the company can know immediately which products will be in short supply, which customers may be affected, and how much revenue is at risk.

Third-party news and social media monitoring services help companies spot events around the globe that may impact any of the company's far-flung network of supply locations. Vakil described how this worked in the context of the pandemic: "We monitor Weibo [a microblogging service like Twitter in China with a half-billion users]. On December 28, 2019, the local government notified all the regional hospitals in Wuhan to keep an eye out for this unknown pattern of pneumonia.... It was captured by Resilinc AI.... And so, on January 4, 2020, we sent out our first custom alert notifying our customers about this unknown pneumonia pattern.... We geofenced the area, and the alert went out to our customers. On their mobile app, they could see how many suppliers, which sites are there, which parts come from there, which products use them, and all of that." She added: "Also, because we do mapping, our customers know what alternate site the supplier has available in other parts of the country or world to recover."[10]

Spotting Risky Diamonds and Clusters

When people who are not supply chain experts think about a company's suppliers, they typically think of its direct suppliers: those who send material to the company and get paid by it. These are known as the company's Tier 1 suppliers. Note that each of a company's Tier 1 suppliers has its own suppliers—they are the company's Tier 2 suppliers. The Tier 2 suppliers have their suppliers, who are the first company's Tier 3 suppliers, and so on. Like a big family tree, a supply chain extends all the way back to the raw materials suppliers, such as the farmers who grow food or miners who extract ore. In a given industry, the competing OEMs often share suppliers, although each OEM might have some unique Tier 1 suppliers, too. Figure 7.1 depicts a schema of an industry's overall supply chain with three OEMs drawing on a deep pyramid of tiers of suppliers.

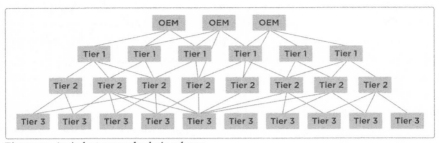

Figure 7.1: An industry supply chain schema

Typically, companies don't know who their deep-tier suppliers are. Direct suppliers tend to be reticent about their own suppliers, because they consider it proprietary information that is part of their competitive advantage. Lack of visibility into the deeper tiers leads companies to encourage (or require) that their suppliers manage their own supplier risks and develop business continuity protocols. A March–April 2020 survey of senior supply chain executives by the World Economic Forum found that 53 percent of companies were supporting suppliers with analysis on their Covid-19 risks in order to mitigate the risks for these suppliers.[11]

Covid-19 also provided an added impetus for many companies to diversify their supply sources by adding second and third suppliers for a given part or service. An April 2020 PwC survey of US CFOs found that 56 percent of companies were planning to develop additional alternate supplier options.[12] Sometimes, however, multi-sourcing doesn't reduce the risk because of two supply chain phenomena that create hidden risks in the supply chain, especially the deeper tiers.

The first issue is that, unbeknown to the OEM, many of its deep-tier suppliers may rely on a single supplier. In other words, instead of a broad pyramid industry supply chain structure as shown in Figure 7.1, the supply chain structure looks more like a diamond in this case, as shown in Figure 7.2.

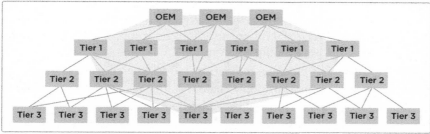

Figure 7.2: A "diamond" supply chain schema

The problem of the diamond structure can be seen in the example of the Evonik disruption. In March 2012, an explosion and devastating fire destroyed an Evonik chemical factory in Marl, Germany.[13] The factory made cyclododecatriene (CDT), a clear liquid that smells like turpentine. Chemical manufacturers use CDT to make cyclododecane and then laurolactam. None of these three obscure chemicals are in the BOMs of any car, which may be why car makers were initially unaware of the event.

However, plastics manufacturers use laurolactam to make polyamide-12, also known as PA-12, a tough plastic used to make strong, lightweight parts. PA-12 helps car makers reduce the weight of vehicles to meet green goals for fuel economy. At the time, cars averaged 46 pounds of PA-12 and related nylons scattered across dozens or hundreds of different parts (tubing, gears, housings, and more) made by many different suppliers. That one Evonik factory had been responsible for about 40 percent of the world's supply of CDT; the loss of the factory severely curtailed supplies of PA-12 to all the makers of parts made from PA-12.

The accident almost brought the entire automobile industry to its knees. Only quick collaboration among eight competing automakers and 50 suppliers helped the industry avoid a significant disruption.

A second category of deep-tier risk comes from an economic phenomenon known as industrial clusters, in which many companies and suppliers in a particular industry co-locate to be near each other in order to take advantage of a talent pool, natural resources, knowledge exchange, or government support. Examples include Detroit for automobiles, Silicon Valley for chips, and Hollywood for movies (Wuhan is one of China's "Detroits," with about 10 percent of the country's auto making industry there).

Clusters are a favorite strategy of government economic development efforts, because once clusters reach a certain scale, they foster a natural positive feedback loop. As they grow, they become more attractive to more industry players, and their rate of growth accelerates. Thus, governments only have to "prime the pump" to achieve economic development. Moreover, clusters attract investment in related infrastructure and education, making the cluster renowned for its signature product.[14]

While clusters can create a competitive advantage,[15] they also create a concentration of geographical supply chain risk. For example, in 2011, floods in Thailand disrupted 35 percent of the entire hard disk industry. Four of the five top suppliers of drives (Western Digital, Seagate Technologies, Hitachi Global Storage Technologies, and Toshiba) all had facilities or key suppliers clustered in Thailand. The shortage of hard disks prevented PC makers from fulfilling demand; for example, Intel lost $800 million in revenue because PC makers couldn't get hard disks.

To this end, Stephen Kaufman, senior lecturer of business administration at Harvard Business School, said, "Supply chain managers who previously focused their attention one or two levels down into their supply chains will have to... develop the systems and discipline to track even more deeply into the chain."[16]

Monitoring the Supply Chain

Early detection of a disruption and recognition of its implications allow a company to find alternative supply sources, alert customers, change manufacturing plans, and, in general, be proactive. This is particularly important as disruptions, such as Covid-19, may affect all suppliers in a given industry. Reacting ahead of competitors may be the difference between a successful response and a failed one. One of the important initiatives a company has to focus on is monitoring and sensing the health of its suppliers. In fact, the April 2020 PwC survey of CFOs in the US found that 54 percent of companies were planning to gauge the financial and operational health of suppliers as a result of Covid-19.[17]

Companies monitor the health of their suppliers via special services (such as Dun & Bradstreet for public companies), banking relationships, news media, social media, and information collected by local tiger teams. They watch for layoffs, scandals, morale problems, turmoil in upper management, and financial troubles. Even something as simple as a dirty or messy factory can signal a potential problem. In many cases, suppliers' operational hiccups (e.g., product defects, late deliveries, incomplete orders) signify that management is preoccupied by issues other than customer service. During the pandemic, supplier monitoring included assessment of the infection risks associated with a supplier's HR practices that might force a facility shutdown, as happened in a number of meatpacking plants in the US, Germany, and elsewhere.[18]

A variety of third-party news filtering services can help gather, curate, collate, and prioritize new events from around the world. In the case of Covid-19-related disruptions, daily data on new infections and government-published criteria for economic reopening or closing can help judge the risks of the infection affecting suppliers. Superimposed on a supply chain map with all the company's BOMs, risks to products and revenues can be assessed quickly.

Monitoring all the news from everywhere can be a hair-raising experience. "I have 14,000 suppliers," said Tom Linton, chief procurement and supply chain officer at Flex in a 2012 interview. "I guarantee that with 14,000 suppliers, at least one of them is not performing well today."[19] A key part of the monitoring process is assessing, filtering, and prioritizing the never-ending stream of bad news to decide which events can be ignored, investigated, or deftly handled with a minor tweak; and which events require alarm bells and all hands on deck.

Mitigating Impacts on Suppliers

As was the case during the 2008 financial crisis, the Covid-19 crisis made companies worry about the financial health of their suppliers. In early 2020, many took steps to support smaller, more vulnerable suppliers. For example, defense contractor Lockheed Martin advanced more than $50 million to small- and medium-size enterprises in its supply chain.[20] Telecom company Vodafone committed to paying its European suppliers within 15 days (down from the standard 30- to 60-day payment terms).[21]

The World Economic Forum survey showed that such practices were quite common.[22] Indeed, 49 percent of companies were guaranteeing purchase of supplies, 46 percent were paying suppliers in advance, and 40 percent were paying suppliers a premium to offset the costs of additional precautions imposed during Covid-19. A scant 1 percent of companies surveyed were taking no actions to mitigate the immediate impact of the pandemic on suppliers.

Rapid Reaction

As demand for granola bars surged among panicked consumers hoarding for a pandemic Armageddon, General Mills was shocked to learn in late March that a supplier wouldn't be able deliver cranberries for a week. "Within 24 hours, we were able to get a new supplier qualified and new product in," said John Church, the top supply chain and logistics executive at the company. Granola bar production never ceased.[23] As the example shows, once a company spots a problem, it can react with urgency before customers are affected. That rapid reaction can include accelerating the deliveries of inventories throughout the supply chain, finding and contracting for materials from alternative suppliers, and securing logistics capacity as needed to manage the disruption. (*See also* Chapter 8, p. 68.)

As mentioned above, redundancy provides the first line of defense in any disruption. For example, Hershey built inventory in anticipation of Covid-19's effects. "As the situation began to unfold," said Michele Buck, CEO at the chocolate maker, "we built inventory in both raw materials and finished goods to mitigate risk and to help us to continue meeting demand."[24] Even without disruptions, and despite companies' focus on lean management principles, inventory kept in various tiers of the supply chain (including in transit) can provide a buffer of days, weeks, or even months.

The other element of redundancy is multi-sourcing. However, many companies found that their sources were concentrated in certain hard-hit areas and thus had to quickly seek alternative suppliers in less-affected regions. This involved determining capacity, validating quality, and quickly negotiating delivery contracts.

A frantic search for additional supplies during a disruption comes with additional risks: counterfeit or substandard parts from unknown suppliers. In March 2020, the Netherlands recalled 600,000 defective N95 masks it had bought from a Chinese supplier.[25] The Centers for Disease Control in the US even created a web page depicting dozens of different kinds of counterfeit N95 respirators that buyers needed to avoid.[26] Desperation is the mortal enemy of prudence and the best buddy of avarice.

Disruptions also often require additional transportation capacity: for instance, to move inventory ahead of a regional Covid-19 shutdown or approaching hurricane; move parts from alternative suppliers; redistribute finished goods to fulfill demand; or bring recovery supplies (e.g., PPE) to the disrupted area. Often, these shipments must be expedited to help accelerate recovery or prevent late deliveries to customers. Thus, rapid reactions to a disruption entail quickly arranging rapid transportation.

Reacting with urgency helps in any large-scale disruption such as Covid-19 that hits multiple companies in an affected region at the same time. As each impacted company seeks resources, those companies with faster reflexes have a better chance of securing all they need and can recover faster than the laggards.

Finally, in situations where supply simply cannot meet total demand, companies have no choice but to deliver less total product than customers would wish for or would have ordered. Managing the demand side of disruptions calls for other methods, as the next chapter describes.

8. Managing for Whack-a-Mole Demand

Amazon prides itself on flawless service and rapid deliveries even during the busiest shopping seasons, but the online demand caused by Covid-19 proved to be a real challenge for the retailer. Brian Olsavsky, CFO at Amazon, told investors at the end of Q1 2020: "While we generally have experience in getting ready for spikes in demand for known events like the holiday season and Prime Day, we also generally spend months ramping up for these periods. The Covid crisis allowed for no such preparation."[1]

News of nurses forced to work without masks, images of empty shelves in grocery stores, and stories of the desperate need for ventilators were pushed by media outlets during the early days of the pandemic. The news was disturbing with regard to medical supply shortages. In general, shortages can be caused by a supply disruption or an increase in demand; sometimes, companies simply cannot fulfill every order and retailers are out of stock.

That inability leads to difficult management challenges. If the company lacks the capacity to fulfill all orders for all types of products, which products should it build? More importantly, which customer(s) should be served partially or completely? All of these decisions have both short-term and long-term implications on the company's relationships with its customers.

Covid-19 caused unprecedented increases in demand for a wide range of consumer goods such as disinfectant products, toilet paper, and fitness equipment. It also caused changes in where consumers bought the products they wanted and when. For example, food suppliers had to change from fulfilling institutional orders (from restaurants, universities, industrial campuses, and office cafeterias) to supermarkets and home deliveries. While some companies could ramp up production, one of their challenges was to determine which of these changes in demand would last beyond the pandemic (and therefore justify capital investment in production capacity) and which was a passing Covid-19 phenomenon. While most companies reined in their capital expenditure to conserve cash, all the main cloud service providers kept investing in server farms. The acceleration of digital transformation of many enterprises by moving applications to the cloud was seen as a long-term phenomenon, and thus the cloud providers kept investing. Retailers also invested in their e-commerce operations, hiring people and planning new distribution centers.[2]

Listening for Signals of Demand

As with managing whack-a-mole supply disruptions, managing whack-a-mole demand fluctuations relies heavily on monitoring the situation to quickly detect the changes. Companies can use a variety of data to anticipate demand, such as point-of-sale data, social media, tiger team reports, online search statistics, and government and business reopening announcements. Walmart, for example, watched and responded to wave after wave of shifting patterns in demand caused by Covid-19, such as the panic hoarding phase, the nesting-at-home phase, the arts-and-crafts phase, the hair dye phase, and the stimulus check phase.[3]

Most companies don't have the benefit of Walmart's treasure trove of more than 1 million retail transactions per hour of real-time point-of-sale data.[4] However, anyone can get a glimpse of the real-time zeitgeist using Google Trends[5] to see what people are searching for.[6] For example, between February 20 and February 25, 2020, searches on Amazon for sanitizer and PPE took over all of the top 10 search spots in a number of countries.[7]

As regions reopen, monitoring the indicators for the return of demand can pay off in handling the resurgent demand. Master Kong, a leading food and beverage producer in China, tracked retail outlets' reopening plans and adapted its supply chain accordingly. When stores actually reopened, Master Kong was able to supply 60 percent of them. In contrast, some of its less agile competitors only supplied a third as many stores.[8]

During any significant supply/demand imbalance—be it owing to a supply disruption or a demand surge—companies will have to prioritize which customers to serve. Past disruptions reveal the ways companies on both ends of the supply chain have handled such challenges, both in terms of the tactics they employed and the considerations they used for their decisions. These examples illustrate the diverse approaches executives can use to determine who gets what. To address this, companies can use allocation schemes, market-based mechanisms, or change the product as discussed in the next three sections.

Allocating Scarce Supplies and Capacity

With allocation, a company directly restricts deliveries by not fulfilling every order as requested. Using allocation immediately raises tough questions of who gets what if customers cannot get everything they want. Factors such as a company's financial situation, customer relationships, fairness, reputation, strategy, and even customer survival are a few of the sometimes conflicting considerations that come into play in these situations. These different factors reflect trade-offs between the company's self-interest to remain financially viable and the customers' interests, as well as between short-term results versus long-term outcomes.

Favor the Most Profitable Customers

A popular allocation criterion is to direct limited supplies to the highest-margin products and customers. For example, General Motors scrambled to find scarce materials in 2011 after a trifecta of disasters—an earthquake, the resulting tsunami, and the related nuclear meltdown—hit Japan and devastated factories there. In GM's crisis room, "Project J" had supply chain professionals scouring the globe to find sufficient parts to keep all of the company's car factories running. Despite the frantic search, at one point, GM could not find enough airflow sensors for its trucks. The team decided to prioritize full-sized trucks over small trucks because the larger vehicles were both more profitable and had smaller retail inventories. Thus, GM temporarily closed a Chevrolet plant in Shreveport, Louisiana, which made the (small) Colorado pickup truck.[9] (As it turned out, shortly before the plant closure, more parts were found, but it was too late and it took another week for the plant to reopen.)

Favor Strategic Customers

A simple product profit margin calculation ignores the long-term importance of a customer to the company. This includes issues such as the customer's growth opportunities or the customer's ability to switch suppliers. Thus, some companies favor their biggest customers based on total revenues or forecasts of lifetime value. During several disruptions to microelectronics suppliers over the past 25 years, the largest PC makers, including HP, Dell and Apple, were high on many suppliers' priority lists.

Assure Supply

During the onset of the Covid-19 crisis, demand for consumer staples outstripped manufacturers' production capacities. Consumers began eating at home more and stocked up for sheltering in place, which drastically increased sales above historical levels. Makers of nonperishable foods had to allocate their overtaxed production capacity across various SKUs.

Many chose to suspend production of low-volume SKUs in order to ensure greater total supplies of products and simplify their supply chains by focusing on fewer products (and SKUs) as well as localized production.[10] (*See also* Chapter 24, p. 214.) General Mills, for example, cut its Progresso soup line from 90 to 50 varieties and eliminated some flavors and package sizes of breakfast cereal.[11]

Downstream, C&S Wholesale Grocers, the biggest food wholesaler in the US, experienced this with their suppliers. Mike Duffy, CEO of C&S, commented, "There were 27,000 items that were suspended in our system, which means manufacturers said, 'I'm not going to make those,' which was about 10 percent of total SKUs. And he added: "I've encouraged our retail partners and manufacturers to take a hard look at them to really see, do we really need some of the SKUs? Because they just clog up the supply chain. I mean, there are a lot of reasons for it. But it was good to see everybody come together to agree to cut those [SKUs] to improve the flow." Eliminating the low-performing products eliminated the time spent on switching production systems to different flavors and sizes. It also reduced the labor needed by C&S and retailers in picking, packing, shipping, and shelving lots of low-volume, niche SKUs. The result increased the total production volumes (and revenues) while reducing costs per unit and assuring availability of the most popular products for consumers.[12]

Fairness to All Customers

Some companies insist on "fair" or uniform allocations of volume because of commercial, cultural, or legal reasons. With a uniform allocation policy, all products or customers get identical treatment, such as the same fraction of ordered volume or the same upper limit on the number of items (e.g., "limit two cartons of eggs"). After the 2011 Fukushima nuclear disaster, many Japanese companies gave every customer the same fraction of their orders. Likewise, Intel, as a large supplier in the PC industry, generally uses a similarly uniform allocation approach to avoid the appearance of favoritism.

But fair fractional allocation isn't easy when customers try to game the system by artificially inflating their orders. To combat this, some companies allocate product based on a portion of pre-disruption historical order volumes. However, in some cases, the disruption does affect actual demand, and some companies take this into account in their allocation algorithms.

For example, AmerisourceBergen, a wholesale distributor of healthcare supplies, published an in-depth explanation of how it manages its allocation.[13] The company faced huge increases in Covid-19-related demand due to existing healthcare facilities stocking up in anticipation of a pandemic outburst; new orders from new or expanded healthcare facilities such as pop-up hospitals and existing hospitals adding more ICU capacity; and consumers seeking longer-term or early prescription refills to handle quarantine conditions. The distributor sought to get as much product as possible to as many providers as possible as quickly as possible, all while being fair to all its customers. At the same time, AmerisourceBergen wanted to prevent hoarding, which could result in supplies of critical healthcare materials becoming stranded in hospital supply cabinets around the country. The company explained the many factors in its allocation algorithm, such as using historical sales data to limit over-ordering and hoarding, being responsive to honest changes in demand by weighing recent order data over older historical order patterns, and favoring customers in known Covid-19 hot zones and with large numbers of ICU beds. The resulting algorithm attempted to be fair to the end patient even as it set unequal allocations among the healthcare providers.

Favor Vulnerable Customers

Allocation by customer vulnerability can be a consideration if the product is essential to the customer's survival (medical or financial). Amazon, for example, prioritized "essential products" such as food and medical supplies in allocating its limited fulfillment and shipping capacity when the Covid-19-related increases in e-commerce outstripped the retailer's abilities to fulfill and ship orders.[14] Similarly, during the pandemic, some retailers catered to vulnerable customers, such as by reserving the first opening hour for the elderly and other at-risk populations to provide favored access to freshly restocked shelves in a freshly cleaned store.

Even if the supplier's preferred allocation method favors larger customers, it may be willing to divert small quantities of supplies to ensure the survival of a smaller enterprise customer. Verifone, a maker of credit card processing equipment, wasn't a large buyer of the electric motors made scarce by the same 2011 floods in Thailand mentioned above, but the company's absolute dependence on these motors led suppliers to fulfill its (small) orders.

Shaping Demand with Prices

Instead of deciding how much to allocate to each customer, some companies use market-based mechanisms to determine who gets what. Economics asserts that increasing price can depress demand (and encourage more supply), and this is the method that these companies utilize.

Differential Price Setting

Rather than refuse to fulfill some or all of each customer's order, a company could change the price of the product to induce customers to order less. For example, to dissuade hoarding, a Danish grocery store priced one bottle of hand sanitizer for a reasonable 40 kroner ($5.75), but if the customer bought more than one bottle, the price increased to 1,000 kroner per bottle ($143).[15]

Similarly, in several instances of PC parts shortages, Dell raised the price of computer configurations that required scarce parts. At the same time, the company balanced those price hikes with lower prices on other machines that used more plentiful parts—and promoted these more readily available machines. This balance of price changes can help manage a shortage without damaging customer relations. Such "demand management" is akin to the revenue management practices used by airlines to fill their seats—allowing price-sensitive leisure travelers to buy some tickets while reserving other seats for customers more willing to pay higher prices.

Going to the Highest Bidder

When flooding in Thailand devastated an industrial cluster of hard disk drive makers in 2011, Seagate Technology became the number-one disk drive maker, taking the crown from its more-disrupted rival, Western Digital Corporation. As demand for Seagate drives soared, it chose to auction off some disk drives to the highest bidder. Seagate also used the threat of these auctions to compel customers to sign long-term supply contracts.

Economists often argue that a well-designed auction improves economic efficiency by ensuring that those who can create the greatest value with a scarce resource (and therefore will pay the highest price for it) get that resource. (This is the usual justification for government auctions of electromagnetic spectrum, as well as for the mechanisms underlying carbon emissions credits).[16] Moreover, customers who can find alternatives to the now-expensive scarce resource will forgo using that resource, thereby conserving supplies for those who have no other options.

However, during a shortage, customers perceive these auctions—despite their theoretical appeal—as profiteering. Indeed, after the flood receded and Western Digital recovered, it took back the lead from Seagate. Unfortunately, the Covid-19 pandemic gave rise to many cases of naked profiteering of much-needed medical supplies.[17] Online auction site eBay banned auctions of Covid-19-related items such as masks and hand sanitizers.[18] In the context of essential consumer goods, auctions seem unjust because they favor the rich over the poor.

Stretching the Supply: Changing the Products

Rather than raise prices or cut off customers, some companies find ways to reduce use of scarce supply by reformulating their products. Such strategies can also be considered market-based mechanisms because the price per value is changed. It can, however, be risky. In February 2013, the boutique distillery Maker's Mark faced a shortage of its premium bourbon. The distiller decided to add a "touch more water," diluting its spirits from the historic level of 90 proof to 84 proof. Outrage ensued. "My favorite bourbon is being watered down so they can 'meet market demand,'" said one super fan, called a brand ambassador, to *Forbes*. "I'll help lower their demand by not buying any more."[19] The company quickly reversed its decision.[20]

When done without affecting the customer experience, such product-altering strategies work well. Intel, for example, diluted some of the chemicals used in chip making during the 2011 Japan crisis, but the company followed strict quality-control protocols to maintain its manufacturing yield and chip performance.[21]

Weigh the Scope and Time Horizon

When choosing among the various strategies to manage scare resources during a supply chain disruption, companies should consider both the scope and the time horizon of their decisions.

Figure 8.1 depicts some of the considerations companies face when making customer prioritization decisions.[22]

Figure 8.1: Scope and time horizon of actions and customer

Clearly, executives in companies fighting for survival have a fiduciary duty to maximize their companies' short-term financial outcomes. In contrast, executives enjoying a strong balance sheet and good credit have the luxury to pursue their values and strategic imperatives. They can make long-term decisions with an expanded scope of how the decisions could align with customers' concerns in order to promote longer-term growth. Strong companies have an advantage during disruptions and can capitalize on it to gain market share (*see* Chapter 26, p. 227).

Regardless of the weakness or strength of the company going into a disruption, a properly managed who-gets-what strategy offers a way to minimize the damage from business interruptions. In the end, well-deliberated decisions about tactics, scope, and time horizon can help a company come out ahead.

9. More Business Resilience Planning and Testing

"Twenty-six years in a job like this, I never had a business plan that was called 'pandemic'. We just never imagined the economy turning off," said Ford's then-CEO Jim Hackett in April 2020.[1] During the Covid-19 pandemic, many a CEO would have been forced to make the same admission. And many an investor, economist, and policy maker who was similarly caught unprepared by the crisis would have excused the oversight. Even world-renowned epidemiologists refused to believe that asymptomatic individuals were contagious and thus missed the conditions that enabled Covid-19 to spread undetected deep into every corner of the world.[2]

Many thought the shutdown of the economy was unprecedented, but they were wrong—it happened during the 1918 flu pandemic. Moreover, recent disease outbreaks such as SARS (2002–03) and H1N1 flu (2009) raised the specter of a pandemic like Covid-19 and sparked small shutdowns here and there. For epidemiologists, a serious global pandemic was a matter of when, not if.[3]

In contrast to Ford, BASF did have a business plan for pandemics. As a global chemical company with an extremely rigorous approach to risk management and safety, BASF had developed a wide range of playbooks for a wide range of possible disruptive events. Although a playbook can never forecast every detail of an actual event, it does provide a broad-brush framework for understanding the likely impacts and likely responses.

Ralf Busche, senior vice president of global supply chain strategy at BASF, recalled the company's approach: "As people got back from ski resorts in Austria and northern Italy, many were infected. It popped up in the news and as we have—and always had—a pandemic plan.... So therefore, we just used what we had basically already planned for and never thought it not serious. And now we have the real test pilot in reality: Okay, does it really work?... We now had to look at the specific situation, which was a little bit different than what we had in the plan—you can't plan for everything."[4]

BASF's preparation meant that none of its major facilities had to be shut down during the Covid-19 crisis, although the company did work out exactly how to do so if it had to. Overall, companies like BASF use tools such as scenario planning, playbooks, simulation exercises, drills, and testing tools to prepare and train for disruption response.

Scenario Planning

Organizations use scenario planning to think about plausible what-if futures and how to operate within them.[5] Scenario planning can be used to prepare for various supply and/or demand disruptions, unexpected technological innovations, tectonic shifts in the competitive landscape, or for long-term social and economic trends. Companies develop scenarios with an intention of exploring a certain focal issue, trends in the world, and unknown future states. Scenarios are also used to acclimate managers to dealing with large-scale uncertainty.[6]

Each scenario is a plausible story about some imagined future with internally consistent details about what the world looks like in that future. The purpose of these scenarios is neither to accurately forecast what is most likely to happen nor to prescribe what action should be taken. Rather, scenario thinking causes managers to realize that the future is uncertain and thus, when possible, make decisions that can be reversed, changed, and adjusted when conditions turn out to be different than expected.

Scenario planning offers two specific strengths to an organization. First, the effort can help the organization "stress test" if its current strategies are robust under all scenarios and possibly adjust its strategies or playbooks accordingly. Second, analysis of the factors leading to each scenario can help create alerts or "sensors in the ground" that may signal which scenario is becoming more likely. Such early warning allows managers to quickly detect impending changes and prepare for them.

Beyond the general "pandemic" scenario, Covid-19 itself sparked a great many pandemic trajectory scenarios, because the exact properties of the disease were unknown (and some are still unknown as of the writing of this book). "I don't think we ever felt like we would be arguing over epidemiological models, and we are," said Michael Hsu, CEO of Kimberly-Clark, which makes PPE, toilet paper, and wipes, to investors. "And we're working through, actually through 11 of them, and they all have different assumptions. And now while that makes it difficult for us to call the business for this purpose, I will tell you, from an operating perspective, we are using those models to predict outcomes to drive scenario planning and contingency plans for all of our operations around the world."[7]

Play It Out: Playbooks, Simulations, and Exercises

Scenarios, as well as experience with disruptions, lead companies to create playbooks. These playbooks outline the roles, processes, and checklists required to effectively cope with each type of disruption. At Rockwell Automation, Tristian Kanwar, vice president of manufacturing operations, said, "Based on various crises in recent years, we have developed playbooks defining actions and measures to take in times of disruption. When Covid-19 hit we kicked these playbooks into action, allowing us to follow pre-defined processes to efficiently deal with the situation."[8]

Playbooks by themselves do not create preparedness. The people who will use a playbook need to understand and debug it by exercising the playbook in drills and simulated tests of disruption response. Simulation exercises have managers work through a disruption scenario and use the playbook to guide action. A facilitator or simulation application then shows the simulated effects of these decisions. After-action debriefings help identify shortcomings of the plan, correct problems with the playbook, uncover hidden risks in the organization, and improve managers' understanding of how that disruption could be handled.

For more technical organizations, advanced simulation software can help manage a complex supply chain or facility in the context of an exercise or actual disruption. BASF's main facility in Ludwigshafen, Germany, has over 2,000 buildings with 200 production plants interlinked by 2,850 kilometers of pipes, 230 kilometers of rail, and 200 kilometers of road.[9] The facility has many vertically integrated systems under a strategy BASF calls Verbund[10] (German for "linked" or "integrated"). This integrated structure means that some of the most important suppliers and customers of BASF plants are other BASF plants. Sophisticated management of all these facilities lets BASF produce thousands of different products. Doing so safely and efficiently involves a complex array of tanks, valves, pumps, pipes, and tanker shipments that interconnect steam crackers, distillation columns, reaction vessels, boilers, and condensers through intricate plumbing across the sprawling campus.

Simulation technology plays a key role in making the Verbund concept work. BASF's Busche explained, "We have a Verbund simulator.... It is a digital mirror of the physical plant with key ingredients—such as raw, auxiliary and operating materials as well as utilities like power supply and steam —built into that simulator. Using the simulator, we look into the most important value chains—those that are critical to keep our Verbund running. We are constantly looking at those—can they technically and commercially still operate?"[11] The simulation software knows all recipes of BASF's products, and how it all connects together. "Supply chain managers, control technicians, plant managers, engineers, etc.—depending on the use case, question, situation—use this software for production planning, capacity adjustments, making new investments, and managing disruptions."[12]

Looking for Vulnerabilities

Finally, some companies automate their disruption drills into an ongoing everyday software system. Netflix created *Chaos Monkey*, an application that intentionally attacks the company's infrastructure by randomly disabling certain bits of it.[13] In theory, Netflix's automated systems should instantly recognize any fault and should reboot, relaunch, or reroute around the affected part. But if the company detects an actual impact to performance or service from the monkeying, it knows that the engineers have work to do to improve their software. Although the idea of company attacking its own systems may seem far-fetched, it forces the company's engineers to write resilient code that is immune to monkey business.[14]

Netflix built Chaos Monkey using the principles of chaos engineering.[15] Chaos engineering relies on A-B testing with experiments that attempt to disturb a system that should be resistant to that disturbance. This type of testing involves the use of one approach with one set of customers, stores, or facilities and a different approach with another set to assess whether treatment A does better/worse than B. By throwing small chaotic disruptions at the system and fixing it anytime a disruption affects performance, the system becomes more and more robust over time. At some level, it is like an automated version of "red team" testing or war games used by military planners and cybersecurity organizations.[16]

The use of digital technology for resilience, such as BASF's Verbund simulator or Netflix's Chaos Monkey, exemplifies a much broader and accelerating trend in using digital systems in supply chains (*see* Chapter 14, p. 119). Specifically, digital technologies can improve supply chain resilience in three ways. First, the technology can both collect and quickly send data about remote systems for better visibility and response time. Second, the technology can use pattern recognition, including AI, to automatically detect specific anomalies. Third, the technology can automatically create and route alerts to managers or other computer systems anywhere in the world.

Based on such simulations, companies can start developing a sense of what the future may look like. More importantly, they can start developing mitigation plans to deal with disruptions and their consequences.

PART 3
ADJUSTMENT REQUIRED

"There are going to be some issues we are dealing with now that are temporary. There will be a lot of things that will be more permanent. Our business leaders need to adapt to them."

—David Gibbs, CEO, Yum Brands Inc.[1]

"It's impossible to overstate the impact of Covid-19 on all of us," Randall Stephenson, CEO of AT&T, told investors. "I expect it will have long-lasting implications for many things we used to take for granted, like how we congregate, work, travel, and interact," he continued.[2] David Abney, CEO of UPS, said in his company's earnings call, "We don't know that we'll ever get back to what we'd call the old normal, but we're not ready to declare what we see today as a new normal either."[3]

For Stephenson, Abney, and other senior executives, figuring out the new normal means thinking through the interconnected feedback loops between their companies' actions, governments' policies, consumers' behaviors, and the spread of the virus. Each affects the other, although none have total control of anything. For decision makers, the challenge is in finding and implementing actions that help control the virus while contributing to job creation and economic growth. Successful companies are likely to be those that find new opportunities for innovation in the new normal.

The entire Covid-19 situation seems unprecedented. But Jeff Harmening, CEO of General Mills, disagrees: "What we're going through now is not unprecedented in the company's history." After going through its archives, General Mills found a 100-year-old company newsletter article on the 1918 Spanish flu, in which the firm's own health department advocated for hand washing and face coverings.[4]

10. Creating Safe Zones

Politicians like to think they are in charge, but in the case of the pandemic, they were third in line at best; in the spring of 2020, the virus and consumers took the reins of power. While politicians dithered over how to control the rapidly spreading virus, citizens took action as they learned more about the disease. Consumers abandoned restaurants, air travel, mass transit, and the like weeks before governments officially announced stay-at-home policies.[1] University of Chicago economists Austan Goolsbee and Chad Syverson used cell phone data to plot the course of the 60 percent drop in consumer traffic to businesses. They reported that only 7 percent could be attributed to legal restrictions.[2] Government orders were not solely responsible for shuttering the economy; in large part, citizens did it on their own.

Likewise, official proclamations of reopenings did not instantly bring back all the workers and customers. Large swaths of many countries' economies depend on discretionary spending at restaurants, bars, theaters, sporting events, and on tourism. Just as the terrorist attacks of 9/11 made many afraid to fly, Covid-19 has made many afraid to take part in any activity that involves large crowds and unavoidable close contact.

People's behavior may change as governments and companies put more mitigation procedures and safety measures in place. After 9/11, the key to getting people back to flying was creating "secure zones." Airports instituted security checks for people, luggage, and vehicles; they also trained airport police and front-line employees to spot suspicious behavior. Airlines bolted cockpit doors and prohibited passengers from congregating at the front of the aircraft.

These steps created a secure travel environment that assuaged travelers' concerns and brought them back to the skies. Bringing Covid-cautious consumers back to stores, restaurants, sports arenas, mass transit, or any other activity involving interactions with others depends on creating "safe zones" where people feel safe from infection. Such safe zones can encourage what economist John Maynard Keynes called the "animal spirits" that boost the economy: "the characteristic of human nature that a large proportion of our positive activities depend on spontaneous optimism rather than mathematical expectations, whether moral or hedonistic or economic."[3]

There is a good chance that even after an effective vaccine becomes widely available, the coronavirus will keep circulating among the world's population for decades to come. "This virus is here to stay," said Sarah Cobey, an epidemiologist and evolutionary biologist at the University of Chicago. "The question is, how do we live with it safely?"[4] In that sense, Covid-19 may become endemic, circulating in the population like HIV, measles, the flu, and chicken pox.

Know Thine Enemy

Just as the air travel industry created secure zones by keeping terrorists away from air travelers, so too can society and companies create Covid-19 safe zones by keeping infectious individuals and the virus away from susceptible people as they work, shop, and learn. Unfortunately, Covid-19 has some insidious characteristics that make this task difficult. People infected with Covid-19 become infectious before exhibiting symptoms; many of the infected only have mild symptoms (while still being infectious), and some never show any symptoms (also while still being infectious). The core implication for business and society is that anyone anywhere—a coworker, fellow shopper, or person in the street—even individuals who seem to be in perfect health—could be spreading Covid-19 to those around them.

Figure 10.1 depicts a way to think about the challenge. In order to control the pandemic and create safe zones, the rate at which susceptible people become infectious (the left arrow) must be *lower* than the rate at which infectious people are prevented from passing on their infection (the right arrow). Most infectious individuals (the middle square in Figure 10.1) are asymptomatic and continue spreading the disease unknowingly. Some, however, may suffer from some symptoms yet continue going out in public due to their need to work, need to buy food, or lack of access to testing.

The mitigation tactics listed on the left side of Figure 10.1 are those intended to avoid infections in the first place. The mitigation tactics on the right are focused on identifying and removing infected individuals from the susceptible population so they will not infect others. Infectious individuals can stop infecting others in three ways: They may become sick enough to self-isolate or seek medical help, they can test positive for the virus and go into quarantine, or they can recover on their own without ever changing their daily activities. The mitigation tactics on the right can help encourage (or force) infectious individuals, including the asymptomatic majority, to avoid infecting others. Of special importance is testing, which is essential to catching asymptomatic infectious individuals as well as symptomatic infectious individuals who refuse to self-isolate.

Indeed, many organizations adopt most of these steps.[5] In many cases, governments mandated several of these practices (along with related signage and training) as a prerequisite to reopening workplaces and public facilities.[6] Brian Niccol, CEO of Chipotle Mexican Grill, said, "You spend a lot of your time ensuring how you can execute your business in this environment in a safe way."[7]

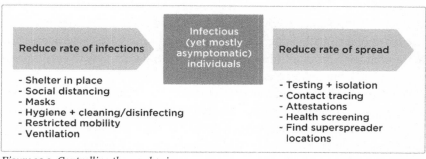

Figure 10.1: Controlling the pandemic

Avoiding the Infectious from the Start

If infectious people do not mingle with susceptible people in the first place, then the rate of infection will drop. Such is the basic logic behind quarantines and several other long-used tactics for stopping the spread of disease. In the absence of a ready means of identifying the infectious, all people must be quarantined. In the case of Covid-19, that is exactly what happened in many countries.

Close Everything and Stay Home

During the 1918 Spanish flu outbreak, the deadliest pandemic in recent history, officials introduced control measures that have become standard for pandemics. These included closing schools, shops, and restaurants; restricting transportation; mandating social distancing; and banning public gatherings. Then, as now, many people refused to comply. In 1918, a San Francisco health officer shot three people when one refused to wear a mandatory face mask. In Arizona, police handed out $10 fines for those caught without the required protective gear.[8] But eventually, those drastic and sweeping measures paid off; in cities that put them into place, death rates plummeted. Those measures were the blueprint for authorities' basic official response to Covid-19.[9]

With Covid-19, the most extreme version of a lockdown took place in Wuhan, the epicenter of the pandemic. When Vice Premier Sun Chunlan visited Wuhan, she declared that the city was facing "wartime conditions" and that "deserters will be nailed to the pillar of historical shame."[10] People were barred from leaving Wuhan, medical workers visited every household to check temperatures and remove infected residents, and authorities severely restricted mobility within the city—people were ordered to stay home. To stop the contagion around China, the lockdown ultimately grew to encompass more than half a billion people.[11]

The American response, however, was far less sweeping. In the US, 42 states mandated some form of stay-at-home orders in March 2020. The orders typically excluded "essential" businesses such as food production and retailing, pharmacies and healthcare, utilities, transportation, banking, law enforcement, emergency services, and news outlets.[12] (Some retailers, such as video game retailer GameStop, tried desperately to be declared "essential" in order to stay open.)[13] However, some states that were not hit hard at the beginning and never implemented control measures—or rolled them back early—started experiencing substantial increases in infections in June and July 2020. On July 10, Atlanta mayor Keisha Lance Bottoms announced that the city would revert back to Phase 1 of its reopening schedule. She had originally issued a stay-at-home order at the end of March and partially reopened the city (moving to Phase 2) in late May before the city's case statistics declined enough, only to again ask citizens to stay at home for any nonessential activity (while enforcing face mask mandates).[14]

In the context of shelter-in-place orders or recommendations, many companies implemented work-from-home policies (see Chapter 11, p. 99). Even as governments lifted restrictions, companies permitted, encouraged, or required work from home to reduce the chance of Covid-19 infections among their employees. Similarly, retailers turned to e-commerce and omnichannel retail (see Chapter 22, p. 198) to enable sales without requiring customers to leave home or enter the store. Restaurants touted curbside takeout and delivery. Thus, many businesses encouraged people to stay at home even as these workers and customers maintained their interactions with the business via online channels.

Mobility Restrictions

Mobility restrictions prohibit those living in or visiting areas with high rates of infection from leaving that location or going to another location. Such restrictions are among the first measures governments use to control the spread of pandemics. These measures also include trade and travel bans, border closures, and even area quarantines, such as the ones implemented in Wuhan. President Trump famously extolled his first action, restricting entry into the US from China, when discussing his handling of the pandemic.[15]

However, according to several studies, such mobility restrictions have had limited success at controlling the spread of viruses. A 2014 WHO study—summarizing 23 other studies—determined that travel restrictions have limited effectiveness and only delay the spread of a virus by about a week. It concluded that "simulated impact is particularly weak in scenarios that involve strains with high transmissibility," such as Covid-19.[16]

Contact Tracing

Contact tracing seeks to identify people exposed to an infected person to ensure they isolate themselves and get tested. Contact tracing is another measure that is not new. During the 16th century, Gabriele Falloppio, chair of medicine at the University of Padua, used Christopher Columbus's journals to track the progression of syphilis from the Americas to hospitals in Barcelona. The disease then spread via soldiers recruited by King Ferdinand II of Aragon, and most significantly through a superspreader event: the siege of Naples in the winter of 1495 by King Charles VIII of France, which gave syphilis a pandemic force.[17] More recently, health authorities used contact tracing among flight passengers during the containment phase of the 2009 H1N1 influenza pandemic.[18]

Determining who has been exposed relies on information about people's activities and locations. In contact tracing, someone typically interviews sick patients regarding their movements and gathers names of people they had contact with. For businesses, contact tracing means logging the workers, customers, and visitors who entered their establishments and who they interact with. Once one of these individuals has been found to test positive, the people who had contact with the individuals can be contacted and, possibly, isolated. Smartphones produce a wealth of location-related information (cell tower location, GPS, WiFi mapping, and Bluetooth proximity) that make these devices ideal data collection systems for contact tracing.[19] Several governments have deployed apps and similar solutions for this purpose.[20]

A number of studies of China's Covid-19 response credited extensive contact tracing as a means of slowing the spread there.[21] Similarly in South Korea, when a coronavirus flare-up was traced to a nightclub in Seoul, a special team of epidemiologists, data scientists, and lab technicians sprang into action. They traced the infections from a nightclubber to a taxi driver and then to a warehouse worker. The team then traced and tested thousands of the warehouse workers, their families and other contacts—almost 9,000 in all.[22] These kinds of teams are the cornerstone of fighting resurgence of the virus and avoiding a spread. South Korea also has laws permitting the government to access records such as mobile phone location data and to publicize the reconstructed movements of infected cases.[23]

In the US and Europe, contact tracing faced difficulties owing to strong privacy laws and cultural norms around privacy. Apple and Google created a system that uses a smartphone's Bluetooth signal to create an anonymized log of the people the phone's user has come into close proximity with, while keeping everyone's identities and locations entirely anonymous.[24] However, the system has seen limited adoption[25] and is not likely to be used in the future because of increasing concerns about how much data that the US tech giants already have on people.

Finding Superspreader Locations

Contact tracing and comprehensive data on infections have a higher-level benefit. Tracing the patterns of infections also uncovers patterns in the locations where infections spread—whether people caught Covid-19 from family members at home, coworkers in the cafeteria, friends at a bar, travel to a particular country, etc. That information helps refine policies and mitigation tactics that have the greatest impact on decreasing the rate of infection while minimizing the impact on everyday life. For example, it can aid in decisions about which categories of businesses (e.g., hair salons, gyms, bars, etc.) to reopen or close.

As explained in Chapter 1 (p. 2), superspreader events (or locations) have an outsized impact on the spread of the infection. A Hong Kong-based study found that only 20 percent of the infected people studied caused 80 percent of all coronavirus transmissions. These individuals infected eight or more people each, on average. In most cases, such sick individuals participated in superspreader events like parties or gatherings at crowded bars, involving close contact with multiple people, many without masks. In contrast, an estimated 70 percent of sick people did not infect anybody else.

As companies open back up, they can take infection data into account by tracing the activities of infected individuals. Universities can find out which local student hangout may be responsible for an outsized number of infections. Offices can detect if their cafeterias are loci of infections, or rather if nearby dining establishments are. Once a superspreader location has been identified, local authorities can be called to act. Information should be given to everybody involved, such as customers, business owners, and law enforcement, so the location can be flagged and avoided. The identification of superspreader locations is one of the important reasons to conduct contact tracing.

Stopping Covid-19 at the Door

From the standpoint of creating a safe space (as well as isolating infectious people from the public), governments, companies, and institutions are looking for ways to screen the infectious as they attempt to enter public spaces. If consumers had confidence that none of the other patrons or staff in a restaurant, store, or aircraft had Covid-19, they would be more likely to return to normal levels of economic engagement. Thus, many organizations are seeking ways to screen people for the disease and reduce the likelihood of a sick person infecting others and the resultant outbreaks.

Health Screening and Attestations

Just as walking through a metal detector has become a common routine at airports, stadiums, and public facilities, so too might pausing for a thermal camera snapshot or a contactless forehead temperature reading become a prerequisite for entry to many places. Already, some retailers, restaurants, salons, and public building owners use temperature screening in this way. Some airlines are lobbying for integrating temperature screening for sick and feverish travelers into security checkpoint processes.[26] (In 2003, amid the SARS outbreak, many airports in Asia screened incoming travelers with thermal cameras.)

Some organizations use attestation: a formal acknowledgement by the customer, worker, visitor, or traveler that they pass a set of criteria related to Covid-19 symptoms and exposure risks. For example, MIT mandates that students and staff answer and submit an online Covid-19 questionnaire the evening before the person intends to come onto campus. The MIT questionnaire system is linked to the campus's building access card readers. Satisfactory answers to the questionnaire (in addition to a recent negative Covid-19 test) allow the person to enter their MIT office or classroom by activating their ID cards for the next 24 hours.

General Motors CEO Mary Barra told investors that, at the company, "When anyone enters a facility they will do a self-assessment questionnaire, and they will have their temperature screened."[27]

Overall, both the evolving science around Covid-19 and the changing cost-effectiveness of different tactics may change what kind of screenings are done. For example, although fever may be a common symptom of Covid-19, it is not universal even among people who have symptoms and are seriously ill. Moreover, by definition, asymptomatic people have no fever at all. Thus, fever monitoring would actually miss most infectious people who are out in public. Likewise, attestation depends on the willingness of the person to truthfully reveal their status. They may have incentives to lie about symptoms in order to make their flight home, avoid losing wages or their job, or not get stuck in quarantine. For truly detecting the infectious, more sophisticated tests are needed.

Virus Testing

Leprosy is a contagious disease that had no cure in biblical times. Biblical texts describe both a medical testing procedure and an isolation procedure. "When anyone has a swelling or a rash or a shiny spot on their skin ... they must be brought to Aaron the priest or to one of his sons who is a priest. The priest is to examine the sore on the skin, and if the hair in the sore has turned white and the sore appears to be more than skin deep, it is a defiling skin disease. When the priest examines that person, he shall pronounce them ceremonially unclean" (Leviticus 13:2–3).

In the thousands of years since Aaron served on the front lines fighting leprosy, medical testing has advanced beyond the subjective eye of the local priest, but testing and isolation still remain a key means of slowing the spread of infections. In the case of Covid-19, a sophisticated test of a nasal or throat sample can show if a person has an active coronavirus infection. The two existing types of tests include reverse transcription polymerase chain reaction (RT-PCR),[28] which detects the genetic material of the virus, and antigen tests, which detect specific proteins on the surface of the virus. The RT-PCR test is processed in a lab and can detect at least 95 percent of cases. The antigen test is much simpler, can be done at home, and gives the results in 15 minutes. It is, however, less accurate and in some cases will give the wrong result half the time.[29] But the test is inexpensive, and frequent multiple tests (for example, daily) can result in higher sensitivity. For example, if four tests (with 50 percent sensitivity) in a row are negative, the likelihood of the test subject not having the virus is 94 percent (assuming independence of the tests and the results).

In an ideal world, everyone in the population would be tested for Covid-19 on a frequent basis—catching almost every Covid-19 case before that infectious person had a chance to spread the disease. Infection rates would plummet even with the economy fully reopened and everyone out and about as normal. However, these tests can be costly; require equipment, supplies, and labor; and take time to return results, which limits their usefulness. The challenge of testing at the national level clearly exceeded the resources (or political will) of many nations which, in turn, allowed the virus to spread. For large companies, institutions, and governments, the challenge is in optimizing the frequency of testing in the context of other infection control measures.

As part of MIT's efforts to reopen for fall 2020, university officials have limited the number of students invited back to campus and, among a plethora of other measures, determined that anybody on campus will be tested twice a week. At MIT, the test results are returned within 24 hours and, in many cases, on the same day. This frequency, coupled with contact tracing, daily attestations, compulsory mask wearing, social distancing and cleaning and sanitizing procedures, allowed the university to open with some degree of confidence. Furthermore, most courses will take place online, research projects that can be done remotely will be required to be done remotely, and on-campus laboratory research will incorporate the guidelines mentioned above. As of this writing, the hope is that the university can function without experiencing uncontrolled spread of the virus.

Proof of Status

Ultimately, what every organization wants from each incoming worker or customer is some proof that the person is not infectious. Iceland, for example, has controlled the virus but is allowing entry of foreign tourists who can prove they do not have Covid-19 or who take a Covid-19 test on arrival. Responding to a business opportunity, biometric identification company Clear, which already offers expedited security lines in airports, is rolling out new health-screening-related products to expedite the process.[30] By allowing registered individuals to be tested quickly, possible infections can be identified quickly. This allows officials to prohibit entry and also to let individuals know they need to isolate and possibly be treated.

In theory, vaccination or having previously had Covid-19 might make someone immune to the disease, suggesting the potential for a kind of "immunity card" as proof of pandemic-free status. The WHO already has an official vaccination card (*Carte Jaune* or Yellow Card) used to document vaccinations and intended to be a medical passport for countries that require vaccination from incoming foreign visitors.[31] Antibody tests (which don't test for a current infection) can detect a person's immune response to a past Covid-19 infection. In the case of some viruses, the presence of these antibodies may imply likely future immunity. As of August 2020, the WHO takes a skeptical view of so-called immunity passports, because the science on immunity to Covid-19 is too young.[32]

The most extensive use of "proof of status" systems is in China, which uses smartphone apps associated with the popular platforms AliPay and WeChat to track every individual's travel, contact history, and biometric data.[33] The app presents a colored QR code for scanning by health authorities: green means the person is free to enter, yellow means they must quarantine at home for 7 to 14 days, and red means they must report to a hospital immediately and quarantine for 14 days. Those without a green code cannot travel, enter shopping malls, use public services, and may even be prohibited from entering their own apartment building. Although Orwellian to some,[34] the system means the economy can fully reopen for the vast majority of people—a February 24 news briefing in one province said 98.2 percent of citizens had a green code.[35]

Isolation of the Ill

The Old Testament mandated not only testing for leprosy, as described above, but also mandated the isolation of lepers. Once the verdict of the priest was "positive," the afflicted person was identified as sick and isolated. "Anyone with such a defiling disease must wear torn clothes, let their hair be unkempt, cover the lower part of their face and cry out, 'Unclean! Unclean!' As long as they have the disease they remain unclean. They must live alone; they must live outside the camp" (Leviticus 13:45–46). Life as a leper was miserable in a time when such diseases were incurable.

With Covid-19, any person who tests positive for the virus is isolated in quarantine—typically in a non-healthcare setting, unless they show severe symptoms. These non-healthcare settings include isolation at home, in a dorm room, or in a group isolation facility.[36] Some jurisdictions also require quarantines of travelers, especially those from countries or states with elevated rates of Covid-19 infections. Typically, they require such travelers to remain in a designated location (e.g., a hotel room).

Countries such as Singapore, China, and Taiwan enforce isolation with digital apps—like mandatory electronic wristbands in Hong Kong—that tip off authorities when a quarantined person leaves their home.[37]

Reducing the Spread Indoors

Because no amount of attestation, fever screening, or virus testing can be 100 percent effective (or feasible 100 percent of the time), companies' second line of defense for safe zones is to reduce the chance that if an infectious person gains entry, they spread the disease to others. That requires using knowledge about how the virus moves from the infected to the susceptible (in the air or on surfaces) and then blocking transmission of the virus.

Back Off, Man!

For many companies, such as NCR, an American technology provider of software, hardware, and services, the shutdown had a brutally simple logic: Everyone must leave the buildings and log into work from home. Marija Zivanovic-Smith, senior vice president of corporate marketing, communications, and external affairs for NCR, described the shift: "In the span of two weeks, we sent 95 percent of our office population... we're talking around 22,000–23,000 people sent safely to work from home, around the world. Despite the change, there was no downtime and commerce kept running for banks, restaurants, and retailers."[38]

In contrast, Zivanovic-Smith explained, reopening entailed much more complex challenges: "Site readiness [for reopening] includes a new employee journey [for] entering and moving about the building and office. How do we regulate that? How do we choose which type of job category should reenter first, and why? How do we manage physical distancing? How do we assign seating, lab space, use of common areas, et cetera? What do we do with the cleaning, and HVAC, PPE? We have outlined 69 activities to be completed before we have sites that are fully ready and operational. And also, we calculated the cost at the end."[39]

Because this new normal of living and working with Covid-19 was so new (and not so normal), NCR decided it needed a pilot project. Stefan Lazarevic, general manager for NCR Serbia and EMEA external affairs director, described the process: "Site preparedness for us means that we have a clear plan with a timeframe [for] how to reach 100 percent site full readiness.... We started with a soft launch, where our leaders came to the office first, made sure that all things were put in place, made sure that we could move forward with all the other employees. And then, the week after, employees from a critical list came back to the office and the number expanded up to 40 percent as required."[40]

Distancing requirements have an even more profound effect on spaces visited by consumers. Distancing requires retailers, restaurants, and entertainment venues to limit the number of customers in the space at the same time, separate them by distance or physical dividers, arrange arrivals by appointment, and more. Before the pandemic, retailers wanted shoppers to linger, browse, try things on, and, perchance, buy more. After Covid-19 hit, restrictions on the number of concurrent shoppers caused retailers to encourage shoppers to move quickly in the aisles—grab and go—to minimize the number of shoppers in the store at any given time and maximize the number of customers per day.

Technological solutions can also be used to promote distancing and other pandemic-thwarting behaviors. Law enforcement agencies have been using aerial drones to enforce distancing, mask use, quarantine violations, and even to detect feverish people.[41] On the ground, Singapore is testing a robotic dog to patrol parks and enforce distancing regulations.[42] In warehouses, Amazon is testing a proximity warning device that workers wear which alerts them if they are about to walk too close to each other.[43] Cameras, sensors, wireless links, and AI enable more sophisticated monitoring.

Contactless Contact

Au revoir to the European kiss on the cheek. Similarly, a traditional handshake now just gets a shake of the head. The pressing need to avoid potential infection has upended centuries-old social traditions as well as newer greetings like the high five. In its place are an evolving panoply of alternatives, such as a nod, hand on heart, namaste bow, and various non-contact hand or foot gestures.[44]

Clever manufacturers have developed many innovative little add-on gadgets to help people open doors without using their hands, such as a foot pedal at the bottom of a door.[45] Consumers can use self-service checkout in stores to avoid having a cashier and a bagger touch their purchases. Elevators have been outfitted with smart speaker systems. A personal smartphone can enable the owner to avoid touching surfaces. Restaurants have posted QR codes with links to their menus, and stores have deployed tap-to-pay systems.

Who Is That Masked Man?

As employees return to the workplace, many of them will be required to wear masks. By spring 2020, more than half (51 percent) of companies in a World Economic Forum survey were mandating the use of PPE for employees.[46] But here, too, many issues are under discussion: Should employers provide masks? Where and when should they be worn? What if employees refuse to wear them? One of the quirks of American federal law is that because face coverings are meant to protect others, not the wearer, employers cannot be required to provide them and train workers in their proper use.[47] Businesses that require masks, however, need to consider the Americans with Disabilities Act and provide an accommodation to employees with disability. However, if the accommodation creates risk to other employees, the employer can be exempted from this requirement.[48]

On April 3, 2020, the CDC recommended that all individuals wear cloth face masks in public and where physical distancing measures were difficult to maintain.[49] While the US federal government considers masks to be voluntary, some states required them for public-facing employees, like receptionists and waiters. Some states and many companies and other organizations required the use of masks indoors at all times while on the premises (with exceptions such as for eating). As China came out of the lockdown, it was still an offense not to wear masks in public.

Japan offers a striking example of the likely efficacy of mask wearing. As of June 30, 2020, the rate of Covid-19 deaths in Japan was only 0.8 per 100,000 population—the rate in the US was 50 times worse.[50] This was despite Japan's dense cities, proximity to China, and that the country never instituted a tough lockdown. Two characteristics of Japanese people stand out. First, their diet may improve their immune systems (despite a high rate of smoking), as evidenced by Japan having the highest concentration of elderly per capita in the world. Second, the Japanese are accustomed to wearing face masks: More than 90 percent of surveyed businessmen (ages 20–50) say they wore masks in public as the country was opening up.[51] Furthermore, a Japanese study assessing the factors affecting Covid-19 death rates suggested mask wearing had the most significant impact; it was responsible for a 70 percent reduction in death rates.[52]

Cleaning and Disinfecting

The horrors of epidemics have often spurred advances in hygiene. The Black Death led local governments in Europe to take more rigorous control of street cleaning, disposal of corpses, and water supply maintenance.[53] A German doctor formulated Lysol in 1889 to combat a cholera epidemic.[54] The 1918 flu pandemic motivated a strong action against spitting in public.

Today, various robot makers are creating germ-zapping bots that can autonomously disinfect a room, hall, or store aisle with bright, sterilizing UV light.[55] In the long term, product makers are looking at better materials or near-permanent surface treatments that can deactivate pathogens without requiring labor-intensive cleaning.

A key element of creating a safe zone for consumers is making sure that not only are they safe in such places, but that they feel safe. For example, Heather Ostis, vice president of supply chain at Delta Air Lines, described how the airline partnered with Purell to provide sanitizing products to passengers: "From the beginning of this pandemic, Delta's strategy, set by our CEO, Ed Bastian, was focused on safety. We added layers of protection, called the Delta CareStandard[SM], to ensure our customers and employees feel safe throughout their travel journey. From the new cleaning and sanitation procedures, to our numerous partnerships—including Purell, Lysol, and the Mayo Clinic—each initiative and partnership is meant to instill confidence back to the customer. Take our partnership with Purell for example. As each customer boards our planes, they are handed an individual Purell wipe for them to use at their seat to wipe down their arm rests, seat buckle, entertainment screen, and more. Even though each plane is cleaned by electrostatic spraying with our proprietary cleaning solution, the added layers of protection—in the form of a Purell wipe—bring about an extra measure of safety and comfort for the traveler."[56]

Ventilation

Ventilation to help sick buildings may be as important as ventilators to help sick Covid-19 patients. In a notorious case from 1974, a single child with measles infected 28 other students in 14 classrooms despite 97 percent of the children being vaccinated. The building's ventilation system recirculated virus-laden, unfiltered air to many of the children in the rest of the school.[57] A 2019 study of influenza transmission found that adding outdoor air to the ventilation system had the same infection-reducing effect as vaccinating 50–60 percent of the people in a building.[58] In its guidelines for opening office buildings, the US CDC recommended, "Increase circulation of outdoor air as much as possible by opening windows and doors if possible, and using fans."[59]

In order to encourage air travel, Delta Air Lines announced, "Many Delta aircraft, including all of our international widebodies, plus many narrow bodies including 737s, 757s, A220s, A319s, A320s and A321s, are equipped with state-of-the-art air circulation systems, blending fresh outside air that is sterilized with a high-temperature compressor and ozone purifier with existing cabin air that has been recirculated through an industrial-grade HEPA filter. HEPA air filters extract more than 99.999 percent of even the tiniest viruses, as small as 0.01 micrometers. Coronaviruses, which range from 0.08 to 0.16 micrometers in size, are filtered by the HEPA filter. Delta's 717s use 100 percent fresh outside air."[60]

Controlling the Virus

"When you start doing testing of one case and it turns out you might have a dozen people impacted by that one person, you're not social distancing enough," said John Church, chief supply chain and global business solutions officer at General Mills, "you're not taking it seriously enough. That's been an important lesson."[61] Feedback is the key part of controlling a complex, evolving risk, such as a novel and growing pandemic with many unknowns. Carefully measuring the number of newly infected people provides a feedback loop on virus control policies such as mask wearing, distancing, health monitoring, and the identification of superspreading locations. For companies, monitoring the numbers of cases typically includes both those within the company and those in the community, as part of a Covid-19 enterprise dashboard. Success depends on reducing and then eliminating new infections.

All of this comes at a cost, however. Implementing anti-virus policies takes time and money, especially in B2C companies with large workforces or numbers of customers. Pandemic management adds costs for materials and new daily duties to employees, such as cleaning and managing PPE. More importantly, the productivity of facilities such as plants, warehouses, and terminals is likely to be reduced by distancing protocols. In many cases, more shifts will be necessary because reducing the density of workers typically means staffing fewer people per shift.

However, in an age of concern about infections, creating safe zones for retail spaces creates a competitive advantage. I learned this from my wife (as I do in most other areas). She was a 25-year patron of a much-loved neighborhood hairdresser but was disappointed to learn that the salon was not taking her safety seriously enough. For example, the establishment was still blow-drying hair, which propels respiratory secretions and virions around the enclosed space. The owners refused to provide accommodation for her concerns.

This lack of concern for safety drove my wife to find a new hair salon. The surrounding Newbury Street area in Boston has more than 50 hair salons within eight short blocks (and many more in the cross streets); the competition is fierce. My wife found a hair salon that agreed to take her very early in the morning, before it opened to other customers, so she could be the only customer in the establishment. Furthermore, the new salon expanded its opening hours to 16 hours a day, seven days a week; it also limited service to a few customers at a time and added a strict disinfecting regimen. As it turns out, the new hairdresser was better on all my wife's hairstyling key performance indicators. She is never going back to her old stylist. Cutting off a 25-year personal and professional relationship was no small step, and it demonstrates the advantage of providing a safe zone to concerned customers.

Of course, hairdressers are not the only businesses to compete on safety. Every service-oriented business, from restaurants advertising their spaced-out outdoor tables to gyms touting plexiglass dividers between machines, competes on being the "safest zone." Airlines, however, never compete on flight safety. They understand that raising doubts in the public's mind about the safety of flying can hurt the entire industry. Yet during the pandemic, the difference between advertising safety and advertising comfort (big seats with dividers between passengers) becomes blurred. Delta Air Lines, for example, is advertising the fact that it is committed to blocking middle seats, as do Alaska Airlines and JetBlue (on larger aircraft). These airlines are betting that blocking the middle seats will give them a competitive advantage among potential passengers worried about full flights.

The Covid-19 case counts of a company (or a community) become the scoreboard for measuring its success in controlling the virus, which has benefits in boosting the confidence of stakeholders. "If enough countries keep the disease under control we could be able to suppress the second wave on a global scale," said Professor Markus Müller, rector of the Vienna Medical University and an adviser to the Austrian government.[62] Vanquishing the threat of more infections and more shutdowns certainly pleases Keynes's "animal spirits" and makes the global economy more active.

11. Cool Home Offices

The combination of stay-at-home orders plus distancing requirements upended how and where office work gets done. The virus forced people out of their usual work stations and into a motley assortment of makeshift home offices. Newly discovered apps allowed workers to communicate, share, and collaborate. For example, engineers developing new systems are accustomed to congregating around a large whiteboard while collaborating and testing each other's ideas. To help them work remotely, many companies developed interactive whiteboard applications for online sessions.[1]

Some workers found they liked working from home, and companies also discovered that it could be a cost-effective strategy for some. However, as with anything involving managing people, the move came with a complex set of trade-offs and priorities. Companies strived to ensure that workers would be productive, socially integrated with their coworkers, and satisfied with their work-life balance so that the company could retain skilled workers and expertise.

Working from Home

As the US shut down, working from home grew by nearly six times (from 7 percent in October 2019 to 41 percent in March 2020), according to data from the Federal Reserve Bank.[2] Similarly, a World Economic Forum survey found that 40 percent of companies mandated working from home to protect employees during Covid-19.[3] Some companies went to extremes in their efforts to move their workforces to home offices. For example, insurance company Nationwide shifted 98 percent of its 27,000 workers to working from home.[4] The pandemic accelerated Nationwide's work-from-home efforts; prior to the pandemic, 20 percent of its employees were home-based.

Many of the technology-adoption changes spurred by Covid-19 accelerated the existing work-from-home trend. A fast-expanding stack of technologies—such as virtual private networks, cloud storage, video-chat apps, and online collaboration tools—enabled many white-collar workers to make a fast transition from working at the office to working from home. "As Covid-19 impacts every aspect of our work and life," said Satya Nadella, CEO of Microsoft, "we have seen two years' worth of digital transformation in two months."[5]

Trends in telecommunications standards such as cellular 5G[6] and WiFi 6[7] promise more speed for work-from-anywhere scenarios (see Chapter 14, p. 119). Both wireless technologies promise very high speeds by using millimeter waves, although the technology comes with trade-offs, including relatively poor range and intolerance of obstacles between the user and the base station.[8] These technologies obviously require investment in new network infrastructure and end-user devices. Yet, in another example of accelerating pre-pandemic trends, Covid-19 has spurred more demand for higher-speed and higher-capacity services both in households and businesses.[9]

The trend spurred sales for other products, too. The shift to working from home, schooling at home, shopping at home, exercising at home, and virtual socializing at home created significant demand for all manner of products such as webcams, monitors, desks, toys, games, and fitness equipment. Of this trend, Dennis Flynn, senior director of supply chain and inventory management at Walmart eCommerce, said, "Sporting goods was one of the first things to start really going up, because people were leaving their gyms. Gyms were closing down. We basically sold out of most of our inventory of health and fitness equipment."[10] Similarly, Intel saw a surge in sales as people upgraded their home computers.[11] Some workers even bought RVs or trailers to do double duty as added space for a distraction-free home office and for Covid-safe travel.

But Are People Working?

Both workers and employers discovered that many types of employees don't need to be tied to a desk and in view of the boss to be productive. Kirt Walker, CEO of Nationwide, explained, "We rely on 10 key performance indicators, and employees can monitor their own work day-to- day, and so can their supervisors." This approach is part of the trend toward data-driven evaluation of workers' output (results) rather than workers' labor input (hours worked). "We don't try to hold people accountable with amount of time they're putting in, but rather how well they are doing on those indicators," Walker said.[12]

The data proved that working from home is a success for many. "We've tracked all of our key performance indicators, and there has been no change," said Walker. "We keep hearing from members, 'If you hadn't announced you were all working from home, we never would have known.'" Many tech companies have extended their work-from-home policies—Facebook, Google, and Twitter plan for at least a year or more of it.[13]

Lynn Torrel of Flex echoed Walker's sentiments: "I think we've really recognized how effective we can be in the work-from-home environment with Zoom meetings, regular calls, and a cadence of communications. A viewpoint that 'you must be in the office from 8:00 to 5:00 so I can see you doing your job' may change. I think that will likely change the perceptions of work from home or work remotely."[14]

Other companies did see productivity differences. Apple's CEO, Tim Cook, said, "In some areas of the company, people may be even more productive. In some other areas, they're not as productive, and so it's mixed depending upon what the roles are."[15] For example, my interviews with NCR and New Balance revealed that although engineers and technicians may be tech-savvy knowledge workers, they often need access to specialized equipment, laboratory gear, prototyping workshops, or manufacturing systems to do their jobs.

According to Kate Lister, president of Global Workplace Analytics, "The biggest holdback against remote work for the past 20 years has been middle managers who didn't trust their employees to do it."[16] Some of those distrustful managers had been insisting on the use of so-called tattleware, which takes screenshots of employees' computer screens, monitors audio for suspicious words, and tracks the apps and websites that employees visit. Some companies even insist on always-on webcams and scheduling multiple daily check-ins to monitor employees.[17] Time will tell whether such practices become more common or whether the trust gap will gradually close as managers get used to home working.

Overall, coming to the office is expensive for both employers and employees. Global Workplace Analytics estimates that for each employee who works remotely half of the time, the typical employer can save about $11,000 per year through increased productivity, lower real estate costs, reduced absenteeism and turnover, and better disaster preparedness. They further estimate working from home half the time saves employees $2,500 to $4,000 per year in reduced costs for commuting, parking, and food (net of added household expenses). Employees also save an hour a day of the average commute by working from home.[18]

Despite the surveys and stories that paint a rosy picture of working from home, the assumptions underlying this analysis are not set in stone. First, after staying away from the office, paranoia about losing one's job may take over, and workers may want to be seen by their managers and coworkers. Second, a company may be concerned about losing its cohesive culture if workers seldom see each other in person. Finally, recall that companies have tried this before (albeit before the ubiquity of current cloud and communications technologies). Companies like Bank of America, IBM, Aetna and, famously, Yahoo embraced working from home for a while but then yanked their employees back to the office.[19]

A Crazy Time to Be Home Alone

Jokes about introverts thriving while working peacefully at home and extroverts going crazy from the lack of daily human contact might be stereotypes, but they do hint at the spectrum of the pandemic's effects on workers' psychological well-being. In interviews for this book, executives reported that some employees preferred working from home because it allowed them to focus on their tasks, enabled better work-life balance, and saved them the commute. Others disliked working at home and could not wait to get back to the office for its social engagement, daily rhythms of life, and structure. BASF's Busche said, "Now we are thinking of how many [people] do we really need in offices." Yet, he added, "The more they worked from home and mobile, the more some people showed some serious signs of needing that social teamwork."

Covid-19 upended people's routines and rituals that had historically enabled many to handle work, family, and the complexities of life. The new normal will see new routines and rituals to promote a workplace mindset, corporate culture, and social bonding while at home. For example, one simple tip for replicating the work routine was to get dressed in work clothing (or at least a nice shirt for a video meeting),[20] in part to signal to family members that it was work time. Some companies began using new platforms such a Breakroom and Walkabout to recreate video-game-like virtual replicas of their offices to give remote workers a sense of being "at work" and seeing avatars of coworkers at their desks or in meeting rooms.[21]

Other organizations sought to replace missing coworker camaraderie with virtual social events. Flex's Torrel said, "I started getting very worried about fatigue with the team. I actually implemented a Monday happy hour. So, every Monday at 4:00 we'll play a game and we take turns hosting these little games. And my team gives me a hard time if I work too much or if I want to talk about work too much." Many other organizations created weekly sessions with breakout groups playing games like Pictionary and scavenger hunt. As the stay-at-home period lengthened, however, these sessions became less frequent. It seems that the initial excitement and newness of online games wore off.

Such a radically new environment and the apprehension about Covid-19 have increased the prevalence of anxiety and depression to above historic norms.[22] To reduce worker stress, companies like Google gave workers extra days off with no meetings around the July 4 holiday in the US. Meri Stevens, worldwide vice president of consumer health supply chain and deliver at Johnson & Johnson, said, "J&J also announced that everybody had to take the weekend around Memorial Day off, Friday to Monday, no emails, nothing. And everybody was good about it, all around the world."[23] A spring 2020 survey by the World Economic Forum found that 47 percent of companies provided advice on mental health to support employees, and 39 percent offered employees voluntary unpaid leave during the pandemic.[24]

Living Wherever

"I had assumed over the course of 20 years that a generation of people would not be tethered to their city... that people will realize over the course of working more remote, they could kind of live anywhere," Airbnb CEO Brian Chesky said. "I never thought that decades would happen in two months."[25] Tech workers in high-cost locations such as Silicon Valley see work from home as a great way to avoid outrageous rents, unaffordable real estate prices, and mind-numbing commutes. "With nothing keeping me here, I can't justify paying the rent prices," said one tech worker.[26] They could move to Hawaii, Sacramento, Michigan, rural America, or anywhere around the globe. Remote work will become even easier with the launch of new satellite broadband services that promise to cover the globe.[27]

An estimated 37 percent of all workers could work from home, with some job categories such as clerical support workers having a 67 percent potential for remote work.[28] Not only will remote working give employees greater freedom to choose a home base, but couples may no longer have to worry that one partner will need to give up their job to follow the other partner to a new and distant job.

The new work-from-home capability will also let companies tap into the best talent residing anywhere. More importantly, such new technology capabilities and companies' processes for working remotely may lead to a new

globalization of labor despite increased nationalism, tariffs, and trade restrictions around the world. While most of the media predicts reshoring of manufacturing to the US and Europe, this may happen only on a limited scale (*see*
Chapter 17, p. 145). At the same time, high-paying white-collar jobholders
may look for places that offer high quality of life anywhere around the world.

The trend is attracting the interest of countries looking to appeal to high-
tech workers with their high-tech salaries. Barbados launched a "Welcome
Stamp" program that includes a one-year visa and no income taxes.[29] Estonia
launched a long-awaited "Digital Nomad" visa program.[30] Countries such
as Germany, Georgia, and Costa Rica offer visa programs for freelancers.[31]
Interest is growing—applications to Portugal's "golden visa" program[32] nearly
tripled in May 2020.[33]

12. Higher Education May Never Be the Same

Classroom education seems tailor-made to spread Covid-19 and other pathogens. It features a large group of people from many different households, often from all over the world, coming together inside the same room for an hour and then dispersing to go to other rooms full of large numbers of other people from other households. In addition to classes, students mingle with still more people for lunch and extracurricular activities, or, in the case of college students, to live packed in dormitories and party the night away. By analogy, as any parent of young children knows, kids bring home more than just homework.

Although technologists have been pushing a vision of remote, computer-aided instruction for decades, it took just a few weeks for Covid-19 to drive the adoption of online learning from niche idea to mainstream reality.

The notion of distance education predates MOOCs (massive open online courses) and the internet. The initial concept began with the availability of reliable, long-distance correspondence offered by the US Postal Service starting in the mid-19th century. It included for-profit "correspondence colleges," which relied on instructional missives mailed between students and professors.[1] The first official correspondence education program, called the Society to Encourage Home Studies, was established in Boston by Ana Eliot Ticknor, now recognized as the pioneer of distance learning in the US. In 1971, the Labour government in the UK launched the country's Open University, offering remote degree education via TV instruction and correspondence.[2]

Following the development of the World Wide Web in 1990 by MIT professor Tim Berners-Lee, the online world took the current form. The first MOOC is usually considered to be a course by David Wiley, at Utah State University. It was open to anyone and enrolled 50 online students from eight countries. The first notably successful MOOC was a 2011 course, "Artificial Intelligence," by Sebastian Thrun and Peter Norvig of Stanford University. It attracted more than 160,000 learners from around the world.

Penn State University, one of the pioneers in online education, launched its first fully online programs in 1998. Penn State World Campus now offers over 100 graduate and undergraduate degrees online, in addition to online certificates and associate's degrees.

Supply Chain Education Online

At MIT, the Center for Transportation & Logistics (CTL) pioneered some of MIT's offerings of online education. In the fall of 2014, Dr. Chris Caplice developed, recorded, and offered the first asynchronous MOOC at MIT, which was an introduction to supply chain management. Despite no marketing budget, the course attracted more than 40,000 learners, taking CTL and MIT by surprise. CTL created and offered a subsequent course in supply chain design in the fall of 2015.

In October 2015, MIT announced a new academic credential for the digital age: the "MicroMasters" in supply chain management.[3] The credential could be earned upon successful completion of the equivalent of one semester's worth of courses and a comprehensive examination. CTL developed three more courses to create a five-course MicroMasters sequence.

The MicroMasters program included one more important feature: Top graduates of the MicroMasters were invited to come to MIT and complete a full master's degree in supply chain management in a single semester. In other words, for those students, the online courses will earn MIT academic credit in a "blended" program combining the MOOC courses with on-campus, in-person classes at MIT.

The MicroMasters program became an overnight success, attracting 350,000 learners from 192 countries by 2020. Fearing a backlash from students whom CTL would not be able to accept into the following residential portion of the blended program, MIT recruited dozens of other universities to recognize the MicroMasters completion credential and allow students to obtain a full academic degree there in a short time.

The first blended class, including learners who finished their MicroMasters program successfully, were accepted to MIT and started their studies on campus in January 2018. Because it was a new program, MIT's teaching laboratory, which is independent of MIT CTL, analyzed the students' performance to ensure that they were "MIT quality." To do this, the lab collected data on the performance of the traditional Supply Chain Management program students and the blended SCM students in all classes they share with other MIT students from all of MIT's schools. The result showed that the blended students in fact outperformed other students in all MIT departments.

This result, which the SCM instructors were anecdotally aware of even before the study, has important implications. First, completing five MIT-level courses (often while working full-time jobs), as the blended students did before they entered MIT, takes a lot of grit and commitment. The assessment demonstrated the importance of such human qualities. Dedication, thirst for learning, and tenacity are important characteristics that show up in the online world but are not always evident in a transcript or standardized test scores. A second, even more important conclusion is the fact that the data on the MOOC students which the admission committee used in their decision was significantly richer than just grades, standardized test results, and letters of recommendation. The online MicroMasters courses yielded a trove of data about each student's performance—because the system logs each keystroke—generating millions of data points that can be used for analysis.

Furthermore, educators can continuously improve the quality of MOOCs using all these data. Instructors can track each student's activities, comprehension, and performance as the class progresses. Those same feedback loops that analyze student performance help fine-tune the MOOC curriculum—if too many students misunderstand the same concepts in the same ways, the problem is the curriculum, not the students. Thus, the curriculum and the teaching processes improve over time.

While many schools are adopting online learning out of pandemic-related necessity, the MIT Supply Chain Management program experience suggests online education has many advantages on its own. As Jeb Bush, the former governor of Florida and founder of the Foundation for Excellence in Education, argued in a *Wall Street Journal* op-ed, "It's time to embrace distance learning—and not just because of the coronavirus." A 2014 MIT-wide task force on the future of MIT education argued, "Innovation in online education and training tools will ultimately lower the cost, boost the efficiency, and broaden the accessibility (and perhaps even the appeal) of educational offerings directed at all age and skill levels."[4]

One of the additional benefits of the MicroMasters courses was in improving MIT's residential education programs. Several classes in the MIT Supply Chain Management program are now offered with an "inverted" instruction style. Students watch lectures at home, take quizzes online, and come to class ready for in-person interactions. These interactions focus on discussing current events, case studies, or guest lectures, where students have to apply the principles explained in the videos to the issues at hand during class discussions.

As the pandemic forced people to stay home, the number of learners in the online programs swelled. With continuing remote sessions, it is inevitable that more resources will be devoted to it, online interactions will only get better, and more students and professors will get comfortable with the medium. Online instruction is bound to be a larger share of future university education.

The Future of Universities

As millions of university students transition from the college experience of dorms and lecture halls to the Covid-19 experience of a tiny screen on the kitchen table, American universities face an existential question. Unlike most universities in Europe and elsewhere, most elite US universities are private institutions. Many rely on revenue from tuition rather than government support. And when *The Atlantic* asked students if they were still willing to pay the same for education delivered remotely, one student's answer was telling: "Would you pay $75,000 for front-row seats to a Beyoncé concert and be satisfied with a livestream instead?"[5]

Technology has affected many other industries. An entire system of making, distributing and pricing movies and television programs has been made obsolete. Movie theaters seem anachronistic as Netflix, Amazon Video, Hulu, Disney+, and dozens of other digital media service providers create award-winning original content to draw in more subscribers at a fast clip.

Forecasts of the death of universities were common in the 2010s. In 2018, the late Harvard Business School professor Clayton Christensen predicted that 50 percent of all colleges and universities in the United States would close or go bankrupt in the next 10 to 15 years.[6] Christensen, who wrote the seminal work on disruptive innovation, argued that online education was the first disruptive innovation in education since the printing press and could lead to many universities' demise. Many observers scoffed at this notion, arguing that universities are not like other businesses. However, a significant number of universities in the US are in dire financial straits, and many have consolidated since the pandemic started, accelerating previous trends.

The Covid-19 period may be the coup de grâce for a large swath of less prestigious institutions of higher education. As millions of students sample online learning, their parents may seriously question the value of a traditional high-cost university degree.[7] The "arms race" among universities in building more palatial accommodations and paying "star" professors more (in many cases with no teaching requirements), increases universities' costs. At the same time, total university enrollments have been decreasing[8] and are likely to decrease further as a result of the natural demographic declines in the number of 18-year-olds, starting around 2026. In order to compete, many universities have turned to the same method used by other struggling businesses: discounting their prices.

Of course, such trends are not going to impact many of the 200 elite universities in the US. Those institutions have lavish endowments, supportive rich alumni, and, more importantly, the cachet and networking opportunities that other universities do not offer. They also get significant revenue from their research activities. Harvard University's endowment of $40 billion (as of 2019) may shrink substantially as a result of the pandemic. And because the financial returns from the endowment support more than a third of Harvard's operating budget, those budgets may shrink as well. However, the large endowment ensures that Harvard can withstand the higher costs associated with the coronavirus and the lower revenues resulting from the recession. Other well-endowed universities with substantial endowments include Yale, Stanford, Princeton, and MIT.

In his widely read 2015 book, *The End of College: Creating the Future of Learning and the University of Everywhere,* Kevin Carey argued that coming-of-age experiences would persist for undergraduate students outside of a campus setting, and higher education would consist of many online courses as well as various certificates, internships, boot camps, and other credit-collecting experiences.[9] As it turned out, Carey's predictions did not come to pass. Students and their parents seem resigned to the traditional in-residence college model despite the high costs and exploding student debt. Carey, however, may have simply been too early—before the sophistication of existing online communication tools and the experience of forced remote learning.

The pandemic may be changing students' and parents' minds as a result of students being stripped of the on-campus, in-class experience. The end of the traditional on-campus college experience as we know it is suddenly not a speculation or a theoretical argument, but a reality. That rich and symbiotic social environment of face-to-face, day-and-night interaction is no more during the pandemic. Only the high tuition costs remain. And now that parents and students have experienced this environment, will they go back to the bundled college experience? Will universities change their offerings to a combination of part-time on-campus and online offerings? Will universities craft a different childhood-to-adulthood transition experience, possibly involving other ways to come of age such as some form of national service?

It is difficult to see the end state of this unfolding change while living it. As with many other industries, the pandemic will likely accelerate previous trends in higher education. It seems unlikely that the education industry can somehow escape the technological forces that wreaked havoc in retail, book publishing, entertainment, the media, and even changed defense and healthcare.

As some higher education institutions go out of business and others consolidate, online competition will become more and more fierce. Courses that attract more students will gain from capturing better data with which to improve the course and higher revenues to justify investment in its production. New 3D gaming concepts and augmented-reality methods are likely to push online learning to improve, provide more engaging content, and deliver better results. Steadily growing production values (and higher production budgets) will create much richer education but ultimately favor only those few institutions that can attract the largest audiences. Sooner or later, it may be difficult for the traditional model of one bored professor lecturing to 30 bored students to compete with a razzle-dazzle superstar presenter with a Nobel Prize and a million online learners.

Education.com and the Future of the Public Mind

The $671 billion higher education industry in the US[10] will likely attract more corporate interest over time. The potential revenues in higher education could be too big for the likes of Google, Amazon, Microsoft and Facebook to not enter this market, or, for that matter, new Silicon Valley startups. Naturally, such enterprises will gain more than just tuition from the students. They will also monetize data collected from online learners as well as marketing other goods and services such as exclusive social networks (Facebook started at Harvard), class-related ancillary media (Amazon), career services (Microsoft owns LinkedIn), and advertising to future high-income young adults as they start making their own choices of consumer brands.

One can imagine a single or a few dominant "social education networks" offering thousands of learning modules, curated by AI, and customized individually to each student's learning goals, learning styles, and abilities. Or these companies might offer more targeted certificate programs that replace traditional four-year degree programs. For example, Google is creating Google

Career Certificates, an online six-month program designed to teach foundation skills for in-demand jobs.[11] Kent Walker, senior vice president of global affairs at Google, said, "In our own hiring, we will now treat these new career certificates as the equivalent of a four-year degree for related roles."

All these developments may have many benefits. These include greater inclusivity and bringing quality education to the masses. However, it may have two unfortunate drawbacks: the decline of liberal education and the increase of inequality.

As more corporations enter the education market, and as parents and students question the value of an expensive college education, preferences for college majors will shift. Both the supply and demand sides of education might focus more on pragmatic degrees—essentially white-collar vocational education—that land well-paying jobs. This shift has been under way for some time, but the pandemic has accelerated it. The result will be a further acceleration in the decline of liberal arts education. Many small liberal arts colleges are closing, others are likely to follow, and liberal arts departments in large universities will likely see continued declining enrollment. However, as the last several years have shown, critical thinking and effective information analysis—the hallmarks of traditional liberal arts education—have never been more important.

The second drawback is possibly an increase in inequality due to two phenomena. A small number of elite institutions will still offer traditional residential education to wealthy and gifted students willing to pay. At these colleges, students will build their exclusive social networks that benefit them personally and professionally throughout life. Others who rely on less costly online degree programs (even with much-improved future technologies), will lack these social network development opportunities. Whether online programs can replicate the social networking elements of traditional colleges remains to be seen.

Another, more serious, level of inequality has already shown itself during the pandemic. Some students lack access to adequate computers, broadband, or a home environment that is conducive to learning. This is part of a deeper gap that has implications not only for education but for participation in an ever more digital economy (*see* Chapter 13, p. 112). This last group will likely be completely left behind without massive efforts to correct the problem.

13. Wider Social, Economic, and Information Gaps

Healthy, wealthy, and wise could be the shorthand descriptors for those groups who were least impacted by Covid-19. The healthy were less likely to die from the disease. The wealthy were more likely to be healthy (and afford better care),[1] had more resources to be able to avoid exposure, and were less likely to be impacted by Covid-19's economic effects. The wise (i.e., those with college degrees) were also similarly blessed with Covid-resistant jobs and more likely be healthy enough to withstand the virus. In short, the impacts of Covid-19 hit the poor much harder than they did rich, educated people.

These inequalities impact supply chains both during and after Covid-19 in at least four ways. First, inequality affects consumption in terms of both who can spend and how much they can spend. Second, it impacts productivity and employment in terms of the likelihood that workers can be employed and productive while distancing. Third, at the country level, poor countries are likely to suffer more and longer. These countries will have more deaths and lower economic growth, both short term and long term. Finally, inequality can trigger social unrest and political turmoil that add risks and costs to doing business in the affected areas.

The Rich Get Richer

"At the end of the day," said Mark Cohen, director of retail studies at Columbia Business School, "the 'haves' have more, and the 'have nots' have less—or have nothing, and therein lies the crisis."[2] Pandemic-related job losses fell disproportionately on the poor as the spread of the virus knocked out millions of service economy jobs in restaurants, nonessential retail, hair salons, and housecleaning. Data from the Federal Reserve found that 40 percent of households with incomes below $40,000 reported job loss in March 2020. That was more than double the 19 percent job loss figure reported for households with income between $40,000 and $100,000 and triple that of the mere 13 percent job loss among of upper-income households earning more than $100,000.[3]

Analysis of data from 175 countries and five past pandemics suggests that Covid-19 will increase overall income inequality and worsen unemployment among the less educated.[4] This effect was worldwide as the pandemic swept the globe and battered economies both rich and poor. Especially distressing is how the pandemic could reverse advances in wealth creation and create new classes of poverty. A United Nations study estimated that the pandemic could push 420 million to 580 million people back into poverty. The result would undo 10 to 30 years of the world's progress in reducing poverty.[5] David Beasley, executive director of the UN's World Food Programme, said, "I want to stress that we are not only facing a global health pandemic but also a global humanitarian catastrophe."[6]

The effect also occurred at the country level. Countries such as Germany, the US, and the UK could afford fiscal stimulus measures many times larger (in percent of GDP terms) than Hungary, Greece, and Italy could.[7] Richer countries had both the deep tax bases and good access to global capital markets that enabled them to support their economies with considerable stimulus packages. The situation was most dire in the poorest African, South American, and Asian countries. In many of these places, healthcare systems were inadequate even before the pandemic and were hit hard by Covid-19.[8] At both household and country levels, the poor were less resilient.

Distancing Is a Luxury Good

The opportunity to work from home was not afforded to all workers equally. Data from the Federal Reserve showed that, during April 2020, 63 percent of college graduates worked entirely from home, while only 20 percent of those with a high school education or less did so.[9] Moreover, the wealthy could afford more space at home and the many appliances, technologies, and toys that make being stuck at home more livable. The wealthy could afford more services such as delivered meals, groceries, and other products, so they weren't forced to go out in public. In big cities, if the wealthy did need to go out, they were more likely to own cars and thus could avoid mass transit. In essence, the well-off could stay healthy by using their money to insulate themselves and their families from Covid-19.

The same pattern happened around the world. The ability to work from home varies from country to country depending on the composition of the country's economy.[10]

In Switzerland, which has an economy dominated by knowledge-based industries (e.g., financial services and pharmaceuticals), an estimated 45 percent of the population can work from home. In contrast, less than a third of the population can work from home in other European countries due to dependence on tourism (e.g., Greece and Spain) or manufacturing (e.g., Slovakia).

The rich also had more resources and opportunity to get away from Covid-19 hotspots. Wealthy New Yorkers fled Manhattan in March 2020 for second homes and tony resorts in the Hamptons, Connecticut, and Florida.[11] As a result, real estate prices in Manhattan plummeted.[12] In China, rich and well-connected citizens could find ways around travel bans and leave locked-down Covid-19 hotspot locations.[13] Similarly, wealthy US citizens could buy citizenship and a second passport in another country to escape the Covid-pariah status of the US.[14]

Digital Slums by the Information Superhighway

"As people are sheltering in their homes," said Evan Spiegel, CEO of the sharing app company Snap, "they are increasingly turning to digital behaviors across every aspect of their lives, including communication, commerce, entertainment, fitness, and learning. We believe that this will accelerate the digital transformation across many businesses, and that the heightened levels of activity we are seeing today will lead to a sustained uplift in the digital economy over time."[15] That's a rosy forecast for the e-economy, but all these new digital behaviors and the related opportunities for work, commerce, education, and entertainment depend on good broadband internet access, which can be costly or inaccessible to the poor.

In the US, an estimated 42 million Americans cannot get broadband because it's simply not available in their area.[16] Telecommunications providers have not built out their high-speed networks to serve all rural and poor areas. The FCC is working to subsidize broadband service to underserved areas, but it will take years. Even if providers built the infrastructure, affordability of home computing equipment and monthly access charges would still remain a challenge for poor households.

What's particularly problematic are the 9.7 million US students who don't have internet access at all—essential in the Covid-era use of online education to reduce or replace in-person classes. Without equal access to online educational systems, poor children are likely to be worse off than their parents. In Los Angeles, 13 percent of high school students had no online contact with their school three weeks into the schools' physical closings, and one-third of high school students were not participating regularly in online classes.[17]

The digital divide spans the globe. Less than half (45 percent) of people worldwide have smartphones,[18] although two-thirds (66 percent) do have a mobile phone.[19] As of 2017, there were only 1 billion broadband connections serving the world's 7.8 billion people.

Countries also vary in the quality of their internet infrastructure, according to an analysis by researchers at Tufts University's Fletcher School.[20] The researchers analyzed 42 countries on three technology attributes that are required in a digital world of working, shopping, and learning from home: the robustness of key digital platforms, internet infrastructure resilience to traffic surges, and the proliferation of digital payment options to facilitate transactions. Wealthy countries such the US, the UK, the Netherlands, and Norway rated high on all dimensions. Poorer countries such as India, Indonesia, and Chile lagged on all three.

Many of the countries of the EU had digital surge resilience that was below the median, owing to aging internet infrastructure. When Covid-19 sent people home and internet use skyrocketed, EU authorities asked video streaming services such as Netflix, YouTube, and Amazon Prime to reduce their bandwidth consumption, which they did.[21] Streaming entertainment might seem like a luxury, but this same electronic infrastructure enables advanced business and supply chain uses of the internet such as video calls, collaboration tools, Internet of things (IoT) sensing, virtual and augmented reality, and rich media e-commerce. As such, advanced e-commerce, work from home, and intensive supply chain visibility may be harder in countries, companies, and households that lack broadband connections and sufficient overall bandwidth.

Race Gap

All of these gaps fell disproportionately on minorities. "Unemployment has tended to go up much faster for minorities, and for others who tend to be at the low end of the income spectrum," said Jerome Powell, chair of the Federal

Reserve, at a news conference in April 2020.[22] Minorities were more likely to work in low-paid service industry jobs that were cut during the pandemic and more likely to work in on-site, physical labor jobs that could not be done from home.

Covid-19 infection rates and mortality rates also varied by race. In a statistical comparison without controlling for any explanatory variables, researchers at Yale and the University of Pittsburgh found that black people were more than 3.5 times more likely to die of Covid-19 than white people, and Latino people were nearly twice as likely to die of the virus as white people.[23] However, many of these deaths are associated with comorbid conditions. An analysis published by the US National Institutes of Health examining mortality rates from all causes of death found no significant statistical association between African Americans and mortality risk after controlling for four comorbidity factors (obesity, diabetes, chronic kidney disease, and hypertension).[24] Thus, the long-term challenge is to avoid comorbid conditions through better education, better diets, better healthcare access, and related initiatives. Poor and minority households also had lower adoption of broadband.[25] Countries around the world showed a similar pattern among racial and ethnic minorities.[26]

Mind the Gap

The overall growing gap in resources is more than just an example of inequality. Throughout history, epidemics and the resulting economic fallouts have triggered social unrest and even armed conflicts.[27] Epidemics have spawned conspiracy theories and militant rhetoric about causes of the sickness that led to attacks on minorities, outsiders, authorities, and other countries. Likewise, unemployment and economic recession bring latent social anger to the boiling point, such that local incidents can generate national unrest. "Unless we take action now, we should be prepared for a significant rise in conflict, hunger and poverty," said Mark Lowcock, head of the UN's Office for the Coordination of Humanitarian Affairs.[28] He warned that the Covid-induced economic ruins wrought by the pandemic could ultimately kill more people than the pandemic itself.

PART 4
SUPPLY CHAINS
FOR THE FUTURE

"The degree of automation and digitalization
is a big advantage in such a crisis. In one of our
factories that is around 80 percent automated we
only faced minor capacity losses."

—Gunter Beitinger, Vice President of
Manufacturing, Siemens[1]

In the months before Covid-19, issues such as US–China trade tensions, Brexit, perennial Persian Gulf problems—plus the continuous drumbeat of typhoons, hurricanes, and many other local dramas, kept supply chain managers up at night. Most consumers slept soundly, confident in the cornucopia of modern consumer economies—that everything would be available in stores and supermarkets in the morning. The disruptive effects of the pandemic on both supply and demand, however, brought the role of supply chains into the public eye. Journalists, consumers, and politicians suddenly wondered where all the goods they took for granted came from. Many people had knee-jerk reactions about their country's apparent over-reliance on China for supplying these goods.

While these pandemic dramas played out, companies were accelerating efforts to automate their supply chains. The greater need for digital technologies in supply chains was driven by a combination of numerous factors: the need to respond to rapidly changing consumer buying habits; the requirements to reduce human contact and reduce the density of workers in offices, plants, and warehouses; and the recession-intensified need to control costs. In addition, ongoing advances (and declining costs) of key technologies such as Internet of things (IoT), mobile internet, robotics, cloud computing, and AI aided this quiet revolution in the infrastructure of commerce that was making supply chains faster and more efficient through automation.

14. An All-Seeing, No-Touch Future

Between the deep uncertainties wrought by the pandemic and the inability to travel or even go to the office, companies and managers sought understanding—and, in particular, visibility— into what was taking place throughout their global supply chains, and some semblance of control through data. Where is the shipment? When will the part be in stock again? How much product does the customer really need? Is the quality of a new supplier as good as they claim? Can the supplier make the quantity it promised by the deadline?

In the computer era, data has always been a source of competitive advantage. "Technology and digitalization enable end-to-end visibility across the supply chain," said Joachim Christ, head of procurement at Merck. "Having this visibility—ideally in real time—is key to proactively run risk analyses and react fast when a crisis hits."[1]

With Covid-19-imposed restrictions on in-person gatherings, data and its analysis became even more important. More than ever before, people wanted and needed to know what was really happening in the supply chain to separate fact from fiction and fear from reality. More broadly, the trend toward more data from more parts of the supply chain is a trend toward more control of the supply chain through digital technologies. Those technologies also enable contact-free operations—reducing the need for workers to touch potentially infectious surfaces or come close to other workers. Importantly, the technologies create data streams that enable process improvements.

Better Shipment Visibility

Express parcel carriers like UPS and FedEx pride themselves on offering almost real-time shipment movement visibility for shippers and consignees. By scanning every package at handover points along the journey, these carriers can show the customer the progress of their shipment at certain intervals. Unfortunately, the workaday world of larger shipments of ordinary goods moving between commercial enterprises does not provide such simple visibility. Whereas UPS, for example, has direct end-to-end control of almost all of the facilities, conveyances, and people involved in transporting a parcel, the same cannot be said for most freight shipments, especially in global trade. For global trade, each shipment typically involves a series of independent truck, rail, and ocean movements managed by both independent carriers and intermediaries. Moreover, shipments might sit for a time in the no-man's-land of a port's container yard awaiting customs approval or the pickup for the next leg of the journey. The result is that most businesses cannot track a shipment seamlessly from an overseas factory to its destination.

Shippers (the beneficial owners of the cargo, like manufacturers, retailers, distributors, and hospitals) and carriers (the owners and operators of transportation assets) are working on improving visibility in transportation using technology. Smartphones put an internet-connected optical code scanner, machine vision camera, and GPS locator in every pocket. As shipments get scanned, images get processed, and conveyance location positioning gets updated. The data can be used for near-real-time shipment location information and stored for later analysis. Companies store more and more such data in the cloud, where users anywhere can find relevant data sets and related specialized applications. These visibility applications are typically part of event management systems designed to alert companies to deviations from the normal (or planned) patterns of shipments and movements.

In the broader world of supply chains, technology adoption faces a special challenge. Unlike the situation with the integrated carriers (UPS, FedEx, DHL, TNT, and postal services), shipment visibility—even just from a factory in Asia to a retailer in the US—requires more than just one company to have the needed sensors and other hardware and software to achieve continuous visibility into goods' flows. Supply chain visibility also needs all (or at least enough) participants to adopt compatible technology and agree on a set of standards so that they can all use the data.

As mentioned in Chapter 7 (p. 58), many companies have not mapped their inbound supply chains and may not even know the physical locations of their direct (Tier 1) suppliers' manufacturing and distribution facilities. However, what supply chain and material handling managers really want is more than just visibility of the inbound shipment from Tier 1 suppliers into their facility. They would like to know as early as possible if there is a problem—late shipment, quality issues, shipment damage, customs delays—anywhere in the supply chain, so they have time to react. For this to happen, they need visibility beyond their Tier 1 suppliers into deeper tiers of their supply chain (*recall* Figure 7.1).

Visibility into deeper tiers of the supply chain is a perennial challenge that, as yet, almost no manufacturer or retailer has cracked. The reasons for this are not so much technological (even though conflicting standards and non-cooperating software platforms do not help). Rather, as mentioned in Chapter 7 (p. 58), most companies do not know who their deep-tier suppliers are. Tier 1 suppliers consider the identity of *their* suppliers (who are Tier 2 suppliers to the OEM) a trade secret. And even in cases where an OEM can identify its deep-tier suppliers, it has no leverage over these suppliers and cannot compel them to share data, because the OEM itself is not a customer of these deep-tier suppliers. Furthermore, parts made by deep-tier suppliers may end up at higher-tier suppliers, serving not only many companies but also multiple industries. As a result, it can be impossible for an OEM to pinpoint deep-tier suppliers that make specific parts.

Other companies are using more technology to gain visibility on the retail and consumer ends. For example, while many companies are wondering what panicked consumers are doing with all the products they bought during Covid-19 hoarding, Procter & Gamble knows. The company knows that people aren't just buying more product such as Tide detergent in order to hoard it; they really are doing more loads of laundry during the pandemic. P&G gets this insight from data collected directly from the washing machines of a select sample of consumers.[2]

P&G has long invested in efforts to gain more visibility into how consumers use its products. Its marketing mantra is grounded in two "moments of truth" for products. The first moment is when a consumer chooses a product in the retail environment from among the competing products. The second is when the consumer actually uses the product. P&G monitors the first moment of truth through interviews, Nielsen data, and point-of-sale data. Previously, P&G would ask a select set of consumers to keep diaries of their experiences using its products in order to understand the second moment of truth, but technology now enables a paperless process. "Why do a laundry diary study when you can put a device on somebody's washer and dryer that tells you exactly when they're doing laundry, how many loads, what type of loads, etc.?" said Michael Lancor, Procter & Gamble's director of consumer fundamentals and insights.[3]

The P&G example illustrates another trend accelerated by Covid-19. This kind of seamless, contactless digital data collection is enabled by IoT, which combines specialized sensors, low-cost computer chips, and ubiquitous wireless networking such as home WiFi or cellular phone networks. These technologies are becoming more sophisticated and less expensive, leading to the presence of sensors everywhere to measure, gather, and transmit data continuously to analysts and managers who can act on it.

Tackling the Shipment Visibility Challenge

Every automobile has an average of 30,000 parts made by thousands of component suppliers scattered across the globe. The parts flow from these suppliers into automotive assembly plants using every mode of transportation and hundreds of transportation carriers. To coordinate the flow of parts, material handling managers need to know when those parts are going to arrive at the plant. In fact, they often need these arrivals to be prescheduled in order to manage the dock doors where the incoming trucks unload the shipments.

While carriers serving commercial enterprises can give shippers an estimated time of arrival of their vehicles to a plant, a store, a warehouse, or a hospital, this does not address the needs of transportation and material handling managers. What they really need to know is when particular parts needed to make particular products at a particular time will arrive. For this, they need to know which parts are loaded on each of the hundreds of trucks, railcars, ocean vessels, or airplanes transporting those parts.

In 2014, former Ford material handling manager and serial entrepreneur Lorne Darnell launched FreightVerify Inc. to tackle the challenge of merging the carriers' information (about the location of their conveyances) with suppliers' data (about the contents of their shipments) and cross-linking these data to the shippers' SKU numbering schemas. He started by focusing on some of the most daunting inbound transportation challenges—those of the automotive industry. By 2017, the company was offering a cloud-based platform on which an automotive manager could look up any SKU number and find where all those in-transit parts were at any given time. For example, some may be on a truck at the plant's yard waiting to be unloaded, others may be several hours away on a truck heading to the plant, still others may be on a railcar several days away, and even others may be offloading at a port. In all cases, Freight-Verify gathers the data on the location of the parts (and the specific trailers, railcars, vessels, airplanes, and the containers these parts are in) and transmits it directly and frequently from the vehicle to its platform for the receiving plant to see. In addition to providing key information such as the location of the part number and the vehicle carrying it, the software provides a very accurate estimated time of arrival, accounting for road congestion, weather delays, highway construction, border crossing problems, and so forth. Each shipment movement is based on a plan that the platform follows in real time, noting any deviation, since many of the loads follow complex routes involving multiple stops and relays.

Naturally, companies also use the platform as a source of business intelligence, to evaluate carrier performance, and to identify long-term bottlenecks.

In 2019, General Motors adopted the software for all movements into its assembly plants as well as for tracking finished vehicle deliveries and after-market parts. Ford followed suit, and FreightVerify began serving other automotive companies and then other manufacturers—and even hospitals.

Extending the use of shipment visibility beyond tracking, FreightVerify builds on it to minimize the use of expedited freight, a source of significant expenditures for all manufacturers. The FreightVerify platform has visibility into both the daily production schedule at an OEM automotive plant and to the inventory levels of all needed parts. It is common in manufacturing to face problems of low inventory of several parts each day. The software identifies the shortages of specific parts given the production schedule and the available inventory, and then scans all the tens of thousands of trucks moving in the OEM's system in real time. Since it knows the contents of each truck, it can identify the location of each needed part; choose the best truck to divert (or offload the part); and finally, schedule or divert another truck to pick it up to ensure not only that the shortage will not be a problem, but that no new shortage will result from the diversions at any plant in the system. This entire process is handled by AI-infused optimization software, replacing personnel and drastically reducing expensive expedited shipments. The result is many fewer calls to suppliers to expedite the needed parts by flying them to the plant or trucking them using specialized (and expensive) carriers.[4]

FreightVerify also integrates the in-transit tracking of SKUs with indoor tracking. Using a new generation of sensors, the company tracks movement of items inside various facilities. For automotive companies, the platform tracks returnable transport containers (the rigid containers carrying engines, transmissions, gas tanks, and other large parts inside the truck) from the supplier, through the OEM plant and back, reducing substantial losses due to shrinkage. For hospital systems, it tracks supplies from suppliers to the patient's bed.[5]

As the pandemic was creating havoc in the reliability of transportation movement, such shipment visibility became more important than ever. Furthermore, going forward, such capabilities allow companies to improve service while cutting costs.

Preparedness = Visibility + Transparency

Supply chain problems such as supplier product fraud (*see* Chapter 7, p. 58) or customers gaming order allocation systems (*see* Chapter 8, p. 68) mean that to be relevant, supply chain visibility requires transparency on the part of supply chain partners. That is, suppliers and customers must be willing to share timely and accurate data with partner companies. Transparency on the part of suppliers means sharing essential data on their capacities, sourcing of key materials, and deeper-tier suppliers that might affect the supplier's ability to deliver quality and quantity on time. Transparency on the part of customers means sharing downstream inventory and sales patterns so the supplier can plan its production.

Transparency enables cost-effective resilience. Correcting for unplanned situations requires physical resources in the form of both redundancy and flexibility of assets, labor, and processes. The ability to deal with unplanned events also depends to a large extent on the amount of forewarning—the time lag between receiving data about a disruption and the impact of that disruption. Such a lag can be used to redirect shipments, find alternative sources of supply, release inventories, alert customers, and more. Without it, a company will have to keep redundant capacity and large inventories in order to avoid stock-outs, production disruptions, backordering, or worse: lost customers. Transparency provides greater forewarning.

In essence, transparency and visibility provide the eyes, ears, and nose for the supply chain while physical resources provide the muscles. The brains of the organization then connect the sensory apparatus of transparency to the muscles of resilience. Those brains include both people and technology (*see* Chapter 15, p. 132).

Trust Between Customers and Suppliers

Transparency requires trust—a company must be willing to share some of its sensitive data with its key trading partners. During a crisis, the bond of trust between buyers and sellers is typically put to the test. A definition of trust is "the willingness to accept vulnerability based on positive expectations of the intentions or behavior of the counter party."[6]

Per this definition, Figure 14.1 illustrates the two dimensions of trust: expectation of outcomes and vulnerability. The riskiest quadrant is where vulnerability is high and there is little expectation that the counterparty will fulfill its obligations and abide by the agreement (Low Expectation/High Vulnerability).

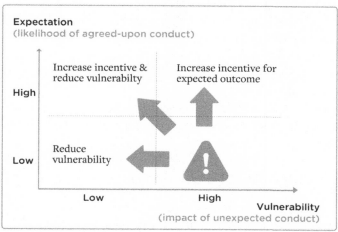

Figure 14.1: Vulnerability and expectations of trust

Increasing Trust

The two principal ways to increase trust are either to increase the incentives for a good expected outcome or to reduce the vulnerability (or both). A company can increase the likelihood of getting what it needs from a supplier by offering higher payments for better performance, penalizing underperformance, or promising the potential for growing future volumes of business. It can also reduce its vulnerability by having multiple sources of supply or redundant inventory to cover shortfalls from an untrustworthy supplier.

Trust in suppliers can be especially challenging for companies engaged in e-commerce on sprawling multi-supplier platforms such as Etsy (which lets artisans sell direct to consumers). Customers need confidence in product descriptions and supplier reliability. Joshua Silverman, CEO of Etsy, said, "We've talked a lot about trust and the Trust team has been working very hard to gain more reviews, get buyers to leave more and richer reviews."[7]

Suppliers can mitigate trust issues by asking for upfront payment. An early payment reduces the supplier's risk, especially if the payment covers the raw material cost and the work. An early payment also creates an incentive for the customer to follow through with the order, since it has already paid for it (in full or in part).

In a crisis, parties can get away with not fulfilling obligations by, for example, shipping subpar products, not paying on time (or at all), or canceling orders and leaving suppliers stuck with sizeable raw material inventory. The crisis provides a ready excuse for nonperformance, including invoking *force majeure* clauses. It also creates many opportunities for one-time deals where there are no ongoing relationships and, therefore, lower incentives to deliver the expected outcome.

In contrast, during day-to-day business, these risks are limited because trading between the supplier and customer is ongoing, and neither side desires to cause a breakup in the relationship.

Building Value-Added Relationships

One of the results of the coronavirus crisis is that companies have gained a deeper appreciation of the importance of trust built over a long period.

As Lynn Torrel, chief procurement and supply chain officer at the giant contract manufacturer Flex, explained, "We've had a few escalation calls with suppliers, and you get on a call and there are critical needs. Often, it's someone I've known for many years. We had a hard negotiation and then had a really good dinner and spent time together, and we're always seeing each other at different events. I think that personal side is important, especially the relationships and trust that build over time."[8]

Similarly, Meri Stevens, worldwide vice president of consumer health supply chain and deliver at Johnson & Johnson, described the importance of trust between suppliers and J&J people, saying emphatically, "Game changing. Game changing. And actually, what's really interesting is that when I went into Deliver about a year ago, one of the big things that we did is really up our game with our major providers. We really changed the way we're doing business. We've done a lot more strategic conversations... The company's commercial teams have worked with customers such as retailers, distributors, and hospitals to put commercial relationships on a more candid footing," she explained.[9] The existence of trust in supply chain relationships means that a customer does not have to pay extra or look for new suppliers to reduce its vulnerability in a crisis. And suppliers will not have to raise their prices or demand early payments to cover a nonpayment risk.

Such relationship building can be even more important when business contacts are based in faraway countries. Trust is key to overcoming cultural, geographic, and language differences between trading partners. The value of personal relationships in creating trust may be difficult to build through video calls. As a result, businesspeople will still have to board airplanes, stay in hotels, and share meals with distant suppliers and customers to continue building the personal relationships that create trust.

However, in today's Covid-19 world, remotely gathered digital data and virtual meetings are here to stay and can replace some of the time-wasting business travel and in-person gatherings that plague many workplaces and business-to-business relations. Online collaboration platforms will continue to improve, as will people's ability to use virtual meeting places to transact business and carry out day-to-day managerial tasks.

But there is still no substitute for personal contact when it comes to building business relationships, and this is unlikely to change in the foreseeable future. As Flex's Torrel added, "I think that we're in a business where we do need to travel. We need to go to the sites, we need to work with our suppliers and customers. But I think there can be less travel, because we've shown we can be effective working from home."

Making Hand-Offs That Are Hands-Off

"You are still handing them [drivers] paper bills, and they are signing them and exchanging them," said Tiffany Parker, a potato grower in Florida. "There's a lot of contact you could probably avoid."[10] Covid-19 pushed small shippers like Parker Produce Co. and the 3.5 million truckers in the US to look for ways to eliminate paperwork.

Before Covid-19, people thought nothing of touching a keypad, signing in on a clipboard, or handing a credit card or photo ID to a cashier or lobby security officer. The fact that the SARS-CoV-2 virus can survive on surfaces for hours (sometimes days) applies pressure on supply chains to go paperless and, even further, contactless. Although supply chains do use a lot of electronic communications and documentation, some steps still require paper documents, especially in transportation and import/export transactions. Both of these activities involve legal or government documents such as purchase orders, bills of lading, and inspection certificates that must be scrutinized and signed by different parties as the goods travel.

One key example of supply chain documentation that is still often maintained in paper form is the bill of lading, which is the legal record of the traded goods. It goes with every shipment and must be signed by the carrier's driver (in triplicate) and the consignee (after comparing the information on the bill of lading to the information in the purchase order). After many years of running

21st century companies with 19th century technology (bills of lading actually originated in the 16th century),[11] almost every loading dock, warehouse, and logistics management office is looking to replace paper documents with digital versions.

Part of the challenge to going fully paperless (and contactless) is universal adoption of standardized electronic document systems among all the parties. At the very least, this involves the supplier, the carrier(s), the consignee, and government authorities. For international shipments, the parties can also include banks, multiple carriers, and various government bodies such as customs, export control, import inspections, and others at both ends of the trip. To be digital, all of these parties must all be able to access the right documents, enter data into them, be able to provide legally binding signatures, and yet not be able to tamper with the underlying information in the document. Such a system must be fully secure in order to manage trillions of dollars in trade and be acceptable to competing parties and all participating governments. One approach, being developed and tested by various companies, uses the blockchain technologies popularized by cryptocurrencies (such as Bitcoin) to create a secure, tamper-resistant, distributed database. Blockchain-based systems do not require a central managing authority and can ensure the integrity of the transactions without it.[12]

Another typical supply chain activity that requires hands-on, in-person interaction happens as companies work with suppliers to develop, refine, and manufacture new products. Representatives of the customer and supplier fly to present product designs, review materials, inspect prototypes, and assess manufacturing samples. Covid-19 brought an instant end to all that travel and even made express-air shipments of samples an expensive and unreliable process.

Though the trend of virtual product development existed before Covid-19, the pandemic greatly accelerated its rise. Instead of travel and express parcels, virtual product development uses instantly delivered digital files, 3D models, and high-resolution video for collaboration. Even before the pandemic, some companies (especially those in apparel) had been adopting virtual product development for speed: the shorter the development time, the better the company can handle fickle market trends. Digital design processes enable around-the-world, 24-hour, rapid development—an Asian supplier or innovation center can work during their day (overnight for US headquarters) on a new product and send the digital results for early morning review at headquarters. The review staff—marketing, sales, customer representatives—can take all day and send end-of-day feedback that arrives early the next morning (local time) at the supplier.

Retail is another arena looking for contactless transactions. Walking into one of Amazon's Go grocery stores seems like stumbling upon a sedate and lei-surely looting incident. People seem to be plucking items off the shelf, putting them in their bags, and then walking out without paying. But that's exactly what Amazon wants customers to do. The posted instructions say, "Use your app as you enter. Bag as you shop. JUST WALK OUT."[13] Scanning a customer's smartphone on entry identifies the customer for billing purposes. Cameras and sensors throughout the store record everything and use computer vision to know exactly who is taking what (or putting it back). The store needs no checkout counters, cashiers, or baggers.

Remote Control Supply Chains

Two-way flows of data enable both remote visibility and remote control. For example, contract manufacturer Flex created *Flex Pulse*, which is both a software-based system and a network of physical "control tower" facilities for using supply chain visibility to manage and improve supply chain perfor-mance. The software enables real-time visibility and control for some 6,000 users on their desktops, laptops, and mobile devices.

Nine Flex Pulse centers around the world have walls of large interactive touchscreens that display a wide range of user-selectable information, such as real-time news of supply chain disruptions, social media streams, maps of global in-transit shipments, heat maps of inventory levels, percent-of-revenue pie charts, maps of exceptions, graphs of lead times, and other supply chain data. Each Flex Pulse center acts as a network operations center. Operational information is also available on user desktops, which helped users navigate the situation during the pandemic. Flex's Torrel and her associates used Flex Pulse to manage the supply chain during the Covid-19 crisis: "We created some specific dashboards to address Covid-19 so that we could understand at a cus-tomer level, at a site level, and at a part-number level where there potentially could be impacts," she said.[14]

Covid-related physical distancing, limited travel, and restrictions on group gatherings all accelerated the trend toward using telepresence technol-ogies for control and management. For example, even before the pandemic, Walgreens used in-store sensors to monitor each of its 9,500 US locations—mostly for security. But it also uses the system for other critical situations. For instance, electrical power sensors alert Walgreens to blackouts, which lets the company quickly contact the power company, supply backup generators, or send refrigerated trucks to recover perishable inventory. High-definition cameras allow managers to monitor inventory and manage personnel to serve customers faster. The video signals can feed into AI-based image recognition systems that either help measure the normal ebb and flow of activity or spot anomalies that need attention. These exceptions could include a wet cleanup in Aisle 5, a forgotten pallet by a dock door, a blocked conveyor belt, or a surge in customer arrivals in the parking lot that portends the need for more check-out lines in the next 30 minutes.

Video cameras and sensors also allow a worker to be at home and in the factory, warehouse, or store at the same time. The next step is the remote control of simple facility functions, leading to remotely operated robots, and even the science fiction concept of a "dark facility," which is fully automated and operates on its own (*see* Chapter 15, p. 132).

The Doctor Will "See" You Now

While contactless, physically distanced interactions increased in all areas and industries when the Covid-19 crisis erupted, they exploded in healthcare. To serve their patients without spreading the virus (or catching it), doctors and nurses renewed the practice of house calls, but with a modern twist: Telemedicine over the internet let doctors see patients in their own homes without physically visiting them. Home-delivered sampling kits enabled patients to collect and send routine body fluid samples for lab analysis. Even new Covid-19 tests can now be done by patients at home and sent to laboratories for analysis.

Patients bought and used blood pressure monitors, pulse oximeters, glucose monitors, thermometers, and heart rate monitors to measure key health parameters. Many of these devices can connect to the internet, smartphones, or phone lines to automatically upload data for review by healthcare providers. In addition, smartwatches and fitness devices used by 21 percent of Americans can collect health-related data 24 hours a day, 365 days a year.[15] These wearable digital devices—personal IoT—can track everyday patterns in physical activity and heart rate to spot changes in energy levels, body stability, heart health, and coughing/sneezing. Such data is fast becoming part of patients' health records to provide visibility to doctors and alerts that trigger a timely diagnosis and treatment.

Secure, online health portals let patients access nurses, doctors, lab results, and health information at any time. They also let them access their prescriptions; Covid-19 spurred a big increase in pharmaceutical e-commerce.[16] Overall, most patients using telehealth seemed to like it. Almost half of US adults have used telemedicine since the beginning of the pandemic, mostly for convenience as well as to reduce anxiety about infection risk.[17]

Digitizing healthcare creates torrents of data on individuals, diseases, treatments, outcomes, and population health trends. Covid-19 has accelerated the use of big data and AI in healthcare for prediction, screening, contact alerts, faster diagnoses, automated deliveries, and laboratory drug discovery.[18] For example, AI platform BlueDot "uses big data analytics to track and anticipate the spread of the world's most dangerous infectious diseases" and was able to warn its clients about the Covid-19 outbreak as early as December 31, 2019.[19] BlueDot's founder, Kamran Khan, said, "On one hand, the world is rapidly changing, where diseases are emerging and spreading faster. On the other hand, we happen to have growing access to data we can use...to generate insights and spread them faster than the diseases spread themselves."[20]

As with so many other technologies mentioned in this book, telemedicine predates Covid-19 by decades, but it needed the pandemic to drive widespread adoption by motivating both patients and healthcare providers to use it. The pandemic has been forcing people to adopt new habits, some of which are likely to persist even as the virus recedes. And as with so many other technologies in this book, telemedicine still needs more development. Any US patient who has tried to coordinate care for themselves, children, or aging parents has probably experienced the frustrating lack of integration between different medical facilities.

15. Automation Increases

Robots do not have to be physically separated, wear masks, or take time off. Companies don't have to worry about robots getting sick. Concerns for worker health, distancing requirements, the threat of facility shutdowns from a Covid-19 outbreak, plus customer worries about disinfecting items touched by other people, all motivate companies to look for more ways to automate their businesses.

Similarly, Covid-19 and its related impacts on physical retail have suddenly made competent e-commerce an existential necessity (*see* Chapter 22, p. 198). E-commerce competition was already pushing companies to automate for speed purposes. Automation is the only way a company can cost-effectively deliver customers' orders within the ever-tightening expectations for delivery within two days, one day, four hours, two hours, and so on.

Industry Gets Hot for Bots

Tyson Foods was among the meat processing companies hit by Covid-19 outbreaks, shutdowns, and productivity declines caused by distancing requirements. "Our industry is heavily dependent on people," said CEO Noel White, "but our company is investing aggressively in automating the most difficult jobs in our processing plants."[1] In 2019, the company opened a new Tyson Manufacturing Automation Center—part of the company's $215 million investment in automation and robotics in the last five years.[2] Automation efforts include foreign object detection, deboning, packaging, and palletizing.

"Automation provides really a lot of things, but one of the things that I would stress is flexibility," said Dean Banks, president of Tyson.[3] The company had installed Multivac packaging systems in some businesses for products like beef and pork, which helped in handling the process with no human touch. Banks added, "Those businesses' ability to very quickly shift those products from foodservice to retail... has been really beneficial." White said he expected the use of automation to accelerate: "I believe it's not only us as a company, I think the industry will continue to look for solves through automation."[4]

From the outside, a BMW car factory is a big building where plain old boxes of car parts go in one end and sleek new cars come out the other. On the inside, the factory is like a bustling city comprised of all the installation locations where workers (and robots) assemble parts into subassemblies that go into cars. Linking these locations are all the connecting routes that handle the flow of parts, subassemblies, and cars. To work at the highest level of efficiency and quality, each factory worker and robot needs constant "home deliveries" of the specific parts they need to do their jobs. Moreover, because 99 percent of BMW's German customer orders are customized, each worker needs exactly the right part that goes with each customer's unique configuration of car design options.

"Ultimately, the sheer volume of possible configurations became a challenge to BMW Group production in three fundamental areas—computing, logistics planning, and data analysis," said Jürgen Maidl, BMW's senior vice president of logistics.[5] To solve this challenge, BMW developed five types of robots: SplitBots unpack pallets of parts, PlaceBots load goods onto shelves, PickBots collect parts as needed, SortBots manage empty containers for reuse, and two sizes of self-driving Smart Transport Robots (STR) move parts containers and rolling parts carriers from place to place.[6]

All of this hardware needs smart control systems to function. Each type of bot uses machine vision and AI to "learn" to grip and move many different kinds of containers and parts. This training uses images of all the containers, parts, racks, shelves, and other factory resources that each bot is expected to work with. BMW has trained the SplitBots to handle 450 different types of parts containers, and PickBots can learn how to handle up to 50,000 different types of parts. To track everything, BMW developed a paperless, contactless system using unique QR codes on the parts containers. Workers wear gloves with integrated scanners, and displays tell them what's in each container.

While a meatpacking plant and a car plant are different types of factories, they are both bustling facilities where employees work in close proximity to each other and hence subject to the constraints imposed by Covid-19. It is not surprising, therefore, that manufacturing industries are actively redoubling their efforts to reduce their reliance on manual labor through automation.

Pick-It, Pack-It, Ship-It

"If there are two topics that are now at the top of grocery boardroom agendas worldwide, they are Covid-19 and how to build successful online capabilities," said Luke Jensen, CEO of Ocado Solutions, which makes robots for grocery store e-commerce fulfillment centers. Even before the pandemic, traditional retailers were ramping up efforts to ring up online sales in an existential fight to compete with Amazon and other online retailers. In 2019, e-commerce made up 16 percent of all US retail sales,[7] and more than 9,300 traditional retail outlets closed.[8] Covid-19 intensified that trend. Although the pandemic-related recession meant that overall consumer spending fell nearly 13 percent in April 2020, e-commerce during that same period grew 49 percent compared to 2019. US retail outlet closures are expected to more than double to between 20,000 and 25,000 stores in 2020.[9]

In addition to the growing volume of e-commerce orders that retailers must now handle, they must also satisfy consumers' unquenchable thirst for fast deliveries. Before Covid-19, companies such as Alibaba and Amazon reinforced their competitive advantage by encouraging consumers to expect free, faultless, fast delivery services. The promise of next-day delivery no longer impresses consumers in a world where same-day and even two-hour services are becoming more common. Automation holds the promise of faster processing and delivery without increased costs.

Ocado's online grocery fulfillment center in Andover, England, is a cross between a chessboard, a beehive, and an inscrutable stacking puzzle.[10] Near the rafters of the huge facility is a chessboard grid of rails. Over a thousand washing-machine-sized robots move north, south, east, and west on the grid, barely missing other robots running on adjacent tracks. Each robot pauses over some cell and seems to squat like a cubical bird laying an egg before moving on. But instead of an egg, the robot will have laid or retrieved a crate containing some category of grocery items. One crate might be filled with raspberry chocolate bars, another with bottles of ketchup, or maybe cans of corn—anything a grocery store might carry. Looking down on the grid from above reveals that each cell is really a deep hole that can hold up to 17 crates.

When a customer's order comes in to Ocado, computers churn through 3 million routing calculations per second to dispatch a swarm of these robots that fan out across the grid in a race to retrieve all the crates that have the SKUs sought by that customer. The robots take the retrieved crates to chutes that go to picking stations. Most of the packaged goods can be picked by other robots with suction-cup grippers that pluck the desired item, present it for scanning, and then place it in a bag in a second crate that will carry the customer's order out to the truck for delivery. Crates with more delicate goods go to human picking stations. End to end, the robot swarm system can retrieve, pick, and pack the average 50-item order in only five minutes.

In addition to being faster than a human picker wandering the aisles, the robots do not take breaks, worry about Covid-19, or complain about poor working conditions (as Amazon experienced in Europe and the US). Barring the odd computer virus, they are immune to communicable diseases and the hullabaloo of contact tracing, testing, quarantining, and disinfection.

Currently, humans are no match for robots when it comes to speed, accuracy, and endurance, but humans beat machines hands down on dexterity. Tell a warehouse robot to fetch a can of beans, and it will perform supremely well; tell it to fetch a ripe avocado, and the fruit will take a bruising. Delicate objects still require either human motor skills or wasteful protective packaging. But this is changing. Consider, for example, work underway at MIT to make robots more dexterous through softer, finger-like gripper materials and better tactile sensors. MIT researchers are giving robots the fine motor control and soft touch needed to manipulate delicate items such as wine glasses and fruit.[11]

In the logistics industry, robots form the core of a worldwide movement to automate warehouses. Leading companies have invested billions of dollars in automation, spearheaded by the deployment of robots that make picking and packing more efficient and continuously track inventories using earthbound robots or flying drones.[12]

For example, in 2018, JD.com, the Chinese e-commerce and logistics giant, opened an automated warehouse on the outskirts of Shanghai. That facility fulfills 200,000 orders a day but employs only four people. And Cainiao, an Alibaba affiliate, operates a fulfillment facility in Wuxi (also outside Shanghai) where 700 automated guided vehicles pick up parcels and deliver them to waiting vehicles. China is the world's largest robotics market, with a 36 percent share of total worldwide installations in 2018.[13]

Overall, sales of service robots for professional use increased by 32 percent to $9.2 billion in 2018, according to the International Federation of Robotics, with logistics systems accounting for 41 percent of the units sold. By 2022, estimates suggest that the worldwide market for warehouse and logistics robots will quadruple. "Right now there is a real business need, so there's urgency and it's easier to get things pushed through," said Melonee Wise, CEO of Fetch Robotics, which makes robots that can pick up objects, self-navigate, and place the objects somewhere else.[14]

Machines on the March

An unassuming box on wheels rolling down the sidewalk might be the future of urban last-mile delivery. With the explosion of both e-commerce and restaurant home deliveries amid the pandemic came the need for more last-mile deliveries of goods and food along with more safety and distancing concerns for both drivers and customers.

That's where autonomous sidewalk robots, such as those made by Starship, come in.[15] The company currently operates in several localities and plans to expand to 100 locations by the summer of 2021.[16] "We saw that business double overnight as a result of the region's coronavirus lockdown," said Ryan Touhy, senior vice president of business development at Starship.[17] Customers use an app to order food or other goods, place a pin on a map where they want the delivery, and can monitor the app for real-time progress of their order and the robot. When the robot arrives, it alerts the recipient, who then uses the app to unlock the robot's cargo door to retrieve the delivery.

Sidewalk robots are but one such solution and are suitable for short-distance deliveries in densely populated areas. Street-legal self-driving versions of conventional delivery vehicles such as vans and trucks could handle urban, suburban, rural, and long-distance freight transportation needs. These larger, faster vehicles will require further engineering developments (and regulatory approvals) to reach higher standards of safe, all-weather self-driving performance that is still some years away.

Small aerial delivery drones—in development by Amazon, UPS, and others—offer the potential for faster delivery of time-sensitive products.[18] Zipline, an American company, has been delivering 170 types of vaccine, medication, and blood products to 2,500 healthcare facilities across Rwanda and Ghana using small aerial delivery drones with a range of up to 75 miles.[19] Zipline is looking to expand to several other countries and in May 2020 received conditional FAA approval for long-range drone deliveries in North Carolina, in a distribution collaboration with Novant Health.[20] In September 2020, Zipline teamed up with Walmart to deliver items on demand from Walmart stores.[21] Larger aerial cargo drones might carry hundreds of pounds over hundreds of miles both for express delivery and humanitarian aid scenarios.[22] Some companies propose using van-sized motherships that can drive to a neighborhood and then dispatch a multitude of sidewalk robots or aerial drones to handle the last few blocks.[23] However, many issues have to be resolved—such as how to safely manage fleets of drones in urban areas—before these aerial robots become common on delivery routes.

Robotic Process Automation

At the same time that a ramified supply chain might be moving millions of shipments of physical parts to make millions of products for millions of customers, it is also moving even more packets of data. These include the orders, invoices, status messages, and reports associated with all those activities. While robotic arms, pickers, placers, sorters, transporters, and autonomous vehicles automate factory floor jobs in the supply chain, white-collar knowledge work can be automated, too. Robotic process automation (RPA) is software designed to replicate and thus automate the routine work of an office worker at their computer or mobile device. RPA involves creating a software bot consisting of scripted actions and simple rules that can handle repetitive tasks of office work such as approving invoices, collating data for weekly reports, sending out reminders, and reordering supplies. Anything that a worker might do over and over again with their keyboard and mouse can be a candidate for RPA.

Leading financial and insurance companies are among the successful adopters of RPA. Zurich Insurance Group used RPA to handle the underwriting of standard boilerplate policies, allowing commercial underwriters to devote their time to more complex policies.[24] Similarly, China Minsheng Bank was able to streamline its cumbersome and time-consuming manual loan application process that was just not working for organizations looking for loans to help their businesses survive Covid-19. To solve the problem, the bank invested heavily in RPA and automated its loan application process to encompass online application review, verification, online lending, and automated approval. This reduced the approval process time to 30 minutes, making it an attractive offering for businesses.[25]

As with physical robots, RPA bots beat human workers on speed but lack the cognitive dexterity of humans. Thus, the RPA bots typically handle repetitive tasks while the person handles the exceptions and works to improve the process rather than simply carry it out.

The adoption of RPA does involve a change in how people view their jobs. Johnson & Johnson's Meri Stevens explained how Covid-19 changed the mindset on using digital tools like RPA: "If you need to make 1,000 decisions a minute, and you can't possibly do that without having your digital aid, your self-worth is no longer tied to the fact that you can manage a lot of [manufacturing] lines. Your self-worth is now tied to the fact that you're keeping product moving for patients." And, she added, "The need for faster decision making, the need to get those insights, forced people into these new ways of working, and they will never go back."[26]

In essence, an RPA bot is a virtual subordinate employee to the employees who create and use it. In one company interviewed, RPA bots are managed by HR because the company treats the bots as employees. HR tracks the task performance of the bots and manages the bots' access credentials just like it does for human employees.

These are just a few examples of how supply chains are automating. In 2021, supply chains will have to steer through the twists and turns of a highly uncertain world, and the hand on the wheel (or on the keyboard) is less likely to be human.

16. Just-in-Time Gets Just-a-Tweak

Following shortages of medical supplies, spot shortages of food, and temporary closures of industrial plants in the US and elsewhere, many in the media sought a scapegoat and several blamed the just-in-time (JIT) system of manufacturing as the culprit. The Australian Broadcasting Company proclaimed, "Coronavirus pandemic exposes fatal flaws of 'just-in-time' economy." They suggested that JIT is about avoiding inventory and warehousing to cut cost and suggested that industries should move to keeping large inventories just in case.[1] This call was echoed, for example, in an article in *The Conversation*, arguing, "We need to build in more redundancies, buffers and firewalls into the systems we depend on for life."[2]

Inventory: The Good, the Bad, and the Costly

At its heart, inventory decouples (or isolates) each process along the supply chain so that each can operate at its own optimal rate or batch size. For example, a very large crude oil carrier (VLCC) "supertanker" vessel might deliver 82 million gallons of crude oil to a refinery every couple of months. There, the oil sits in a storage tank while the refinery steadily churns out 3 million gallons of gasoline per day. The gasoline then sits in another big tank waiting for fuel delivery trucks to take 10,000 gallons at a time to gas stations. At the gas station, the fuel sits in an underground tank waiting for cars to buy 5–15 gallons at a time. Finally, the fuel sits in the car's tank as the engine slowly sips about a gallon of gas per hour in city driving. All of the inventory in all of the tanks along the way lets each process start and stop as needed and allows them to be relatively independent of the other processes. The crude oil vessel, refinery, fuel truck, gas station fuel pump, and car engine all get to produce, move, or use gasoline at their ideal rate or batch size with the various inventories of fuel decoupling all these processes.

The amount of inventory kept in each tier of a supply chain is the sum of three types of inventory. The example above demonstrates the role of so-called *cycle stock*, which allows transportation of crude to move efficiently in huge tankers on a periodic cycle of deliveries to refineries operating continuously. *Seasonal stock* helps decouple a steady, continuous source of supply (e.g., the refinery) from seasonal or periodic cycles of demand (e.g., high gas demand during summer). Thus, the refinery operates continuously, building inventories that are stored in gasoline tanks during the winter season for the summer gasoline demand. *Safety stock* helps a gasoline retailer to decouple (possibly disrupted) scheduled deliveries of gasoline from unpredictable demand surges (e.g., a coming snowstorm causes a run on gasoline). The sum total of all these kinds of inventory is the amount needed to ensure that no link in the chain runs out of the product.

Companies that employ JIT try to eliminate some of the inventory by coordinating their processes rather than allow each process run at its own optimal rate. As such, some processes may be operating at less than optimal rates (for example, trucks may run half-full), but overall, the costs are lower due to the savings in inventory levels and other bigger but less obvious savings described below.

Critics of JIT focus on its lack of safety stock for major events like pandemics. Companies, even those using JIT, do routinely keep some added inventory beyond just the amount needed for cycle stock and seasonal stock, owing to the vagaries of demand patterns (which can spike unexpectedly), problems with suppliers (due to floods, strikes, accidents, or whatever), or issues with transportation (due to border crossings, weather delays, accidents, etc.). However, the amount of safety stock they keep depends on the company's estimates of the chances of unexpected (and therefore unknown) variations in processes, the economics of holding inventory, and the service goals of the company.

One way to arrive at the correct safety stock level is to balance the inventory carrying costs with the costs of lost sales, lost customers, or penalties for non-delivery of goods. These costs are difficult to figure out. Thus, most companies choose a service level they can "live with." A typical safety stock calculation balances service level (the probability of running out of stock) with the costs of keeping extra inventory. For example, having, say, a 95 percent service level means that a company will not be able to serve a customer only 5 percent of the time. Given the statistical distribution of unexpected events, companies can calculate the level of required safety stock to achieve a given service level. To have a 100 percent service level covering any eventuality, including major events such as Covid-19, would require enormous inventory levels, many times the normal amounts. As a result, companies try to keep a "Goldilocks inventory": just enough to handle supply chain interruptions and variations in customer orders, yet not too much to be too expensive and risky.

As any episode of *Hoarders* can show, too much inventory can be a problem. These costs of more inventory include the capital tied up in the inventory and the operating costs of servicing, managing, and storing it. But the problems with adding more inventory go beyond the costs. Inventory also adds risks that the inventoried goods may become obsolete, damaged, or unsalable in the future. Extra inventory also has a detrimental effect on product quality, as mentioned in Chapter 7 (p. 58).

Flex's Torrel described the company's love-hate relationship with inventory: "We cannot just stockpile everything in a just-in-case kind of scenario when that's not the way the supply chain or the margins work." When Covid-19 triggered the first shutdowns in late January, Flex became concerned and had vigorous discussions about boosting inventory due to the uncertainty involved. Torrel spoke of the supreme challenge "to have something [Covid-19] go across the world with the unpredictability that it had, not knowing the speed or the potential devastation it would have, how our factories would be shut down, how long they would be shut down, when we would be able to ramp them up. How could we make sure that we had the right parts in our factories to be able to ramp up production when we did, while at the same time understanding we really do need to be very focused on inventory?" Flex added inventory to respond to the risks of disruption only where necessary but stopped pushouts until they understood the actual demand changes. Later, after the first waves of disease and closures eased in some parts of the world and the environment became somewhat more predictable, the company had further intense discussions about when and where to return to lower, cost-efficient levels of inventory.[3]

Doing Justice to Just-in-Time

The irony about criticisms of JIT-caused shortages in grocery stores is that Toyota developed JIT starting in the 1950s to avoid parts shortages—by emulating US supermarkets. Previously, Toyota used mass production of large batches of auto parts and subassemblies that were sent to the next step of the assembly line in order to make large batches of the next assembly or the final car. Often, at the beginning of the month, Toyota faced shortages of some parts if some batches lagged behind others. At the end of the month, when all the batch production processes had caught up, Toyota had to frantically assemble cars to meet its final goal.

Toyota learned of US supermarkets where consumers shopped and frequently bought "(1) what is needed, (2) at the time needed, (3) in the amount needed," wrote Taiichi Ohno, creator of the Toyota Production System.[4] His insight led to a system in which Toyota workers took only the parts they needed for immediate production while the maker of the part replenished the "supermarket" in response to demand.

Although JIT certainly reduced inventories and associated costs, elements of what became the Toyota Production System (TPS) were really the tip of the performance-improvement iceberg. With small quantities of parts being made and provided just in time, any mistakes or quality problems with the parts or their production could be caught and corrected immediately before more defective parts or cars were made. Just-in-time production enabled continuous improvement of parts and production that created higher-quality cars. Thus, JIT reduced waste and costs caused by uncaught defects, obsolete or unwanted parts, rework, and warranty repairs. Toyota, in essence, innovated around the usual trade-off between cost and quality—TPS delivered higher-quality cars without the higher costs typically associated with higher quality.

Contrary to the assertion that JIT reduces resilience, the TPS actually improved the resilience of its supply chain by making production systems more flexible. Replacing big, "as-scheduled" batch production with small, "as-needed" production meant the factory could more easily switch production among many different products as demand changed. Rather than ending up creating a big batch of an unneeded product while being short of another in-demand product, JIT systems could more flexibly change quantities to match changes in demand.

JIT also fostered tight connections between suppliers, manufacturers, and customers; it furthered continuous communications between companies as well as between labor and management; and it led to worker empowerment, all of which helped to avoid errors and increase quality. TPS and JIT spun off or were associated with many related management concepts, such as lean manufacturing, Kaizen, and Six Sigma that have been implemented in almost every industry. Overall, the TPS is one of the most important manufacturing and supply chain innovations ever, with immense benefits. Consequently, despite its vulnerability to exceptionally disruptive events, the practice is not going away.

Adding Just-in-Case to Just-in-Time

For all of JIT's benefits, it clearly failed to satisfy the extraordinarily high demand associated with the pandemic-induced healthcare crisis, paper product hoarding, and changing consumer food shopping patterns. While the headlines screaming about food shortages were widely exaggerated (*see* Chapter 1, p. 2), there was an actual shortage of personal protective equipment in the US and other countries. That worrisome supply shortfall prompted calls for "just-in-case" inventories in healthcare (and food) supply chains to prepare for outbreaks. Yet the benefits of just-in-time operations—quality, flexibility, waste reduction—are just too significant to forgo. So, the question is how companies in certain crucial industries can enjoy the benefits of JIT while ensuring that they have enough inventories just in case disaster strikes.

Johnson & Johnson faced this issue when the Pentagon contracted the company for keeping stockpile inventory for emergency military needs.[5] As a major provider of medical supplies, J&J serves many hospitals and pharmacies. Because the demand for its products ebbs and flows with the flu, hay fever, and cold seasons, as well as outbreaks of various diseases, J&J keeps inventory in several warehouses it can call on when needed. Such safety stock provides a buffer against imperfect forecasts in demand as well as imperfect supplier performance. The flipside is that if inventory can cover for imperfections, a big pile of inventory makes it easy to ignore or not correct more imperfections. Too much inventory lets management become sloppy because inattention has no consequences.

To meet its contractual obligation to the Pentagon, J&J had two major challenges: how to keep the extra stockpile inventory fresh and up to date and how to ensure that all that extra inventory did not infect J&J's processes with sloppiness, which would lead to expensive quality problems. J&J solved the problem with a "sell-one-stock-one" (SOSO) inventory replenishment policy that essentially made the company replace any inventory it sold just in time as it sold it, rather than dip into the stockpile.[6] Under the SOSO strategy, J&J did not set aside the Pentagon's inventory to molder in a dedicated warehouse; instead, the company commingled the inventory with the rest of J&J's stock.

To keep its commitment, J&J used the Pentagon's stockpile requirements to configure its inventory software with a "red-line" inventory level for each product. Only Pentagon-authorized orders had access to inventory below the red line. Routine, everyday orders could only tap into inventories above the red line. Because going below the red line required explicit Pentagon approval, J&J could not use this inventory to compensate for day-to-day variations or process imperfections.[7]

The requirement of a Pentagon-authorized order to dip into the stockpile parallels the requirement of a US presidential directive necessary to release oil from the US Strategic Petroleum Reserve. In both cases, this requirement prevented managers from using the inventory to manage day-to-day fluctuations.

The J&J story points to the way companies can maintain the advantages of JIT and yet—in cases where demand is very high and no alternative supplier or alternative product will do—ensure that they can still adequately serve customers. The essence of the strategy is to continue all aspects of JIT while maintaining sufficient inventories of finished goods and parts. The secret is first to ensure that the inventory keeps turning and therefore remains fresh and current, and second, that the inventory cannot be used to cover for ordinary production and supply chain failures by requiring a special authorization for its use.

Faster! Faster!

Finally, some key items in crucial industries such as food actually need *more* JIT. When it comes to fresh fruits and vegetables that top the charts of recommended healthy foods, the perishability of many of these foods makes JIT essential. Consumers could not have fresh salad any day of the week and every week of the year without just-in-time systems for growing, picking, packing, and shipping lettuce and similar fresh ingredients. In fact, the leaner the inventories along the supply chain for fresh foods, the more days of "freshness" the product will have on the retailer's shelves or in the consumer's home and the less total waste from spoiled or expired goods.

Overall, Covid-19 accelerated—and necessitated—an ongoing trend toward faster and more agile supply chains for better response to changing conditions of supply and demand. Darius Adamczyk, chairman and CEO of Honeywell, said, "Having agile supply chain processes is more important than ever to manage our expenses and cash investments. Therefore, we condensed our sales, inventory and operations planning process from a traditional monthly cycle to a weekly cycle."[8] Similarly, a PwC survey of US CFOs found that 72 percent believe their companies will be more agile going forward.[9]

17. The China Question

When China became the epicenter of the coronavirus outbreak, many hoped that what was happening in China would stay in China. It didn't. Moreover, the economic ripples spread faster than the virus did. Shutting down manufacturing in Wuhan and other affected Chinese locations sent shockwaves around the world. Even if only 1 percent (hypothetically) of a car's parts come from disrupted suppliers in China, a car maker cannot make and sell cars that are 99 percent complete.

Companies and countries realized just how dependent they had become on China. Professor Beata Javorcik, chief economist at the European Bank for Reconstruction and Development, was quoted in a BBC analysis titled "Will Coronavirus Reverse Globalization?" She noted that between the SARS epidemic in 2003 and the Covid-19 pandemic of 2020, China's share of global output exploded from 4 percent to 16 percent. "So that means that whatever is happening in China affects the world to a much larger extent," she said.[1]

China exports a multitude of products and parts to the US. For example, the US depends on China for 40 percent of its apparel, 65 percent of its footwear, and 80 percent of its accessories.[2] Of course, the real question about such dependencies is, "So what?" It is difficult to conceive of a national emergency rooted in not having enough footwear. What is alarming, however, is China's role in medical products, including about 150 critical pharmaceuticals and medical supplies not made in the US. India's restriction on exports of 26 drug ingredients[3] further heightened US calls for more self-sufficiency when these dependencies came into focus during the Covid-19 pandemic.

Some media outlets reported that a corporate exodus out of China had already begun. For example, CNBC quoted reports that a significant number of companies were moving operations out of China. One commentator claimed that the production of toys and cameras was going to Mexico, the manufacture of personal computers was moving to Taiwan, and automotive manufacturing was finding new locations in Thailand, Vietnam, and India.[4] According to *Forbes*, "New data shows US companies are definitely leaving China."[5] In particular, another *Forbes* commentator argued, "China will never be the same once this pandemic is over."[6]

Leaving for Cheaper Shores

The decision to do business in China involves multiple considerations. In fact, many companies had been leaving China well before the pandemic due to increasing labor costs. Between 2011 and 2016, labor costs in China increased by 64 percent.[7] They climbed again by 30 percent from 2016 to 2020,[8] resulting in a doubling of labor costs in a decade. Even before the US imposed tariffs on imports from China, labor-dependent companies were leaving the country. In particular, apparel manufacturers were moving in substantial numbers to countries like Sri Lanka and Bangladesh, where the labor costs as of 2020 were one-seventh those in China.

Also, apparel manufacturing is labor-intensive, but the skills and worker training it requires are relatively basic. In addition, apparel is less capital-intensive than other industries. Consequently, setting up shop outside of China is neither complicated nor expensive for apparel businesses. In fact, many Chinese apparel companies themselves have moved operations to other Asian countries, a trend evident since at least 2010.[9] Many of the clothes made in these relocated factories are exported back to China as well as the rest of the world.

Some companies in other industries have reacted to souring trade relations between the US and China by relocating some operations outside of China. The trend gained some momentum during the 2018–2020 trade war between the two countries as companies looked for ways to avoid higher tariffs and the risk of further trade disruptions.

US administration officials were hopeful about reshoring following the pandemic. "The fact is," said Secretary of Commerce Wilbur Ross, "it does give business yet another thing to consider when they go through their review of their supply chain... So, I think it will help to accelerate the return of jobs to North America."[10] And the Japanese government announced a subsidy for Japanese companies who move some of their production lines out of China to Southeast Asia or back to Japan.[11]

Although national self-sufficiency has an instinctual attractiveness in anxious times, the real story of China is more complex.

China's Fast Recovery

China was the first country to get the coronavirus, the first to botch the initial response, and the first to lock down the affected areas (strongly!). The shock of Chinese suppliers going down hard and the follow-up of Chinese resource nationalism led supply chain managers, journalists, and politicians to call for companies to leave China. However, China was also the first to suppress the spread and the first to reopen factories and its economy while controlling the virus. China's authoritarian shutdown—leading to early reopening while other countries were closing or struggling—revealed China to be a more reliable source of supply than many other countries. "Our supply chain in certain parts of the world are almost fully recovered, including China, Taiwan and South Korea," said Dave Mosley, CEO of data storage company Seagate Technology.[12] As of September 11, 2020, the US's per-capita death toll from Covid-19 was 181 times that of China (with US cases and deaths still rising rapidly).

Wall Street analysts were skeptical that China's short-lived economic disruption would really have long-term effects on companies' reliance on Chinese suppliers. "Technology vendors are encouraged by the pace at which China's production has ramped up post the Covid-19 shock, and this has reinforced their belief in locating the production of their high-volume products in China. This provides reassurance that China will remain a large base for manufacturing in these products," said Katy Huberty of Morgan Stanley at the end of April.[13] More than 70 percent of companies surveyed by the American Chamber of Commerce in China in March 2020 said they had no plans to relocate manufacturing, their supply chains, or sourcing out of China due to the pandemic.[14] China's strong supply base and large and growing consumer population are the reasons why most companies are likely to stay there.

China: More Than Just a Low-Cost Supplier

An *Economist* story about Zhuangzhai, China, illustrates the evolution of Chinese industry from low-cost provider to something harder to replace.[15] More than 20 years ago, this town of 100,000 began making parts for coffins for export to Japan. Chinese labor at the time cost less than one-tenth that of Japan. What began as labor arbitrage evolved as Chinese coffin makers innovated to use less wood per coffin and develop flat-pack coffins that are easier to ship. By 2020, this small town supplied about half of all the coffins used in Japan.

When Chinese labor costs increased over the years, some Japanese buyers tried to switch to cheaper Southeast Asian suppliers but switched back. "Price-wise, talent-wise, this place is pretty far ahead," said Li Ruqi, the 56-year-old founder of Yunlong Woodcarving, the largest local firm. The town's ecosystem of workshops and suppliers made it a competitive supplier even if labor costs were higher. Zhuangzhai also had two other natural advantages over other possible factory locations: their native, fast-growing paotong trees produced a lightweight, creamy wood favored for Japanese coffins, and the moderate humidity of the region was good for woodworking. Even in a seemingly simple industry, there are relationships, assets, and knowledge that give that region competitive advantage and make it hard to relocate elsewhere. A similar pattern shows up in high-technology products, too.

Flat-panel displays are in many products: phones, tablets, cars, cameras, computers, TVs, household appliances, even ventilators. These ubiquitous components are essentially very large semiconductor chips plus some exotic chemicals fabricated into a sandwich between thin sheets of high-quality glass and other materials. Just as chip makers race to put more components on the smallest possible chip of silicon, display makers race to put more components on the largest possible sheet of glass. As of 2019, China produced 46 percent of the world's flat panel displays and was expected to reach 62 percent market share (four times larger than any other region) by 2023.[16]

Moving panel production out of China would be quite an undertaking. A new factory to build the latest generation of flat-panel displays costs on the order of $6 billion, but that's just the start of the investment. That factory also needs a supporting cast of sophisticated suppliers to make the large sheets of glass, rolls of polarizing film, backlighting systems, display driver chips, and the flexible circuit boards that route the high-speed digital signals to the millions of pixels on the display. In this industry and others, China has become a nexus for sophisticated manufacturing. Reshoring would mean replicating an entire ecosystem of factories, suppliers and sub-suppliers that have unique know-how and scale.

China as a Growth Market

For many companies, reshoring would actually put the company farther from customers, not closer. China represents a market too important to lose. In 2019, Chinese consumers bought more than 20.7 million passenger cars,[17] handily beating sales to US consumers, which were only 17 million vehicles in 2019,[18] or the EU at 15.8 million.[19] Overall, China has the second-highest GDP in the world and consumes about 20 percent of the world's output. In 2020, the number of Chinese among the top 10 percent of the world's wealthiest exceeded the number of Americans, making China an extremely attractive prospect for companies marketing upscale goods. As such, many companies will stay in China for the growth opportunities associated with the country's 1.4 billion consumers.

Although many companies might be satisfied serving mature markets such as the US or EU, other companies see China, India, and other growing countries as the next big opportunities for growth. To support that goal, they want to be local, especially as China is becoming more nationalistic. Commercially, a greater geographic footprint gives companies more access to more suppliers, more customers, and more experience. Even for American companies, the US grows less and less important as more and more people around the world join the middle class and the ranks of the wealthy.

Being Local Comes Back in Fashion

Despite the preceding reasons for staying in China, some companies were reshoring to places such as the US or EU for various reasons even before Covid-19.[20] These companies found that rising foreign wages, tariffs, and logistics costs had increased the landed costs of outsourced manufacturing. Reshoring also improved speed. Closer proximity to markets and customers reduced the latencies in the supply chain and accelerated time to market. Finally, some sought better control over product and material quality by reshoring. But that does not mean that everything must be reshored.

For example, Spanish fast-fashion retailer Zara is vertically integrated (it manufactures, distributes and sells in its own stores and online). It splits its manufacturing of garments for Europe into two segments to have an off-shore-plus-local hybrid strategy. The first includes basic perennial items (like undergarments, T-shirts, and jeans), which do not change frequently and whose sales can be forecasted relatively accurately. Those are made in China or elsewhere in Southeast Asia, because a long lead time is not a problem for products with relatively stable demand. The second are fashion items whose sales are difficult to forecast because they depend on the fleeting tastes of Zara's young customers. Those products are made locally in Europe or near-shore in Turkey.

Another hybrid strategy is late customization, also known as postponement, which splits the manufacturing process for each product into a low-cost, offshore, mass production portion and a fast, local customization portion.[21] An example is CafePress, which uses postponement to be the ultimate gift shop for the online, at-home era. The e-commerce-only store offers more than one billion different products spanning dozens of categories, such as apparel, accessories, home decor, drinkware, stationery, and even face masks. Each product can come decorated with any of a vast array of images and graphic designs such as internet memes, brand logos, popular entertainment images, clever sayings, or a customer's own design of images and words.

Rather than attempt the impossible of producing and storing inventory of all the possible designs and products, CafePress postpones the final manufacturing step of imprinting the design onto the blank object. With postponement, CafePress can use low-cost, overseas suppliers to mass produce blank objects such as plain T-shirts, water bottles, flip-flops, or notebooks. These items can be sourced from anywhere and shipped in bulk via slower, cheaper modes of transportation to the company's warehouse. Once the customer clicks "Place your order," the final manufacturing step happens in a Louisville, Kentucky, industrial park, which is a US Foreign Trade Zone (and hence affords the company certain tax advantages), and the customized item is shipped to the customer from UPS's nearby Louisville Worldport hub.

The main benefits of postponement are in allowing companies to deal effectively with the large number of variants of a product. Such proliferation makes it difficult to forecast the demand for each variant (such as graphics on a T-shirt, the color of a sweater, or the exact configuration of parts a consumer may order in a PC). To solve the forecasting challenge, manufacturers can combine two truisms of forecasting: First, aggregate forecasts are always more accurate than disaggregate forecasts, and second, forecasts over shorter timeframes are more accurate than forecasts over a longer period.

The reason that CafePress can ship the blank objects from overseas is because the forecast of the number of blank objects is an aggregation of the forecast of all the variants a customer may order. The underlying phenomenon is called *risk pooling*. As the demand for one design variant may be high, the demand for another may be low, and these variations are likely to cancel each other.[22] Consequently, the demand for the blank items is stable and can be forecasted well in advance.

The other truism of forecasting is that short-term forecasting is more accurate than long-term forecasting. With postponement, the final customization step can be taken shortly before the selling season when trends are known, or, as in the case of CafePress, once the order is in hand, obviating the need for a forecast of the finished product.

Of Travel Bubbles and Trade Barriers

US–China trade tensions, US–EU trade tensions, Brexit, and other regional disputes introduce added risks and added costs into supply chains. The tit-for-tat of punitive tariffs creates random collateral damage in multiple industries. For example, the US–China trade war hurts African economies by reducing Chinese manufacturing activity, which leads to reduced demand for African commodities.[23] Such trade wars also cause companies to avoid investment and sourcing in both places involved in a trade war. The result is risk for companies trading between the combatants, but also opportunities for companies in non-combatant countries that avoid the tariffs by acting as intermediaries in routing trade around the barriers (*see* Chapter 18, p. 157).

Then, Covid-19 added to the patchwork map of free and less-free trade zones.

On May 5, 2020, in a historic meeting, Jacinda Ardern, New Zealand's prime minister, met with Australia's cabinet (virtually) to discuss the concept of a "Trans-Tasman travel bubble."[24] The pact would enable free travel and trade between the two neighbor countries who had successfully (at the time of the initial negotiations) limited the spread of the virus. It's one example of a trend where countries were beginning to relax travel bans and traveler quarantine rules, but with key provisos—countries with poor pandemic control are not invited. Thus, for example, the EU opened its borders to 15 countries at the end of June but excluded the United States, Brazil, and Russia, among others.[25] Per-capita Covid-19 case counts in the US were nearly seven times higher than in the EU at the time. And in early August, the "Trans-Tasman bubble" was put on hold following a Covid-19 outbreak in the Australian state of Victoria.

Covid-19 travel bubbles create a new kind of fragmentation in trade patterns beyond the usual geopolitical squabbling of who's being unfair to whom. Although goods can certainly move from Covid-19 hotspot countries without significant worries of infection (the virus won't survive journeys of more than a day or so), the salespeople, installation technicians, and support staff who are needed to sell, deliver, and maintain the product may not be able to travel. Manufacturers in hotspot countries are at a competitive disadvantage if they cannot visit customer countries, and customers from other countries are loath to travel to a hotspot location. Countries such as the US, Brazil, Russia, India, and others may lose market share to suppliers in countries with better pandemic controls.

China + 1 or More

Some companies are considering a "China + 1" strategy of diversifying their facilities and suppliers to at least one other country.[26] As Chinese wages have risen, these companies have sought other low-cost countries in the region but have also retained their presence in China.

As mentioned earlier in this chapter, the apparel industry has been doing this for some time. They've moved labor-intensive cutting and sewing operations to other lower-cost South Asian countries like Bangladesh and Sri Lanka. As a result, China's share of clothing exports declined from 37 percent in 2010 to 31 percent in 2018. However, the companies have left machine-intensive textile production in China. Over the same period, China's share of global exports of textiles—which are made into apparel—rose from 30 percent to 38 percent. Thus, the apparel industry has become more dependent on China even as fewer finished goods carry a "Made in China" label. The point is that manufacturers worldwide still rely on Chinese intermediate goods, such as electrical wiring for cars made in Europe and electronic components for mobile phones made in Brazil.

Several companies refer to the China + 1 strategy as a way to consider the next capital investment project. These companies are not considering uprooting their China operations, which rely on an entire ecosystem of suppliers and sub-suppliers. As Flex's Lynn Torrel said, "That supply chain has been decades in the making." Instead, some companies are considering the next, incremental capital investment and looking at nearby Asian countries instead of China.

As companies think about risk-balancing their supply chains, some are going to reshore to the US or Europe. Most, however, will be looking for "near reshoring"—Mexico to supply the US while Eastern Europe and Turkey supply the EU. Yet other companies will be moving some operations out of the US and EU to balance risks in those locations. And it is not clear that substantial investment will be made while the pandemic is still in force. "While there will be some diversification in the supply chain to economies like India, Vietnam, Mexico and Taiwan, companies are currently focused on cash preservation and costs, which will limit the scope of such diversification moves in the near term," said Katy Huberty of Morgan Stanley at the end of April 2020.[27]

Resilient Networks for Virtual Capacity

Some companies are unlikely to reshore because they have already optimized a global portfolio of locations. "We will produce in China because we produce in China for China or for Asia," said Ralf Busche, senior vice president of global supply chain strategy and management at BASF.[28] Busche described how, in general, BASF locates its upstream plants (which make large quantities of common key ingredient chemicals) near sources of the raw materials (such as crude oil and natural gas). This minimizes the costs of transporting raw materials. BASF then locates the downstream plants (which make complex, value-added chemicals) near their customers to maximize service levels and delivery speed. As such, the company carefully places its networks of plants all around the world, because the best places for raw materials and those for customers are scattered all around the world.

Such networks of facilities can provide resilience through the redundancy inherent in having multiple plants around the globe. BASF can redeploy the network capacity in support of changing needs or recovery from disruption. Walmart's distribution network illustrates this kind of resilient network architecture made possible by managing a pool of resources. The company operates more than 150 distribution centers in the US[29] that serve the company's 4,756 stores.[30] At times, natural disasters affect distribution in one region by, for example, damaging a facility or creating a surge in pre-disaster or post-disaster demand.

To handle disruptions, the retailer seamlessly shifts how the unaffected portions of the distribution network share capacity with the affected portions in a neighbors-helping-neighbors pattern. Neighboring DCs cover the impacted DC, and neighbors of immediate neighbors share their capacity with the immediate neighbors who are most involved in handling the disruption. In essence, all the service areas of the DCs shift toward the affected zone. This strategy means that Walmart needs only minimal surplus capacity (or overtime activity), because every DC is chipping in a small slice of capacity to cover for the disrupted part of the network.

In a whack-a-mole world where pandemics, nationalistic trade policies, and local disasters hit different locations at different times to impede the production, flow, or consumption of goods, no single source location can be safe. Instead, a multi-shore network of locations provides local presence to serve local customers (and appease local government) as well as the resilience required to manage risks of disruptions to capacity. "One of the lessons learned," said Mourad Tamoud, executive vice president of global supply chain at Schneider Electric, "is the importance of developing stronger business continuity plans and operating shorter, regional supply chains oriented closer to the point of demand."[31]

PART 5
OF POLITICS AND
PANDEMICS

"Given the nature of the crisis, all hands should be on deck, all available tools should be used."

—Christine Lagarde,
President of the European Central Bank[1]

The pandemic triggered massive responses from governments intent on fighting the virus and mitigating its impact on their institutions, their businesses, and their citizens. Unprecedented regulations limited travel, closed businesses, prohibited exports, modified consumer financial contracts, and limited personal freedoms. Stimulus spending injected trillions of dollars into consumers' wallets, ailing businesses, and financial markets. In many ways, governments demonstrated their immense power and resources, which may lead to new future expectations. This included initiatives such as the US Federal Reserve's direct purchasing of corporate debt and backstopping the corporate bond market, "the first nongovernment bond-buying in the Fed's history."[2]

Covid-19 had many societal and economic effects that will impact supply chains now and in the future. The pandemic exacerbated inequalities between rich and poor. It affected people's disposable income and laid bare the inequalities in terms of access to the technology needed for working, shopping, and studying from home. Around the globe, the pandemic intensified economic nationalism, especially in the arena of healthcare-related products, and it has accelerated ongoing trends in global trade patterns. The crisis also pulled attention and resources away from other pressing societal issues, such as climate change, poverty, inequality, corruption, food security, clean water availability, and religious conflicts. Finally, the high costs and regulatory upheaval created by the pandemic will have long-term effects on taxation, inflation, and business regulations.

18. The Folly of Trade Wars and Economic Nationalism

During the second quarter of 2020, GDP in the US declined by a staggering 33 percent on a seasonally adjusted annualized rate, according to the advance estimate of the US Bureau of Labor Statistics.[1] The consumer reaction to Covid-19 and government measures taken to contain the outbreak resulted in an unprecedented shuttering of businesses and a dizzying increase in unemployment.

Governments around the world have used the crisis to erect trade barriers and "bring manufacturing home." Whether it is "Buy American" in Washington, "Buy Canadian" in Ottawa, or "Time to Buy British" in London, governments have been encouraging their citizens to buy local products for a long time. The coronavirus, however, was used to put some teeth into such slogans, and the shortage of PPE and medical products helped "socialize" such actions in the population.

The Siren Song of Protectionism

Governments' protectionist actions in the wake of the pandemic followed a well-worn script. Throughout history, many governments have responded to domestic economic problems by battening down the import hatches through higher tariffs or quotas on foreign goods. The objective has always been to protect domestic producers from the downturn, thereby maintaining or increasing employment in those industries.

Alas, the net effects of protectionism have mostly been the opposite of the intended ones, as demonstrated by the infamous Smoot–Hawley Tariff Act, signed into law on June 17, 1930.[2] The act was intended to protect domestic industry and national employment by raising the already high tariffs the United States levied on imported goods by an average of 40 percent. "As we learned after President Herbert Hoover signed the Smoot–Hawley tariff at the

outset of the Great Depression, vibrant international trade is a key component to economic recovery; hindering trade is a recipe for disaster," said Asa
Hutchinson, governor of Arkansas.[3]

Smoot–Hawley may not have caused the stock market crash in the fall
of 1929 (even though many economists argue that the forward-looking stock
market declined because it anticipated the effects of Hoover's plans for tariffs).
However, it certainly was a major catalyst for the Great Depression and led
to economic misery spreading around the world as other countries retaliated
and raised tariffs too. International trade plunged by more than 50 percent,
unemployment shot up to 25 percent, and worldwide GDP fell by 15 percent.[4]
The economic pain lingered and, even as late as 1940, the unemployment rate
in the US did not fall below 15 percent.

Only with the Reciprocal Trade Agreements Act of 1934 did world trade
start to recover. This act gave the US president the authority to negotiate
tariffs and bilateral trade agreements, as well as the authority to adjust tariff
rates. It helped to speed the recovery from the Great Depression by reducing
tariffs over time, culminating in the 1947 General Agreement on Tariffs and
Trade (GATT).[5]

The situation during the fall of 2020—a severe recession and calls for
economic nationalism by both political parties in the US—closely parallels
the situation at the end of the 1920s. Such nationalism can already be observed
in the mid-2020 plans of countries to hoard vaccines produced by domestic
pharmaceutical companies as well as to forward-buy vaccines just for their
own populations.[6] Yet, conquering the pandemic requires international cooperation. As several political leaders commented, a vaccine is a "public good."[7]
Unfortunately, when the first batches of vaccine are in short supply, politicians
are likely to revert to "my country first."

Such hoarding is not new. After a vaccine was developed for the H1N1 flu
virus, Western countries bought up virtually all the supplies of the vaccine.
Peter Navarro, leader of the US supply chain response to Covid-19, said, "If we
have learned anything from the coronavirus and swine flu H1N1 epidemic of
2009, it is that we cannot necessarily depend on other countries, even close
allies, to supply us with needed items, from face masks to vaccines."[8]

The behavior of countries during the first few months of the coronavirus
pandemic bears this out. In the face of global shortages of PPE, China, European countries, and the United States hoarded supplies of respirators, surgical masks, and gloves for their own front-line healthcare workers. More than
70 countries plus the EU imposed export controls on local medical supplies
during the first four months of the pandemic.[9] The EU encouraged movement
of supplies among member states, but exports outside the bloc needed special

authorization.[10] And in June 2020, the US bought up virtually all the supplies of remdesivir, one of the first Covid-19 therapeutics, leaving none for the most of the rest of the world for three months.[11] All such actions exacerbated the situation around the world, leading other countries to hoard their own supplies, resulting in further shortages and increased prices.

In this environment, the World Trade Organization (WTO) lost the little influence it had before the pandemic as arbiter of world trade disputes. There was little chance that the organization could lead a multilateral round of tariff reductions with a trade rulebook[12] updated to reflect pandemic-related changes. Consequently, without world leadership but with countries resorting to beggar-thy-neighbor policies, many observers expect a continued deterioration of free world trade. According to a UN report, world trade was down 28 percent in the second quarter of 2020,[13] and foreign direct investment was expected to fall by 40 percent.[14]

Before taking a look at 2020–2021 and beyond, the following two sections first explain why trade is good for the economy.

Why Trade?—The Theory

In the 17th and 18th centuries, many countries practiced a trading strategy of mercantilism, which called for maximizing exports through subsidies while minimizing imports through tariffs. Adam Smith, the father of modern economics, realized that mercantilism could not create economic growth for all nations at the same time, because one nation's subsidized export is another nation's tariffed import. In his 1776 work *The Wealth of Nations,* Smith introduced the concept of absolute advantage, using country-to-country differences in labor productivity to explain how all nations can simultaneously get rich if they focus on their absolute advantages and practice free trade.[15]

To understand his argument, imagine that the fertile farms of the United States can produce more wheat per worker-hour than farms in the United Kingdom, while the well-developed textile mills of the UK can produce more yards of cloth per worker-hour than can the US. If the labor wages are the same in both countries, then the US should produce all the wheat for both countries, the UK should produce all the cloth, and the two should trade them freely. Both nations will be better off (workers being gainfully employed in the most productive activities and consumers enjoying lower overall prices) compared to each nation attempting to be self-reliant but producing some goods inefficiently.

Of course, trade grows naturally if there are no local substitutes. Japan buys oil from Saudi Arabia because Japan has few oil deposits. Similarly, China buys Chilean copper because China doesn't have enough local copper ore to meet local demand. Ditto aluminum, steel, gold, wheat, fruit, and so on.

Absolute advantage, however, is only half the story of trade, because some nations may have no absolute advantage in any product (all of their products are expensive) while other nations have many kinds of absolute advantage (most of their products are cheap). A familiar scenario for this is when one country has high wages while another has low wages. Intuition would suggest that if a country has no absolute advantage, it would import everything and export nothing, while the country with total absolute advantage would import nothing and export every kind of product. This intuition, however, is wrong because of the effects of comparative advantage, which explains how trade across geographies can create value for both trading parties, even if one party could potentially produce all goods with fewer resources than could the other. Comparative advantage refers to the fact that even if a certain country is more (or less) efficient than any other country at making everything, there are still some things that each country is better or worse at making.

The notion of comparative advantage is attributed to the English political economist David Ricardo, who used England and Portugal as representative examples in his 1817 book *On the Principles of Economy and Taxation*.[16] Ricardo supposed that Portugal could produce both wine and cloth cheaper than could England, but the relative costs of production were different within the two countries. In Ricardo's example, the English could produce cloth at moderate cost but wine only at a very high cost. In contrast, the Portuguese could make both wine and cloth very inexpensively.

With these relative production cost structures, Portugal would benefit from producing more wine for high-profit exports to England, even if it meant sacrificing local cloth production and importing the high-cost English cloth. That is, the Portuguese economy would do better to convert fields of flax, cotton, and sheep to more vineyards for making highest-profit exports. Therefore, while it would be cheaper to produce cloth in Portugal than England, it would be more profitable for Portugal to produce more wine and trade that for English cloth. England would also benefit, because while its costs of producing cloth remain unchanged, it could get wine at a lower price, closer to the cost of cloth. As this example shows, countries gain by specializing in the goods in which they have comparative advantage and trading those goods for the other.

The following numerical example was suggested by the writer Matt Ridley[17] (used here in a different context): Jack and Jill each prepare a meal. Suppose it takes Jack 30 minutes to make a loaf of bread and 40 minutes to make an omelet. However, it takes Jill only 20 minutes to make a loaf of bread and 10 minutes to make an omelet. For one meal with both dishes, Jack will spend 70 minutes and Jill 30 minutes. With these productivity numbers, Jill has an absolute advantage for both dishes, but it still pays for her to get her bread from Jack. She can spend 20 minutes in making two omelets and Jack can spend 60 minutes making two loaves of bread. As they trade one omelet for one loaf of bread, both are better off. Jill only has to spend 20 minutes on her meal (instead of 30) and Jack only has to spend 60 minutes instead of 70 when they trade.

Why Tariffs Are Terrible

Tariffs are examples of economic nationalism: government policies that penalize the products of foreign countries or subsidize the products of domestic producers. Naturally, one country's imposition of tariffs causes other countries to retaliate and impose tariffs on the first country, thereby reducing its exports. This can lead to escalating rounds of tariffs and counter tariffs, leading to the collapse of trade and deepening recessions. There are many arguments against tariffs and for free trade.

Scale

If a firm operates in a world of restrictive tariffs and quotas, then that firm is largely restricted to selling only in the modest volumes needed by its own home market. With complete free trade, by contrast, each domestic producer can potentially sell higher volumes to the entire world. In many industries, the average per-unit production cost decreases as output increases.[18] The result of greater trade is lower per-unit costs for companies and lower prices for consumers, leading to higher standards of living.

One key benefit of scale is that companies can make greater varieties of products. At low volumes of sales, new niche products cannot recoup the fixed costs of adding the proposed new product (e.g., R&D, specialized equipment, changeovers in manufacturing, marketing, and overhead) to meet the firm's required ROI or payback thresholds. As scale increases, however, more low-volume products become viable. This enriches consumers' choices, by having a wider variety of products to satisfy many budgets, tastes, and international markets.

An especially important benefit of increased scale is the increased ability to invest in research and development. The costs of such investments can be spread out over a large number of products, leading to more innovation and also tending to augment product variety.[19] In turn, customers in countries that lack tariffs gain access to additional innovation from all the producers in the world, not just the domestic ones. Thus, nationalists impoverish their own countries by denying their citizens access to the global economies of scale and global sources of innovation.

The Virtues of Competition

One of the stated goals of economic nationalism and tariffs is to protect domestic industries from foreign competition. However, firms that do not compete can become complacent and inefficient, providing subpar products and services, as happened in many cases to government services and monopolies such as postal services.[20] For example, the competition in smartphones between Apple, Samsung, and many others drives continuous innovation at both leading companies and at their competitors. In addition to better products, this competition has led to a gargantuan growth in the market for mobile phones as well as related products and services. In 2019, the World Bank reported that while only 70 percent of the world population had access to basic sanitation services such as toilets, almost 97 percent had access to a mobile phone.[21]

As any entrepreneur of a new category of product or service knows, the market (both of customers and investors) needs more than one player to "validate" the need for this new type of product or service. As more companies join the fray, the market becomes more aware of the products offered, and well-managed companies win and grow. This is the case with almost any innovative product. The more competition, the more awareness is created. At the same time, competition keeps productivity growing while keeping prices in check, allowing the market to grow. In contrast, economic nationalism fragments the market, reduces the total opportunities for entrepreneurs, and thus stifles innovation of new product categories.

Tariffs are a Tax on Citizens

"For economists, tariffs operate like taxes, increasing the price of goods to consumers and often costing jobs, not creating them," tweeted economist Teresa Ghilarducci.[22] For a case in point, note the retaliatory tariffs that the European Union put on (among other things) Kentucky bourbon producers, sending a message to Republican senate majority leader (and Kentucky senator) Mitch McConnell. The president of the Kentucky Distillers' Association noted, "This is a 25 percent tax increase—tariffs are taxes, no doubt about it."[23]

What's more, higher prices for tariffed imported goods mean consumers have to ration their spending. That's the tariff "tax" economists speak of. As Alan Greenspan, former Federal Reserve chairman, said, "Whatever you tax, you get less of." Higher tariffs mean less trade.[24] The knock-on effects are lower total consumption. Whether a European consumer chooses to buy the higher-priced tariffed Kentucky bourbon or switch to a (presumably more expensive) domestic distilled beverage, that consumer will have less discretionary income to spend on all other goods and will thus have a lower standard of living because of tariffs.

Standards

One of the long-term effects of the lack of international cooperation is the damage to the development of international standards for products and trade. To see the importance of such standards, consider the maritime container, the standardization of which provided a crucial boost to world trade. Another example is the International Commerce Terms (Incoterms) that define transactions between an importer and an exporter such that both sides understand the terms of the deal. These details cover the task to be accomplished, costs, timing, risk allocation, and who is responsible for what. Incoterms cover the entire movement of the item from the exporter's facility to the importer's facility.

Standards allow buyers of goods and services to feel confident the sellers understand the quality and safety specifications they expect. Standards also provide a language with which buyers and sellers can communicate about the supplied or demanded attributes of products and services. As countries retreat from international engagement, fewer standards will be developed and maintained, hampering trade for years to come.

Competitive Disadvantage for Domestic Companies

HUSCO International is a $450 million Wisconsin-based private company, providing engineering, development, and manufacturing of various fluid power valves and hose fittings for the automotive and off-highway vehicle industries. (The name of the company derives from Hydraulic Unit Specialty Company.) It has nine sales and manufacturing locations around the world, including in China. In a July 2020 Bloomberg webinar, CEO Austin Ramirez explained how the 25 percent US tariffs on Chinese automotive parts are hurting his company and the US automotive industry.[25]

For example, in the short run, the tariffs mean higher costs for parts. In order to remain competitive, HUSCO pressures suppliers for lower prices, reduces its own margins, and passes some of the increased costs to its customers. Ramirez's main concern, however, was for the long run. US tariffs mean that competing Japanese and German auto parts and automobile makers can purchase cheaper Chinese parts and become more competitive on the world stage, hurting jobs in the United States. Once these competitors' products take hold in the automotive industry, future car and heavy equipment designs will be specified around these products, and American jobs will have to be cut.[26]

Retaliation

Once a tariff is put in place, the other country is likely to retaliate. For example, when President Trump imposed levies on Canadian steel and aluminum, Canada responded in kind. It imposed a 25 percent tariff on assorted US metal products. In addition, Canada imposed tariffs of 10 percent on over 250 other US goods like beer kegs, whiskey, and orange juice.[27]

An example of direct tit-for-tat retaliation took place between China and the US in late 2019. In response to the Trump administration's tariffs on Chinese goods, China imposed tariffs ranging from 5–10 percent on $75 billion worth of US goods in two batches, effective on September 1 and December 15, 2019. Those were the exact same dates that the Trump administration's tariffs on Chinese goods were set to take effect. China also added a 25 percent tariff on US cars and a 5 percent tariff on auto parts and components, both going into effect December 15.[28]

Earlier trade wars between the US and China caused American agricultural exports to China to fall from $15.8 billion in 2017 to $5.8 billion in 2018, and these exports remained depressed in 2019.[29] Farmers were doubly affected when the 2019 US tariffs on Canadian aluminum and steel increased the price of these imports, raising farmers' costs for vehicles, equipment, and other metal products. The Trump administration rescinded these tariffs but reimposed them in August 2020, only to see Canada imposing a dollar-for-dollar retaliatory tariff. Canadian deputy prime minister Chrystia Freeland stated, "The last thing Canadian and American workers need is new tariffs that will raise costs for manufacturers and consumers, impede the free flow of trade, and hurt provincial and state economies."[30] On September 16, the Trump administration rescinded these tariffs.[31]

Retaliation can also come through mutual export bans tied to trading dependencies. In April 2020, the Trump administration invoked the Defense Production Act and threatened to ban exports of respirators made by US company 3M to Canada and Mexico. Canada was prepared to retaliate by halting exports of hospital-grade pulp that US companies needed to produce surgical masks and gowns. Canada also could have stopped Canadian nurses and hospital workers from crossing the border into Michigan, where they were desperately needed to treat American patients. Mexico, for its part, could have cut off the supply of motors and other components that US companies needed to make ventilators. The White House seemed unaware of these potential vulnerabilities. Once it realized the costs of these actions, the Trump administration backed off.[32]

Tariffs can become a self-reinforcing cycle—once imposed, domestic political considerations can make it difficult to stop the momentum of successive retaliations as trade plummets and all countries become worse off.

Jobs in Developing Countries

The popular press abounds with anecdotes about greedy multinationals exploiting impoverished workers in poor countries—paying low wages, imposing atrocious working conditions, and using child labor—in order to produce cheap goods for Western consumers. An empirical study published by the National Bureau of Economic Research disputes these impressions based on a thorough analysis. In fact, its authors argue that the data shows that the opposite is true. They argue, "Foreign ownership raises wages both by raising labor productivity and by expanding the scale of production and, in the process, improves the conditions of work. Furthermore, there appears to be some evidence that foreign-owned firms make use of aspects of labor organizations and democratic institutions that improve the efficiency characteristics of their factory operations."[33]

The corollary of this empirical finding is that when multinationals leave less-developed countries, they leave a hole; that is, they take with them employment opportunities that employees in these countries may find difficult to replace. This is especially true for industries that employ women (e.g., textiles), for whom employment alternatives are particularly limited or unsavory. Thus, reshoring from a less developed country to a rich Western country may end up throwing many people out of a job, thus increasing poverty and exploitation in those countries.

The Craziness of It All

To exemplify the absurdity and unintended consequences of tariffs, consider Alaskan salmon. Alaska sells and processes more seafood than any other state in the US. Preparing frozen wild salmon for US supermarkets involves filleting and then removing multiple pin bones that "float" inside the meat. The latter is a delicate process that has to be done by hand and is very labor-intensive. Chinese processing centers have both the scale and the low labor costs to make the operation affordable.

The two biggest markets for Alaskan frozen salmon are China and the lower 48 states. Thus, frozen Alaskan filleted salmon is shipped to China for processing and then back to the US for consumption. Unfortunately, in response to US tariffs on Chinese goods, China levied retaliatory trade tariffs of 30–40 percent on Alaskan seafood. Yet the Chinese appetite for Alaskan salmon kept that market mostly intact, and total revenues dropped by only 10 percent. Of course, when the cleaned Alaskan salmon is sent back from China to the US, it is a different product according to the Harmonized Tariff Schedule of the United States (HTSUS). Consequently, it is subject to American trade tariffs on Chinese products. Thus, Americans are made to pay more for Alaskan frozen seafood than Chinese consumers are.

Globalization Increases Resilience

The Covid-19 pandemic did not prove that doing business in China was bad or dangerous (*see* Chapter 17, p. 145). What it did prove is that companies should not keep all their supply eggs in one basket. In other words, any place in the world can become inaccessible as a result of pandemic, natural disaster, armed conflict, or unwise government policies. As companies are updating their post-pandemic supply networks, they are indeed spreading out their own facilities as well as the locations of their suppliers around the world. "A global supply chain is a resilient supply chain," said HUSCO's Ramirez. "HUSCO needs to be more global, not less."[34]

Indeed, as part of building resilience throughout their supply chains, a number of companies have been relocating operations and buying more from suppliers outside of China. This is an acceleration of a trend that predated the pandemic, fueled by increasing labor costs in China as well as trade tensions. The main beneficiaries of this movement are other Southeast Asian nations, led by Vietnam, Taiwan, and Malaysia; as well as India, Mexico, Eastern Europe, and Turkey. The lower tariffs between these places and the US encourages geographical resilience at a relatively low cost.

American companies did not bring significant business back to the US after the Covid-19 outbreak in China. Instead, to the extent that they did not invest in China, they spread manufacturing and procurement around the world. Furthermore, the diversification movement included reducing dependence on the US itself by investing incremental capital in other parts of the world. Similarly, many Chinese suppliers are setting up manufacturing operations outside China in order to increase their own resilience (and avoid tariffs). As mentioned in Chapter 17 (p. 147), companies are not leaving China en masse, because suppliers in that country offer unique capabilities, large manufacturing ecosystems, and a huge, growing market.

In contrast, the effects of economic nationalism evident during the pandemic—the increasing tariffs, reduced trade, and the expected intense resentment against vaccine-hoarding countries—do not enhance resilience. Self-reliance is a risky all-things-in-one-domestic-basket strategy. The selfishness of economic nationalism does not bode well for the other challenges facing humanity, such as the fight against climate change.

The Downside of Globalization

The saying "In theory, theory and practice are the same. In practice, they are not," has been attributed to many scholars from Albert Einstein to Richard Feynman.[35] Many of the thoughtful detractors of globalization and free trade argue that the problem with it is in the implementation, not the concept. That is, the devil is in the details. Assumptions about the incentives, behaviors, and outcomes in the real world don't match the theoretical ideals presented by the proponents of free trade. Understanding those failings doesn't imply rejecting globalization, only that it needs leaders and institutions to mitigate its shortcomings.

Labor (Im)mobility

Traditional free trade theories assumed that workers displaced by foreign competition could move to a new job. Moreover, the displaced workers were expected to benefit from moving from low-productivity jobs (which had been protected by trade restrictions) to higher-productivity jobs in the growing companies that could sell competitively around the world. In theory, any unemployment caused by opening up to free trade would be short-lived and counterbalanced by better times ahead.

In practice, such labor mobility is not so easy or as prevalent. Jobs have become much more specialized since Adam Smith and David Ricardo first articulated the fundamental advantages of trade in terms of maximizing worker productivity. Modern companies in competitive industries prefer to hire trained and experienced workers in their own industry rather than untrained and inexperienced workers coming from declining industries. Older, highly paid workers from displaced industries face the unpleasant prospect of accepting entry-level wages when switching industries. The result is structural unemployment.

The Nobel Prize-winning economist Joseph Stiglitz argued that when there is high unemployment, many workers simply cannot find a new job anywhere, and thus free trade leads to even higher unemployment. The result, he argued, further increases inequality; although corporations may profit, workers take a hit. In this context, Stiglitz stated emphatically that while companies do benefit from free trade, "Trickle-down economics is a myth."[36]

Regulatory Race to the Bottom

Corporations routinely bemoan the lack of consistent regulatory frameworks and standards around the world. Non-uniform product regulations create inefficiencies for global sales, while non-uniform production regulations create an unlevel playing field in the context of competition with foreign firms. In theory, having strong environmental, social-justice, and labor-protection standards around the world would be a boon to all involved. Consumers would get the protections they desire, and corporations would get the level playing field they argue for.

In the absence of strong regulation, companies do not bear all the costs of their natural resource consumption, operations, and byproducts such as pollution, carbon emissions, environmental degradation, and toxic waste in end-of-life products. Known as negative externalities, these costs are borne by society. In a non-globalized, strictly local economy, such costs may be somewhat self-limiting, because local consumers, voters, investors, and politicians directly experience the societal costs of each company's local production and can decide whether such costs are worth it. With globalization, in contrast, the locations of supply, manufacturing, management, investment, and consumption may be so far removed from each other that local decision makers don't directly experience all the negative externalities.

In practice, Stiglitz argued, "one could, of course, get regulatory harmonization by strengthening regulations to the highest standards everywhere. But when corporations call for harmonization, what they really mean is a race to the bottom."[37] Analyses of foreign direct investment find support for the so-called pollution haven hypothesis, by which companies or countries outsource polluting activities to countries with lax regulations.[38] In turn, this creates perverse incentives for developing countries to compete on lax regulations in order to attract foreign investment.

Thus, in a world in which regulations are not harmonized at the highest level, free trade amounts to a forced movement of jobs out of countries that have strong environmental, health and safety, minimum wage, labor protection, and related regulations to countries that do not.

The Free Market Isn't

Labor mobility and regulations are not the only questionable assumptions behind free trade theories. The central assumption is that the world economy operates on pure market forces of fair competition on the basis of offering the best products at the best prices. Longtime IBM executive Ralph Gomory and eminent labor economist William Baumol argue that consumers do not live in such a utopian world.[39] In contrast, instead of competing fairly through better products and prices, companies can pursue anticompetitive strategies to forestall the predicted utopia of ever better prices (and ever better wages) predicted by the theory of free trade with free markets.[40]

Thus, arguing for abolishing tariffs is meaningless when countries use other means to restrict trade. The real world involves the following (and more):

- nations manipulating their currencies for advantage in exports
- supporting state-owned and politically favored enterprises, which enables them to underprice and drive competitors out of the market
- imposing non-tariff trade under the cover of health and safety inspections or national security considerations in order to increase the price of imports
- favoring domestic firms over foreign firms in legal rulings
- forcing foreign companies to merge with local companies, thereby transferring their intellectual property and technology to a potential future rival

In a world where markets are manipulated, the argument goes, not manipulating markets and not setting up trade barriers leaves a country at a disadvantage. And, of course, once manipulation gets into gear with actions and counteractions, it is difficult to stop, and all sides lose.

Supporting Emerging Markets

German-American economist Friedrich List argued in 1841 that there is room for some tariffs in support of emerging markets.[41] He argued in favor of enabling developing countries to transform themselves from low-GDP agrarian societies into high-GDP industrial societies. To this end, developing countries were justified in using temporary commercial restrictions to protect their nascent industrial efforts until they could compete head to head with more established countries. List accused developed countries of hypocrisy—historically pursuing protectionism when they originally needed it but then trying to force free trade on their developing competitors when the latter needed some protection.

Of course, List's theory about the laudable ethics of allowing developing countries to raise their standards of living (and industries) up to developed-world levels has its own issues in practice. In particular, there is the challenge of determining when newly developed countries should wean themselves off protectionism and how to convince them (or force them) to do so. In many ways, List's 19th century writings are applicable to the behavior of China and other emerging economies today.

Moving Forward

Although the preceding examples show how the free trade baby soils the international bathwater, throwing the former out with the latter is shortsighted. Free trade does offer distinct advantages for those countries that participate, and it is possible to offset the downsides described above. It is an exchange of one surplus for another surplus that fills needs for both participating parties. To restrict trade to within arbitrary lines on a map is to limit all citizens' access to all the innovations, new products, and best prices available from around the world and to limit domestic companies' access to global customers.

Trade, when done right, can also bring peace dividends as well as corporate dividends. In 1795, Immanuel Kant argued that "the spirit of commerce... sooner or later takes hold of every nation, and is incompatible with war."[42] More prosaically, in 1999, Thomas Friedman observed, "No two countries that both had McDonald's had fought a war against each other since each got its McDonald's."[43] Economic ties bring people together—each side must learn much about the other in order to make the best deal. And with an ongoing bilateral flow comes mutual dependence and a preference for stability over conflict. The mutual profits from trade become mutual incentives for peace.

In addition, while globalization has increased inequality in the US and other Western countries, it has substantially increased equality between countries. In China and other Asian countries, years of globalization resulted in lifting billions of people from poverty to the middle class. So, while the US median income in 2013 was a mere 4 percent higher than in 2008, Chinese and Vietnamese median incomes more than doubled, while Thailand's median income increased by 85 percent and India's by 60 percent. The Covid-19 pandemic is on track to further these trends as Chinese and other Asian economies are likely to come out of the pandemic-induced recession better than the US and Europe.[44]

The obvious advantages and just-as-obvious disadvantages of world trade suggest the need for something between unfettered globalization and fully shackled localization. The arguments for protecting young economies, the need to raise people out of poverty, the societal costs of rapid change on those left behind, and the environmental costs of unregulated overdevelopment all imply the need for balanced processes to create mutually beneficial long-term outcomes in the face of conflicting short-term incentives. By extension, it also appears that there is a need for leadership and trusted institutions that can arbitrate disputes to equal satisfaction or, at least, grudging acceptance.

In the decades since the end of World War II, the United States has led the creation of a set of trade rules and institutions that enforce them. Unfortunately, that system is coming undone for a number of reasons, such as the rise of populism across the globe and a concomitant decline in the influence of key supranational organizations such as the WTO. The disruptions caused by the Covid-19 pandemic have quickened this trend. The world now awaits its next leader.

19. Strengthening the Medical Supply Chain

As society struggles to come to terms with the scale of the Covid-19 pandemic, one of the most tragic sights has been front-line healthcare workers begging for more masks and protective gowns to save the lives of those who are saving lives. With Covid-19 came story after story of shortages of masks, tests, swabs, testing reagents, testing equipment, ventilators, and intensive-care beds. Hidden behind all these stories were shortages of literally thousands of items that hospitals needed to care for critically ill patients.

Bindiya Vakil, CEO of Resilinc, an American supply chain risk management software company, commented that at the height of the first wave of infections in the US, healthcare supply chains faced shortages of 10,500 different items. However, the shortages were unevenly distributed among hospitals, so the company built a hospital-to-hospital exchange platform. She explained, "We built that exchange as kind of a dating tool that hospitals could join, post the things they were offering, post the things they were requesting, and the system would do a match. And then they could text each other directly through the exchange."[1]

Certain items, however, were in short supply everywhere, rendering an exchange among healthcare providers impossible. These items included personal protective equipment items like medical-grade respirator masks (e.g., N95 masks), surgical gowns, eye gear, as well as medical equipment, namely ventilators. Failures of leadership in Europe, the US, and elsewhere to pool purchasing at the national level forced hospitals and local governments into a brutal competition for PPE and ventilators. That competition raised the prices charged by vendors, introduced unpredictability into procurement processes, and allowed unscrupulous suppliers to sell shoddy PPE. While the standard for N95 masks is to filter 95 percent of airborne particles, tests showed that some masks filtered only 35 percent of particles and others tested at only 15 percent.[2] "This is why we need a nationally led response," said Virginia governor Ralph Northam.[3]

To make sure that the United States (or any country) does not find itself in the same situation, governments need to improve pandemic preparedness. Supply chains designed to provide the most cost-effective healthcare products and services for normal variations of demand struggle to cope with a global emergency demand surge associated with a global healthcare crisis. Thus, governments need to invest in national reserves of inventory, manufacturing, and labor, combined with healthcare delivery systems able to handle the stress of a global pandemic.

Strategic Medical Inventories

During the years in which the US was a net importer of oil and in response to the Arab oil embargoes of the 1970s, the US created the Strategic Petroleum Reserve to store oil for times of crisis when the country could not procure or produce all the oil it needed for its daily energy needs. Covid-19 painfully proved that in a global pandemic, the US and most other countries could not procure or make all the medical supplies they needed to save lives. Furthermore, while many manufacturers can turn to making some of these items, it takes time. Thus, nations need to keep a large, centrally managed inventory of healthcare supplies in several locations around the country to supplement the ordinary inventories maintained for everyday use by manufacturers, distributors, and hospitals.

The US has a Strategic National Stockpile (SNS) of medical supplies, but these reserves were woefully inadequate for the Covid-19 crisis. The Clinton administration started the stockpile with an October 1998 budget authorization "for pharmaceutical and vaccine stockpiling activities at the Centers for Disease Control and Prevention."[4] The George W. Bush administration obtained more funding for the stockpile and bolstered it significantly. Unfortunately, it was not replenished properly during either the Obama or Trump administrations, leading to the 2020 shortages. The same shortages were evident in other countries. France, for example, has been dealing with Covid-19 with no inventory of PPE, following years of neglecting to stockpile this vital resource, mainly for budgetary reasons.[5]

The challenge with stockpiles is that most medical products have limited shelf lives beyond which the product may no longer be safe and effective. Even simple products like face masks degrade over time—the straps lose elasticity, and the specially treated filter fabrics lose their particle-trapping effectiveness over the years.

As detailed in Chapter 16 (p. 139), Johnson & Johnson faced this issue of the cost of obsolete inventory under its contract to the Pentagon for keeping a stockpile of medical supplies for emergency military needs.[6] The challenge was in integrating everyday JIT management of inventories for civilian needs with management of emergency, just-in-case stockpile inventories—serving two very different objectives without compromising either. As mentioned previously, the solution was a "sell-one-stock-one" (SOSO) inventory discipline that physically commingled the emergency stockpile with civilian supplies so that day-to-day use of the supplies kept the large inventory fresh. A digital "red line" in the inventory management system prevented J&J from using the stockpile without Pentagon authorization. The requirement of a Pentagon-authorized order to dip into the stockpile parallels the requirement of a US presidential directive necessary to release oil from the US Strategic Petroleum Reserve. In both cases, this requirement prevented managers from using the inventory to deal with day-to-day fluctuations.

The structure of the US healthcare supply chain includes several large distributors. Similar to J&J's role, these distributors could be the keepers of the strategic national stockpile. Since these distributors manage the day-to-day needs of hospitals, they can be tasked with keeping a strategic reserve. The inventory carrying costs can be paid by the government, the inventory can be kept fresh by using it to replenish regular orders, and dipping below a "red line" can be permissible only with presidential approval. This process ensures safety stock without undermining those companies' quality processes. Managing a national stockpile from within the existing commercial distribution networks for healthcare products has an added benefit: It can use the natural and established channels between the thousands of makers of medical supplies and the thousands of healthcare facilities in the country.

Distributed Inventory

Bank runs and product hoarding have the same fundamental cause. Customers' fears that a bank or supplier won't be able to provide cash or products, respectively, causes the customers to rush to that bank or supplier and get money or products now. In essence, if the customers do not trust the supplier to be able to meet the customers' future demand, then they will try to take control by immediately attempting to obtain all the inventory they believe they will need. If a throng of customers suddenly takes this action, the resulting demand creates a self-fulfilling prophecy: The customers' fears of suppliers being unable to fulfill orders or experiencing stock-outs are realized.

Financial policy makers have known about this self-destructive mob dynamic for a long time—runs on banks are almost as old as banks themselves. Over the past century or so, governments have created two solutions to reduce the chance of bank runs. The first is requirements for bank reserves: Regulators require each bank to maintain sufficient inventory of cash against fluctuations in depositor withdrawals or defaults on loans made by the bank. The second is government money-supply guarantees in the form of direct lending to banks and deposit insurance. These two policies help reassure the bank's customers that their money will always be there.

By analogy, a national emergency inventory of medical supplies is like a government money-supply guarantee. Correspondingly, hospitals also need their own reserves of key supplies as a front-line of defense against any health-care crisis. This would require each hospital to maintain a local SOSO inventory of supplies and equipment. Such local reserves augment national reserves in two ways. First, a local buffer gives authorities and commercial partners (distributors and manufacturers) time to coordinate resupply. Second, a local buffer helps handle any disruptions in replenishment logistics created by natural disasters or shortages of logistics capacity.

In preparation for a second Covid-19 wave, 90 percent of hospitals and health systems were building safety stocks of about 20 critical medications over the summer of 2020. More than half are building a month's supply of sedatives and painkillers based on their usage during the height of the pandemic. The increased demand caused distributors to put some of these drugs on allocation, meaning that orders are filled only partially (*see* Chapter 8, p. 68).[7]

In the wake of the 2008 financial meltdown, financial authorities discovered that simple bank reserves and deposit insurance do not suffice on their own. Systemic financial risks imply that even if each bank is strong enough on its own, a larger-scale disruption could provoke a domino effect that brings many of the banks down. Thus, financial regulators created and imposed bank stress-testing protocols whereby banks must show they can weather disruptive scenarios such as a depression, stock market crash, real estate downturn, natural disaster, and the like.[8]

Similarly, governments should include stress-testing requirements for hospitals as part of their license to operate. Such tests typically involve working through some emergency scenarios and validating the organization's capacity to respond. In the process, a hospital will both learn the gaps in its preparedness and train people for what to expect in an emergency. The result is both greater preparedness and resilience on the part of hospitals and greater overall confidence in the healthcare system to handle major events (*see* Chapter 9, p. 76).

Medical Products Manufacturing

"In times of crisis, we can no longer switch from one production zone to another to get our essential products," warned Louis Gautier, the former director of the French General Secretariat for Defense and National Security.[9] The Covid-19 crisis showed that although global supply chains for medical products were vast, they could not handle every country's simultaneous increases in demand for a wide range of essential medical products when Covid-19 spread around the world.

To many observers, these PPE shortages seemed like a market failure in which neither for-profit hospitals nor medical product suppliers maintained sufficient inventories and capacities to serve the public as they were supposed to during the pandemic. As such, many called for governments to step in. And governments have stepped in for ages to promote certain industries and projects they deem to be in the national interest. Examples include governments' support for green technology and strategic industries such as chip design and manufacturing,[10] as well as the Pentagon's support for US weaponry R&D and manufacturing.

In response to Covid-19, countries are pouring resources into local manufacturing of healthcare products. For example, with help from the French government, Sanofi has been building a vaccine production site and a new research center in France. But the French are not alone; the EU Foreign Policy Chief Joseph Borrell announced that the European Union will seek to diversify its supply chains of medicines to reduce its reliance on other nations. "In practice this will mean stockpiling some crucial assets. It is not normal, for example, that Europe does not produce even one milligram of paracetamol," he said.[11] And talking about the shortages of medical supplies during the Covid-19 pandemic, Ngozi Okonjo-Iweala, chair of the board at the vaccine alliance GAVI, and Nigeria's former minister of finance, said, "This will lead to a surge of nationalism with respect to the need to produce pharmaceuticals, medical supplies, and equipment domestically. Even countries that traditionally had no capability in these areas will seek to develop the same."[12]

However, the siren call of self-sufficiency may lead to a rockier future than people believe. Chapter 17 (p. 145) delved into the many reasons that, contrary to intuition, reshoring of manufacturing would not improve resilience. In fact, it would likely worsen resilience if only for the fact that a pandemic would likely impair domestic production of medical products right at the time that domestic demand surges. Moreover, the specialized industrial ecosystems employed in manufacturing of all of the materials in each product make self-sufficiency costly and difficult. Restrictive trade policies on exporting domestic production would be more likely to create mutual beggar-thy-neighbor responses that end up reducing global production at a time when that capacity is needed most. Instead, multi-sourcing from multiple countries provides a more robust base.

An in-depth OECD analysis of supply and demand for global mask production uncovered both the magnitude of the challenge and limits to production. The study suggested that normal global demand for masks before the pandemic was about 48 million masks per day. During the pandemic, the volume of masks needed just to protect China's essential workers increased to 240 million masks per day (and that figure doesn't include consumer demand for masks). Normalized for population, this suggests mask consumption was 27 times higher in the pandemic than in normal times and exceeded global mask production capacity by a factor of 10.[13] Even China, maker of 41 percent of all masks in the world, could not make enough masks to save the healthcare workers of Wuhan.[14]

That is, the world would need a stockpile of 27 years' worth of normal demand of PPE to handle just one year of Covid-19, and that assumes the pandemic only lasts 12 months. Given that masks don't last 27 years, maintaining such a stockpile would be quite expensive.

However, the response of the world's companies to Covid-19 shows that countries don't need enormously deep stockpiles to cover the entire pandemic. As detailed in Chapter 3 (p. 21), many companies far outside the mask and medical products industry repurposed their production systems to bridge critical shortages. Haute couture clothing makers, shoe companies, and producers of T-shirts switched to making masks. Car makers made ventilators,[15] and distilleries made hand sanitizer.[16]

The OECD mapping of mask supply chains did uncover the bottlenecks that limit mask production, especially for the much-coveted N95 masks. For the most part, mask production depends on simple materials and manufacturing steps that are widely found among various suppliers in various industries. The one crucial material that truly was in short supply[17] was polypropylene electret melt-blown non-woven fabric.[18]

Polypropylene production itself wasn't the bottleneck—global production churns out 16 pounds a year of this versatile plastic per man, women, and child on earth.[19] It goes into bottles, yogurt tubs, cereal box bags, and even cars. What limited N95 mask production was the melt-blown non-woven fabric production systems and high-voltage treatment systems needed to make a breathable filter layer that electrostatically traps very tiny particles.

Having governments spend inordinate sums building giant stockpiles that are expensive and rarely called upon in just-in-case mask factories makes little sense. Instead, pandemic response strategies can depend on (and encourage) the flexible use of the vast global production systems for discretionary consumer goods. Governments would only need to stockpile a large, but not enormous, supply of masks and crucial machinery for the bottleneck materials or stages of mask production. This stockpile would only be required to cover a few weeks or months of high-volume PPE consumption (less if governments listen to their epidemiologists rather than waiting for shortages of PPE) during which the government activates a flexible response.

Medical National Reserve Labor

In the event of war, many countries need a much larger force than their peacetime national armed forces. To this end, these countries use reservists under various schemes. For example, South Korean males who finish their military or police service are automatically enrolled in the national reserve force for seven years. In Finland, all men belong to the armed forces reserve until age 60. And in Israel, all citizens finishing military service are automatically part of the reserves until age 54 for men and 38 for women. Reservists get regular training and are called to service when needed. The US operates a reserve for each military branch as well as the Army and Air Force National Guards. All reservists train one weekend a month plus two weeks a year and can be called upon in case of a war.

Reserves of weapons and ammunition alone are not enough in the event of war; reservists provide a surge capacity of labor to use those reserve weapons. Similarly, inventories of medical equipment and supplies are not sufficient without corresponding reserves of nurses, technicians, and other trained medical personnel to use them. Thus, a key part of a country's long-term pandemic strategy should be a new reserve force: a Medical National Reserve.

Medical National Reserve members would be volunteers trained in basic nursing or medical technician duties needed for a pandemic. Such a medical reserve would provide trained personnel in cases of pandemics and other national disasters that threaten to overwhelm local healthcare resources. It could be part of the Department of Homeland Security, the Federal Emergency Management Administration, or a newly constituted pandemic-preparedness organization. Members would regularly train on new equipment and work in hospitals one weekend a month (or as required by the hospitals), shadowing doctors, nurses, and technicians and helping where possible. The US needs weekend healers to complement its weekend warriors.

These ideas for creating a more robust healthcare system may require legislation to flesh out the details and principles, such as how hospital licensing rules may change, how reserve supplies would be allocated, and how the Medical National Reserve volunteers would be managed and compensated. These new or expanded government programs may appear extreme, but global crises such as the Covid-19 pandemic should serve as a warning sign that traditional practices simply aren't enough.

20. Green Takes a Back Seat to Recovery

The coming debate about climate change was summarized by Jean Pisani-Ferry, an economist and former aide to President Emmanuel Macron of France: "Die-hard green militants regard it as obvious: the Covid-19 crisis only strengthens the urgent need for climate action. But die-hard industrialists are equally convinced: there should be no higher priority than to repair a ravaged economy, postponing stricter environmental regulations if necessary. The battle has started. Its outcome will define the post-pandemic world."[1]

Governments' efforts to combat Covid-19 have much in common with the effort to curb global climate change. In both cases, society faces a danger that is large and consequential. Also, in both cases, a primary weapon is reducing economic activity while striking a balance between economic growth and mitigating the danger. Likewise, the challenge in both cases is to reduce inequality as the poor are already suffering more and are about to go through more pain. In addition, both challenges are global and yet governments are retreating to a "me first" stance, creating a "tragedy of the commons" on a global scale.

The measures taken by governments, companies, and consumers to fight or avoid the Covid-19 pandemic have significantly reduced greenhouse gas (GHG) emissions around the world. Global emissions plunged by 17 percent in April 2020, according to a peer-reviewed study.[2] However, said Robert Jackson, a Stanford professor and one of the authors of the study, "History suggests this will be a blip.... The 2008 [financial] crisis decreased global emissions 1.5 percent for one year, and they shot back up 5 percent in 2010. It was like it never happened."[3] In fact, as an early indicator, the coal industry in China returned to pre-pandemic levels within six weeks of the lifting of the lockdown.[4] The conclusion is that the world is still facing the climate change challenge and will continue to face it beyond the current health crisis.

"We are already experiencing the impact of climate change today, and virtually every day,"[5] said Martin Brudermüller, chairman of BASF. There is little question that man-made activities have loaded the atmosphere with greenhouse gases, chief among them is carbon dioxide (CO_2), causing the earth's climate to change. In 1988, the UN established the Intergovernmental Panel on Climate Change (IPCC). This scientific panel reviewed the state of knowledge of climate science, assessed the social and economic impact of climate change, developed recommendations for response strategies, and planned future international conventions on the climate.[6] Over the years, the IPCC issued five assessment reports (ARs). The latest (as of this writing) was AR5 in 2014 (AR6 is under preparation for release in 2022). Its headline statement was: "Human influence on the climate system is clear, and recent anthropogenic emissions of greenhouse gases are the highest in history. Recent climate changes have had widespread impacts on humans and natural systems."[7]

The headline statement encapsulates both the problem and the main difficulties in rising to the climate challenge. The situation is dire, yet emissions keep growing.

The Difficulty in Curbing Emissions

Despite the increasing evidence of climate change and its growing consequences, green promises have outpaced green actions even before the pandemic. Most consumers, companies, and governments have made only minor, marginal changes to their behavior. Even the promised changes, if actually enacted, are, at best, ineffective and, at worst, will ensure that the planet continues on its current destructive path.

Although the Paris Agreement was signed in 2016, global CO_2 emissions increased by 4.3 percent by 2018.[8] A follow-up climate conference in Madrid in 2019 failed to reach a comprehensive agreement. Furthermore, emissions will continue increasing because of consumers' behaviors and the march of economic development.

The Real Inconvenient Truth: Consumer Apathy

When it comes to sustainability, consumers (and citizens) claim one thing but do another.[9] In a Nielsen survey, 66 percent of global consumers claimed they were willing to pay more for sustainability;[10] other surveys find similar numbers. However, studies of actual consumer purchasing behavior at the store find that only 5–12 percent of consumers opt for sustainable product options,[11] despite the typically small price differences. This finding was confirmed in a study I conducted in 2019 with my students at four supermarkets in New England, using "consumer observation and intercept" at the point of choice, right in the supermarket aisle.[12]

Most consumers also show their true colors (not green) at the ballot box. One of the most promising avenues for reducing emissions is a carbon tax, which aligns economic and sustainability incentives. Yet a carbon tax proposal failed for the second time in 2018 in Washington state—one of the most progressive states in the US.[13] Australians repealed their carbon tax and kicked out the Labor government when the opposition campaigned on "axe the tax."[14] Ultimately, most consumers seem to want good jobs, affordable products, and a better life for their children today. They either do not believe the science, or they do not seem to be willing to sacrifice even minimally for the sake of the planet and future generations.

Citizens' real-world choices bind the hands of governments on climate-related matters. If consumers can't use the ballot box to vote out disliked climate policies, they use the picket lines, as seen in the months-long violent demonstrations in Paris and other French cities triggered by a proposed carbon tax of only 12 cents per gallon of fuel (about 2 percent).[15]

Can Corporations Lead?

Companies face even tighter constraints than governments. Companies lack the printing press of fiat currencies and the strong arm of the tax collector to raise money for sustainability. If consumers don't like the price and performance of one company's green products, they can switch suppliers more easily than citizens can switch home countries or political leaders. Thus, companies are even less able to pick up the climate change slack left by apathetic consumers and politically constrained governments.

To placate a vocal green minority, most companies offer "sustainability theater": highly visible but relatively minuscule improvements. Restaurants stop using plastic straws, even though the environmental effect is negligible[16] and paper straws are not recyclable (unlike plastic straws);[17] hotels ask guests to forgo daily fresh towels (but don't charge for them); and retailers eschew single-use bags even though those are the wrong environmental choice —all in the name of "pretend" sustainability.[18] Companies tout their commitments to reducing carbon footprints and other environmental impacts, but these initiatives are, for the most part, just cost-saving initiatives with a green marketing veneer. These much-marketed incremental solutions often act as a fig leaf for corporations and governments to cover their lack of substantive actions.

To see corporate sustainability theater in action, consider, for example, the much-celebrated statement by the CEO of BlackRock, the world's largest money manager at the time of this writing. The company said it will divest from companies that generate more than 25 percent of their revenue from coal production used for power generation.[19] Careful examination of the policy, however, shows that it is really just "greenwashing." (Why more than 25 percent and not, for instance, 10 percent? Or zero?) Furthermore, the policy applies only to the company's $1.8 trillion "active fund." As a result, the divestiture will affect only $500 million in holdings, or a tiny fraction (0.007 percent) of its $7 trillion in assets.[20] Finally, on May 17, 2020, the *Financial Times* reported that BlackRock refused to back environmental resolutions of Australian oil companies. Its headline read, "BlackRock Accused of Climate Change Hypocrisy."[21]

The Developing World

Even if consumers in the developed world suddenly embraced emissions-restricting measures, nearly half of humanity still lives on less than $5.50 per day, according to the World Bank.[22] For the poor half of the world, environmental sustainability is a luxury good.

Moreover, as the poor strive to improve their lives in the long term, they will expect to live in buildings made of concrete, use air conditioning, own home appliances, eat more meat, and drive cars—changes that inevitably increase GHG emissions in the short term. Darren Woods, CEO of oil and gas giant Exxon Mobil, said, "Despite the current uncertainty and volatility, the fundamentals that underpin our business remain strong." And he added, "Why do I say that? We know that in the coming decades, populations will grow to more than 9 billion people by 2040, up from just over 7 billion today. Billions of people will enter the middle class and seek lifestyles and products that require energy. Economies will expand once again."[23]

The "China miracle" shows both the human gains and the environmental costs of this trend. China moved from a 99 percent extreme poverty rate in 1978 to essentially eliminating extreme poverty in 2014. However, as the country industrialized and moved hundreds of millions of people into the middle class, CO_2 emissions surged more than 2,000 percent between 1978 and 2017. In January 2018, the *New York Times* reported that "China's emissions are more than US plus Europe and still rising."[24] In India, the government plans to continue to produce electricity with coal "for decades to come." It issued a nine-point plan in 2017 to increase coal production, aiming to provide electricity to an additional 304 million people.[25]

Post-Covid-19 Sustainability

The global economic shutdown to fight Covid-19 improved many environmental metrics dramatically. Cleaner air, less congestion, lower noise, and more. Delhi residents were so shocked to see their normally hazy, gray skies replaced by clear blue horizons that they posted pictures on social media.[26] Owing to the shutdown, the International Energy Agency (IEA) said that the world would use 6 percent less energy in 2020—equivalent to losing the entire energy demand of India.[27] These reductions were attained, however, at enormous economic costs.

Economic Recession versus Environmental Progress

Reports from the OECD[28] and the European Commission[29] concluded that Covid-19 would cause an even deeper recession of the European economy than originally thought. The OECD report concluded that job losses have been 10 times greater than those inflicted during the first months of the 2008 global financial crisis, making it very unlikely that employment in Europe, the United States, and other developed economies would return to pre-pandemic levels before 2022 at the earliest. Stefano Scarpetta, the OECD's director of employment, labor, and social affairs, said, "In a matter of a few months, the Covid-19 crisis wiped out all improvements in the labor market made since the end of the 2008 financial crisis."[30]

Policy makers, the media, think tanks, and academics are locked in a debate about the post-pandemic world. Ursula von der Leyen, president of the European Commission, said in April 2020 that the bloc's green goals should be "the motor for the recovery."[31] She added, "The European Green New Deal is about investing billions of euros in restarting the economy. We should avoid falling back on old, polluting habits."[32] Seventeen European environmental ministers signed a statement to "make the EU's recovery a Green Deal,'" and "to build the bridge between fighting Covid-19, biodiversity loss and climate change."[33]

On July 14, 2020, the Democratic nominee for the US presidency, Joe Biden, outlined a similar far-reaching version of climate policy, which included most of the elements of the so-called Green New Deal. It called for investing $2 trillion over the next four years while committing the US to net-zero greenhouse gas emissions by 2050, investing in clean infrastructure and industry, expanding public transit and high-speed rail, and increasing federal support for research and development in no-carbon energy generation.[34]

While such statements arise from good intentions, they miss the biggest obstacle to implementation: more unemployed people, more poor people, more bankrupt companies, and bare government coffers. Anand Menon, professor of European politics at King's College London, concluded, "I suspect the next value clash in politics will be between environmentalism and those who favor economic growth, and I fear the economy will be the winner in this." A comment by Stefan Lehne, a former EU official, supports Menon's prediction: "Every day, letters from powerful industrial organizations, from cement to plastic to the car industry, arrive in the Commission, saying that we need relief on standards for emissions, on regulations."[35]

Future Cooperation—Not

Countries' behavior regarding an eventual vaccine for Covid-19 may serve as a bellwether for progress on climate change. As mentioned in Chapter 18 (p. 157), under stress, countries are reverting to "me first" behavior, even though vaccinating the world, like solving climate change, requires global cooperation.

The behavior of countries during the first several months of a vaccine becoming available may resemble the well-known game theory concept of the prisoner's dilemma. In this two-person game, the winning strategy is to be selfish, even though cooperation would result in a better outcome for both players. Countries will play a similar game when a Covid-19 vaccine arrives. Fearing a lack of cooperation by other nations, each one will hoard vaccines and other crucial supplies. Given the pressure of the citizenry on politicians and the difficulty of understanding the benefits of sharing a vaccine, this outcome is virtually inevitable.

The result will be long-simmering resentments and recriminations between countries, which are likely to hamper international cooperation for years to come on the epic challenge of climate change. And this is despite the fact that climate change is a worldwide problem and solving it is a true public good. As was happening already, countries may refuse to introduce meaningful changes that will hamper their own growth because they do not trust other countries to do the same.

Loose Talk

The doomsday talk by environmentalists and well-meaning researchers and policy makers may be the undoing of many mitigation plans. Such dire warnings have become fodder for politicians eager to burnish their green credentials. For example, in a speech outlining his climate policy, Joe Biden declared, "We have nine years before the damage is irreversible."[36] This was a repeat of US Representative Alexandria Ocasio-Cortez's mistaken reading of the IPCC special report *Global Warming of 1.5°C*,[37] which concluded that "humanity should cut global carbon dioxide emissions by 40 to 50 percent by 2030 to have a good chance of limiting future average warming to below 1.5 degrees Celsius by 2100."[38] Yet, no catastrophe is likely to take place even if the planet does become more than 1.5 degrees Celsius warmer. Climate researcher Zeke Hausfather explained, "Climate change is a problem of degrees, not thresholds."[39]

One can only imagine the headlines in certain media outlets when the year 2030 rolls around and no climate-induced catastrophic event takes place and humanity is still standing. Much of the public's trust, sans the most ardent environmentalists, will evaporate and make it harder to marshal the world for a serious Green New Deal.

Less Attention to Climate

As a result of the Covid-19-induced economic crisis, economic growth will likely take center stage in a post-pandemic world. Financially stressed consumers will flock to cheap products with less focus on how they are made. Companies' priorities will be revenue increases, cost control, and risk management and resilience. Sustainability may not be among the top three concerns, regardless of lofty statements. And governments will be preoccupied with reviving their economies and reining in huge deficits and debts incurred during the Covid-19 crisis (*see* Chapter 21, p. 191). John Sawers, former head of MI5, said it best: "The harsh realist in me says that we'll emerge more divided, less capable and poorer than before, and that will make governments less inclined to invest in problems that will emerge years and decades down the line." And he concluded, "I would say that government will pay less attention to climate."[40]

Room for (Some) Optimism?

In my writing, I have always argued that in the end, the solution to the climate challenge will be rooted in technology. Some technologies are already bearing fruit—specifically renewables. A 2019 report by the International Renewable Energy Agency estimates that "more than half of the renewable capacity added in 2019 achieved lower electricity costs than new coal. New solar and wind projects are undercutting the cheapest of existing coal-fired plants." However, while solar and wind sources have been growing at a fast clip, they accounted in 2018 for only 4 percent of all energy used in the US.[41]

The environmental movement's multi-decade educational and persuasion efforts aimed at consumers have met with limited success. CO_2 emissions per dollar of GDP have been declining in many countries. At the same time, however, global GDP has been rising at a faster rate. In addition, adding billions of people from the developing world to the middle class will doom any such climate mitigation efforts. Future technological solutions have to rely on more than mitigation and reductions in the rate of emissions. They have to focus on negative emissions technologies—taking carbon out of the atmosphere and reversing the effects of climate change. These methods include bioenergy carbon capture and storage, direct air capture and storage, vegetation-based capture, and several others.[42]

The world's pandemic experience may help the future climate fight in four ways: (1) supporting the role of technology, (2) marshaling the availability of money, (3) promoting international cooperation, and (4) reinforcing the role of scientific and professional predictions.

Role of Technology

The Covid-19 crisis will have demonstrated that when the chips are down, the world relies on the ingenuity of scientists and engineers to develop technological solutions. During the pandemic, it became clear that policies used since biblical times—identifying the sick and quarantining them, as well as lockdowns—have unsustainable economic costs. The world has turned to technology to develop vaccines and therapeutics. As mentioned above, the role of breakthrough technology in tackling climate change is critical in reducing the carbon intensity of the economy and removing excess carbon from the atmosphere. The successful development and application of Covid-19 vaccines and therapeutics may demonstrate the power of technology and unlock enough resources for the development of new technologies to fight climate change.

Money Is No Object

The second conclusion from the Covid-19 experience is that when society sees clear dangers, it can marshal huge sums of money to address the challenge. Governments and companies are spending many billions of dollars to understand the virus; reveal its modes of transmission; and develop tests, vaccines, and therapeutics. Thousands of scientists around the world are working in a mad dash as the world shelters in place. Governments and nongovernmental organizations are spending billions more on preparing the manufacturing and supply chain management capabilities to be ready for a vaccine when it becomes available. Finally, governments are spending orders of magnitude more—trillions of dollars—mitigating the economic consequences of mandates that sought to control the pandemic by shutting down social and economic activities.

Unprepared governments had to spend vast amounts of money mitigating the pandemic's consequences because they had allowed the virus to spread almost unhindered in their communities. Many governments focused too much on the minuscule numbers of sick and dying in the early days rather than the dangerous projected growth trends. In letting the virus spread to catastrophic levels, they incurred catastrophic human, medical, and economic costs. The lesson here is that preparation and timely response to the warnings of scientists is much less expensive than mitigation after the fact. "Pathogens are inevitable, but that they turn into pandemics is not," said venture capitalist and political economist Nick Hanauer.[43]

International Cooperation

Despite economic nationalism at the government level during Covid-19, several important signs of scientific cooperation have emerged. Not only did researchers and health professionals the world over share technical details and processes that work, but some countries changed their postures with regard to cooperating. For example, China—which is expending significant sums to develop a vaccine—announced that "vaccines China develops will become a 'global public good' once they are ready for use, and it will be China's contribution to ensuring vaccine accessibility and affordability in developing countries."[44]

IMF Chief Economist Gita Gopinath said, "This is a virus that doesn't respect borders: it crosses borders. And as long as it is in full strength in any part of the world, it's affecting everybody else. So, it requires global cooperation to deal with it." Carbon dioxide does not respect borders, either. Emissions in any part of the world affect everybody. Just like fighting a pandemic, climate change requires worldwide cooperation among scientists and engineers, even when some governments are not doing their part.

A particularly hopeful sign may be the European Recovery Fund. Toward the end of July 2020, European leaders, led by Angela Merkel and Emanuel Macron, were able to push the deal through despite opposition from several member states. This landmark agreement gives Brussels the unprecedented power to borrow hundreds of billions of euros in the financial markets and distribute the funds to hard-hit member states.[45] While initially designated to help mitigate the economic consequences of the pandemic's impacts, the EU has taken a one-way step toward an "ever closer union."[46] The Recovery Fund has introduced mutual risk sharing across Europe and may even open the door to central tax collection.[47] All these developments mean that the EU may come out of the crisis stronger, more cohesive, and more powerful.

Despite that, as part of the budget negotiations, funds for the European Green Deal were slashed, such funds will likely be restored once the pandemic is under control. The combination of European desires for a climate initiative and the newfound financial muscle demonstrated by the Recovery Fund, means that Europe is likely to act more cohesively and forcefully in the future on issues ranging from mutual national defense to climate change.

Listening to the Experts

The final lesson from the pandemic that may apply to global warming may be that scientists' warnings should be taken seriously by decision makers. Some covers of *Time* magazine since 2003 included prescient warnings based on scientific reports:

- 2003 – The Truth About SARS: China's Coverup; How Scared Should You Be?
- 2004 – Bird Flu: Is Asia Hatching the Next Human Pandemic?
- 2005 – Avian Flu Death Threat
- 2009 – H1N1: How Bad Will It Get? As Students Head Back to School This September, Swine Flu Could Infect Millions
- 2009 – Why You'll Be Wearing Masks Again: The World May Have Dodged a Deadly Flu Pandemic This Time. We Won't Always Be So Lucky
- 2017 – Warning: We Are Not Ready for the Next Pandemic

Others who sounded the alarm include Bill Gates in a 2015 TED talk and the 2019 *Worldwide Threat Assessment* by the US Intelligence Community. Less than a year before the Covid-19 crisis, the intelligence report stated, "We assess that the United States and the world will remain vulnerable to the next flu pandemic or large-scale outbreak of a contagious disease that could lead to massive rates of death and disability, severely affect the world economy, strain international resources...."[48]

It is possible that as awareness of the global warming threat grows, regrets over not listening to experts' warnings could surface and the vast sums of money invested in fighting the pandemic might set a new spending precedent, forcing decision makers to reconsider the climate fight. The lesson learned from the Covid-19 crisis that global threats must be met with global cooperation may also help to turn the tide. Critically, these attitudinal shifts might also provide the impetus for the technological breakthroughs that are our best hope of overcoming the climate change challenge.

21. Government and the Post-Covid-19 Economy

The experience of Covid-19 around the world has, most likely, created an inflection point in the forward march of humanity. Such inflection points often change the way people perceive the world around them. One example of such a pivotal event is the Great Depression. The Depression led to an array of programs known as the New Deal[1] and was also one of the reasons for the rise of fascism and the Nazi party, leading to World War II.[2] World War II itself gave rise to new multinational organizations, such as the United Nations, the International Monetary Fund, and the North Atlantic Treaty Organization, as symbols of a "rules-based international order."[3]

Many large-scale events have generated inflection points in the serpentine arc of history. The rise of the two largest religions—Christianity after the death of Jesus and Islam following Muhammad—had far-reaching consequences into the modern era. Another turning point in religion was the Protestant Reformation, which started the decline of the Catholic Church and encouraged free thought. The American Revolution also was an agent of freedom in that it was pivotal in spreading the ideas of equality and fairness. Gutenberg's printing press brought learning to the masses, and with it, independent thinking. The year 2020 is likely to lead to another inflection point, and future historians may divide the 21st century to BC and AC: "Before Covid-19" and "After Covid-19."

Big Government Is Back

In his 1996 State of the Union address, President Bill Clinton declared, "The era of big government is over." Although the United States never really had "big government" compared to other major countries, many big shocks to the system have expanded the role of the US government through the years. For example, the Great Depression spurred the growth of social programs; World War II spawned the Department of Defense; the Cold War triggered construction of the Interstate Highway System; the 9/11 attacks led to the creation of the Department of Homeland Security; and the 2008 financial crisis engendered acceptance of enormous deficits as the Federal Reserve (and other central banks) fought the financial meltdown.[4]

The Covid-19 pandemic was no different. To fight the economic effects of the virus, the US Congress appropriated trillions of dollars for the biggest US government spending program ever. The Federal Reserve launched an array of financial market interventions to inject even more liquidity into the financial system. New laws mandated temporary prohibitions on evictions due to unpaid rent and provided the right to forbearance of mortgage payments.[5]

The United States, however, was not alone in pumping unprecedented amounts of money into the economy, nor was its aid package even the most generous. As of June 2020, the Japanese government's stimulus package amounted to 21.1 percent of its GDP and Canada's was 15 percent, while the US's was "only" 13.2 percent.[6] Most governments were expected to increase their stimulus spending to support their economies, especially as new Covid-19 cases popped up and new shutdowns were announced. More money in all countries was provided by states and local authorities. And, as mentioned above, European leaders pushed a €750 billion European Recovery Fund for rebuilding hard-hit European economies.

Increased Expectations of Governments

The speed with which governments around the world developed and implemented gargantuan financial stimulus packages was not the only area of accelerated government activism during the pandemic. When Emmanuel Macron declared that France was "at war," he was not the only national leader using this metaphor. Other political leaders moved with warlike speed to solve social problems that had bedeviled their societies for many years. For example, with the stroke of a pen, the city of London ended the problem of people sleeping on the streets by providing free hotel rooms, at state expense, to all those in need—1,400 in all.[7]

Such swift interventions prompted some to ask why these measures were not adopted earlier.[8] London's claim that "these are extraordinary times" sounded flat given that Finland had started a similar program well before the pandemic. The point is that government *can* accomplish a lot and very quickly when there is a will and unity of purpose.

As a side effect of implementing major changes, governments likely create increased expectations among their constituents. The result is the so-called Ratchet Effect, in which surges in government spending during a crisis do not taper back down after the crisis to pre-crisis levels.[9] Likewise, short-term regulation enacted in a crisis often lingers on the books long after life has returned to normal.

A Pew Research Center survey in 2019 found broad support for maintaining or increasing a wide array of government programs.[10] Even among "small government" Republican-leaning individuals, the Pew survey found that more than half of respondents wanted higher spending on veterans' benefits, infrastructure, education, military defense, and counterterrorism.[11] The implication is that citizens will simply expect more from their governments in many areas of life.

Once a government increases spending, even to address a short-term issue, turning off the faucet of largesse is not easy. Austerity is seldom popular, and it is rare that any institution shrinks by choice. Governments, not being subject to market forces, can continue to grow regardless of their spending exceeding their income.

Transformative Policies and Regulations

The coronavirus responses described above demonstrated the might and necessity of governments. Governments assumed greater control over citizens' lives, closing borders, enforcing quarantines, mandating testing, as well as tracking and surveilling citizens. It is likely that, even as the pandemic comes under control, many governments will be loath to let go of their newfound powers and capabilities.[12] In many countries, people's movements will be tracked using face recognition, as is done in China already. The justification may go beyond health monitoring to security requirements and, possibly, more nefarious political objectives. The era of bigger and more intrusive government may affect all countries, but it may show first in sophisticated, capable countries that are relaxed about privacy, such as Japan and South Korea.

Another area in which governments will increase involvement is in setting industrial policy. The sad state of the World Trade Organization means that governments are likely to continue the "beggar-thy-neighbor" policies of tariffs and export restrictions in order to reduce their dependence on manufacturing in foreign lands. For example, Japan has a $2.3 billion fund to pay companies to leave China.

Governments are also likely to double down and intervene in purchasing and inventory policies, providing subsidies to industries considered critical, increasing "buy local" requirements, and so forth. While some of these policies existed in the past, the type of manufacturing deemed essential to national security is likely to be much broader.

The pandemic laid bare the inequality in most Western societies (*see* Chapter 13, p. 112), and the next few years are likely to see higher taxes in order to fund expansion of social services. Large, transformative initiatives were taken by governments, and not only will it be difficult to step back, but people will expect more. As always, outlays are likely to run ahead of government collections, and so deficits will mushroom even beyond the elevated levels of 2020.

The pandemic has highlighted the division of roles and responsibilities of national vs. local governments in the US. The latter include subnational governments (state governments) as well as county and city governments. The focus of state governors and mayors is on health, safety, education, and all other essential services. In many ways, the role of governors and mayors has been elevated during the pandemic because businesses and institutions have to adhere to local rules and regulations, such as which categories of locations are open or closed, occupancy limits, distancing requirements, and so on. Moreover, during the crisis a federal government policy was to shift responsibility for managing the pandemic response to state governments.

The Growing Web of Regulation

Governments have grown larger in more ways than just spending. For example, in the US, a steadily accumulating body of regulations, such as the Sherman Antitrust Act (1890), Fair Labor Standards Act (1938), Clean Air Act (1963), Occupational Safety and Health Act (1970), Consumer Product Safety Act (1972), Food Safety Modernization Act (2011) have imposed a growing number of restrictions and obligations on businesses. These acts, plus innumerable other regulatory activities, have enlarged the accumulated corpus of US federal regulations from 10,000 pages in 1950 to 186,000 pages in 2019. Moreover, the number of pages of new regulatory changes each year has also swollen from 10,000 pages per year in 1950 to over 70,000 pages a year in 2019.[13]

Other governments are not far behind. Since the Treaty of Rome in 1957, which created the European Economic Community (a forerunner of the

European Union),[14] the EU has adopted more than 100,000 legislative acts, including directives, regulations, and decisions.[15] This figure does not include the additional national and local regulations adopted by each member country and jurisdiction. For example, Denmark regulates baby names, which must be picked from a list of 7,000 preapproved names.

The trend of increasing regulations shows no sign of abating—US federal regulations have grown in 55 of the last 69 years. Despite campaigning on an anti-regulation platform, the Trump administration wrote nearly 200,000 pages of new language in its first three years, and the total body of regulatory code at the end of 2019 was no smaller than it was at the end of the Obama administration in 2017. The size of the regulatory system will inevitably increase in 2020 in response to the pandemic and as the country recovers from the crisis.

In addition to more regulatory language on Covid-19 and recovery-related issues, future regulations that impact businesses might appear in areas such as customer data privacy, autonomous vehicles (both ground and air), trade, cybersecurity, gig-economy labor, and the environment. The direction and nature of some future regulations—such as on trade or the environment—may go in diametrically opposite directions in different countries as well as in the aftermath of the 2020 elections in the US. The growing complexity of technology, business, and world affairs will likely spur a growing complexity in regulations.

Calamitous Government Finances

"The steep contraction in economic activity and fiscal revenues, along with the sizable government support, has further stretched public finances, with global public debt projected to reach more than 100 percent of GDP this year," the IMF said in its *World Economic Outlook Update* in June 2020. As of mid-May 2020, The G10 countries, plus China, had unveiled an estimated $15 trillion in combined stimulus spending and loan guarantees, with more stimulus in sight as Covid-19 showed signs of resurgence.[16] Average financial liabilities in the OECD countries are expected to rise from 109 percent of GDP to 137 percent by the end of 2020.

So, while many governments may have ambitious spending plans—be it a "Green New Deal," new social protections, or beefed up military—the money may not be there. In particular, the world was set back in fighting other diseases while suppressing Covid-19. These include a host of neglected and reemerging tropical diseases (e.g., schistosomiasis, echinococcosis, leishmaniasis, trypanosomiasis).[17] Most disconcerting is the comeback of diseases that humanity was in the process of controlling. These include tuberculosis (which kills 1.5 million annually around the world), HIV, and malaria (which kills 1–3 million per year).[18] Resources will have to be dedicated to control these diseases.

Some governments face especially serious fiscal constraints. In the US, state and local governments cannot borrow money to handle increased spending and decreased tax revenues.[19] Most must balance their budgets, which forces them to either cut spending or raise taxes and fees in a crisis. Similarly, developing countries face constraints tied to high sovereign debt levels even before Covid-19 struck.[20] Servicing the preexisting debt constrains what these countries can do to recover from the pandemic and damages their long-term financial stability.

Ultimately, government debts must be unwound through either taxes, inflation, or default. All three strategies can have negative effects on future economic growth. Even if countries choose to roll these debts over in perpetuity, the interest payments will be money the government must extract from someone but which they cannot use for other beneficial purposes. Thus, post-pandemic, one can expect a period of slower growth around the world, with the only "positive" aspect being possibly reduced carbon emissions for a while. "Our economic strategy is using a considerable amount of money, and honestly speaking it's going to be a big fiscal problem in the future," said Hiroaki Nakanishi, executive chairman of Hitachi in an interview with the *Financial Times*.[21]

The world has struggled to cope with the uncertainties created by the Covid-19 crisis and determining the balance between public health and economic viability. Unfortunately, the post-pandemic road promises to be just as rocky—perhaps even rockier—as societies grapple with the ripple effects of the pandemic as well as the various global-scale problems that existed before the coronavirus erupted.

PART 6
THE NEXT
OPPORTUNITIES

"You look back on history, and after [the] 1918 flu came the roaring '20s. We got through it then, and we can get through it now. People are resilient."

—Brian Niccol, CEO,
Chipotle Mexican Grill[1]

Andrew Savikas, chief strategy officer at getAbstract (a provider of business book summaries for corporate learning) hopes the pandemic will provide "one of those rare opportunities to radically rethink the way we work and live." His vision includes having "less time spent in cars, less pollution and a chance for people to reclaim some flexibility and have more work-life balance."[2] Such changes in the coming years will present existential difficulties for some companies but offer growth opportunities for others.

22. More E-Commerce

"E-commerce was already a big thing. Home grocery delivery was already a thing, and working from home was already a thing [for some]," said Andrew Savikas.[1] The pandemic accelerated all that, he added: "We've encountered five years' worth of change in five weeks and that can be a little bit jarring."[2]

While fears of contagion kept people out of brick-and-mortar stores, it sent them online to buy all the essentials (and luxuries) for their shelter-at-home lifestyles. In an example of the bullwhip effect (*see* Chapter 2, p. 14), suppliers of e-commerce technologies, such as mobile payment company Square, saw even faster changes. "Overnight, doing business in person was not really an option anymore, so everyone scrambled to get online," said David Rusenko, head of e-commerce at the company.[3] "We saw a three-year adoption cycle get compressed to three weeks."

On August 3, 2020, the oldest department store in the United States filed for bankruptcy protection. In 1826, Samuel Lord and George Washington Taylor, both English immigrants, founded Lord & Taylor, a dry goods store on Manhattan's Lower East Side. The company grew into a chain and in 1914 opened its grand flagship store on New York's Fifth Avenue.[4] A leader in innovation for decades, it was the first retailer to introduce a lunch counter, provide animated window displays during the Christmas season, allow employees to become company stockholders, and introduce new American designers. In its bankruptcy announcement, the company said that it will liquidate if a buyer is not found.[5]

Industry analysts say the pandemic was the final nail in the coffin of many brick-and-mortar retailers. "The traditional retail sector has been distressed for many years, and now this intense shock is pushing more companies to the brink," said Sarah Wyeth, sector lead analyst for retail and restaurants at S&P Global.[6] In April 2020, S&P Global categorized 30 percent of retailers as "distressed" (implying at least a 50 percent probability of default), double the number since the pandemic began.[7] In particular, department stores have been in decline for two decades. Between March 1999 and February 2020, US department store revenues declined 70 percent.[8] And then Covid-19 hit.

By mid-2020, other notable retailer bankruptcies in the US included Neiman Marcus, Brooks Brothers, J. Crew, J.C. Penney, and Pier 1.[9] High debts and low cash levels meant that these retailers lacked the financial resources to survive the pandemic-induced interruption in revenues or to invest in quickly adapting to more online sales. Moreover, these were just the early victims. Bankruptcies typically peak some 10 months after companies weaken and become distressed.[10] That said, most US retail bankruptcies in 2020 have been of the Chapter 11 type, which gives the company protection from creditors while it tries to reorganize, keep some top-performing stores open, and figure out how to use the assets of the company to make money.

Omnichannel Retail

Omnichannel retailing is one of the main strategies for utilizing the assets of retailers with physical outlets within the context of digital retail. For example, Shanghai-based Lin Qingxuan is a retailer with 300 outlets that sells cosmetics made from traditional Chinese herbs. Chinese New Year was a big shopping season for the retailer, but then Covid-19 hit, shuttering 40 percent of the company's locations right at the start of the holiday and causing a 90 percent collapse in sales at their brick-and-mortar stores. The company faced bankruptcy. "Suddenly," said founder Sun Laichun, "the old environment is no longer viable due to the coronavirus outbreak. We had no choice, and we had to take the new digital path."[11]

With so many stores closed, the company redeployed a key retail asset, namely more than 100 of its in-store beauty advisors.[12] The advisors used digital tools such as WeChat, DingTalk, and Taobao Livestreaming for online events that engaged with at-home customers.[13] A pre-Valentine's Day online event yielded revenues 45 percent higher than in the previous year; sales in Wuhan were triple the prior year's, and an International Women's Day event in early March produced a fivefold jump in online sales.[14] "And now," Laichun said, "we've realized that we can do business in this new digital path."[15]

Other retailers adapted to Covid-19 (and e-commerce) with virtual versions of fitting rooms and product testing. Nashville-based Savas specializes in made-to-measure leather jackets—a high-touch retail experience made impossible by the pandemic. The company created a virtual-fitting package with a self-measuring kit, a packet of fabric swatches, and video consultations.[16] Beauty product retailer Sephora created a "Virtual Artist" app and website that uses images of the customer's face to let cosmetics shoppers try on different colors of makeup, eyelashes, and so forth.[17] Similarly, IKEA's augmented reality app lets customers see how IKEA's furniture would look in their homes.

The term "omnichannel" refers to an integrated retail communications and fulfillment strategy in which a customer can interact with the retailer via any physical or electronic channel (in-store, web, phone, mobile app, text message, video, etc.) and buy (or return) products via any physical channel (off the shelf, curbside, home delivery, lockers, etc.). "Our omnichannel strategy, enabling customers to shop in seamless, flexible ways, is built for serving the needs of customers during this crisis and in the future," Walmart CEO Doug McMillon said in the management commentary part of its Q1 2020 earning release, as the company reported a 74 percent increase in e-commerce sales.[18] Other strong retailers reported similarly impressive growth in e-commerce. For example, in April 2020, Target saw a 282 percent increase in digital sales compared to April 2019.[19]

For the customer, in theory, omnichannel creates a smooth retail experience that brings together the best of both e-commerce and brick-and-mortar retail. For the retailer, in practice, creating this smooth experience across all the different customer-facing technologies and the back-end physical fulfillment systems can be daunting. Dennis Flynn, senior director of supply chain and inventory management at Walmart eCommerce, explained the complexity of the product flows required to serve omnichannel consumers. Given the surge in both e-commerce sales and overall demand for some products, Flynn described how Walmart sought "creative ways to get product out, whether it was through ship-from-store or through our fulfillment centers or increasing what we call DSV (drop ship vendors), where the manufacturer ships direct to a customer."[20]

Managing omnichannel logistics requires holistic inventory management: having visibility into all the inventory wherever it is and having optimization algorithms to determine from where and how best to fulfill orders. Due to its need to compete with Amazon, Walmart has developed many of these underlying technologies, while other retailers were caught flat-footed.

To imagine the complexity, consider a simple order of a sweater by a customer in Boston from a local retailer. The retailer may fulfill the order from the nearest Boston store; from another store in the national chain; from the closest regional fulfillment center in, say, Connecticut; from a national fulfillment center; or direct from the maker of the sweater. The considerations go beyond stock availability and transportation distance to include factors such as the relative rates of sales in various locations. For example, if the sweater sells well in the northeastern US but not in California, the company may decide to fly the sweater from California to Boston to avoid discounting the sweater later where it was not selling well. The net profit from a full-price sale in Boston minus transportation costs from California might exceed the uncertain profits on a discounted sale in California.

The challenge becomes significantly larger if the order includes multiple items. Furthermore, the decision also depends on whether the order is destined for a Boston store for customer pickup or shipped directly to their home. In the former case, transportation costs may be lower due to consolidation with other items bound for the store. In the latter case, individual packages will be sent to the customer's home, increasing the transportation costs and possibly biasing the decision in favor of using a local distribution center or local store.

BOPIS (Buy Online, Pick up In Store) is a popular omnichannel fulfillment practice. BOPIS more than tripled during Covid-19 shutdowns and remained at more than double the 2019 levels as the US economy reopened in June 2020.[21] BOPIS avoids the costs of last-mile delivery, albeit with some relatively minor added expenses in labor and floor space at the store. Although BOPIS certainly enables low-contact transactions, it also encourages additional in-store shopping—85 percent of shoppers have made additional in-store purchases during a BOPIS pickup, and 15 percent say that they do so "somewhat frequently."[22]

Another mode of digital sales involves BOSFS (Buy Online, Ship From a Store). This mode was popularized by retailers such as Walmart, which have large networks of brick-and-mortar outlets as a way to use their physical stores as a competitive advantage in their battle with Amazon and other online retailers. Ship-from-store allows for faster delivery, because, unlike distribution centers, such stores are located in cities and towns close to the customer.[23] Responding to the threat, Amazon has been in discussions with Simon Property Group, the biggest mall operator in the United States, about taking over space abandoned by ailing department stores in malls.[24] Amazon intends to use these spaces as forward fulfillment centers, allowing it to cut delivery times even further.

Who Shops Online

During May and June 2020, the MIT Center for Transportation & Logistics conducted a survey of grocery shopping habits in the US.[25] The survey was administered by Dr. Lisa D'Ambrosio and Dr. Alexis Bateman from two CTL research facilities: AgeLab and Sustainable Supply Chains. The survey, part of a *Covid-19 Generational and Lifestyle Study*, elicited 1,320 responses. (The results shown here are pre-publication and not peer reviewed as of this writing.)

The survey questions focused on buying behavior, distinguishing between shopping in a store and an array of online shopping modes (home delivery, BOPIS, locker pickup, curbside pickup, and having someone else do the shopping).

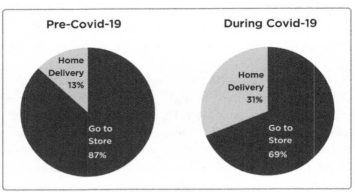

Figure 22.1: *Home delivery before and during Covid-19*

As depicted in Figure 22.1, home delivery's share of shopping increased from 13 percent to 31 percent of all shopping trips. Shoppers in large cities were already more inclined to use home delivery before the pandemic, and they increased their use of home delivery more than others during the pandemic, as shown in Table 22.1. This is likely due to the high density of urban areas, which have more home delivery service availability and also pose a higher risk for in-store shopping during the pandemic.

	Pre-Covid-19	During Covid-19
Large city	26.0%	60.1%
Suburb near large city	8.2%	19.9%
Small city or town	2.7%	10.3%
Rural	1.7%	6.9%

Table 22.1: Location of grocery shopper impact on e-shopping

Shopping behavior also varied across generations, as shown in Figure 22.2.

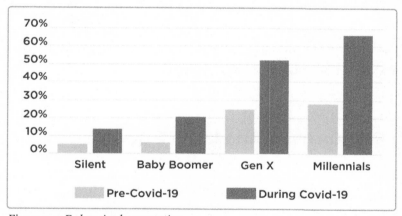

Figure 22.2: E-shopping by generation

All generations more than doubled their shopping online during Covid-19. Cross-generational patterns did not change (in that more younger people shopped online than older people both before and during Covid-19). The definitions of each generation used here were the ones used by the Pew Research Center: Silent Generation, born 1945 or earlier; Baby Boomers, born 1946–1964; Generation X, born 1965–1980; Millennials, born 1981–1996.

Another question in the survey probed for "stickiness": Were those who shifted their shopping mode likely to stay with it or shift back after the pandemic? Nearly one-third (31 percent) of those who shifted planned to stay with the new mode of shopping.

Out of those who shifted from in-store shopping to home delivery—the largest group to shift their shopping mode—31 percent stated that they were likely to continue with home delivery, as depicted in Figure 22.3. While this

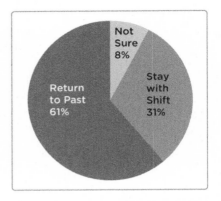

Figure 22.3: Percent staying with shopping choice

is good news for all the gig workers involved in home delivery operations, note that the total percentage of people who shifted to home delivery is only 18 percent. Thus, the long-term percentage of shoppers added to home delivery due to Covid-19 may only be about 5.6 percent.

Big Platforms for the Little Guys

Technology is lowering barriers to entry for small suppliers who want to sell online directly to consumers. While the generic "Face Mask, Pack of 50" was becoming the number-one bestselling product on Amazon, consumers of a more stylish bent turned to Etsy to find handcrafted face masks made by some of Etsy's 2.7 million artisans and sellers. "When the CDC changed its guidelines... we all of a sudden saw overwhelming amounts of demand come on to our site," said Joshua Silverman, CEO of Etsy. "It's as if we woke up and it was suddenly Cyber Monday, but everyone in the world wanted only one product and it was a product that basically didn't exist two weeks before."[26]

Online platforms like Etsy offer a dynamic and flexible retailing channel for selling in more volatile and less predictable environments. Consumers can search for anything, and that search data (along with data about what consumers did or did not click on or buy) provides powerful, real-time visibility into demand, including demand for entirely new products. In the case of Covid-19, Etsy saw within hours a change in search behavior and adjusted its systems to reflect the new interest in protective face masks rather than Halloween masks or decorative tribal masks. The company also had to recruit face-mask makers, educate them on delivery expectations, and allocate demand so it wasn't too concentrated on a few sellers. By its May earnings call, Etsy had 60,000 shops selling face masks, with sales totaling 12 million units worth $133 million in April alone (representing at least 10 percent of Etsy's gross merchandise sales).[27]

"Why am I going into so much detail about masks?" Silverman told investors. "It's not because I'm convinced that masks are going to be an enduring category for months to come," he continued. "The reason I wanted to tell the story is because I think it really highlights the dynamism of the Etsy model and our Etsy sellers."[28] Not only did this new product category surge to the fore, but sales in non-mask categories grew 79 percent in April, too, despite a serious slump in wedding- and party-related products, which had been big sellers.

Some have argued that Covid-19 has accelerated the consolidation of retail toward giants such as Amazon, Walmart, and Target. "The best brands that have taken the friction out of online shopping are going to get more of our time and our wallet, putting more pressure on the smaller ones," said Eric Clark, a manager of the Rational Dynamic Brands mutual fund.[29] However, third-party platforms such as Etsy counter that simple chain of logic.

Platforms enable independent stores to compete online. For example, C&S Wholesale Grocers teamed up with Instacart to offer e-commerce and same-day delivery solutions to more than 3,000 C&S independent grocery retailers across the United States.[30] Similarly, Bookshop is a third-party platform used by 750 independent bookstores for online sales.[31] Book distributor Ingram handles fulfillment for Bookshop orders, and the local bookstore gets 30 percent of the list price without the costs of inventory or shipping.

These online platforms are part of the same accelerating technology trends that created cloud computing, Airbnb, Uber, and TaskRabbit. Scalable online technologies mean that a third party can create a system that lets anyone perform some function, such as a gig job, or one that offers e-commerce capability (allowing small retailers to build an online catalog of products, offer online shopping with a shopping cart, provide order tracking, etc.). "We should be able to shop an entire mall from one app," said Deborah Weinswig, CEO and founder of Coresight, a retail and technology advisory firm. "Each mall in a way is ultimately a platform, and if you're Simon [Property Group], you have many different Amazons."[32]

Facebook for E-Commerce

Even though Amazon is the largest player in the Western e-commerce universe, that universe may be growing at a faster rate than even Amazon can adjust to. This became patently obvious during the pandemic. Amazon's much-touted same-day, overnight, and two-day deliveries became two-week deliveries without a guarantee. The flood of e-commerce volume overwhelmed the giant retailer.

Taking advantage—and taking a page from Amazon's playbook—Facebook announced a new e-commerce initiative on May 19, 2020. Ignoring the physical side of the equation (warehouses, planes, trucks, and a huge inventory), Facebook will allow businesses to build virtual shops on its Facebook and Instagram platforms, as well as allow other platforms (e.g., Spotify) to sell goods and services via its sites.[33] The virtual storefronts will be free for any business. Facebook will generate revenue by charging for the use of its payment system and from an expected increase in advertising from merchants looking to increase their visibility.

The pandemic demonstrated Amazon's struggles to keep up, even as it prioritized some items over others. At the same time, traditional retailers reported dramatic growth in online sales for the second quarter of 2020. These included Walmart (up 97 percent), Home Depot (100 percent), Lowe's (135 percent), and Target (195 percent), among others. Merchants and manufacturers looking to sell online are likely to prefer using platforms that do not compete with them (as Amazon does both as a store and as a manufacturer of Amazon Basics products). Thus, Facebook is using its popular social media platforms to expand into a lucrative adjacent area, with the potential of a substantial increase in its core advertising and new payment-system businesses.

The Increasing Dollars and Cents of Fulfillment and Delivery

No matter how long the pandemic lasts, people will continue to need goods, and those goods will require warehouses for efficient distribution and fulfillment. Prologis, the largest developer, owner, and operator of warehouses in the US, notes that the surge in online shopping has been keeping warehouse vacancy rates low despite the impacts of Covid-19 on jobs and the economy.

Large retailers such as Walmart and Amazon are increasing their warehouse footprint. "We're not seeing those guys slow down, they continue to be very active in making new deals," said Hamid Moghadam, CEO of Prologis. "The strong continue to be taking a lot of space."[34]

Whereas few wanted to share a ride with Uber or Lyft at the height of the pandemic, other gig jobs in fulfillment and delivery surged. While Uber rides slumped 80 percent in April 2020, Uber Eats food delivery service saw an 89 percent increase.[35] To boost business in that growing food delivery sector, Uber bought Postmates for $2.65 billion in July 2020.[36] (Uber also cut 3,700 staffers, including some from Uber Eats in international markets.)[37] Downloads of delivery service apps such as Instacart, Peapod, and Shipt jumped between 300 and 600 percent between February and April 2020.[38] Instacart saw a staggering tenfold rise in grocery orders —twentyfold in California and New York. The company boosted its network of shoppers from 200,000 to 750,000.[39]

However, e-commerce fulfillment and deliveries also add costs for packaging, last mile-transportation, and labor. In many cases, consumers are loath to pay extra for shipping. Studies show that 54 percent of shoppers have abandoned their carts due to expensive shipping, while 39 percent did so due to no free shipping. In addition, 26 percent abandoned their cart because shipping was too slow.[40] Over time, automation of the last mile (*see* Chapter 15, p. 132) may reduce delivery costs, although the diversity of delivery locations (high-rises; urban, suburban, and rural homes) implies a diversity of delivery systems.

Synchronizing Commerce

Two examples show how mobile technology trends are improving service in the physical world. First, Chipotle is bringing BOPIS to burritos by expanding its Chipotlanes concept from 10 locations to 100 locations as of June 2020. With this system, consumers order their food via a mobile app and select a pickup time. There are no long lines of idling cars waiting to get to the "order here" station and then waiting for their order to be completed at the pickup window. "You pull to the window and they should hand you the bag and you drive away," said chief restaurant officer Scott Boatwright. "The digital experience has just exploded with Covid.... And, that business has been really sticky."[41] (The lack of queuing also enables Chipotle to more easily get permission for "drive-through" service from retail development owners who don't want the congestion of a traditional drive-through lane.)

Second, parking is the bane of last-mile logistics in cities. Delivery personnel have no idea how long it will take to find a space near the customer's address or if they will be forced to double-park or park far away. For last-mile logistics companies, the result is low delivery productivity, unreliable delivery timing, and added costs from parking fines. To address this problem, startups such as CurbFlow are working with cities to manage curb space on a by-appointment basis.[42] A mobile app lets delivery drivers and logistics companies schedule curbside loading and unloading activities. This system reduces unsafe double-parking and the time-consuming hunt for parking or walking to and from distant spaces.

The CurbFlow concept is a step beyond the ongoing work of urban planners to control and manage urban curb space.[43] Such contested spaces are used for storage of cars (parking), commercial deliveries, temporary workers' vehicles (such as various contractors), bus stops, shared ride services, and even outdoor dining. The fundamental difference with CurbFlow is the dynamic management of the curb, opening up capacity for shared use.

At a deeper level, both of these examples show the value of synchronizing activities in supply chains—a customer and supplier both benefit from prearranging when some item (a food order, a parking space, etc.) should be available. Both of these examples also show the accelerating use of mobile platforms to accomplish this. With synchronization, the customer gains visibility and confidence over the timing and availability of their burrito or parking slot, while the service provider gains visibility into real-time demand and can smooth their resource consumption. This contrasts sharply with traditional approaches to drive-through lanes and parking that depend on customers arriving randomly at the resource and queueing until it is available.

23. Remaking the City

High-density living made cities such as Wuhan and New York City juicy targets for Covid-19. Worse, elevators in big-city high-rise buildings seemed like unavoidable sources of contagion. Wealthy city dwellers fled the pandemic,[1] and companies sent employees home to work. Working from home enabled many to think about relocation and using their big-city salaries to buy much larger homes outside of the city. Thus, big Covid-19-infected cities and big high-rises are likely to lose population due to the pandemic.

Cities have come back from the impact of disasters before. After 9/11, office rents in Manhattan and Washington, D.C., declined, especially for space on what had been previously coveted upper floors. However, when further attacks failed to materialize, fears faded, and downtown, upper-floor rents bounced back. In the future, today's refugee city dwellers may end up missing the hustle-and-bustle lifestyle of big cities even if it means forgoing the lower costs of living (and larger houses) in suburbs, smaller towns, and less expensive states or countries. Thus, urban lifestyles might ultimately survive Covid-19.[2]

The Great Emptying Out

Companies, however, emphasized cost more than lifestyle when making location decisions. "The notion of putting 7,000 people in the building may be a thing of the past," said Jes Staley, CEO of Barclays.[3] "There will be a long-term adjustment to our location strategy." Similarly, at Nationwide Insurance, remote work has gone so well that the company is shutting down five regional offices[4] and has plans to shrink from 20 physical offices to just four.[5] Likewise, Morgan Stanley's CEO, James Gorman, told Bloomberg TV, "We've proven we can operate with effectively no footprint."[6] Expensive city office buildings just don't look as attractive anymore.

As long as the pandemic rages, physical distancing requirements will give companies a stark choice: Continue work-from-home policies for most of their staff or pay for more office space to reduce the chance of infection. In the last decade, companies have crammed more and more workers into their offices. In 2010, offices averaged 44 workers per 10,000 square feet. By 2017, they averaged 66 workers per 10,000 square feet.[7] To the extent that the pandemic creates economic recession and financial uncertainty, most companies will opt to minimize real estate costs rather than add more real estate.

Elevators enabled the modern high-rise but might now contribute to their downfall. First introduced in 1857 in Manhattan, elevators made the vertical growth of cities possible. "Elevators are the epicenter of urban density," said Andreas Bernard, a professor of cultural studies and the author of *Lifted: A Cultural History of Elevators*.[8] Without this vertical mode of transportation for people (and cargo), cities would be constrained to the Parisian style of urban architecture—five stories being the comfortable limit for taking the stairs. Between the impossibility of physical distancing in a small elevator during busy times, the need to touch unsanitized buttons, and the threat of lingering aerosols from previous passengers, elevators make the high-rise office, apartment building, or hotel even less attractive during the pandemic.

The availability of efficient telecommuting and online collaboration technology means that even if some workers need to be in an office, those offices can be relocated to less expensive suburbs and secondary cities where real estate, costs of living, and wages will be lower. Consider, for example, MIT, Harvard, and Stanford. All three universities occupy some of the most expensive real estate in the world. Whereas faculty and students need to be co-located on campus for the traditional college experience (*see* Chapter 12, p. 105), the supporting administrative functions could be relocated to less expensive locales, performed via remote work, or even moved offshore. Similarly, while sales executives need to be close to their customers (some of whom may still be in expensive city centers), corporate support functions could be relocated.

Most importantly, employees who can work from home—such as computer programmers, accountants, lawyers, telemarketers, transportation brokers, and financial advisors—are deciding to do just that. People are leaving large cities like New York[9] and high-cost urban areas like California's Bay Area, which had been losing population even before the pandemic.[10] Despite the uncertain economy, in June 2020, homebuilders enjoyed their highest sales in 15 years—55 percent above the previous year's levels. Buyers sought suburban and rural areas, high-tech homes, and extra rooms for home offices and homeschooling.[11]

Even if Covid-19 just disappeared, as some have wished, the telecommuting genie is out of the bottle and will have profound effects. Office space, especially expensive space in downtown areas, will likely lose substantial value, and the effects on the urban landscape will go beyond just vacancies in high rise offices. To the extent that fewer people will live in cities and work downtown, city economies will support fewer restaurants, shops, parking garages, transit services, and hot dog vendors.[12] For big cities and big skyscrapers, Covid-19 has brought Yogi Berra's words to life: "Nobody goes there anymore, it's too crowded."

Spreading Out and Slowing Down

Restaurants and retailers around the world also suffered during the pandemic due to business models that assume modest margins made on large volumes of business, often associated with high-foot-traffic locations. Closure mandates, occupancy limits, and consumer reluctance to gather in crowds have thrown these business models into the red for many consumer-focused companies. Few restaurants, shops, and hair salons can afford to pay 100 percent of their pre-Covid-19 rents while operating at 50 percent capacity or less during partial-opening limbo phases. "Given that recovery to pre-crisis levels may be gradual," said Coresight founder and CEO Deborah Weinswig, "retailers that were struggling to stay in business pre-crisis are unlikely to have the wherewithal to stay the course on the road to recovery."[13]

A Yelp analysis of business closures found that nearly 16,000 restaurants in the US have permanently closed, and another 10,000 are temporarily shut as of July 10.[14] Coresight estimates that US retailers will shutter 20,000 to 25,000 stores in 2020, representing 5–6 percent of the total physical stores in the US.[15] Fifty-five to sixty percent of closures are expected to take place in America's malls.[16] The downward trends over the last decades for the department stores that anchor those malls—namely reductions in sales and more bankruptcies—have accelerated during the pandemic and will likely drag these fading cathedrals of consumption to their graves.

The survivors (and the city) may find a way forward through remaking the urban landscape. As long as the pandemic creates either government mandates or consumer demand for distancing, facilities such as restaurants, bars, barber shops, gyms, and coffee shops will need more space per customer. Many cities are repurposing civic spaces to enable social gatherings while maintaining person-to-person distances from a health standpoint. For the duration of the pandemic, cities are converting parking spaces, and even entire streets, into pedestrian spaces for restaurant tables and other public uses.[17] These actions are more than just good-hearted gestures; many cities depend on sales tax revenues—throttled by the pandemic—for a large portion of their budgets.

In New York City (and many other locations), bicycle use surged because it was the best personal transportation alternative to the high infection risk posed by mass transit and the high cost of cars (less than half of New York City households have a car). Furthermore, work from home reduced the number of commuters and reduced congestion. More than 200 cities have announced road closures to expand pedestrian zones, add bicycle lanes, and enable restaurants to expand outside.[18] Others are designating some streets as "slow streets" to encourage safe, mixed use.[19]

Some see these adaptations to Covid-19 as a welcome and potentially permanent change to the urban environment. "There are certain byproducts that, if we take advantage of them, will let us be more of an open city, more of a city that's usable by all sorts of people, cafés, and cyclists," said councilmember Mary M. Cheh of Washington, D.C. "It's an opportunity to stop doing things in the old polluting and unhealthful ways."[20]

The Light at the End of the Tunnel for Dark Stores

Creative retailers are also playing a part in changing the face of cities by repurposing assets in response to changes wrought by the pandemic. In many cases, adapting assets to other uses is part of the shift toward omnichannel retailing (*see* Chapter 22, p. 198).

For example, Walmart reopened a shuttered Sam's Club in North Carolina and even doubled the number of employees there. However, no customers are coming through the doors, because the facility is now an e-commerce fulfillment center (also known as a "dark store" because it is not open to customers).[21] Similarly, shoe retailer DSW started shipping orders out of its closed shoe stores. "We essentially turned them into 'mini-warehouses' to fulfill our increased digital demand," said Bill Jordan, chief growth officer of the chain's parent company, Designer Brands.[22] With the growth of e-commerce and the expectation of fast delivery comes the need for more fulfillment centers spread out all around the country, close to customers.

Grocers across the country have decided to repurpose their brick-and-mortar stores. Kroger, Stop & Shop, Whole Foods, and other grocers have temporarily closed some of their retail outlets to shoppers and dedicated them to their delivery services.[23] (These repurposed stores are often stores that had been set to close, have not yet opened, or are located where the company has another store nearby.) Such stores then act as "forward fulfillment centers" where online order picking activities are not commingled with shoppers. This makes the stores less crowded, enabling order pickers to be more efficient and accurate in order fulfillment. It also allows for better stock control.

Logistics startups, such as Ohi, are also capitalizing on vacant urban real estate. For example, Ohi converted a former office in New York City's Garment District into a micro-warehouse for e-commerce fulfillment.[24] The startup offers micro-warehouse services and software that enable brands and retailers to be closer to their customers. As offices and retail outlets go dark, e-commerce fulfillment activities may fill many of these spaces.

24. And the Winner Is...The Big Unknown

The pandemic came with many quirky shifts in winning and losing products. "We're seeing increased sales in tops, but not bottoms," said Dan Bartlett, Walmart's executive vice president of corporate affairs.[1] Although chocolate sales were up, Hershey saw declines of 40–50 percent of its gum and mint products.[2] Unilever's sales of hand and home hygiene products (as well as ice cream) increased, while sales of deodorant and hair and skin care products declined.[3] Working from home but meeting on videoconferencing systems meant that only people's tops were visible, and any bad breath or body odor was not detectable. "These behaviors are going to continue to change and evolve as people get accustomed to this new lifestyle," said Bartlett.

Some Big Financial Forks in the Road

The growing wealth gap (*see* Chapter 13, p. 112) and disparate pandemic experiences between well-paid professionals working from home and unemployed service workers sitting at home affects which products and retailers will make it through the pandemic. Products at the high end and the low end are likely to sell well, while those in the middle might languish. Stores that cater to lower-income households will likely do well, because growing numbers of unemployed and financially insecure people will trade down to cheaper brands bought from discount-oriented retailers.

Walmart fared well in the 2008 recession and has done well so far in 2020. Dollar stores have done even better. While Walmart had a 10 percent annual gain in sales in the first quarter, Dollar General raked in a 21.7 percent gain. Dollar General's CEO, Todd Vasos, said, "We do very good in good times and we do fabulous in bad times." Similarly, Mike Witynski, enterprise president at Dollar Tree, which also owns Family Dollar, told analysts, "When people are unemployed and they don't have that source of income, they will need value more than ever."[4]

The effects on the high-end side are more complicated. As of June 10, 2020, high-income households had reduced spending by 17 percent, whereas low-income households only reduced their spending by 4 percent. Unlike prior recessions, which saw large declines in durable goods spending and relatively unchanged spending on services, the Covid-19 recession saw a large reduction in spending on services.[5]

Covid-19 crushed spending on restaurants, entertainment, travel, hair salons, spas, spectator sports, and all the other services that depend on in-person experiences—all of which are activities enjoyed by high-income households. The virus also decimated sales of luxury-brand products. Consummate French luxury conglomerate LVMH Moët Hennessy Louis Vuitton saw revenues slump by 28 percent in the first half of 2020.[6] With travel, weddings, parties, and social gatherings all curtailed, the wealthy had little reason to buy LVHM's high fashion products—if you can't flaunt it, why buy it?

Instead, the US savings rate surged from an average of less than 8 percent in 2019 to 33 percent in April 2020 (nearly double the previous record set in 1975).[7] As of mid-2020, high-income households are sitting on a growing pile of cash. Whether, when, and how they might spend that money in the future remains unknown. Given how much high-end retail sales are linked to travel and social events, spending at the high end will be especially sensitive to consumers' perceptions of personal health and safety (*see* Chapter 10, p. 83). Accentuating that sensitivity is the concentration of wealth, savings, and spending in the generation of people who are near to retirement age. This older cohort is especially susceptible to serious illness or death from Covid-19.

The Search for Simplicity

Chapter 8 (p. 68) described how companies were cutting down on the number of items they sell due to the need to assure supply. As companies are gearing up for a possibly long time of continuously changing "new normal," they continue to cut down on the variety of products they offer. For example, McDonald's has limited its menu in order to simplify its operations. "We are working on making our business simpler," said Dirk Van de Put, chairman and CEO of snacking company Mondelez, in late April.[8] IGA CEO John Ross added, "We may not need 40 different choices of toilet paper."[9] Mondelez, Coca-Cola, General Mills, and Proctor & Gamble all reduced the number of their SKUs to reduce downtime in switchovers, enable longer production runs of popular products, and thus maximize production of the most popular products in the face of consumer hoarding.

"There's potential for this to result in a cutting of the long tail of inefficient SKUs and brands in our categories," said Jon Moeller, Procter & Gamble's COO and CFO.[10] Nielsen data in mid-June showed a 7.3 percent overall decline in grocery store SKUs, with declines as high as 30 percent in some categories, such as baby care, bakery, and meat.[11] Thus, while during the pandemic panic, the SKU reductions were driven by the need to increase supply, as the world has been adjusting to pandemic conditions, the SKU reductions have been driven by the need to cut costs amid the economic devastation to consumer spending.

Mondelez is planning to remove a quarter of its SKUs to focus on the most important brands, according to Van de Put. "We are using this opportunity to significantly reduce the number of SKUs... we are [also] reducing significantly our innovation projects," he said in a Q1 2020 earnings call.[12] The move will simplify the company's supply chain operations and reduce costs as well as inventories. The dropped SKUs represent only 2 percent of the company's revenues but a much larger percent of the cost, creating a drag on the financial performance of the company. The culling of the offerings also leads to higher customer service, mainly in terms of on-shelf availability of the remaining SKUs and "cleaner-looking" shelves, according to Van de Put.[13]

SKU simplification isn't new; it happens during every recession and in every financially stressed company. (Mattel began such efforts in the aftermath of the closure of Toys R Us.) When times are good, it's easy for companies to keep making and selling minor product variants with marginal financial returns just to maximize market share, retain loyal customers, and hold onto retail shelf space. Then a crisis or recession prompts a culling of the low-volume and low-margin products. Once the economy or company recovers, however, the firm inevitably starts funding innovation, introducing new products, and increasing the number of SKUs again. Some refer to this phenomenon as "accordion retailing": introducing a breadth of products in good times and then narrowing it when times are tough, only to broaden it again when the business cycle turns.[14]

Many of the technologies being adopted faster as a result of Covid-19 enable both greater rates of product innovation and more flexibility in manufacturing. For example, virtual product development and cloud-based design platforms make it easier to come up with new products. Additive manufacturing can quickly produce prototypes, low-volume test-market quantities, and support highly flexible manufacturing systems. Robotics and automation can be programmed to handle innumerable SKUs. IoT-driven visibility into consumer product usage enables better forecasting of local demand of niche quantities. Thus, once the crisis is over, some companies will be looking to add SKUs to meet new needs and wrest market share from companies that are relying on a curtailed set of aging SKUs.

There's No Place Like Home

Home improvement retailers such as Lowe's actually beat bellwether retailer Walmart in terms of sales growth in the first quarter of 2020.[15] Government stay-at-home edicts, employers' work-from-home policies, homeschooling, and staycations fostered an upgrade-the-home movement. Moreover, with a recession going on and a reluctance to let strangers into the house, homeowners turned to do-it-yourself efforts to make being home more enjoyable or, at least, more tolerable.

Almost every room in the house got upgrades: bigger TVs in the den,[16] bread makers in the kitchen,[17] new mattresses in the bedroom,[18] bidets in the bathroom,[19] new desks in the home office, fitness equipment in the basement, and backyards filled with gardens, trampolines, and inflatable pools. With the long-term trends toward working from home and people moving from cramped cities to more spacious abodes, sales of durable goods for the home and yard are likely to continue even after the virus abates.

The closure (or avoidance) of restaurants especially impacted home kitchens. Fragrant herb gardens bloomed and smelly jars of sourdough starter began to appear as people ate more meals at home. (Home cooking also boomed during the 2008 recession.) Meal kit delivery companies, such as HelloFresh and Blue Apron, saw a surge in customers along with competition from restaurants that were also preparing kits. Blue Apron CEO Linda Findley Kozlowski said, "Even as restrictions on consumer behavior begin to ease, we expect that there will be a shift to new economic and social norms, reflecting the changes in cooking and eating habits developed during the weeks or months consumers spend at home, and these will persist for some time."[20] These sales trends illuminate business opportunities amid the doom and gloom of panic-stoking media reports.

What this means for future sales is hard to predict. Take exercise equipment sales. They boomed under the effects of gym closures and people's desperate need to burn off stress without leaving the house. As mentioned in Chapter 8 (p. 68), sales of fitness equipment typically peak during the holidays, but how these products will sell at the end of 2020 is anyone's guess (as of this writing). Although it's unlikely that people who bought a treadmill in March will buy another one in December, they might buy other equipment, or perhaps households that could not afford such equipment in March will be especially inclined to buy fitness equipment as holiday gifts. Similar buying patterns may emerge with bread makers, big TVs, and the other durable goods that boomed early in the pandemic.

The upshot is that companies need to be ready for anything, whether it's another surge of toilet paper hoarding or a second Roaring '20s boom of hedonistic excess.

25. Flexibility for the Future

A famous quote attributed (erroneously) to Charles Darwin says, "It is not the strongest of the species that survives, nor the most intelligent that survives. It is the one that is most adaptable to change." During the onset of the Covid-19 pandemic, some companies that were quick to adapt and change did well. In doing so, these businesses found another kind of resilience: Instead of simply bouncing back to the original "normal" as quickly as possible, they were flexible; they bounced forward to create something new to supplement or replace what had been disrupted. Other companies employed or created flexible business systems that enabled them to change what they made or how they operated.

Go Direct to Consumer: Farms and Wholesalers

J.W. Lopes is small New England fresh produce distributor serving restaurant chefs, institutional directors, neighborhood grocers, and even prison cooks. It is a family-owned and operated business run by Jeff Kotzen and his father Peter. Elyssa, Jeff's wife, joined the business in March 2020. In an interview for this book, Jeff shared, "My great grandfather, a first-generation immigrant from Russia, came to the US and started as a fruit peddler in Faneuil Hall. He worked his way up, ended up taking over the business he was working at."[1] The business went through ups and downs and in 2016, Jeff and his father went into this new, local wholesale business, J.W. Lopes. That was the year Jeff and Elyssa met each other.

At the end of January 2020, Jeff was meeting with his accountant and feeling bullish about the business. He had just built a processing center that could make 1,000 pounds of broccoli florets, among other pre-cut produce—a value added service that his wholesale customers were asking for due to labor shortages. Jeff was glad to fill the need and grow the business.

Then the virus hit. The governor of Massachusetts ordered people to stay at home, and 75 percent of the company's customers closed down. Big customers who had been ordering $30,000–$40,000 per week dropped to $200 a week. Some restaurants tried to stay open, but takeout service did not come close to offsetting the lost dine-in volumes. J.W. Lopes had to lay off most of its staff, including people who had worked with his family for decades.

Elyssa joined her husband and became a J.W. Lopes employee while continuing to work at her job at a Boston-based international health NGO that focused on sub-Saharan Africa (and supporting her children's remote learning). Jeff continued, "And Elyssa had this idea of selling produce direct to consumers, which we started doing. It was a pretty simple concept. A $74.95 produce box—taking advantage of our logistics network, because we have about 20 trucks and we have 20 drivers. So, we had the logistics in place to kind of take advantage of that." Elyssa and Jeff relied on word of mouth, social media posts, and email blasts aimed at people looking for high-quality fresh, locally grown produce. "It's almost like you're going to a farmer's market on our website, but we can bring the products directly to your door," Jeff said.

Then, a local distributor suggested they also sell fish to customers. "We had such positive feedback on the fish as an addition to our produce that we started growing one week at a time by reaching out to local companies: bakeries, butchers, dairy farms, the list goes on," Jeff said. J.W. Lopes added some of those companies' items to their home delivery offerings.[2] As their product line grew, it was important to differentiate the direct-to-consumer service from the wholesale business, so, the new service was called New England Country Mart. As they added more local suppliers, direct-to-consumer sales blossomed, and the company rehired all the employees it had laid off and even added more staff.

Along the way, the Kotzens needed to develop new capabilities to provide service to consumers, such as an upgraded e-commerce website, building a social media following, routing technology, inventory management, barcoding, and so forth. "Almost every day, either we figure something out and we identify a new process, a new Google doc, and a new method of communication between all of us—some of whom are working from home," said Elyssa. Jeff added, "Our stack of technology and the packaging that we use are getting better and better." The company also rented smaller refrigerated delivery trucks, because the bigger wholesale delivery trucks had a hard time in smaller neighborhood streets.

Jeff highlighted their competitive advantage relative to large supermarkets: "Wegmans has a big distribution center in upstate New York, right? Around Rochester. So, the farms are shipping produce to Rochester. Going into

Rochester, all the produce is getting handled again, separated to go to various stores. Goes on another truck, gets to the store. The produce manager's going to start breaking it down, putting the produce on the stands. Now you have consumers going and touching the produce—what they want, what they don't want. And then your Instacart driver comes by and picks whatever they want. So really, your product has been touched five, six times."

"I don't think we initially thought that this would be a long-term business idea," Jeff continued. The success of the new business changed that. "We're kind of all-in on this direct-to-consumer model right now." As restaurants and institutions slowly reopen, the Kotzens are running two teams of people. "We're going to build both businesses, work hard, and see where it takes us," Jeff concluded.[3]

Other companies, especially in the food industry, did a similar pivot from wholesale to direct-to-consumer sales. For some produce farmers, Covid-19 and the direct-to-consumer model has been a boost to business. "We had a reporter call here and say, 'We want to see some produce rotting in the field and milk going down the drains,'" said Judith Redmond, a longtime farmer in California's Capay Valley, northwest of Sacramento. "And I said, 'Well, actually, that's not what's happening in the Capay Valley.'"[4] Farmers there were using community-supported agriculture (CSA) programs, in which consumers subscribe directly to a local farm and get boxes of in-season produce direct from that farm, either delivered or for pickup. Covid-19 brought a boom in new subscribers looking for a shorter food supply chain, which means that fewer people touch the produce and the consumer gets fresher produce sooner.

Recently available technologies and platforms play a key role in enabling this flexible shift from wholesale to direct-to-consumer for companies of all sizes (but especially the smaller ones). For example, Joseph Boo helped his dad convert a wholesale Asian vegetable business to direct-to-consumer.[5] Boo built the website with Shopify, shot product photos with his iPhone, marketed the business on Instagram and Facebook, hired help using Upwork, and arranged delivery logistics through Onfleet. Until the advent of mobile phones, apps, cloud services, and digital platforms, such a shift would have been virtually impossible for a small business.

From Emergency to Opportunity

In 1906, a British immigrant to the US, William Riley, founded the New Balance Arch Support Company in Boston to make inserts that improved the comfort and fit of any shoe. Many of his early customers were first responders such as police and firefighters who had to stand on their feet for long periods of time. Over the years, the company expanded into related product lines. Thirty years later, the company started making shoes, and in 1978, it released its first sports apparel products.

When Covid-19 hit, "We got calls from MGH [Massachusetts General Hospital], Partners HealthCare down here in Boston, as well as the state; they really needed PPE," said Dave Wheeler, COO of New Balance, who described the company's response to the pandemic in an interview for this book. "We put our heads together over one weekend and looked at what equipment we have, what kind of skills we have, what kind of raw material supply domestically we have." The company quickly pivoted to making protective masks.

"We designed a mask that was unique to New Balance. It has a little bit of a New Balance look to it." Wheeler added, "It's put together with no-sew fabric, which is what we use on our 1540 shoe. You can see this no-sew holds the shoe together in certain parts. And then similar fabric, and we inserted some foam filtration. We worked with the MIT folks to help us understand filtration requirements. We started on a Friday, brainstormed over the weekend, created a 3D image, and then had a physical prototype on Monday. By Friday, we were in production."

Without much fanfare, on March 30, 2020, the company tweeted, "Made shoes yesterday. Making masks today," along with a photo of the sturdy-look-ing face mask with elastic curly-shoelace straps. "The ad became the biggest social media hit in New Balance's history just with those two lines," Wheeler said, "because the company did something in the moment, took action for taking care of people—the greater good," by answering the call for help from the medical community. He added, "There were also a ton of comments about the look. Like, 'I want to buy one of those.' 'That's the coolest thing ever.' 'That's definitely New Balance.' And so, even though we didn't have the design guys design it, the supply chain guys did pretty well, I think."[6]

Figure 25.1: New Balance advertisement

Whereas many companies temporarily repurposed their manufacturing assets and supply chains to make PPE and ventilators just for the pandemic response, New Balance took the foray into mask-making further. They turned this emergency humanitarian effort into a new product line. Although the company had not been in the mask business before, they began to consider a longer-term strategy for creating masks for runners and other related products that tie into the core brand. In June, after having made 1 million masks for healthcare workers, New Balance launched a redesigned NB Face Mask V3 for the public, and announced future plans for "athletics-ready" face masks.[7]

This example also illustrates that while supply chains often span long distances and involve collaboration around the globe, sometimes proximity is the key to agility. In an era where digital tools can enable ever more people to work remotely from anywhere in the world, some tasks may work better with physical presence. Half of New Balance's mask team did their work in the local factory, because that's where the raw materials and equipment were. Relationships with nearby MIT allowed for quick understanding of filtration requirements. New Balance also tapped longtime local suppliers to get quick shipments of needed materials despite the shutdown. Similarly, the mask team could get rapid feedback on the fit and functionality of its masks because the lead user (Massachusetts General Hospital) was only a half-hour down the highway. Finally, with local production in Massachusetts, masks could be quickly distributed to local hospitals, first responders, and others.

Multiplying Capacity with Additive Manufacturing

Additive manufacturing, also known as 3D printing, shined during the pandemic. Firms and individuals used additive manufacturing to make face shields, face masks, nasal swabs, ventilator parts, and more. "We're collectively doing all we can to activate our 3D printing technology, expertise, ecosystem, and production capacity to help front-line medical personnel in the battle against Covid-19," said Christoph Schell, chief commercial officer of HP.[8] Not only was 3D printing used in response to Covid-19, but it was used in a distributed way to recruit designers and source available capacity over the internet.

For example, the US Food and Drug Administration (FDA), Department of Veterans Affairs (VA), National Institutes of Health (NIH), and America Makes formed a public-private partnership for Covid-19 response.[9] The partnership solicited needs from the healthcare community, approved product designs among stakeholders, and coordinated 3D manufacturing among 3D printer owners. The NIH managed the designs, the VA tested designs for safety and efficacy, and the FDA wrote Emergency Use Authorizations for effective designs that were then printed and shipped by participating printer owners. As of mid-June 2020, the partnership had made nearly half a million pieces of PPE.[10]

Overall, additive manufacturing is the most flexible manufacturing technology. Within the physical limits of the printing materials and printer size, a given 3D printer can potentially make almost anything for any product in any industry. With digital designs transmitted instantaneously across the internet, anyone with a compatible printer anywhere can contribute capacity. Although each printer may be glacially slow (compared to specialized, automated, mass production systems), a large number of pooled printers (often called "printer farms") can multiply the production capacity. Moreover, compared to specialized mass production systems, the setup time to make a new kind of part is negligible for additive manufacturing. "3D printing and digital manufacturing help bridge supply chain gaps, accelerate design-to-production, and enable localized manufacturing of critical parts when and where they're needed," said HP's Schell.[11]

Flexible Warehousing and Fulfillment Anywhere

The need for more warehousing and fulfillment is not just a matter of building more and bigger warehouses. Two key supply chain trends are shaping the demand for these resources vital to the future of retail.

The first is the volatile and dynamic nature of commerce (especially e-commerce) caused by seasonal demand, promotional demand, product launches, company growth, and, of course, disruptions. The second trend is the increasing demand for faster delivery times, which requires the deployment of inventory close to the many population centers of the world. The result is that more companies will need flexibility, juggling many spaces in warehouses and related services that vary in size over months and years to come.

These growing dynamics of demand for warehousing flexibility in terms of locations and capacities, especially for e-commerce, do not match the supply of warehousing that is typically offered via long-term commitments to large facilities. Moreover, both large companies and hopeful startup firms that do sign multi-year leases for large warehouses often have underutilized space in these cavernous buildings while they build up the demand or use the space only for seasonal products.

That's where technology platform companies such as Flexe come in. Flexe provides a platform that matches short-term demand for storage with the supply of surplus warehouse space—an Airbnb for warehousing. Its customers include both warehouse owners who have extra space and companies looking for storage space. Flexe installs its proprietary warehouse management system in the warehouses that have space available for a short-term lease, so it can onboard new customers looking for space in the region of their choice very quickly. The system uses cloud-based software for warehousing, fulfillment, and logistics services. While not owning any physical buildings, Flexe can offer additional room to any customer who needs warehouse space in any one of more than 1,000 facilities anywhere in the US.

One of Flexe's fast-growing startup customers sells large, bulky objects and had to change distribution and fulfillment constantly as the company grew. They started small in a single East Coast warehouse, expanded to a few warehouses nationwide to offer two-day delivery, expanded more to provide one-day delivery, changed distribution when they inked a deal with a major retailer, and reconfigured again when they added a return center. For this startup, said Flexe co-founder and CEO Karl Siebrecht, "Flexe is like this big switchboard, and over the course of over four years, they have probably reconfigured their network over 50 times to account for their growth, the growth in their SKU mix, their different channel initiatives, you name it."[12]

"It turns out that in times of great disruption and uncertainty, flexibility is really valuable," Siebrecht continued. Companies used Flexe to handle the pandemic-related boost in e-commerce and to offload slow-moving merchandise (e.g., apparel) to free up space for in-demand products like food and home-related products. Even before Covid-19, companies used Flexe to manage disruptions such as hurricanes and winter storms, as well as to manage both growth (looking for extra space) and contraction (renting out unused space).

26. Adversity and Strength Will Build the Future

The crucible of a crisis can help make people and companies more resilient. During a significant crisis, successful companies adapt quickly and learn to operate in the "fog of war." In the face of significant uncertainty, unclear signals from the market, and pressure from customers and suppliers, companies become more alert and agile. If prediction is impossible, deft reaction is essential. Agile reactions enable companies with ample financial resources to invest in the future when prices for assets and supplies are at their lowest.

Doing Business in Argentina

Many developing countries have chaotic and uncertain business environments. For example, businesses in Argentina face rampant corruption, seemingly arbitrary regulations that appear without warning, runaway inflation, and financial crises (including currency devaluations, which are common and frequent). Businesspeople have little choice but to live through the chaos, changing regulations, lack of modern financial systems, and an undeveloped business credit infrastructure. Interest rates for small business loans run up to 45 percent. Through it all, however, entrepreneurs start companies and build them in an environment in which a North American or European entrepreneur would not even try. (The Spanish-language publisher of my last three books is an Argentinian family-owned company, and I could see how the chaos of their home country has helped them manage the chaos in the book publishing industry in the digital age.)

The persistence and ingenuity of Argentinian businesspeople makes them, in many ways, more resilient in times of crisis compared to their counterparts in more stable commercial environments. First, because crises are nothing new, and second, because they are always preparing for crises of all kinds, they build in flexibility that serves them well. Naturally, this business resilience is not unique to Argentina; it exists in many developing countries.

Boeing Lives to Fly Again

The year 2019 was one of the best for Airbus and the worst ever for Boeing. While Airbus delivered an all-time record 863 aircraft for the year, Boeing delivered only 380 aircraft (out of an original target of 810–815). A design defect in Boeing's popular 737 MAX aircraft (which was the cause of two crashes killing 346 people), forced the grounding of that model and led many airlines to cancel orders.[1] Then, the pandemic all but grounded air travel, put Boeing's customers in a financial tailspin, and created zero visibility on the future of airlines' purchasing plans.

Boeing may be down, but it can't be counted out. In fact, the experience may strengthen the company. Pain is an excellent (if unpleasant) teacher, and Boeing has had a tough year enrolled in the school of hard knocks. As such, it will likely graduate with a set of deeply engrained "lessons learned" from the fiasco.

In the long term, the crisis may create a nimbler and more competitive Boeing. More broadly, the adversity being foisted on the world's companies and citizens is forcing them out of their comfortable patterns of existence. The result may be that some will find ways to thrive in the new environment. Companies undergoing Chapter 11 bankruptcy can reorganize and move forward into the future, as did General Motors after the 2008 financial crisis or Delta Air Lines after its 2005–07 bankruptcy. GM made a record $9.7 billion in net income in 2014, while Delta hit a record revenue of $47 billion in 2019.

The Strong Respond with Strength

"If you're a shareowner in Amazon, you may want to take a seat, because we're not thinking small," said Jeff Bezos, CEO of Amazon, in a late April 2020 press release. Bezos explained, "Under normal circumstances, in this coming Q2, we'd expect to make some $4 billion or more in operating profit. But these aren't normal circumstances. Instead, we expect to spend the entirety of that $4 billion, and perhaps a bit more, on Covid-related expenses getting products to customers and keeping employees safe."[2]

On the personnel side, the company added 159,600 employees in the second quarter of 2020, bringing its total head count to 1 million.[3] On the physical asset side, Amazon was planning to add 306 more distribution facilities in the following couple of years to its 1,248 existing DCs.[4] To bolster its transportation capabilities, the company added 12 widebody Boeing 767 cargo aircraft in June 2020 to boost its total fleet to more than 80.[5] The growing number of aircraft parallels a growing number of Amazon air hubs in California, Kentucky, Texas, Florida, and Puerto Rico.

Texas Instruments learned from the 2008 financial crisis to not overreact to bullwhip gyrations created by disruptions. During the company's Q1 2020 earnings call, CEO Richard K. Templeton recalled how, in 2008, "Our customers overcorrected for the downside, and we then spent one-and-a-half years chasing backup to support demand." For this crisis, the company chose not to try to predict the recession or recovery. "Instead," Templeton said, "we want to ensure that we have the highest degree of optionality so that we can deal successfully with any outcome."[6] In the subsequent quarter, the company reported being pleased with that decision, because it enabled them to serve unforecasted demand caused by a surge in personal electronics sales associated with the work-from-home trend.

Procter & Gamble is another large company making the most of the situation going into the future. "This shift to e-commerce, which we've seen during the crisis big-time in China [and] big-time in the US.... is a great set up for the future," said the company's CFO, Jon Moeller. The company makes many of the cleaning and personal care products sought by consumers, but it also faces competition from other branded and generic suppliers. "We have to stay on our toes and we have to execute every day—we have to have superior offerings at superior values—but there's nothing I see in the ecosystem as it's either evolving or being revolutionized that we can't take advantage of," Moeller said.[7]

Making the Most of the Worst

"Overall, I think during a period like this, there are a lot of new things that need to get built," said Mark Zuckerberg, CEO of Facebook. In his call to action, Zuckerberg stressed that "it's important that, rather than slamming on the brakes now, as I think a lot of companies may, that it's important to keep on building and keep on investing and building for the new needs that people have, and especially to make up for some of the stuff that other companies would pull back on." And Zuckerberg concluded, "In some ways that's an opportunity, in other ways, I think it's a responsibility to keep on investing in the economic recovery."[8]

An example of doing exactly this is Chipotle. The company is debt-free and has almost $1 billion in cash. It is continuing to expand, building new restaurants and remodeling old ones to improve service for digital orders (including its Chipotlanes BOPIS-like drive-through service described in Chapter 22, p. 198).[9] It is enjoying less competition for new building sites and is planning to take over other companies' shuttered retail locations once the immediate coronavirus crisis has passed.[10]

Many companies now realize that their most important assets leave the office every day (and don't even return to the office in the morning now that they are working from home). That has some companies (those who aren't in the maelstrom of pandemic-induced demand) looking at how to upskill their workforce or tackle useful projects that were hard to perform during times of normal business volumes.

Similarly, dozens of forward-thinking governments crafted economic mitigation programs that supported companies to maintain employment rather than merely support jobless workers during unemployment. Rather than have a company lay off workers in the downturn, these governments subsidized retention of employees by employers. Retaining and enhancing a company's human portfolio will allow it to emerge faster from the pandemic-induced recession.[11]

Finally, as the pandemic amply demonstrates, a crisis is a terrible thing to waste. It provides an opportunity for tough business decisions, such as reorganization or cutting underperforming products, retail outlets, or customers. The crisis can be used to overcome resistance to change, because the crisis itself has disrupted the status quo and created a burning platform that demands the organization make changes. Some of these restructuring activities are likely to take place under bankruptcy protection, yet others are taken by companies to shore up their finances. In any case, some companies are doing more than just riding out the storm: They are actively working to make the most of the post-pandemic environment, with its many changes in how people work, shop, and live.

Building a Stronger, More Flexible Web of Connections

The economic effects of Covid-19 surprised many people, managers, and politicians by revealing everyone's dependence on a previously hidden web of complex interconnections inherent in the global economy. That a virus in China could halt car production or affect supplies of PPE in the US shocked many Americans. Numerous members of the media, as well as politicians, reacted to this news with a cry for self-reliance, to disconnect from what they saw as foreign unknowns and foreign risks.

As seductive as self-reliance seems, it is an all-eggs-in-one-basket strategy. Relying entirely on domestic production to serve domestic consumption fails if production is closed by a pandemic (or other disruption), or if consumers' wallets are closed by a recession. In a world in which resurgent disease and political whims can make any country an unreliable supplier or a fickle customer, companies must diversify their suppliers and their customers. That means striving for more (and better) connections, not fewer.

Many of the trends accelerated by Covid-19 are rooted in improvements in connectivity and its utilization. IoT connects people to data about distant things. Cloud computing connects people and companies to data storage, applications, and computing power. Mobile devices, video teleconferencing, and collaboration apps connect people to people anywhere at any time. Supply chain visibility and transparency connect companies to other companies around the globe. E-commerce and omnichannel retail connect consumers to distant and local retailers. Technological platforms enable people and companies to easily access needed resources or services as well as offer their resources to others.

Thus, the true lesson from Covid-19 is in the emerging opportunities for companies to *grow and improve* connections. These connections give companies a deeper understanding of their suppliers (and suppliers of suppliers) and customers. The connections enable visibility, remote management, working from home, buying from anywhere, and selling to anywhere. And fast, better connections foster the flexibility and agility companies need to deal with disrupted supply, disrupted demand, and hoarding, and to capture long-term, global opportunities. Although Covid-19 may have exposed the fragile links lurking in the global economy, it also accelerated the adoption of a great many technologies and practices that will make the global economy more robust over time.

REFERENCES

Part 1: What Happened

1. Justin Davidson, "The Leader of the Free World Gives a Speech, and She Nails It," *Intelligencer* (blog), *New York Magazine,* March 18, 2020, https://nymag.com/intelligencer/2020/03/angela-merkel-nails-coronavirus-speech-unlike-trump.html.

Chapter 1: The Virus Goes Viral

1. Suzanne Nossel, "Coronavirus Lies by China, Trump Administration a Risk for Public Health," *Foreign Policy,* March 9, 2020, https://foreignpolicy.com/2020/03/09/truth-coronavirus-china-trump-pence.

2. Chris Buckley, "Chinese Doctor, Silenced After Warning of Outbreak, Dies From Coronavirus," *New York Times,* February 6, 2020, https://www.nytimes.com/2020/02/06/world/asia/chinese-doctor-Li-Wenliang-coronavirus.html.

3. Radio Free Europe/Radio Liberty, "Iran Says 3,600 Arrested For Spreading Coronavirus-Related Rumors," RadioFreeEurope/RadioLiberty, April 29, 2020, https://www.rferl.org/a/iran-says-3600-arrested-for-spreading-coronavirus-related-rumors/30583656.html.

4. Radio Free Europe/Radio Liberty.

5. Donald Trump, "Remarks by President Trump in Meeting with African American Leaders" (The White House, February 27, 2020), https://www.whitehouse.gov/briefings-statements/remarks-president-trump-meeting-african-american-leaders.

6. Matt Apuzzo, Selam Gebrekidan, and David D. Kirkpatrick, "How the World Missed Covid-19's Silent Spread," *New York Times,* June 27, 2020, https://www.nytimes.com/2020/06/27/world/europe/coronavirus-spread-asymptomatic.html.

7. Camilla Rothe et al., "Transmission of 2019-NCoV Infection from an Asymptomatic Contact in Germany," *New England Journal of Medicine* 382, no. 10 (March 5, 2020): 970–971, https://doi.org/10.1056/NEJMc2001468.

8. Tangi Salaun, "Special Report: Five Days of Worship That Set a Virus Time Bomb in France," *Reuters,* March 30, 2020, https://www.reuters.com/article/us-health-coronavirus-france-church-spec-idUSKBN21H0Q2.

9. Smriti Mallapaty, "What the Cruise-Ship Outbreaks Reveal about COVID-19," *Nature* 580, no. 7801 (March 26, 2020): 18, https://doi.org/10.1038/d41586-020-00885-w.

10. Idrrees Ali and Phil Stewart, "Exclusive: In Navy Study, 60 Percent of Carrier Volunteers Have Coronavirus Antibodies," *Reuters,* June 9, 2020, https://www.reuters.com/article/us-health-coronavirus-usa-navy-exclusive-idUSKBN23F29Z.

11. "Coronavirus Disease (COVID-19) Situation Report 73," Coronavirus Disease (COVID-19) Situation Reports (Geneva: World Health Organization, April 2, 2020), https://www.who.int/docs/default-source/coronaviruse/situation-reports/20200402-sitrep-73-covid-19.pdf?sfvrsn=5ae25bc7_6.

12. Apuzzo, Gebrekidan, and Kirkpatrick, "How the World Missed Covid-19's Silent Spread."

13. Kai Kupferschmidt, "Study Claiming New Coronavirus Can Be Transmitted by People without Symptoms Was Flawed," *Science,* February 3, 2020, https://www.sciencemag.org/news/2020/02/paper-non-symptomatic-patient-transmitting-coronavirus-wrong.

14. Robert Dillard, "The COVID-19 Pandemic: Fauci Calls Out WHO on Asymptomatic Carriers Comment; Global Economy Suffering Worst Peacetime Recession in a Century; and More" *DocWire News,* June 10, 2020, https://www.docwirenews.com/home-page-editor-picks/the-covid-19-pandemic-fauci-calls-out-who-on-asymptomatic-comment-global-economy-suffering-worst-peacetime-recession-in-a-century-and-more.

15. Apuzzo, Gebrekidan, and Kirkpatrick, "How the World Missed Covid-19's Silent Spread."

16. "Update: King County COVID-19 Case Numbers for March 6, 2020," Government, King County Public Health News and Blog, March 6, 2020, https://www.kingcounty.gov/depts/health/news/2020/March/6-covid-19-case-updates.aspx.

17. Laura Geggel, "How a Superspreader at Choir Practice Sickened 52
     People with COVID-19" LiveScience, May 14, 2020, https://www.
     livescience.com/covid-19-superspreader-singing.html.

18. Richard Read, "A Choir Decided to Go Ahead with Rehearsal. Now
     Dozens of Members Have COVID-19 and Two Are Dead," *Los Angeles
     Times*, March 30, 2020, https://www.latimes.com/world-nation/
     story/2020-03-29/coronavirus-choir-outbreak.

19. Nicole Brown, "What Is a Coronavirus 'Super-Spreading' Event?," *CBS
     News*, May 15, 2020, https://www.cbsnews.com/news/super-spreader-
     coronavirus.

20. Lea Hamner et al., "High SARS-CoV-2 Attack Rate Following Exposure at
     a Choir Practice — Skagit County, Washington, March 2020," Morbidity
     and Mortality Weekly Report (Atlanta: Centers for Disease Control and
     Prevention, May 15, 2020), https://www.cdc.gov/mmwr/volumes/69/wr/
     mm6919e6.htm.

21. Neel Patel, "What's a Coronavirus Superspreader?," *MIT
     Technology Review*, June 15, 2020, https://www.technologyreview.
     com/2020/06/15/1003576/whats-a-coronavirus-superspreader.

22. Farah Stockman and Kim Barker, "How a Premier U.S. Drug Company
     Became a Virus 'Super Spreader,'" *New York Times*, April 12, 2020,
     https://www.nytimes.com/2020/04/12/us/coronavirus-biogen-boston-
     superspreader.html.

23. Christie Aschwanden, "How 'Superspreading' Events Drive Most
     COVID-19 Spread," *Scientific American*, June 23, 2020, https://www.
     scientificamerican.com/article/how-superspreading-events-drive-most-
     covid-19-spread1.

24. Choe Sang-Hun, "Shadowy Church Is at Center of Coronavirus
     Outbreak in South Korea," *New York Times*, February 21, 2020, https://
     www.nytimes.com/2020/02/21/world/asia/south-korea-coronavirus-
     shincheonji.html.

25. Raphael Rashid, "Being Called a Cult Is One Thing, Being Blamed for
     an Epidemic Is Quite Another," *New York Times*, March 9, 2020, https://
     www.nytimes.com/2020/03/09/opinion/coronavirus-south-korea-church.
     html.

26. Aylin Woodward, "70% of People Infected with the Coronavirus Did Not
     Pass It to Anyone, Preliminary Research Shows. Superspreading Events
     Account for Most Transmission," *Business Insider*, June 4, 2020, https://
     www.businessinsider.com/super-spreader-events-account-for-most-
     coronavirus-transmission-2020-6.

27.   Dillon Adam et al., "Clustering and Superspreading Potential of Severe
      Acute Respiratory Syndrome Coronavirus 2 (SARS-CoV-2) Infections
      in Hong Kong," pre-print available on Research Square, May 22, 2020,
      https://doi.org/10.21203/rs.3.rs-29548/v1.

28.   Aschwanden, "How 'Superspreading' Events Drive Most COVID-19
      Spread."

29.   Arnold Barnett, "Covid-19 Risk Among Airline Passengers: Should the
      Middle Seat Stay Empty?," pre-print available on medRxiv (Public and
      Global Health, July 5, 2020), https://doi.org/10.1101/2020.07.02.20143826.

30.   "World Air Transport Statistics 2019," World Air Transport Statistics
      (Montreal: International Air Transport Association, 2019), https://www.
      iata.org/contentassets/a686ff624550453e8bf0c9b3f7f0ab26/wats-2019-
      mediakit.pdf.

31.   "France's First Coronavirus Case 'Was in December,'" *BBC News*, May 5,
      2020, https://www.bbc.com/news/world-europe-52526554.

32.   Kate Kelland, "Italy Sewage Study Suggests COVID-19 Was There in
      December 2019," *Reuters*, June 19, 2020, https://www.reuters.com/article/
      us-health-coronavirus-italy-sewage-idUSKBN23Q1J9.

33.   Bill Chappell, "1st Known U.S. COVID-19 Death Was Weeks Earlier Than
      Previously Thought," *NPR*, April 22, 2020, https://www.npr.org/sections/
      coronavirus-live-updates/2020/04/22/840836618/1st-known-u-s-covid-19-
      death-was-on-feb-6-a-post-mortem-test-reveals.

34.   Michelle A. Jorden et al., "Evidence for Limited Early Spread of
      COVID-19 Within the United States, January–February 2020," Morbidity
      and Mortality Weekly Report, Morbidity and Mortality Weekly Report
      (Atlanta: Centers for Disease Control and Prevention, June 5, 2020),
      https://www.cdc.gov/mmwr/volumes/69/wr/mm6922e1.htm.

35.   Mark Arsenault et al., "How the Biogen Leadership Conference in Boston
      Spread the Coronavirus," *Boston Globe*, March 10, 2020, https://www.
      bostonglobe.com/2020/03/11/nation/how-biogen-leadership-conference-
      boston-spread-coronavirus.

36.   Jacob Lemieux and Bronwyn MacInnis, "Introduction and Spread of
      SARS-CoV-2 in the Greater Boston Area," *Broadminded* (blog), Broad
      Institute of MIT and Harvard, June 4, 2020, https://www.broadinstitute.
      org/blog/introduction-and-spread-sars-cov-2-greater-boston-area.

37.   "Health Equipment: Hospital Beds," Organisation for Economic Co-
      operation and Development, accessed July 28, 2020, http://data.oecd.org/
      healtheqt/hospital-beds.htm.

38.   Raymond Zhong and Paul Mozur, "To Tame Coronavirus, Mao-Style Social Control Blankets China," *New York Times,* February 15, 2020, https://www.nytimes.com/2020/02/15/business/china-coronavirus-lockdown.html.

39.   David Cyranoski, "What China's Coronavirus Response Can Teach the Rest of the World," *Nature* 579 (2020): 479–480, https://doi.org/10.1038/d41586-020-00741-x.

40.   Raymond Zhong and Vivian Wang, "China Ends Wuhan Lockdown, but Normal Life Is a Distant Dream," *New York Times,* April 7, 2020, https://www.nytimes.com/2020/04/07/world/asia/wuhan-coronavirus.html.

41.   Gwynn Guilford and Sarah Chaney, "Nearly Three Million Sought Jobless Benefits Last Week," *Wall Street Journal,* May 14, 2020, https://www.wsj.com/articles/unemployment-benefits-weekly-jobless-claims-coronavirus-05-14-2020-11589410374.

42.   Federal Reserve Bank of St. Louis, "Unemployment Rate," FRED Economic Data, accessed July 28, 2020, https://fred.stlouisfed.org/series/UNRATE.

43.   "Aptiv PLC (APTV) Q1 2020 Earnings Call Transcript," The Motley Fool, May 5, 2020, https://www.fool.com/earnings/call-transcripts/2020/05/05/aptiv-plc-aptv-q1-2020-earnings-call-transcript.aspx.

44.   Alan Tovey, "Ford Chief: 'There Is No Future,'" *Telegraph* (London), April 29, 2020, https://www.telegraph.co.uk/business/2020/04/29/no-future-says-ford-chief.

45.   Blake Schmidt, "Shortage Rumors Spark Toilet Paper Panic Buying in Hong Kong," *Bloomberg,* February 5, 2020, https://www.bloomberg.com/news/articles/2020-02-05/hong-kong-went-from-face-mask-shortage-to-run-on-toilet-paper.

46.   Farah Master, "Hong Kong Shoppers Snap up Rice and Noodles as Coronavirus Fears Mount," *Reuters,* February 7, 2020, https://www.reuters.com/article/us-china-health-hongkong-supermarkets-idUSKBN2010Q6.

47.   Frances Mao, "Why Are People Stockpiling Toilet Paper?," *BBC News,* March 4, 2020, https://www.bbc.com/news/world-australia-51731422.

48.   Daniel Piotrowski, "Woman Pulls out a Knife during Fight over Toilet Paper," *Daily Mail,* March 4, 2020, https://www.dailymail.co.uk/news/article-8072347/Horror-Woolworths-shopper-pulls-KNIFE-near-toilet-paper-aisle.html.

49.   Corina Knoll, "Panicked Shoppers Empty Shelves as Coronavirus Anxiety Rises," *New York Times*, March 13, 2020, https://www.nytimes.com/2020/03/13/nyregion/coronavirus-panic-buying.html.

50.   Bill Morrissey, "Leveraging Environmental Sustainability for Growth" (Sustainable Brands Conference, Monterey, Calif., June 3, 2008).

51.   Nathaniel Meyersohn, "Egg Prices Are Skyrocketing Because of Coronavirus Panic Shopping," *CNN*, March 25, 2020, https://www.cnn.com/2020/03/25/business/egg-prices-supermarkets-coronavirus/index.html.

52.   Julia Rentsch, "Coronavirus-Fueled Panic Buying Cleared the Shelves of Eggs. What's next for Egg Markets?," *USA Today*, April 6, 2020, https://www.usatoday.com/story/money/2020/04/06/egg-demand-wipes-shelves-clean-raises-prices-covid-19/2954400001.

53.   Janelle Nanos, "Coming to a Grocery Store near You: Meat Shortages," *Boston Globe*, April 29, 2020, https://www.bostonglobe.com/2020/04/29/business/coming-grocery-store-near-you-meat-shortages.

54.   David Yaffe-Bellany and Michael Corkery, "Dumped Milk, Smashed Eggs, Plowed Vegetables: Food Waste of the Pandemic," *New York Times*, April 11, 2020, https://www.nytimes.com/2020/04/11/business/coronavirus-destroying-food.html.

55.   "Food Waste FAQs," U.S. Department of Agriculture, accessed August 15, 2020, https://www.usda.gov/foodwaste/faqs.

56.   "The United States Meat Industry at a Glance," North American Meat Institute, accessed September 21, 2020, https://www.meatinstitute.org/index.php?ht=d/sp/i/47465/pid/47465.

57.   "Poultry & Eggs," Economic Research Service, U.S. Department of Agriculture, August 21, 2019, https://www.ers.usda.gov/topics/animal-products/poultry-eggs.

58.   "The United States Meat Industry at a Glance."

59.   "Turkey Sector: Background & Statistics," Economic Research Service, U.S. Department of Agriculture," November 20, 2019, https://www.ers.usda.gov/newsroom/trending-topics/turkey-sector-background-statistics.

60.   Jen Skerritt and Deena Shanker, "Food Rationing Confronts Shoppers Once Spoiled for Choice," *Bloomberg*, April 21, 2020, https://www.bloomberg.com/news/articles/2020-04-21/food-rationing-is-new-reality-for-buyers-once-spoiled-for-choice.

61. Jenni Styrk, "Top 100 Fastest Growing & Declining Categories in E-Commerce," Stackline, March 31, 2020, https://www.stackline.com/news/top-100-gaining-top-100-declining-e-commerce-categories-march-2020.

62. Hardy Graupner, "Coronavirus Scare: When Will 'hamsterkauf' Become an English Word?," *Deutsche Welle*, May 3, 2020, https://www.dw.com/en/coronavirus-scare-when-will-hamsterkauf-become-an-english-word/a-52635400.

63. "The Great Toilet Paper Scare," editorial, *Wall Street Journal*, March 22, 2020, https://www.wsj.com/articles/the-great-toilet-paper-scare-11584918854.

64. Kelvin Chan, Beatrice Dupuy, and Arijeta Lajka, "Conspiracy Theorists Burn 5G Towers Claiming Link to Virus," *ABC News*, April 21, 2020, https://abcnews.go.com/Health/wireStory/conspiracy-theorists-burn-5g-towers-claiming-link-virus-70258811.

65. Kate Gibson, "Feds Charge Phony Church with Selling Toxic Bleach as COVID-19 Cure," CBS News, July 9, 2020, https://www.cbsnews.com/news/feds-charge-phony-church-with-selling-toxic-bleach-mms-as-covid-19-cure.

Chapter 2: Eruptions of Supply Chain Disruptions

1. Matthew Heller, "Walmart Gets Big Boost From Pandemic Panic," *CFO*, May 19, 2020, https://www.cfo.com/financial-performance/2020/05/walmart-gets-big-boost-from-pandemic-panic.

2. Jenni Styrk, "Top 100 Fastest Growing & Declining Categories in E-Commerce," Stackline, March 31, 2020, https://www.stackline.com/news/top-100-gaining-top-100-declining-e-commerce-categories-march-2020.

3. Melissa Repko and Courtney Reagan, "Walmart Earnings Soar as E-Commerce Sales Jump, Shoppers Flock to Stores," *CNBC*, May 19, 2020, https://www.cnbc.com/2020/05/19/walmart-wmt-earnings-q1-2021.html.

4. "How CEOs See Today's Coronavirus World," *Wall Street Journal*, June 11, 2020, https://www.wsj.com/articles/how-ceos-see-todays-coronavirus-world-11587720600.

5. Norihiko Shirouzu and Yilei Sun, "As One of China's 'Detroits' Reopens, World's Automakers Worry about Disruptions," *Reuters*, March 8, 2020, https://www.reuters.com/article/us-health-coronavirus-autos-parts/as-one-of-chinas-detroits-reopens-worlds-automakers-worry-about-disruptions-idUSKBN20V14J.

6.   Shirouzu and Sun.

7.   Benjamin Franklin, "The Way to Wealth," *Poor Richard's Almanack*, June 1758 (Waterloo, Iowa: U.S.C. Publishing Company, 1914), 22.

8.   Jack Ewing, Neal E. Boudette, and Geneva Abdul, "Virus Exposes Cracks in Carmakers' Chinese Supply Chains," *New York Times*, February 4, 2020, https://www.nytimes.com/2020/02/04/business/hyundai-south-korea-coronavirus.html.

9.   Chris Paukert, "Nissan First to Halt Japanese Plant over Coronavirus Issue," *Roadshow*, February 10, 2020, https://www.cnet.com/roadshow/news/nissan-coronavirus-kyushu-plant-stoppage-parts-shortage.

10.   Heather Ostis, Vice President of Supply Chain, Delta Air Lines, interview by Yossi Sheffi, June 3, 2020.

11.   Mike Duffy, CEO, C&S Wholesales Grocers, interview by Yossi Sheffi, June 4, 2020.

12.   Johanna Mayer, "Where Does the Word 'Quarantine' Come From?," Massive Science, accessed July 29, 2020, https://massivesci.com/articles/quarantine-coronavirus-covid19-etymology-science-friday.

13.   Dave Roos, "Social Distancing and Quarantine Were Used in Medieval Times to Fight the Black Death," HISTORY, March 25, 2020, https://www.history.com/news/quarantine-black-death-medieval.

14.   "Amazon (AMZN) Q1 2020 Earnings Call Transcript," Rev, May 1, 2020, https://www.rev.com/blog/transcripts/amazon-amzn-q1-2020-earnings-call-transcript.

15.   Federal Reserve Bank of St. Louis, "Imports of Goods and Services," FRED Economic Data (FRED, Federal Reserve Bank of St. Louis), accessed July 28, 2020, https://fred.stlouisfed.org/series/IMPGS.

16.   Robert Peels et al., "Responding to the Lehman Wave: Sales Forecasting and Supply Management during the Credit Crisis," working paper, BETA Working Paper Series no. 297 (Eindhoven: Beta Research School for Operations Management and Logistics, December 5, 2009), https://www.researchgate.net/publication/228718119_Responding_to_the_Lehman_wave_sales_forecasting_and_supply_management_during_the_credit_crisis.

17.   Ciara Linnane, "China Government Orders State Banks to Issue More Loans to Small Businesses Hurt by Coronavirus," *MarketWatch*, February 25, 2020, https://www.marketwatch.com/story/china-government-orders-state-banks-to-issue-more-loans-to-small-businesses-hurt-by-coronavirus-2020-02-25.

18.   Jan C. Fransoo and Maximiliano Udenio, "Exiting a COVID-19
      Lockdown: The Bumpy Road Ahead for Many Supply Chains," pre-print
      available at SSRN, May 1, 2020, https://doi.org/10.2139/ssrn.3590153.

Chapter 3: Their Finest Hour

1.   Jenna Tsui, "How the Grocery Industry Is Responding to New
      Consumer Behavior," *Supply Chain Brain*, July 24, 2020, https://www.
      supplychainbrain.com/blogs/1-think-tank/post/31659-how-the-grocery-
      industry-is-responding-to-new-consumer-behavior.

2.   Eric Boehm, "Federal Regulations Are Making the Grocery Store Supply
      Crunch Worse," *Reason*, April 20, 2020, https://reason.com/2020/04/20/
      federal-regulations-are-making-the-grocery-store-supply-crunch-worse.

3.   Jessica Fu, "FDA Loosens Nutrition Facts Labeling Requirements to Help
      Restaurants Sell Unused Food," *The Counter*, March 30, 2020, https://
      thecounter.org/fda-nutrition-facts-labeling-restaurants-unused-food-
      covid-19-coronavirus.

4.   Lela Nargi, "Covid-19 Has Forced Large-Scale Farms That Supply
      Institutions to Dump Produce They Can't Sell. Why Can't It Just Feed
      Hungry People? We've Got Answers," *The Counter*, April 27, 2020, https://
      thecounter.org/covid-19-produce-dumping-food-banks.

5.   Jake Bittle, "Beef Producers Are Grinding up Their Nicest Steaks, While
      Retailers Can't Meet Demand for Cheaper Cuts," *The Counter*, May 6,
      2020, https://thecounter.org/beef-producers-grinding-steaks-ground-
      beef-coronavirus-covid-19-usda.

6.   Kate Gibson, "Filet Mignon Is Cheapest in Decade as Coronavirus
      Upends Meat Supplies," *CBS News*, April 28, 2020, https://www.cbsnews.
      com/news/coronavirus-supply-filet-mignon-lowest-cost-decade.

7.   Hannah Ritchie and Max Roser, "Crop Yields," Our World in Data, 2019,
      https://ourworldindata.org/crop-yields.

8.   James Wong, "The Food Workers Producing Miracles in a Crisis," *Follow
      the Food, BBC*, accessed August 15, 2020, https://www.bbc.com/future/
      bespoke/follow-the-food/the-food-workers-producing-miracles-in-a-
      crisis.html.

9.   International Foodservice Distributors Association (IFDA), "Food
      Industry Groups Form Partnership to Ensure Sufficient Food Supply
      Amid COVID-19 Crisis," *Food Logistics*, March 19, 2020, https://www.
      foodlogistics.com/transportation/press-release/21123237/international-
      foodservice-distributors-association-ifda-food-industry-groups-form-
      partnership-to-ensure-sufficient-food-supply-amid-covid19-crisis.

10. Jessica Donati and Alicia Caldwell, "U.S. Keeps Processing Seasonal Worker Visas After Warning From Farmers," *Wall Street Journal*, March 19, 2020, https://www.wsj.com/articles/u-s-keeps-processing-seasonal-worker-visas-after-warning-from-farmers-11584652889.

11. Evan Ramstad, "For General Mills, Outbreak Spurred a Run on Its Products and Rush in Its Factories," *Star Tribune* (Minneapolis), May 3, 2020, https://www.startribune.com/for-general-mills-outbreak-spurred-a-run-on-its-products-and-rush-in-its-factories/570162402.

12. Connor D. Wolf, "Food Distributors Play Key Role in Coronavirus Crisis," *Transport Topics*, March 26, 2020, https://www.ttnews.com/articles/food-distributors-play-key-role-coronavirus-crisis.

Chapter 4: Finding the Agility to Defeat Fragility

1. "How to Rebound Stronger from COVID-19: Resilience in Manufacturing and Supply Systems" (World Economic Forum, May 1, 2020), https://www.weforum.org/whitepapers/how-to-rebound-stronger-from-covid-19-resilience-in-manufacturing-and-supply-systems.

2. Evan Ramstad, "For General Mills, Outbreak Spurred a Run on Its Products and Rush in Its Factories," *Star Tribune* (Minneapolis), May 3, 2020, https://www.startribune.com/for-general-mills-outbreak-spurred-a-run-on-its-products-and-rush-in-its-factories/570162402.

3. Scott Horsley, "At The Frozen Pizza Factory That Never Closed: Social Distancing In A Tent," *NPR*, May 7, 2020, https://www.npr.org/sections/coronavirus-live-updates/2020/05/07/850707023/at-the-frozen-pizza-factory-that-never-closed-social-distancing-in-a-tent.

4. General Mills Inc., "General Mills Reports Results for Fiscal 2020 and Outlines Fiscal 2021 Priorities," news release, July 1, 2020, https://s22.q4cdn.com/584207745/files/doc_financials/2020/q4/General-Mills-Fiscal-2020-Fourth-Quarter-Earnings-Press-Release-(1)-(1).pdf.

5. "Helping the World Respond to COVID-19," 3M, accessed July 29, 2020, https://www.3m.com/3M/en_US/company-us/coronavirus.

6. Saabira Chaudhuri, "Unilever Capitalizes on Coronavirus Cleaning Boom," *Wall Street Journal*, July 23, 2020, https://www.wsj.com/articles/americans-in-lockdown-buy-cleaning-products-and-ice-cream-lifting-unilever-11595495473.

7. David Williams, "More than 40 Employees Lived at Their Plant for 28 Days to Make Material to Protect Health Care Workers," *CNN*, April 20, 2020, https://www.cnn.com/2020/04/20/us/coronavirus-workers-go-home-trnd/index.html.

8.   Jeff Fleck, Senior Vice President – Chief Supply Chain Officer for the Consumer Products Group, Georgia-Pacific, interview by Yossi Sheffi, June 15, 2020.

9.   Sarah Nassauer, "Walmart Sales Surge as Coronavirus Drives Americans to Stockpile," *Wall Street Journal,* May 19, 2020, https://www.wsj.com/articles/walmart-sales-surge-as-coronavirus-drives-americans-to-stockpile-11589888464.

10.   "Amazon Hiring on Once Again to Handle Pandemic's Online Shopping Surge," *Retail Customer Experience,* April 14, 2020, https://www.retailcustomerexperience.com/news/amazon-hiring-on-once-again-to-handle-pandemics-online-shopping-surge.

11.   Annie Palmer, "Amazon Gives Front-Line Workers a $500 Coronavirus Bonus," *CNBC,* June 29, 2020, https://www.cnbc.com/2020/06/29/amazon-gives-front-line-workers-a-500-coronavirus-bonus.html.

12.   Caroline Delbert, "With Few Willing to Fly, Airliners Are Transforming Into Cargo Planes," *Popular Mechanics,* March 24, 2020, https://www.popularmechanics.com/flight/airlines/a31914424/passenger-airliners-cargo-planes.

13.   Meri Stevens, Worldwide Vice President, Consumer Health Supply Chain and Deliver, Johnson & Johnson, interview by Yossi Sheffi, June 4, 2020. (On the day of the interview, J&J announced that Stevens was also given the responsibility to run the company's consumer health supply chain.)

14.   Ian Duncan, "Drug Industry Warns That Cuts to Passenger Airline Service Have Put Medical Supplies at Risk," *Washington Post,* May 2, 2020, https://www.washingtonpost.com/local/trafficandcommuting/drug-industry-warns-that-cuts-to-passenger-airline-service-has-put-medical-supplies-at-risk/2020/05/02/d34a7c96-83ff-11ea-ae26-989cfce1c7c7_story.html.

15.   "Coronavirus & Shipping: Air Freight, Trucking & More," Freightos, accessed July 28, 2020, https://www.freightos.com/freight-resources/coronavirus-updates.

16.   Heather Ostis, Vice President of Supply Chain, Delta Air Lines, interview by Yossi Sheffi, June 3, 2020.

17.   Ostis.

18.   James Graham, "Cargo Seat Bags for the Pax Cabin Launched," *Air Cargo Week,* April 7, 2020, https://www.aircargoweek.com/cargo-seat-bags-for-the-pax-cabin-launched.

19.   Eric Kulisch, "Delta Air Lines Cabins to Go Naked," *FreightWaves*, August 14, 2020, https://www.freightwaves.com/news/exclusive-delta-air-lines-cabins-to-go-naked.

20.   Thomas Pallini, "Air Canada Is Ripping Seats out of Aircraft across Its Fleet to Turn Them into Cargo Planes. See inside the New Boeing 777 and Dash 8-400 Temporary Conversions," *Business Insider*, April 28, 2020, https://www.businessinsider.com/coronavirus-air-canada-converting-three-boeing-777s-to-cargo-only-2020-4.

21.   Kyunghee Park, "Korean Air Bucks Virus Challenges to Post Quarterly Profit," *Bloomberg*, August 6, 2020, https://www.bloomberg.com/news/articles/2020-08-06/korean-air-bucks-virus-challenges-to-post-quarterly-profit?sref=KgV4umfb.

22.   Russell Redmann, "C&S Wholesale Grocers Partners with US Foods and Performance Food Group as Coronavirus Disrupts Jobs," *Supermarket News*, March 24, 2020, https://www.supermarketnews.com/retail-financial/cs-wholesale-grocers-us-foods-partner-coronavirus-disrupts-jobs.

23.   Redmann.

24.   Mike Duffy, CEO, C&S Wholesale Grocers, interview by Yossi Sheffi, June 4, 2020.

25.   "Frequently Asked Questions," Walmart Inc., accessed August 15, 2020, https://corporate.walmart.com/frequently-asked-questions.

26.   Coral Murphy, "Walmart to Turn 160 Parking Lots into Drive-in Movie Theaters in August," *USA Today*, July 2, 2020, https://www.usatoday.com/story/money/2020/07/02/walmart-turn-160-parking-lots-into-drive-movie-theaters/5366693002.

27.   Lauren Thomas, "Mall Owners Renting out Parking Lots during the Coronavirus Pandemic," *CNBC*, July 14, 2020, https://www.cnbc.com/2020/07/14/brookfield-other-us-mall-owners-rent-out-parking-lots-during-pandemic.html.

28.   Tom Ryan, "Can Parking Lots Save the Mall?," *RetailWire* (blog), April 26, 2017, https://retailwire.com/discussion/can-parking-lots-save-the-mall.

29.   Christina Jewett, Melissa Bailey, and Danielle Renwick, "Exclusive: Nearly 600 — And Counting — US Health Workers Have Died Of COVID-19," *Kaiser Health News*, June 6, 2020, https://khn.org/news/exclusive-investigation-nearly-600-and-counting-us-health-workers-have-died-of-covid-19.

30. Donald G. McNeil Jr., "Mask Hoarders May Raise Risk of a Coronavirus Outbreak in the U.S.," *New York Times,* January 29, 2020, https://www.nytimes.com/2020/01/29/health/coronavirus-masks-hoarding.html.

31. Keith Bradsher and Liz Alderman, "The World Needs Masks. China Makes Them, but Has Been Hoarding Them," *New York Times,* March 13, 2020, https://www.nytimes.com/2020/03/13/business/masks-china-coronavirus.html.

32. "Walmart (WMT) Earnings Call Transcript Q1 2020: Q1 FY2021 Earnings Release," Rev, accessed July 29, 2020, https://www.rev.com/blog/transcripts/walmart-wmt-earnings-call-transcript-q1-2020-q1-fy2021-earnings-release.

33. Robert Sherman, "Over 600 Distilleries, Big and Small, Now Making Hand Sanitizer during Coronavirus Outbreak," *Fox News,* April 9, 2020, https://www.foxnews.com/food-drink/distilleries-hand-sanitizer-coronavirus-hundreds.

34. Sherman.

35. Kacey Culliney, "COVID-19: LVMH Perfumes & Cosmetics to Produce Hydroalcoholic Gel for France," CosmeticsDesign-Europe, March 16, 2020, https://www.cosmeticsdesign-europe.com/Article/2020/03/16/LVMH-Perfumes-Cosmetics-producing-hydroalcoholic-gel-for-France-amid-COVID-19.

36. Thomas Parker, "880,000 Ventilators Needed to Meet Coronavirus Demand, Says Analyst," *NS Medical Devices,* March 25, 2020, https://www.nsmedicaldevices.com/analysis/coronavirus-ventilators-global-demand.

37. Dan Robinson, "Companies Helping to Plug Shortage of Ventilators and Other Medical Kit," *NS Medical Devices,* April 1, 2020, https://www.nsmedicaldevices.com/analysis/companies-ventilators-shortage-coronavirus.

38. Royal Philips N.V., "Philips Joins Forces with Flex and Jabil to Speed the Production of Hospital Ventilators," news release, April 14, 2020, https://www.philips.com/a-w/about/news/archive/standard/news/articles/2020/20200414-philips-joins-forces-with-flex-and-jabil-to-speed-the-production-of-hospital-ventilators.html.

39. "Flex Ltd. Sets Goal of 30,000 Ventilators a Month," *Evertiq,* April 7, 2020, https://evertiq.com/news/48046.

40. Lynn Torrel, Chief Supply Chain and Procurement Officer, Flex, interview by Yossi Sheffi, June 1, 2020.

41. Vyaire Medical, "Vyaire Medical and Spirit AeroSystems Partner to Greatly Increase Ventilator Production in Response to COVID-19 Pandemic," news release, May 4, 2020, https://www.vyaire.com/news-events/vyaire-medical-and-spirit-aerosystems-partner-greatly-increase-ventilator-production.

42. Brad Templeton, "Car Companies Are Making Ventilators, But Ventilator Companies, Hackers And CPAP Companies Are Working Harder," *Forbes*, April 20, 2020, https://www.forbes.com/sites/bradtempleton/2020/04/20/car-companies-are-making-ventilators-but-ventilator-companies-hackers-and-cpap-companies-are-working-harder.

43. Mike Colias, "Detroit Auto Makers Near Finish Line in Covid-19 Ventilator Push," *Wall Street Journal*, August 15, 2020, https://www.wsj.com/articles/detroit-auto-makers-near-finish-line-in-covid-19-ventilator-push-11597489200.

44. Selina Hurley, "The Man Behind The Motor – William Morris And The Iron Lung," *Science Museum Blog*, March 7, 2013, https://blog.sciencemuseum.org.uk/the-man-behind-the-motor-william-morris-and-the-iron-lung.

45. David Chandler, "Inside MIT's Low-Cost Ventilator Project," *MIT Technology Review*, June 16, 2020, https://www.technologyreview.com/2020/06/16/1002980/inside-mits-low-cost-ventilator-project.

Part 2: Living with Uncertainty

1. Simon Farrant, Olivier Le Peuch, and Stephane Biguet, "Schlumberger First-Quarter 2020 Results Prepared Remarks," https://investorcenter.slb.com/static-files/62d4b006-39dd-464a-b3f5-ce913c079d93.

Chapter 5: The Whack-a-Mole Recovery

1. Marc Santora, "Europe Braces for New Phase in Pandemic With Cases Surging," *New York Times*, August 21, 2020, https://www.nytimes.com/2020/08/21/world/europe/coronavirus-second-wave.html.

2. Heather Haddon, "McDonald's Sales Fall as Coronavirus Pandemic Changes Dining Habits," *Wall Street Journal*, April 30, 2020, https://www.wsj.com/articles/mcdonalds-sales-drop-6-11588248343.

3. Meri Stevens, Worldwide Vice President, Consumer Health Supply Chain and Deliver, Johnson & Johnson, interview by Yossi Sheffi, June 4, 2020.

4. Rob Stein, Carmel Wroth, and Alyson Hurt, "U.S. Coronavirus Testing Still Falls Short. How's Your State Doing?," *NPR*, May 7, 2020, https://

www.npr.org/sections/health-shots/2020/05/07/851610771/u-s-coronavirus-testing-still-falls-short-hows-your-state-doing.

5. Christina Maxouris, "US Could Be in for 'a Bad Fall and a Bad Winter' If It's Unprepared for a Second Wave of Coronavirus, Fauci Warns," *CNN*, April 29, 2020, https://www.cnn.com/2020/04/29/health/us-coronavirus-wednesday/index.html.

6. Kristine A. Moore et al., "COVID-19: The CIDRAP Viewpoint" (Minneapolis: University of Minnesota Center for Infectious Disease Research and Policy, April 30, 2020), https://www.cidrap.umn.edu/sites/default/files/public/downloads/cidrap-covid19-viewpoint-part1_0.pdf.

7. Stacey L. Knobler et al., The Story of Influenza, The Threat of Pandemic Influenza: Are We Ready? Workshop Summary (Washington, D.C.: National Academies Press, 2005), https://www.ncbi.nlm.nih.gov/books/NBK22148.

8. Moore et al., "COVID-19: The CIDRAP Viewpoint."

9. James Hadfield et al., "Narrative: August 2020 Update of COVID-19 Genomic Epidemiology," Organization (Nextstrain, August 14, 2020), https://nextstrain.org/narratives/ncov/sit-rep/2020-08-14.

10. Yudith Ho and Claire Jiao, "Southeast Asia Detects Mutated Virus Strain Sweeping the World," *Bloomberg*, August 16, 2020, https://www.bloomberg.com/news/articles/2020-08-17/malaysia-detects-virus-strain-that-s-10-times-more-infectious?sref=KgV4umfb.

11. Jan Hoffman and Ruth Maclean, "Slowing the Coronavirus Is Speeding the Spread of Other Diseases," *New York Times*, June 14, 2020, https://www.nytimes.com/2020/06/14/health/coronavirus-vaccines-measles.html.

12. Hoffman and Maclean.

13. James Gallagher, "When Will the Coronavirus Outbreak End?," *BBC News*, March 23, 2020, https://www.bbc.com/news/health-51963486.

14. Gallagher.

15. Sharon Begley, "Covid-19's Future: Small Outbreaks, Monster Wave, or Ongoing Crisis," *STAT*, May 1, 2020, https://www.statnews.com/2020/05/01/three-potential-futures-for-covid-19.

16. Gallagher, "When Will the Coronavirus Outbreak End?"

17. "Draft Landscape of COVID-19 Candidate Vaccines" (Geneva: World Health Organization, August 13, 2020), https://www.who.int/publications/m/item/draft-landscape-of-covid-19-candidate-vaccines.

18. Tung Thanh Le et al., "The COVID-19 Vaccine Development Landscape," *Nature Reviews Drug Discovery* 19 (April 9, 2020): 305–306, https://doi. org/10.1038/d41573-020-00073-5.

19. Tyler Clifford, "Developing a Vaccine Takes 10 Years. Sanofi Seeks to Do so within 18 Months," *CNBC,* March 27, 2020, https://www.cnbc. com/2020/03/27/vaccine-development-takes-10-years-sanofi-seeks-to-do-so-in-18-months.html.

20. Matt Simon, "Why Creating a Covid-19 Vaccine Is Taking So Long," *Wired,* May 20, 2020, https://www.wired.com/story/why-creating-a-covid-19-vaccine-is-taking-so-long.

21. Associated Press, "Only Half of Americans Would Get a COVID-19 Vaccine, Poll Shows," *CBS News,* May 27, 2020, https://www.cbsnews. com/news/coronavirus-vaccine-half-americans-would-get.

22. Nils Karlson, Charlotta Stern, and Daniel B. Klein, "Sweden's Coronavirus Strategy Will Soon Be the World's," *Foreign Affairs,* May 12, 2020, https://www.foreignaffairs.com/articles/sweden/2020-05-12/swedens-coronavirus-strategy-will-soon-be-worlds.

23. Bojan Pancevski, "Coronavirus Is Taking a High Toll on Sweden's Elderly. Families Blame the Government," *Wall Street Journal,* June 18, 2020, https://www.wsj.com/articles/coronavirus-is-taking-a-high-toll-on-swedens-elderly-families-blame-the-government-11592479430.

24. Gallagher, "When Will the Coronavirus Outbreak End?"

25. Antonio Regalado, "What If Immunity to Covid-19 Doesn't Last?," *MIT Technology Review,* April 27, 2020, https://www.technologyreview. com/2020/04/27/1000569/how-long-are-people-immune-to-covid-19.

26. Sergio Correia, Stephan Luck, and Emil Verner, "Pandemics Depress the Economy, Public Health Interventions Do Not: Evidence from the 1918 Flu," pre-print available at SSRN, June 5, 2020, https://doi.org/10.2139/ssrn.3561560.

27. Chris Isidorre, "A Flood of Corporate Debt Could Make the Economic Recovery More Difficult," *CNN,* April 25, 2020, https://www.cnn. com/2020/04/25/economy/corporate-debt/index.html.

28. "Corporate Bonds and Loans Are at the Centre of a New Financial Scare," *Economist,* March 12, 2020, https://www.economist.com/finance-and-economics/2020/03/12/corporate-bonds-and-loans-are-at-the-centre-of-a-new-financial-scare.

29. Matthew Fox, "Delinquent Mortgages Spike to the Highest Level in 21 Years as COVID-19 Stress Freezes Payments," *Business Insider,*

July 17, 2020, https://markets.businessinsider.com/news/stocks/
delinquent-mortgages-spike-covid19-stress-freezes-payments-past-due-
coronavirus-2020-7-1029405332.

30.   Cortney Moore, "Coronavirus Made 40% of Major Retailers Skip May
      Rent Payments," *Fox Business,* June 8, 2020, https://www.foxbusiness.
      com/money/coronavirus-retailers-skip-may-rent-payments.

31.   Heather Long, "The next Big Problem: Businesses Can't or Won't Pay
      Their Rent. It's Setting off a Dangerous Chain Reaction," *Washington Post,*
      June 4, 2020, https://www.washingtonpost.com/business/2020/06/03/
      next-big-problem-businesses-cant-or-wont-pay-their-rent-its-setting-off-
      dangerous-chain-reaction.

32.   Andrew Soergel and Shelbi Austin, "The 10 Countries With the Most
      Debt," *U.S. News & World Report,* December 19, 2019, https://www.
      usnews.com/news/best-countries/slideshows/top-10-countries-with-the-
      heaviest-burden-of-debt.

33.   "How Deep Will Downturns in Rich Countries Be?," *Economist,* April 16,
      2020, https://www.economist.com/finance-and-economics/2020/04/16/
      how-deep-will-downturns-in-rich-countries-be.

34.   Emily Badger and Quoctrung Bui, "The Recession Is About to Slam
      Cities. Not Just the Blue-State Ones," *The Upshot* (blog), *New York Times,*
      August 17, 2020, https://www.nytimes.com/2020/08/17/upshot/pandemic-
      recession-cities-fiscal-shortfall.html.

35.   Carmen Reinhart and Vincent Reinhart, "The Pandemic Depression,"
      Foreign Affairs, August 6, 2020, https://www.foreignaffairs.com/articles/
      united-states/2020-08-06/coronavirus-depression-global-economy.

36.   Carmen M. Reinhart and Kenneth S. Rogoff, "Recovery from Financial
      Crises: Evidence from 100 Episodes," working paper, NBER Working
      Paper Series no. 19823 (Cambridge, Mass.: National Bureau of Economic
      Research, January 2014), https://www.nber.org/papers/w19823.pdf.

37.   Federico Caniato, Antonella Moretto, and James B. Rice Jr., "A Financial
      Crisis Is Looming for Smaller Suppliers," *Harvard Business Review,* August
      6, 2020, https://hbr.org/2020/08/a-financial-crisis-is-looming-for-smaller-
      suppliers.

38.   "A Crisis Like No Other, An Uncertain Recovery," *World Economic
      Outlook Update* (Washington, D.C.: Interrnational Monetary Fund, June
      2020), https://www.imf.org/en/Publications/WEO/Issues/2020/06/24/
      WEOUpdateJune2020.

39. Richard Javad Heydarian, "The Economics of the Arab Spring," *Foreign Policy In Focus* (blog), April 21, 2011, https://fpif.org/the_economics_of_the_arab_spring/; Andrew Lilico, "How the Fed Triggered the Arab Spring Uprisings in Two Easy Graphs," *Telegraph* (London), May 4, 2011, https://www.telegraph.co.uk/finance/economics/8492078/How-the-Fed-triggered-the-Arab-Spring-uprisings-in-two-easy-graphs.html.

40. "Defund Police, Watch Crime Return," editorial, *Wall Street Journal*, June 8, 2020, https://www.wsj.com/articles/defund-police-watch-crime-return-11591658454.

41. "How CEOs See Today's Coronavirus World," *Wall Street Journal*, June 11, 2020, https://www.wsj.com/articles/how-ceos-see-todays-coronavirus-world-11587720600.

42. Ed Yong, "America's Patchwork Pandemic Is Fraying Even Further," *Atlantic*, May 20, 2020, https://www.theatlantic.com/health/archive/2020/05/patchwork-pandemic-states-reopening-inequalities/611866.

43. Yossi Sheffi, "Are You Prepared to Manage a Whack-A-Mole Recovery?," *LinkedIn Influencer* (blog), April 24, 2020, https://www.linkedin.com/pulse/you-prepared-manage-whack-a-mole-recovery-yossi-sheffi.

44. Will Douglas Heaven, "Our Weird Behavior during the Pandemic Is Messing with AI Models," *MIT Technology Review*, May 11, 2020, https://www.technologyreview.com/2020/05/11/1001563/covid-pandemic-broken-ai-machine-learning-amazon-retail-fraud-humans-in-the-loop.

45. "Dana Incorporated (DAN) Q1 2020 Earnings Call Transcript," The Motley Fool, April 30, 2020, https://www.fool.com/earnings/call-transcripts/2020/04/30/dana-incorporated-dan-q1-2020-earnings-call-transc.aspx.

46. "Aptiv PLC (APTV) Q1 2020 Earnings Call Transcript," The Motley Fool, May 5, 2020, https://www.fool.com/earnings/call-transcripts/2020/05/05/aptiv-plc-aptv-q1-2020-earnings-call-transcript.aspx.

47. "How CEOs See Today's Coronavirus World."

48. Mike Bird, "The Coronavirus Savings Glut," *Wall Street Journal*, June 23, 2020, https://www.wsj.com/articles/the-coronavirus-savings-glut-11592905053.

49. Oscar Jorda, Sanjay R. Singh, and Alan M. Taylor, "Longer-Run Economic Consequences of Pandemics," working paper (Federal Reserve Bank of San Francisco, June 30, 2020), https://www.frbsf.org/economic-research/publications/working-papers/2020/09.

Chapter 6: Managing for Ongoing Disruptions

1.   "Honeywell International Inc. (NYSE: HON) Q1 2020 Earnings Call Transcript," AlphaStreet, May 1, 2020, https://news.alphastreet.com/honeywell-international-inc-nyse-hon-q1-2020-earnings-call-transcript.

2.   Simon Farrant, Olivier Le Peuch, and Stephane Biguet, "Schlumberger First-Quarter 2020 Results Prepared Remarks," https://investorcenter.slb.com/static-files/62d4b006-39dd-464a-b3f5-ce913c079d93.

3.   Sarah O'Brien, "Dividend Cuts May Mean Rethinking Your Retirement Income Strategy," *CNBC*, July 16, 2020, https://www.cnbc.com/2020/07/16/dividend-cuts-may-mean-rethinking-your-retirement-income-strategy.html.

4.   Heather Long and Andrew Van Dam, "Pay Cuts Are Becoming a Defining Feature of the Coronavirus Recession," *Washington Post*, July 1, 2020, https://www.washingtonpost.com/business/2020/07/01/pay-cut-economy-coronavirus.

5.   Kelly Yamanouchi, "Delta Cuts 70% of Flights, 10,000 Employees to Take Unpaid Leave," *Atlanta Airport Blog, Atlanta Journal-Constitution,* March 18, 2020, https://www.ajc.com/blog/airport/more-than-000-delta-air-lines-employees-take-unpaid-leave/czzGXjjvfv8GQhDSzV4mIP.

6.   "How CEOs See Today's Coronavirus World," *Wall Street Journal,* June 11, 2020, https://www.wsj.com/articles/how-ceos-see-todays-coronavirus-world-11587720600.

7.   Mike Colias, "In Detroit, Scramble for Cash Upends High-Profile Vehicle Rollouts," *Wall Street Journal,* May 6, 2020, https://www.wsj.com/articles/general-motors-posts-profit-on-strong-trucks-sales-11588767852.

8.   Ben Foldy and Mike Colias, "Auto Makers' Reopening Complicated by Worker Absences Amid Covid Cases," *Wall Street Journal,* June 13, 2020, https://www.wsj.com/articles/auto-makers-reopening-complicated-by-worker-absences-amid-covid-cases-11592074008.

9.   Colias, "In Detroit, Scramble for Cash Upends High-Profile Vehicle Rollouts."

10.   Adam Hayes and Margaret James, "Cash Conversion Cycle (CCC) Definition," Investopedia, April 12, 2020, https://www.investopedia.com/terms/c/cashconversioncycle.asp.

11. Federico Caniato, Antonella Moretto, and James B. Rice Jr., "A Financial Crisis Is Looming for Smaller Suppliers," *Harvard Business Review,* August 6, 2020, https://hbr.org/2020/08/a-financial-crisis-is-looming-for-smaller-suppliers.

12. Lynn Torrel, Chief Supply Chain and Procurement Officer, Flex, interview by Yossi Sheffi, June 1, 2020.

13. Torrel.

14. Olaf Schatteman, Drew Woodhouse, and Joe Terino, "Supply Chain Lessons from Covid-19: Time to Refocus on Resilience" (Sydney: Bain & Company, April 27, 2020), https://www.bain.com/insights/supply-chain-lessons-from-covid-19.

15. Daniel Biran, Vice President, Security, Biogen, interview by Yossi Sheffi, June 26, 2020.

16. Torrel, Chief Supply Chain and Procurement Officer, Flex.

17. Mike Duffy, CEO, C&S Wholesale Grocers, interview by Yossi Sheffi, June 4, 2020.

18. Yossi Sheffi, *The Power of Resilience: How the Best Companies Manage the Unexpected* (Cambridge, Mass.: MIT Press, 2015), 64, https://mitpress.mit.edu/books/power-resilience.

19. Ralph Keyes, *The Quote Verifier: Who Said What, Where, and When* (New York: St. Martin's Griffin, 2006), 165–166, https://ralphkeyes.com/book/quote-verifier.

20. Yossi Sheffi, *The Resilient Enterprise: Overcoming Vulnerability for Competitive Advantage* (Cambridge, Mass.: MIT Press, 2005), 348, https://mitpress.mit.edu/books/resilient-enterprise.

21. Evan Ramstad, "For General Mills, Outbreak Spurred a Run on Its Products and Rush in Its Factories," *Star Tribune* (Minneapolis), May 3, 2020, https://www.startribune.com/for-general-mills-outbreak-spurred-a-run-on-its-products-and-rush-in-its-factories/570162402.

22. Dave Wheeler, Chief Operating Officer, New Balance, interview by Yossi Sheffi, May 27, 2020.

23. Jonathan Tilley, "Analysis: Malaysia Airlines' Mishandled Response to the MH370 Crisis," *PRWeek,* March 21, 2014, http://www.prweek.com/article/1286333/analysis-malaysia-airlines-mishandled-response-mh370-crisis?utm_source=website&utm_medium=social.

24. Ramstad, "For General Mills, Outbreak Spurred a Run on Its Products and Rush in Its Factories."

Chapter 7: Managing for Whack-a-Mole Supply

1. Mayra Rodriguez Valladares, "U.S. Corporate Debt Continues To Rise As Do Problem Leveraged Loans," *Forbes,* June 25, 2019, https://www.forbes.com/sites/mayrarodriguezvalladares/2019/07/25/u-s-corporate-debt-continues-to-rise-as-do-problem-leveraged-loans/#7a45d17d3596.

2. "Honeywell International Inc. (NYSE: HON) Q1 2020 Earnings Call Transcript," AlphaStreet, May 1, 2020, https://news.alphastreet.com/honeywell-international-inc-nyse-hon-q1-2020-earnings-call-transcript.

3. Yossi Sheffi, *The Resilient Enterprise: Overcoming Vulnerability for Competitive Advantage* (Cambridge, Mass.: MIT Press, 2005), https://mitpress.mit.edu/books/resilient-enterprise.

4. Yossi Sheffi, *The Power of Resilience: How the Best Companies Manage the Unexpected* (Cambridge, Mass.: MIT Press, 2015), https://mitpress.mit.edu/books/power-resilience.

5. Yossi Sheffi, "A Quake Breaks a Supply Chain," in *The Power of Resilience: How the Best Companies Manage the Unexpected* (Cambridge, Mass.: MIT Press, 2015), 1–26, https://mitpress.mit.edu/books/power-resilience.

6. Sheffi, *Power of Resilience,* 97.

7. Bindiya Vakil, CEO, Resilinc, interview by Sheffi Yossi, June 11, 2020.

8. Ravi Anupindi, "Supply Chain Risk Management at Cisco: Response to H1N1" (Ann Arbor, Mich.: WDI Publishing, July 17, 2012), https://wdi-publishing.com/product/supply-chain-risk-management-at-cisco-response-to-h1n1.

9. Vakil, CEO, Resilinc.

10. Vakil.

11. "How to Rebound Stronger from COVID-19: Resilience in Manufacturing and Supply Systems" (World Economic Forum, May 1, 2020), https://www.weforum.org/whitepapers/how-to-rebound-stronger-from-covid-19-resilience-in-manufacturing-and-supply-systems.

12. Tim Ryan et al., "PwC's COVID-19 CFO Pulse Survey" (PricewaterhouseCoopers, April 27, 2020), https://www.pwc.com/us/en/library/covid-19/pwc-covid-19-cfo-pulse-survey-4.html.

13. Sheffi, *Power of Resilience,* 97–99.

14. Yossi Sheffi, *Logistics Clusters: Delivering Value and Driving Growth* (Cambridge, Mass.: MIT Press, 2012), https://mitpress.mit.edu/books/logistics-clusters.

15. Michael E. Porter, "Clusters and the New Economics of Competition," *Harvard Business Review,* December 1998, https://hbr.org/1998/11/clusters-and-the-new-economics-of-competition.

16. Dina Gerdeman, "How the Coronavirus Is Already Rewriting the Future of Business," *Harvard Business School Working Knowledge,* March 16, 2020, http://hbswk.hbs.edu/item/how-the-coronavirus-is-already-rewriting-the-future-of-business.

17. Ryan et al., "PwC's COVID-19 CFO Pulse Survey."

18. Kate Connolly, "Meat Plant Must Be Held to Account for Covid-19 Outbreak, Says German Minister," *Guardian* (Manchester), June 22, 2020, https://www.theguardian.com/world/2020/jun/22/meat-plant-must-be-held-to-account-covid-19-outbreak-germany.

19. Sheffi, *Power of Resilience,* 129.

20. Rachel Jewett, "Lockheed Martin to Advance $50M to Supply Chain Businesses in COVID-19 Response," *Via Satellite,* March 27, 2020, https://www.satellitetoday.com/business/2020/03/27/lockheed-martin-to-advance-50m-to-supply-chain-businesses-in-covid-19-response.

21. Vodafone Group, "Vodafone Launches Five-Point Plan to Help Counter the Impacts of the COVID-19 Outbreak," news release, March 18, 2020, https://www.vodafone.com/news-and-media/vodafone-group-releases/news/vodafone-launches-five-point-plan-to-help-counter-the-impacts-of-the-covid-19-outbreak.

22. World Economic Forum, "How to Rebound Stronger from COVID-19."

23. Evan Ramstad, "For General Mills, Outbreak Spurred a Run on Its Products and Rush in Its Factories," *Star Tribune* (Minneapolis), May 3, 2020, https://www.startribune.com/for-general-mills-outbreak-spurred-a-run-on-its-products-and-rush-in-its-factories/570162402.

24. Micah Maidenberg, "Fewer Products, Localized Production—Companies Seek Supply-Chain Solutions," *Wall Street Journal,* April 26, 2020, https://www.wsj.com/articles/coronavirus-disrupted-supply-chains-that-companies-are-still-fixing-11587893401.

25. Stuart Lau, "Netherlands Recalls 600,000 Face Masks from China Due to Low Quality," *South China Morning Post,* March 29, 2020, https://www.scmp.com/news/china/diplomacy/article/3077428/netherlands-recalls-600000-face-masks-china-due-low-quality.

26.   The National Personal Protective Technology Laboratory, "Counterfeit Respirators / Misrepresentation of NIOSH-Approval," Centers for Disease Control and Prevention, August 7, 2020, https://www.cdc.gov/niosh/npptl/usernotices/counterfeitResp.html.

Chapter 8: Managing for Whack-a-Mole Demand

1.   "Amazon (AMZN) Q1 2020 Earnings Call Transcript," Rev, May 1, 2020, https://www.rev.com/blog/transcripts/amazon-amzn-q1-2020-earnings-call-transcript.

2.   Mike Robuck, "Report: Despite Covid-19 Disruption in 2020, Data Center Capex Poised to Hit More than $200B over next Five Years," Fierce Telecom (blog), July 24, 2020, https://www.fiercetelecom.com/telecom/report-despite-covid-19-disruption-2020-data-center-capex-poised-to-hit-more-than-200b-over.

3.   Alicia Wallace, "Walmart CEO Says We're in the 'Hair Color' Phase of Panic Buying," *CNN Business,* April 11, 2020, https://www.cnn.com/2020/04/11/business/panic-buying-walmart-hair-color-coronavirus/index.html.

4.   Michael Raeford, "Walmart Handles More than 1 Million Customer Transactions Every Hour, Which Is Imported into Databases Estimated to Contain More than 2.5 Petabytes of Data," GrabStats, accessed August 10, 2020, http://www.grabstats.com/stats/2036.

5.   "Google Trends," Google Trends, accessed August 10, 2020, https://trends.google.com/trends/?geo=US.

6.   Alyssa Fowers, "Last Year, We Searched Google for How to Tie a Tie. Now We're Using It to Find Toilet Paper," *Washington Post,* April 17, 2020, https://www.washingtonpost.com/business/2020/04/17/last-year-we-searched-google-how-tie-tie-now-were-using-it-find-toilet-paper.

7.   Will Douglas Heaven, "Our Weird Behavior during the Pandemic Is Messing with AI Models," *MIT Technology Review,* May 11, 2020, https://www.technologyreview.com/2020/05/11/1001563/covid-pandemic-broken-ai-machine-learning-amazon-retail-fraud-humans-in-the-loop.

8.   Martin Reeves et al., "How Chinese Companies Have Responded to Coronavirus," *Harvard Business Review,* March 10, 2020, https://hbr.org/2020/03/how-chinese-companies-have-responded-to-coronavirus.

9.   Yossi Sheffi, "Reducing the White-Space," in *The Power of Resilience: How the Best Companies Manage the Unexpected* (Cambridge, Mass.: MIT Press, 2015), 53–78, https://mitpress.mit.edu/books/power-resilience.

10.   Micah Maidenberg, "Fewer Products, Localized Production—Companies Seek Supply-Chain Solutions," *Wall Street Journal,* April 26, 2020, https://www.wsj.com/articles/coronavirus-disrupted-supply-chains-that-companies-are-still-fixing-11587893401.

11.   Evan Ramstad, "For General Mills, Outbreak Spurred a Run on Its Products and Rush in Its Factories," *Star Tribune* (Minneapolis), May 3, 2020, https://www.startribune.com/for-general-mills-outbreak-spurred-a-run-on-its-products-and-rush-in-its-factories/570162402.

12.   Mike Duffy, CEO, C&S Wholesale Grocers, interview by Yossi Sheffi, June 4, 2020.

13.   Heather Zenk, "How Do Allocations Work for the Pharma Supply Chain?," AmerisourceBergen, April 16, 2020, https://www.amerisourcebergen.com/insights/how-do-allocations-work-for-the-pharma-supply-chain.

14.   Jason Aten, "Amazon Says It Will Prioritize Essentials and Stop All Shipments of Other Products to Its Warehouses," *Inc.*, March 18, 2020, https://www.inc.com/jason-aten/amazon-says-it-will-prioritize-essentials-stop-all-shipments-of-other-products-to-its-warehouses.html.

15.   Michael Bartiromo, "Danish Market Creatively Prices Hand Sanitizer to Discourage Coronavirus Hoarding," *Fox News,* March 23, 2020, https://www.foxnews.com/lifestyle/danish-market-prices-hand-sanitizer-coronavirus-hoarding.

16.   "Auctions," Federal Communications Commission, accessed August 10, 2020, https://www.fcc.gov/auctions.

17.   Nick McKenzie and Anthony Galloway, "Coronavirus: Former CCP General Accused of COVID-19 Mask Mark-Ups," *Sydney Morning Herald,* April 1, 2020, https://www.smh.com.au/national/profiting-from-a-pandemic-former-chinese-officer-accused-of-huge-covid-19-mark-ups-20200401-p54g4h.html.

18.   Suhauna Hussain, "EBay Bans Sales of Masks and Hand Sanitizer in Response to Coronavirus Price Gouging," *Los Angeles Times,* March 6, 2020, https://www.latimes.com/business/technology/story/2020-03-06/ebay-bans-n95-masks-hand-sanitizer-coronavirus-price-gouging.

19.   Larry Olmsted, "Whiskey Or Water? Marketing Nightmare As Bourbon Fans Incensed Over Choice," *Forbes,* February 14, 2013, https://www.forbes.com/sites/larryolmsted/2013/02/14/whiskey-or-water-marketing-nightmare-as-bourbon-fans-incensed-over-choice/#2cfd9ae277fa.

20.   Associated Press, "Whiskey Lovers Cheer as Maker's Mark Restores
      Proof," *CBS News,* February 17, 2013, https://www.cbsnews.com/news/
      whiskey-lovers-cheer-as-makers-mark-restores-proof.

21.   Yossi Sheffi, "Who Gets What When Supply Chains Are Disrupted?," *MIT
      Sloan Management Review,* May 27, 2020, https://sloanreview.mit.edu/
      article/who-gets-what-when-supply-chains-are-disrupted.

22.   Sheffi, "Who Gets What When Supply Chains Are Disrupted?".

Chapter 9: More Business Resilience Planning and Testing

1.   "Ford Motor Co. (F) Q1 2020 Earnings Call Transcript," The
      Motley Fool, April 28, 2020, https://www.fool.com/earnings/call-
      transcripts/2020/04/28/ford-motor-co-f-q1-2020-earnings-call-transcript.
      aspx.

2.   Matt Apuzzo, Selam Gebrekidan, and David D. Kirkpatrick, "How the
      World Missed Covid-19's Silent Spread," *New York Times,* June 27,
      2020, sec. World, https://www.nytimes.com/2020/06/27/world/europe/
      coronavirus-spread-asymptomatic.html.

3.   Christopher Chadwick, The next flu pandemic: a matter of 'when',
      not 'if,' interview by World Health Organization Regional Office for
      the Eastern Mediterranean, February 2019, http://www.emro.who.int/
      pandemic-epidemic-diseases/news/the-next-flu-pandemic-a-matter-of-
      when-not-if.html.

4.   Ralf Busche, Senior Vice President, Global Supply Chain Strategy &
      Management, BASF Group, interview by Yossi Sheffi, June 8, 2020.

5.   Shardul Phadnis, Chris Caplice, and Yossi Sheffi, "How Scenario
      Planning Influences Strategic Decisions," *MIT Sloan Management Review,*
      June 2016, http://sloanreview.mit.edu/article/how-scenario-planning-
      influences-strategic-decisions.

6.   Phadnis, Caplice, and Sheffi.

7.   "Kimberly-Clark Corp. (KMB) Q1 2020 Earnings Call Transcript,"
      The Motley Fool, April 22, 2020, https://www.fool.com/earnings/call-
      transcripts/2020/04/22/kimberly-clark-corp-kmb-q1-2020-earnings-call-
      tran.aspx.

8.   "How to Rebound Stronger from COVID-19: Resilience in Manufacturing
      and Supply Systems" (World Economic Forum, May 1, 2020), https://
      www.weforum.org/whitepapers/how-to-rebound-stronger-from-covid-19-
      resilience-in-manufacturing-and-supply-systems.

9. "Ludwigshafen Site Strong in the Verbund" (Ludwigshafen am Rhein, Germany: BASF SE), accessed August 10, 2020, https://www.basf.com/ global/de/documents/Ludwigshafen/2020_site_brochure_Ludwigshafen_ EN.pdf.

10. "Verbund," BASF SE, accessed August 10, 2020, https://www.basf.com/us/ en/who-we-are/strategy/verbund.html.

11. Busche, Senior Vice President, Global Supply Chain Strategy & Management, BASF Group.

12. Stefan Brüggemann et al., "Support of Strategic Business Decisions at BASF's Largest Integrated Production Site Based on Site-Wide Verbund Simulation," ed. Bertrand Braunschweig and Xavier Joulia, *Computer Aided Chemical Engineering* 25 (2008): 925–930, https://doi.org/10.1016/ S1570-7946(08)80160-5.

13. Jon Brodkin, "Netflix Attacks Own Network with 'Chaos Monkey'—and Now You Can Too," *Ars Technica*, July 30, 2012, https://arstechnica.com/ information-technology/2012/07/netflix-attacks-own-network-with-chaos-monkey-and-now-you-can-too.

14. Lorin Hochstein and Casey Rosenthal, "Netflix Chaos Monkey Upgraded," *Netflix Technology Blog*, Medium, March 24, 2018, https:// netflixtechblog.com/netflix-chaos-monkey-upgraded-1d679429be5d.

15. "Principles of Chaos Engineering," Principles of Chaos Engineering, May 2018, http://principlesofchaos.org.

16. "Red Team vs Blue Team," *EC-Council Blog*, June 15, 2019, https://blog. eccouncil.org/red-team-vs-blue-team.

Part 3: Adjustment Required

1. "How CEOs See Today's Coronavirus World," *Wall Street Journal*, June 11, 2020, https://www.wsj.com/articles/how-ceos-see-todays-coronavirus-world-11587720600.

2. Thomson Reuters, "Q1 2020 AT&T Inc Earnings Call," 2020, https:// investors.att.com/~/media/Files/A/ATT-IR/financial-reports/quarterly-earnings/2020/Final%201Q20%20earnings%20transcript.pdf.

3. "United Parcel Service Inc. (UPS) Q1 2020 Earnings Call Transcript," The Motley Fool, April 28, 2020, https://www.fool.com/earnings/call-transcripts/2020/04/28/united-parcel-service-inc-ups-q1-2020-earnings-cal.aspx.

4.   Evan Ramstad, "For General Mills, Outbreak Spurred a Run on Its
      Products and Rush in Its Factories," *Star Tribune* (Minneapolis), May 3,
      2020, https://www.startribune.com/for-general-mills-outbreak-spurred-a-
      run-on-its-products-and-rush-in-its-factories/570162402.

Chapter 10: Creating Safe Zones

1.   Emily Badger and Alicia Parlapiano, "Government Orders Alone Didn't
      Close the Economy. They Probably Can't Reopen It," The Upshot (blog),
      New York Times, May 7, 2020, https://www.nytimes.com/2020/05/07/
      upshot/pandemic-economy-government-orders.html.

2.   Austan Goolsbee and Chad Syverson, "Fear, Lockdown, and Diversion:
      Comparing Drivers of Pandemic Economic Decline 2020," working
      paper (Becker Friedman Institute for Economics at the University of
      Chicago, June 2020), https://bfi.uchicago.edu/wp-content/uploads/BFI_
      WP_202080v2.pdf.

3.   John Maynard Keynes, *The General Theory of Employment, Interest and
      Money* (London: Macmillan, 1936), 161–162.

4.   William Wan and Carolyn Y. Johnson, "Coronavirus May Never Go
      Away, Even with a Vaccine," *Washington Post,* May 27, 2020, https://www.
      washingtonpost.com/health/2020/05/27/coronavirus-endemic.

5.   "Sharing What We've Learned: A Blueprint for Businesses" (The
      Kroger Co., July 15, 2020), https://www.thekrogerco.com/wp-content/
      uploads/2020/04/Krogers-Blueprint-for-Businesses.pdf.

6.   Christina Prignano, "Read the Safety Standards Workplaces Must
      Implement Once They're Allowed to Reopen," *Boston Globe,* May 11, 2020,
      https://www.bostonglobe.com/2020/05/11/metro/read-safety-standards-
      workplaces-must-implement-before-reopening.

7.   "How CEOs See Today's Coronavirus World," *Wall Street Journal,* June
      11, 2020, https://www.wsj.com/articles/how-ceos-see-todays-coronavirus-
      world-11587720600.

8.   Polly J. Price, "How a Fragmented Country Fights a Pandemic," *Atlantic,*
      March 19, 2020, https://www.theatlantic.com/ideas/archive/2020/03/how-
      fragmented-country-fights-pandemic/608284.

9.   Nina Strochlic and Riley Champine, "How Some Cities 'Flattened the
      Curve' during the 1918 Flu Pandemic," *National Geographic,* March 27,
      2020, https://www.nationalgeographic.com/history/2020/03/how-cities-
      flattened-curve-1918-spanish-flu-pandemic-coronavirus.

10. Amy Qin, Steven Lee Myers, and Elaine Yu, "China Tightens Wuhan Lockdown in 'Wartime' Battle With Coronavirus," *New York Times,* February 6, 2020, https://www.nytimes.com/2020/02/06/world/asia/coronavirus-china-wuhan-quarantine.html.

11. Emily Feng and Amy Cheng, "Restrictions And Rewards: How China Is Locking Down Half A Billion Citizens," *NPR,* February 21, 2020, https://www.npr.org/sections/goatsandsoda/2020/02/21/806958341/restrictions-and-rewards-how-china-is-locking-down-half-a-billion-citizens.

12. Grace Hauck and Jorge L. Ortiz, "Coronavirus in the US: How All 50 States Are Responding – and Why Eight Still Refuse to Issue Stay-at-Home Orders," *USA Today,* March 30, 2020, https://www.usatoday.com/story/news/nation/2020/03/30/coronavirus-stay-home-shelter-in-place-orders-by-state/5092413002.

13. Brian Welk and Samson Amore, "GameStop Says Work From Home Products – Not Just Video Games – Makes Them 'Essential Retail,'" *Yahoo Entertainment,* March 20, 2020, https://www.yahoo.com/entertainment/gamestop-stores-stay-open-amid-221944632.html?guccounter=15.

14. "City of Atlanta Coronavirus Disease 2019 (COVID-19) Response," City of Atlanta, accessed August 11, 2020, https://www.atlantaga.gov/government/mayor-s-office/city-of-atlanta-covid-19-response.

15. Michael Corkery and Annie Karni, "Trump Administration Restricts Entry Into U.S. From China," *New York Times,* January 31, 2020, https://www.nytimes.com/2020/01/31/business/china-travel-coronavirus.html.

16. Ana L.P. Mateus et al., "Effectiveness of Travel Restrictions in the Rapid Containment of Human Influenza: A Systematic Review," *Bulletin of the World Health Organization* 92 (September 24, 2014): 868–880D, https://doi.org/10.2471/BLT.14.135590.

17. Mona O'Brien and Samuel Cohn, "Contact Tracing: How Physicians Used It 500 Years Ago to Control the Bubonic Plague," *The Conversation,* June 3, 2020, http://theconversation.com/contact-tracing-how-physicians-used-it-500-years-ago-to-control-the-bubonic-plague-139248.

18. Mark Zastrow, "Coronavirus Contact-Tracing Apps: Can They Slow the Spread of COVID-19?," *Nature,* May 19, 2020, https://www.nature.com/articles/d41586-020-01514-2.

19. Zastrow.

20. Kelly Servick, "COVID-19 Contact Tracing Apps Are Coming to a Phone near You. How Will We Know Whether They Work?," *Science,* May 21,

2020, https://www.sciencemag.org/news/2020/05/countries-around-world-are-rolling-out-contact-tracing-apps-contain-coronavirus-how.

21.   Mary Van Beusekom, "Study: Contact Tracing Slowed COVID-19 Spread in China," *CIDRAP News*, University of Minnesota Center for Infectious Disease Research and Policy, April 28, 2020, https://www.cidrap.umn.edu/news-perspective/2020/04/study-contact-tracing-slowed-covid-19-spread-china.

22.   Heesu Lee, "These Elite Contact Tracers Show the World How to Beat Covid-19," *BloombergQuint*, July 26, 2020, https://www.bloombergquint.com/coronavirus-outbreak/these-elite-contact-tracers-show-the-world-how-to-beat-covid-19.

23.   Zastrow, "Coronavirus Contact-Tracing Apps."

24.   Russell Brandom, "Answering the 12 Biggest Questions about Apple and Google's New Coronavirus Tracking Project," *The Verge*, April 11, 2020, https://www.theverge.com/2020/4/11/21216803/apple-google-coronavirus-tracking-app-covid-bluetooth-secure.

25.   Sara Morrison, "Perhaps Months Too Late, a Covid-19 Contact Tracing App Comes to America," *Vox*, August 6, 2020, https://www.vox.com/recode/2020/8/6/21357098/apple-google-exposure-notification-virginia-contact-tracing.

26.   Alison Sider and Michelle Hackman, "TSA Preparing to Check Passenger Temperatures at Airports Amid Coronavirus Concerns," *Wall Street Journal*, May 16, 2020, https://www.wsj.com/articles/tsa-preparing-to-check-passenger-temperatures-11589579570.

27.   "General Motors Co. (GM) Q1 2020 Earnings Call Transcript," The Motley Fool, May 6, 2020, https://www.fool.com/earnings/call-transcripts/2020/05/06/general-motors-co-gm-q1-2020-earnings-call-transcr.aspx.

28.   Nicole Jawerth, "How Is the COVID-19 Virus Detected Using Real Time RT-PCR?," International Atomic Energy Agency, March 27, 2020, https://www.iaea.org/newscenter/news/how-is-the-covid-19-virus-detected-using-real-time-rt-pcr.

29.   Kay Lazar, "Do-It-Yourself Coronavirus Testing Sparks Kudos, and Caution," *Boston Globe*, August 22, 2020, https://www.bostonglobe.com/2020/08/22/metro/do-it-yourself-coronavirus-testing-sparks-kudos-caution/?s_campaign=breakingnews:newsletter.

30.   "Health Pass," CLEAR, accessed August 11, 2020, https://www.clearme.com/healthpass.

31. A. Wilder-Smith and D.R. Hill, "International Certificate of Vaccination or Prophylaxis," *Lancet* 370, no. 9587 (August 18, 2007): 565, https://doi.org/10.1016/S0140-6736(07)61291-4.

32. "'Immunity Passports' in the Context of COVID-19" (Geneva: World Health Organization, April 24, 2020), https://www.who.int/news-room/commentaries/detail/immunity-passports-in-the-context-of-covid-19.

33. Shining Tan, "China's Novel Health Tracker: Green on Public Health, Red on Data Surveillance," *Trustee China Hand* (blog), Center for Strategic & International Studies, May 4, 2020, https://www.csis.org/blogs/trustee-china-hand/chinas-novel-health-tracker-green-public-health-red-data-surveillance.

34. Tautvile Daugelaite, "China's Health Code System Shows the Cost of Controlling Coronavirus," *Wired* (UK edition), July 17, 2020, https://www.wired.co.uk/article/china-coronavirus-health-code-qr.

35. Paul Mozur, Raymond Zhong, and Aaron Krolik, "In Coronavirus Fight, China Gives Citizens a Color Code, With Red Flags," *New York Times*, March 1, 2020, https://www.nytimes.com/2020/03/01/business/china-coronavirus-surveillance.html.

36. "COVID-19 Pandemic Planning Scenarios" (Centers for Disease Control and Prevention, July 10, 2020), https://www.cdc.gov/coronavirus/2019-ncov/hcp/planning-scenarios.html.

37. Mozur, Zhong, and Krolik, "In Coronavirus Fight, China Gives Citizens a Color Code, With Red Flags."

38. Marija Zivanovic-Smith, Senior Vice President, Corporate Marketing, Communications, and External Affairs of NCR, interview by Yossi Sheffi, May 26, 2020.

39. Zivanovic-Smith.

40. Stefan Lazarevic, General Manager, NCR Serbia & EMEA External Affairs Director, interview by Yossi Sheffi, May 26, 2020.

41. Alex Williams, "The Drones Were Ready for This Moment," *New York Times*, May 23, 2020, https://www.nytimes.com/2020/05/23/style/drones-coronavirus.html.

42. Jennifer Nalewicki, "Singapore Is Using a Robotic Dog to Enforce Proper Social Distancing During COVID-19," *Smithsonian Magazine*, May 21, 2020, https://www.smithsonianmag.com/smart-news/singapore-using-robotic-dog-enforce-proper-social-distancing-during-covid-19-180974912.

43. Annie Palmer, "Amazon Is Testing a Wearable Device That Lights up and Beeps When Warehouse Workers Get Too Close to Each Other," *CNBC*, June 16, 2020, https://www.cnbc.com/2020/06/16/amazon-tests-wearable-social-distancing-device-for-warehouse-workers.html.

44. Allison Aubrey, "No-Touch Greetings Take Off: People Are Getting Creative About Saying 'Hi,'" *NPR*, March 15, 2020, https://www.npr.org/sections/health-shots/2020/03/15/814540484/no-touch-greetings-take-off-people-are-getting-creative-about-saying-hi.

45. "Google Search: Gadgets for Contactless World," Google, accessed August 11, 2020, https://www.google.com/search?source=univ&tbm=isch&q=gadgets+for+contactless+world.

46. "How to Rebound Stronger from COVID-19: Resilience in Manufacturing and Supply Systems" (World Economic Forum, May 1, 2020), https://www.weforum.org/whitepapers/how-to-rebound-stronger-from-covid-19-resilience-in-manufacturing-and-supply-systems.

47. Nancy Cleeland, "Masks On? What Employers Need to Know About Face Coverings at Work," Society for Human Resource Management, June 15, 2020, https://www.shrm.org/resourcesandtools/hr-topics/employee-relations/pages/face-masks.aspx.

48. "Legal Alert: Businesses That Mandate Masks For Employees And Customers Need To Consider ADA Issues," Fisher Phillips LLP, May 30, 2020, https://www.fisherphillips.com/resources-alerts-businesses-that-mandate-masks-for-employees-and.

49. "Considerations for Wearing Masks," Centers for Disease Control and Prevention, August 7, 2020, https://www.cdc.gov/coronavirus/2019-ncov/prevent-getting-sick/cloth-face-cover-guidance.html.

50. Rupert Wingfield-Hayes, "The Puzzle of Japan's Low Virus Death Rate," *BBC News*, July 4, 2020, https://www.bbc.com/news/world-asia-53188847.

51. Joel Rush, "Mask Use Still Widespread In Slowly Reopening Japan As Coronavirus Cases Remain Low," *Forbes*, June 22, 2020, https://www.forbes.com/sites/joelrush/2020/06/22/mask-use-still-widespread-in-slowly-reopening-japan-as-coronavirus-cases-remain-low.

52. Stephen Chen, "Face Masks Save Lives, Japanese Coronavirus Study Says," *South China Morning Post*, June 25, 2020, https://www.scmp.com/news/china/science/article/3090440/coronavirus-face-masks-save-lives-japanese-study-says.

53.   Thomas Parker, "Will Covid-19 Change the Future of the Hand
        Sanitiser Market?," *NS Medical Devices,* May 20, 2020, https://www.
        nsmedicaldevices.com/analysis/hand-sanitiser-future-market.

54.   Lauren Gelman, "40+ of the Most Trusted Brands In America," *Reader's
        Digest,* September 11, 2018, https://www.rd.com/list/most-trusted-brands-
        america.

55.   Jamie Bell, "Germ-Zapping Robots That Could Clean Offices and
        Hotels after Covid-19," *NS Medical Devices,* May 21, 2020, https://www.
        nsmedicaldevices.com/news/germ-zapping-robots-covid-19-xenex.

56.   Heather Ostis, Vice President of Supply Chain, Delta Air Lines, interview
        by Yossi Sheffi, June 3, 2020.

57.   E.C. Riley, G. Murphy, and R.L. Riley, "Airborne Spread of Measles in a
        Suburban Elementary School," *Journal of Epidemiology* 107, no. 5 (May
        1978): 421–432, https://doi.org/10.1093/oxfordjournals.aje.a112560.

58.   Timo Smieszek, Gianrocco Lazzari, and Marcel Salathé, "Assessing the
        Dynamics and Control of Droplet- and Aerosol-Transmitted Influenza
        Using an Indoor Positioning System," *Scientific Reports* 9 (February 18,
        2019): 2185, https://doi.org/10.1038/s41598-019-38825-y.

59.   "Communities, Schools, Workplaces, & Events," Centers for Disease
        Control and Prevention, April 30, 2020, https://www.cdc.gov/
        coronavirus/2019-ncov/community/office-buildings.html.

60.   Olivia Mayes, "Air Filtration Systems Help Keep Aircraft Cabins Safe,"
        Delta News Hub, Delta Air Lines, March 14, 2020, https://news.delta.com/
        video-air-filtration-systems-help-keep-aircraft-cabins-safe.

61.   Evan Ramstad, "For General Mills, Outbreak Spurred a Run on Its
        Products and Rush in Its Factories," *Star Tribune* (Minneapolis), May 3,
        2020, https://www.startribune.com/for-general-mills-outbreak-spurred-a-
        run-on-its-products-and-rush-in-its-factories/570162402.

62.   Bojan Pancevski, "Countries That Kept a Lid on Coronavirus Look to
        Each Other to Revive Their Economies," *Wall Street Journal,* May 2, 2020,
        https://www.wsj.com/articles/countries-that-kept-a-lid-on-coronavirus-
        look-to-each-other-to-revive-their-economies-11588424855.

Chapter 11: Cool Home Offices

1.   Sarah Moseley, "Top 4 Interactive Whiteboard Apps," *Highfive* (blog),
        accessed August 23, 2020, https://highfive.com/blog/top-4-interactive-
        whiteboard-apps-remote-meetings.

2.   Board of Governors of the Federal Reserve System, "Report on the Economic Well-Being of U.S. Households in 2019, Featuring Supplemental Data from April 2020" (Washington, D.C.: Federal Reserve System, May 2020), https://www.federalreserve.gov/publications/2020-economic-well-being-of-us-households-in-2019-financial-repercussions-from-covid-19.htm.

3.   "How to Rebound Stronger from COVID-19: Resilience in Manufacturing and Supply Systems" (World Economic Forum, May 1, 2020), https://www.weforum.org/whitepapers/how-to-rebound-stronger-from-covid-19-resilience-in-manufacturing-and-supply-systems.

4.   Lee Clifford, "Working from Home Is Going So Well That This Fortune 100 Company Is Going to Keep Doing It—Permanently," *Fortune,* May 11, 2020, https://fortune.com/2020/05/11/permanent-work-from-home-coronavirus-nationwide-fortune-100.

5.   "Microsoft Corp. (MSFT) CEO Satya Nadella on Q3 2020 Results," Seeking Alpha, April 30, 2020, https://seekingalpha.com/article/4341291-microsoft-corp-msft-ceo-satya-nadella-on-q3-2020-results-earnings-call-transcript.

6.   Sascha Segan, "What Is 5G?," *PCMag,* April 6, 2020, https://www.pcmag.com/news/what-is-5g.

7.   Darren Allan, "Wi-Fi 6: Everything You Need to Know," *TechRadar,* October 29, 2019, https://www.techradar.com/news/wi-fi-6-release-date-news-and-rumors.

8.   Jon Brodkin, "Millimeter-Wave 5G Will Never Scale beyond Dense Urban Areas, T-Mobile Says," *Ars Technica,* April 22, 2019, https://arstechnica.com/information-technology/2019/04/millimeter-wave-5g-will-never-scale-beyond-dense-urban-areas-t-mobile-says.

9.   Thomson Reuters, "Q1 2020 AT&T Inc Earnings Call," 2020, https://investors.att.com/~/media/Files/A/ATT-IR/financial-reports/quarterly-earnings/2020/Final%201Q20%20earnings%20transcript.pdf.

10.   Dennis Flynn, Senior Director, Supply Chain and Inventory Management, Walmart eCommerce, interview by Yossi Sheffi, June 12, 2020.

11.   Asa Fitch, "Intel Reports Profit Surge but Warns of Further Delays on Advanced Chips," *Wall Street Journal,* July 23, 2020, https://www.wsj.com/articles/intel-reports-profit-surge-but-warns-of-further-delays-on-advanced-chips-11595536707.

12.   Clifford, "Working from Home Is Going So Well That This Fortune 100 Company Is Going to Keep Doing It—Permanently."

13. Sarah Frier, "Tech Workers Consider Escaping Silicon Valley's Sky-High Rents," *Bloomberg*, May 14, 2020, https://www.bloomberg.com/news/articles/2020-05-14/tech-workers-consider-escaping-silicon-valley-s-sky-high-rents.

14. Lynn Torrel, Chief Supply Chain and Procurement Officer, Flex, interview by Yossi Sheffi, June 1, 2020.

15. "How CEOs See Today's Coronavirus World," *Wall Street Journal*, June 11, 2020, https://www.wsj.com/articles/how-ceos-see-todays-coronavirus-world-11587720600.

16. Uri Berliner, "Get A Comfortable Chair: Permanent Work From Home Is Coming," *NPR*, June 22, 2020, https://www.npr.org/2020/06/22/870029658/get-a-comfortable-chair-permanent-work-from-home-is-coming.

17. Drew Harwell, "Managers Turn to Surveillance Software, Always-on Webcams to Ensure Employees Are (Really) Working from Home," *Washington Post*, April 30, 2020, https://www.washingtonpost.com/technology/2020/04/30/work-from-home-surveillance.

18. "Latest Work-at-Home/Telecommuting/Mobile Work/Remote Work Statistics," Global Workplace Analytics, accessed August 12, 2020, https://globalworkplaceanalytics.com/telecommuting-statistics.

19. Nicole Spector, "Why Are Big Companies Calling Their Remote Workers Back to the Office?," *NBC News*, July 27, 2017, https://www.nbcnews.com/business/business-news/why-are-big-companies-calling-their-remote-workers-back-office-n787101.

20. Joel Stein, "The Video Call Is Starting. Time to Put on Your Zoom Shirt," *New York Times*, June 29, 2020, https://www.nytimes.com/2020/06/29/business/zoom-shirt.html.

21. Katie Deighton, "Miss Your Office? Some Companies Are Building Virtual Replicas," *Wall Street Journal*, May 27, 2020, https://www.wsj.com/articles/miss-your-office-some-companies-are-building-virtual-replicas-11590573600.

22. Kimberly Holland, "What COVID-19 Is Doing to Our Mental Health," Healthline, May 8, 2020, https://www.healthline.com/health-news/what-covid-19-is-doing-to-our-mental-health.

23. Meri Stevens, Worldwide Vice President, Consumer Health Supply Chain and Deliver, Johnson & Johnson, interview by Yossi Sheffi, June 4, 2020.

24. World Economic Forum, "How to Rebound Stronger from COVID-19."

25. Hannah Sampson and Natalie Compton, "11 Ways the Pandemic Will Change Travel," *Washington Post,* June 15, 2020, https://www.washingtonpost.com/travel/2020/06/15/11-ways-pandemic-will-change-travel.

26. Frier, "Tech Workers Consider Escaping Silicon Valley's Sky-High Rents."

27. Magdalena Petrova and Michael Sheetz, "Why in the next Decade Companies Will Launch Thousands More Satellites than in All of History," *CNBC,* December 15, 2019, https://www.cnbc.com/2019/12/14/spacex-oneweb-and-amazon-to-launch-thousands-more-satellites-in-2020s.html.

28. Mark Travers, "What Percentage Of Workers Can Realistically Work From Home? New Data From Norway Offer Clues," *Forbes,* April 24, 2020, https://www.forbes.com/sites/traversmark/2020/04/24/what-percentage-of-workers-can-realistically-work-from-home-new-data-from-norway-offer-clues/#af479c78fee0.

29. Sophie-Claire Hoeller, "Barbados Is Officially Letting People Move There to Work Remotely for a Year, and All You Need to Do Is Fill out an Application," *Insider,* July 23, 2020, https://www.insider.com/work-remote-live-caribbean-barbados-new-visa-2020-7.

30. "Digital Nomad Visa," Republic of Estonia e-Residency, accessed August 23, 2020, https://e-resident.gov.ee/nomadvisa.

31. Adam Taylor, "Barbados Wants You to Work from Its Beaches during the Pandemic," *Washington Post,* July 16, 2020, https://www.washingtonpost.com/world/2020/07/16/barbados-work-remote-coronavirus.

32. "Portugal Golden Visa 2020 Guide," Property Lisbon, February 17, 2020, https://www.propertylisbon.com/portugal-golden-visa-2020-guide.

33. "Golden Visa Investment Almost Triples," *Portugal News,* June 12, 2020, https://www.theportugalnews.com/news/golden-visa-investment-almost-triples/54458.

Chapter 12: Higher Education May Never Be the Same

1. "The History of Online Schooling," OnlineSchools.org, accessed August 12, 2020, https://www.onlineschools.org/visual-academy/the-history-of-online-schooling.

2. "Open University," in *Encyclopedia Britannica,* December 17, 2008, https://www.britannica.com/topic/Open-University-British-education.

3. Steve Bradt, "Online Courses + Time on Campus = a New Path to an MIT Master's Degree," *MIT News*, Massachusetts Institute of Technology, October 7, 2015, http://news.mit.edu/2015/online-supply-chain-management-masters-mitx-micromasters-1007.

4. Institute-Wide Task Force on the Future of MIT Education, "Final Report" (Cambridge, Mass.: Massachusetts Institute of Technology, July 28, 2014), https://jwel.mit.edu/sites/mit-jwel/files/assets/files/document_task_force_foe_final_140728.pdf.

5. Michael D. Smith, "Are Universities Going the Way of the CDs and Cable TV?," *Atlantic*, June 22, 2020, https://www.theatlantic.com/ideas/archive/2020/06/university-like-cd-streaming-age/613291.

6. Michael B. Horn, "Will Half Of All Colleges Really Close In The Next Decade?," *Forbes*, December 13, 2018, https://www.forbes.com/sites/michaelhorn/2018/12/13/will-half-of-all-colleges-really-close-in-the-next-decade/#4325b12852e5.

7. Lydia Saad, "Majority of U.S. Workers Say Job Doesn't Require a Degree," *Gallup*, September 9, 2013, https://news.gallup.com/poll/164321/majority-workers-say-job-require-degree.aspx.

8. Bryan Alexander, "Academia after Peak Higher Education," personal blog, May 29, 2018, https://bryanalexander.org/future-of-education/academia-after-peak-higher-education.

9. Kevin Carey, *The End of College: Creating the Future of Learning and the University of Everywhere* (New York: Riverhead, 2015), https://www.penguinrandomhouse.com/books/314571/the-end-of-college-by-kevin-carey.

10. U.S. Department of Education, National Center for Education Statistics, Integrated Postsecondary Education Data System, "Postsecondary Institution Revenues," The Condition of Education, May 2020, https://nces.ed.gov/programs/coe/indicator_cud.asp.

11. Justin Bariso, "Google Has Announced a Plan to Disrupt the College Degree," Inc., August 19, 2020, https://www.inc.com/justin-bariso/google-plan-disrupt-college-degree-university-higher-education-certificate-project-management-data-analyst.html.

Chapter 13: Wider Social, Economic, and Information Gaps

1. Brian Rosenthal et al., "Why Surviving Covid Might Come Down to Which NYC Hospital Admits You," *New York Times*, July 31, 2020, https://www.nytimes.com/2020/07/01/nyregion/Coronavirus-hospitals.html.

2. Rachel Siegel, "Hard-Hit Retailers Projected to Shutter as Many as 25,000 Stores This Year, Mostly in Malls," *Washington Post*, June 9, 2020, https://www.washingtonpost.com/business/2020/06/09/retail-store-closure-mall.

3. Tami Luhby, "Nearly 40% of Low-Income Workers Lost Their Jobs in March," *CNN*, May 15, 2020, https://www.cnn.com/2020/05/14/economy/low-income-layoffs-coronavirus/index.html.

4. Davide Furceri et al., "COVID-19 Will Raise Inequality If Past Pandemics Are a Guide," *VoxEU* (Centre for Economic Policy Research, May 8, 2020), https://voxeu.org/article/covid-19-will-raise-inequality-if-past-pandemics-are-guide.

5. Vicky McKeever, "Coronavirus Could Push Half a Billion More People into Poverty Globally, UN Warns," *CNBC*, April 9, 2020, https://www.cnbc.com/2020/04/09/coronavirus-could-push-half-a-billion-people-into-poverty-globally.html.

6. "Covid-19 Threatens Europe's Success at Fighting Inequality," *Economist*, June 6, 2020, https://www.economist.com/europe/2020/06/06/covid-19-threatens-europes-success-at-fighting-inequality.

7. "The Covid-19 Pandemic Will Be Over by the End of 2021, Says Bill Gates," *Economist*, August 18, 2020, https://www.economist.com/international/2020/08/18/the-covid-19-pandemic-will-be-over-by-the-end-of-2021-says-bill-gates.

8. "The Covid-19 Pandemic Will Be Over by the End of 2021, Says Bill Gates."

9. Board of Governors of the Federal Reserve System, "Report on the Economic Well-Being of U.S. Households in 2019, Featuring Supplemental Data from April 2020" (Washington, D.C.: Federal Reserve System, May 2020), https://www.federalreserve.gov/publications/2020-economic-well-being-of-us-households-in-2019-financial-repercussions-from-covid-19.htm.

10. "How Deep Will Downturns in Rich Countries Be?," *Economist*, April 16, 2020, https://www.economist.com/finance-and-economics/2020/04/16/how-deep-will-downturns-in-rich-countries-be.

11. Amanda L. Gordon, "They're the Last Rich People Left on the Upper East Side," *Bloomberg*, March 27, 2020, https://www.bloomberg.com/news/articles/2020-03-27/they-re-the-last-rich-people-left-on-the-upper-east-side.

12. Stefanos Chen and Sydney Franklin, "Real Estate Prices Fall Sharply in New York," *New York Times,* July 2, 2020, https://www.nytimes.com/2020/07/02/realestate/coronavirus-real-estate-price-drop.html.

13. Melissa Sou-Jie Van Brunnersum, "Coronavirus Exposes the Divide between China's Rich and Poor," *Deutsche Welle,* February 25, 2020, https://www.dw.com/en/coronavirus-exposes-the-divide-between-chinas-rich-and-poor/a-52526369.

14. Laura Begley Bloom, "Want To Escape From America? 12 Countries Where You Can Buy Citizenship (And A Second Passport)," *Forbes,* July 28, 2020, https://www.forbes.com/sites/laurabegleybloom/2020/07/28/escape-america-countries-buy-citizenship-second-passport.

15. Stephanie Condon, "As Snapchat Use Soars during Pandemic, Infrastructure Costs Also Climb," *ZDNet,* April 21, 2020, https://www.zdnet.com/article/as-snapchat-use-soars-during-pandemic-infrastructure-costs-also-climb.

16. John Busby and Julia Tanberk, "FCC Underestimates Americans Unserved by Broadband Internet by 50%," BroadbandNow Research, February 3, 2020, https://broadbandnow.com/research/fcc-underestimates-unserved-by-50-percent.

17. Dana Goldstein, Adam Popescu, and Nikole Hannah-Jones, "As School Moves Online, Many Students Stay Logged Out," *New York Times,* April 6, 2020, https://www.nytimes.com/2020/04/06/us/coronavirus-schools-attendance-absent.html.

18. Deyan Georgiev, "67+ Revealing Statistics about Smartphone Usage in 2020," *TechJury* (blog), March 28, 2019, https://techjury.net/blog/smartphone-usage-statistics.

19. "July Global Statshot," Digital 2020 (DataReportal, July 2020), https://datareportal.com/global-digital-overview.

20. Bhaskar Chakravorti and Ravi Shankar Chaturvedi, "Which Countries Were (And Weren't) Ready for Remote Work?," *Harvard Business Review,* April 29, 2020, https://hbr.org/2020/04/which-countries-were-and-werent-ready-for-remote-work.

21. Hadas Gold, "Netflix and YouTube Are Slowing down in Europe to Keep the Internet from Breaking," *CNN,* March 19, 2020, https://www.cnn.com/2020/03/19/tech/netflix-internet-overload-eu/index.html.

22. Patricia Cohen and Ben Casselman, "Minority Workers Who Lagged in a Boom Are Hit Hard in a Bust," *New York Times,* June 6, 2020, https://www.nytimes.com/2020/06/06/business/economy/jobs-report-minorities.html.

23. Bill Hathaway, "New Analysis Quantifies Risk of COVID-19 to Racial,
     Ethnic Minorities," *YaleNews,* Yale University, May 19, 2020, https://news.
     yale.edu/2020/05/19/new-analysis-quantifies-risk-covid-19-racial-ethnic-
     minorities.

24. Jonathan Daw, "Contribution of Four Comorbid Conditions to Racial/
     Ethnic Disparities in Mortality Risk," *American Journal of Preventive
     Medicine* 52, no. 1S1 (January 2017): S95–S102, https://doi.org/10.1016/j.
     amepre.2016.07.036.

25. Alvaro Sanchez, "Toward Digital Inclusion: Broadband Access in the
     Third Federal Reserve District" (Federal Reserve Bank of Philadelphia,
     March 2020), https://www.philadelphiafed.org/-/media/egmp/resources/
     reports/toward-digital-inclusion-broadband-access-in-the-third-federal-
     reserve-district.pdf.

26. Clive Cookson, Hannah Kuchler, and Richard Milne, "Nations Look
     into Why Coronavirus Hits Ethnic Minorities so Hard," *Financial Times,*
     April 29, 2020, https://www.ft.com/content/5fd6ab18-be4a-48de-b887-
     8478a391dd72.

27. Frank Snowden, *Epidemics and Society* (New Haven, Conn.: Yale
     University Press, 2019), https://yalebooks.yale.edu/book/9780300192216/
     epidemics-and-society.

28. Ana Ionova, Nabih Bulos, and Kate Linthicum, "The Economic
     Devastation Wrought by the Pandemic Could Ultimately Kill More
     People than the Virus Itself," *Los Angeles Times,* May 11, 2020, https://
     www.latimes.com/world-nation/story/2020-05-11/more-than-a-billion-
     people-escaped-poverty-in-the-last-20-years-the-coronavirus-could-
     erase-those-gains.

Part 4: Supply Chains for the Future

1.   "How to Rebound Stronger from COVID-19: Resilience in Manufacturing
     and Supply Systems" (World Economic Forum, May 1, 2020), https://
     www.weforum.org/whitepapers/how-to-rebound-stronger-from-covid-19-
     resilience-in-manufacturing-and-supply-systems.

Chapter 14: An All-Seeing, No-Touch Future

1.   Jennifer L. Schenker, "How To Rebound Stronger From COVID-19," *The
     Innovator* (blog), Medium, May 8, 2020, https://innovator.news/how-to-
     rebound-stronger-from-covid-19-675b20602178.

2. Sharon Terlep, "The U.S. Consumer Is Nesting. Will That Last?," *Wall Street Journal*, May 2, 2020, https://www.wsj.com/articles/the-u-s-consumer-is-nesting-will-that-last-11588392011.

3. Stephen Whiteside, "How P&G Is Approaching the next Tide of Market Research," *Informa Connect*, March 12, 2019, https://informaconnect.com/how-pg-is-approaching-the-next-tide-of-market-research.

4. Lorne Darnell, Founder and Chairman, *FreightVerify*, interview by Yossi Sheffi, August 21, 2020.

5. Rich Pirrotta, Chief Revenue Officer, FreightVerify, interview by Yossi Sheffi, August 14, 2020.

6. Rephrased from Denise M. Rousseau et al., "Not So Different After All: A Cross-Discipline View of Trust," *Academy of Management Review* 23, no. 3 (July 1998): 393–404, https://doi.org/10.5465/AMR.1998.926617.

7. "Etsy, Inc. (ETSY) CEO Joshua Silverman on Q1 2020 Results - Earnings Call Transcript," Seeking Alpha, May 7, 2020, https://seekingalpha.com/article/4343941-etsy-inc-etsy-ceo-joshua-silverman-on-q1-2020-results-earnings-call-transcript.

8. Lynn Torrel, Chief Supply Chain and Procurement Officer, Flex, interview by Yossi Sheffi, June 1, 2020.

9. Meri Stevens, Worldwide Vice President, Consumer Health Supply Chain and Deliver, Johnson & Johnson, interview by Yossi Sheffi, June 4, 2020.

10. Jennifer Smith, "Coronavirus Upheaval Triggers Corporate Search for Supply-Chain Technology," *Wall Street Journal*, April 29, 2020, https://www.wsj.com/articles/coronavirus-upheaval-triggers-corporate-search-for-supply-chain-technology-11588189553.

11. Daniel E. Murray, "History and Development of the Bill of Lading," *University of Miami Law Review* 37, no. 3 (September 1, 1983): 689–732, https://repository.law.miami.edu/umlr/vol37/iss3/13.

12. Jan Keil, "Blockchain in Supply Chain Management: Key Use Cases and Benefits," *Infopulse* (blog), August 8, 2019, https://www.infopulse.com/blog/blockchain-in-supply-chain-management-key-use-cases-and-benefits.

13. Nick Statt, "Amazon Is Expanding Its Cashierless Go Model into a Full-Blown Grocery Store," *The Verge*, February 25, 2020, https://www.theverge.com/2020/2/25/21151021/amazon-go-grocery-store-expansion-open-seattle-cashier-less.

14. Torrel, Chief Supply Chain and Procurement Officer, Flex.

15. Emily A. Vogels, "About One-in-Five Americans Use a Smart Watch or Fitness Tracker," *Fact Tank* (blog), Pew Research Center, January 9, 2020, https://www.pewresearch.org/fact-tank/2020/01/09/about-one-in-five-americans-use-a-smart-watch-or-fitness-tracker.

16. Sophia Kunthara, "Telemedicine Is Becoming More Popular. That's Good for Prescription Delivery Startups" *Crunchbase News,* May 14, 2020, https://news.crunchbase.com/news/telemedicine-is-becoming-more-popular-thats-good-for-prescription-delivery-startups/?

17. Jeff Bendix and Logan Lutton, "How Doctors Can Develop Patient Relationships Using Just Telehealth Visits," *Medical Economics,* July 21, 2020, https://www.medicaleconomics.com/view/how-doctors-can-develop-patient-relationships-using-just-telehealth-visits.

18. Kat Fu Lee, "Covid-19 Will Accelerate the AI Health Care Revolution," *Wired,* May 22, 2020, https://www.wired.com/story/covid-19-will-accelerate-ai-health-care-revolution.

19. Steve Mollman, "How Artificial Intelligence Provided Early Warnings of the Wuhan Virus," *Quartz,* January 25, 2020, https://qz.com/1791222/how-artificial-intelligence-provided-early-warning-of-wuhan-virus.

20. Mollman.

Chapter 15: Automation Increases

1. "Tyson Foods Inc. 2020 Q2 - Results - Earnings Call Presentation (NYSE:TSN)," Seeking Alpha, May 5, 2020, https://seekingalpha.com/article/4343089-tyson-foods-inc-2020-q2-results-earnings-call-presentation.

2. Tyson Foods Inc., "New Facility to Boost Tyson Foods' Automation and Robotics Efforts," news release, August 8, 2019, https://www.tysonfoods.com/news/news-releases/2019/8/new-facility-boost-tyson-foods-automation-and-robotics-efforts.

3. "Tyson Foods Inc. 2020 Q2 Earnings Call."

4. Dean Best, "Meat Industry to Step up Spending on Automation, Tyson Foods Forecasts," *Just-Food,* May 6, 2020, https://www.just-food.com/news/meat-industry-to-step-up-spending-on-automation-tyson-foods-forecasts_id143641.aspx.

5. David Greenfield, "BMW Outfits Robots with Artificial Intelligence," *Automation World,* June 24, 2020, https://www.automationworld.com/factory/robotics/article/21138274/bmw-outfits-robots-with-artificial-intelligence.

6.   Simon Duval Smith, "BMW – Revolutionising Logistics through Robotics and Virtual Reality," *Automotive Purchasing and Supply Chain,* January 24, 2019, https://weekly.automotivepurchasingandsupplychain.com/210119/features/bmw-future-logistics.php.

7.   Jessica Young, "US Ecommerce Sales Grow 14.9% in 2019," *Digital Commerce 360,* February 19, 2020, https://www.digitalcommerce360.com/article/us-ecommerce-sales.

8.   Hayley Peterson, "More than 9,300 Stores Are Closing in 2019 as the Retail Apocalypse Drags on — Here's the Full List," *Business Insider,* December 23, 2019, https://www.businessinsider.com/stores-closing-in-2019-list-2019-3.

9.   Lauren Thomas, "25,000 Stores Are Predicted to Close in 2020, as the Coronavirus Pandemic Accelerates Industry Upheaval," *CNBC,* June 9, 2020, https://www.cnbc.com/2020/06/09/coresight-predicts-record-25000-retail-stores-will-close-in-2020.html.

10. Tech Insider, "Inside A Warehouse Where Thousands Of Robots Pack Groceries," May 9, 2018, YouTube video, 0:03:20, https://www.youtube.com/watch?v=4DKrcpa8Z_E.

11. "Robot Hand Is Soft and Strong," Education, *Robotics @ MIT* (blog), Massachusetts Institute of Technology, March 16, 2019, https://robotics.mit.edu/robot-hand-soft-and-strong.

12. Gary Wollenbaupt, "Move over Delivery Drones, Warehouse Drones Are Ready for the Spotlight," *Supply Chain Dive,* August 28, 2018, https://www.supplychaindive.com/news/move-over-delivery-drones-warehouse-drones-are-ready-for-the-spotlight/531038.

13. International Federation of Robotics, "Robot Investment Reaches Record 16.5 Billion USD – IFR Presents World Robotics," news release, September 18, 2019, /2019-09-18_Press_Release_IFR_World_Robotics_2019_Industrial_Robots_English.pdf.

14. Jennifer Smith, "Coronavirus Upheaval Triggers Corporate Search for Supply-Chain Technology," *Wall Street Journal,* April 29, 2020, https://www.wsj.com/articles/coronavirus-upheaval-triggers-corporate-search-for-supply-chain-technology-11588189553.

15. Starship Technologies, "Starship Campus Delivery Service with Robots," April 30, 2018, YouTube video, 0:02:57, https://www.youtube.com/watch?v=P_zRwq9c8LY.

16. Kirsten Korosec, "Starship Technologies Is Sending Its Autonomous Robots to More Cities as Demand for Contactless Delivery Rises,"

TechCrunch (blog), April 9, 2020, https://techcrunch.com/2020/04/09/
starship-technologies-is-sending-its-autonomous-robots-to-more-
cities-as-demand-for-contactless-delivery-rises/?_guc_consent_
skip=1594259929.

17. Timothy B. Lee, "The Pandemic Is Bringing Us Closer to Our Robot
    Takeout Future," *Ars Technica,* April 24, 2020, https://arstechnica.com/
    tech-policy/2020/04/the-pandemic-is-bringing-us-closer-to-our-robot-
    takeout-future.

18. Joanna Stern, "Like Amazon, UPS Also Considering Using Unmanned
    Flying Vehicles," *ABC News,* December 3, 2013, https://abcnews.go.com/
    Technology/amazon-ups-drone-delivery-options/story?id=21086160.

19. Miriam McNabb, "Drone Delivery Heroes Zipline Launch World's Largest
    Vaccine Delivery Network in Ghana," *DroneLife,* April 24, 2019, https://
    dronelife.com/2019/04/24/drone-delivery-heroes-zipline-launch-worlds-
    largest-vaccine-delivery-network-in-ghana.

20. Jake Bright, "Zipline Begins US Medical Delivery with Drone Program
    Honed in Africa," *TechCrunch* (blog), May 27, 2020, https://social.
    techcrunch.com/2020/05/26/zipline-begins-us-medical-delivery-with-
    uav-program-honed-in-africa.

21. Anne D'Innocenzio, "Walmart to Test Drone Delivery with Zipline
    in Latest Deal," *ABC News,* September 14, 2020, https://abcnews.
    go.com/Business/wireStory/walmart-test-drone-delivery-zipline-latest-
    deal-72999412.

22. Felicia Shivakumar, "Giant Cargo Drones Will Deliver Packages
    Farther and Faster," *The Verge,* June 10, 2019, https://www.theverge.
    com/2019/6/10/18657150/autonomous-cargo-drones-delivery-boeing-
    aircraft-faa-regulation.

23. Aaron Brown, "Mercedes-Benz Turns a Van Into a Delivery Drone
    Mothership," *The Drive* (blog), September 7, 2016, https://www.thedrive.
    com/news/5118/mercedes-benz-turns-a-van-into-a-delivery-drone-
    mothership.

24. Jared Wade, "RPA: How 5 Financial Firms Are Using Robotic Process
    Automation," *Finance Americas* (blog), September 3, 2017, https://
    financetnt.com/rpa-real-world-practical-ways-5-financial-services-firms-
    use-robotic-process-automation.

25. Kasey Panetta, "How Chinese Companies Successfully Adapted to
    COVID-19," *Smarter with Gartner* (blog), Gartner Inc., June 16, 2020,
    //www.gartner.com/smarterwithgartner/how-successful-chinese-
    companies-adapted-to-covid-19.

26.   Meri Stevens, Worldwide Vice President, Consumer Health Supply Chain and Deliver, Johnson & Johnson, interview by Yossi Sheffi, June 4, 2020.

Chapter 16: Just-in-Time Gets Just-a-Tweak

1.   Stephen Long, "'Just-in-Time' Economy out of Time as Pandemic Exposes Fatal Flaws," *ABC News* (Australian Broadcasting Corporation), May 1, 2020, https://www.abc.net.au/news/2020-05-02/coronavirus-pandemic-exposes-just-in-time-economy/12206776.

2.   Evan Fraser, "Coronavirus: The Perils of Our 'Just Enough, Just in Time' Food System," *The Conversation*, March 16, 2020, http://theconversation.com/coronavirus-the-perils-of-our-just-enough-just-in-time-food-system-133724.

3.   Lynn Torrel, Chief Supply Chain and Procurement Officer, Flex, interview by Yossi Sheffi, June 1, 2020.

4.   Taiichi Ohno, *Toyota Production System: Beyond Large-Scale Production,* trans. Productivity Press (New York: Taylor & Francis, 1988), https://www.amazon.com/Toyota-Production-System-Beyond-Large-Scale/dp/0915299143.

5.   Yossi Sheffi, *The Resilient Enterprise: Overcoming Vulnerability for Competitive Advantage* (Cambridge, Mass.: MIT Press, 2005), 173–174, https://mitpress.mit.edu/books/resilient-enterprise.

6.   Yossi Sheffi, "Supply Chain Management under the Threat of International Terrorism," *International Journal of Logistics Management* 12, no. 2 (July 2001): 1–11, https://doi.org/10.1108/09574090110806262.

7.   Sheffi, *Resilient Enterprise,* 174.

8.   "Honeywell International Inc. (NYSE: HON) Q1 2020 Earnings Call Transcript," AlphaStreet, May 1, 2020, https://news.alphastreet.com/honeywell-international-inc-nyse-hon-q1-2020-earnings-call-transcript.

9.   Tim Ryan et al., "PwC's COVID-19 CFO Pulse Survey" (PricewaterhouseCoopers, April 27, 2020), https://www.pwc.com/us/en/library/covid-19/pwc-covid-19-cfo-pulse-survey-4.html.

Chapter 17: The China Question

1.   Jonty Bloom, "Will Coronavirus Reverse Globalisation?," *BBC News*, April 2, 2020, https://www.bbc.com/news/business-52104978.

2.   Rick Helfenbein, "Retail Set To Revolt – As President Trump Plays Politics With China," *Forbes*, May 10, 2020, https://www.forbes.com/sites/

rickhelfenbein/2020/05/10/retail-set-to-revoltas-president-trump-plays-politics-with-china.

3. Alexandra Harney, "China's Coronavirus-Induced Supply Chain Woes Fan Concerns of Possible Drug Shortages," *Reuters*, March 11, 2020, https://www.reuters.com/article/us-health-coronavirus-pharmaceuticals-ap-idUSKBN20Y1C7.

4. Huileng Tan, "China Is Producing Higher Value Goods — Even as Factories Are Shifting Away from the Mainland," *CNBC*, May 14, 2020, https://www.cnbc.com/2020/05/14/china-is-producing-higher-value-goods-even-as-factories-shifting-from-mainland.html.

5. Kenneth Rapoza, "New Data Shows U.S. Companies Are Definitely Leaving China," *Forbes*, April 7, 2020, https://www.forbes.com/sites/kenrapoza/2020/04/07/new-data-shows-us-companies-are-definitely-leaving-china.

6. Kenneth Rapoza, "China Set To Lose Tons Of Businesses Post-Pandemic," *Forbes*, April 20, 2020, https://www.forbes.com/sites/kenrapoza/2020/04/20/china-set-to-lose-tons-of-businesses-post-pandemic.

7. Sophia Yan, "'Made in China' Isn't So Cheap Anymore, and That Could Spell Headache for Beijing," *CNBC*, February 27, 2017, https://www.cnbc.com/2017/02/27/chinese-wages-rise-made-in-china-isnt-so-cheap-anymore.html.

8. Erin Duffin, "Manufacturing Labor Costs per Hour: China, Vietnam, Mexico 2016-2020," Statista, August 9, 2019, https://www.statista.com/statistics/744071/manufacturing-labor-costs-per-hour-china-vietnam-mexico.

9. Ethirajan Anbarasan, "Chinese Factories Turn to Bangladesh," *BBC News*, August 29, 2012, https://www.bbc.com/news/business-19394405.

10. "Trump Official: Coronavirus Could Boost US Jobs," *BBC News*, January 31, 2020, https://www.bbc.com/news/business-51276323.

11. "Japan Reveals 87 Projects Eligible for 'China Exit' Subsidies," *Nikkei Asian Review*, July 17, 2020, https://asia.nikkei.com/Economy/Japan-reveals-87-projects-eligible-for-China-exit-subsidies.

12. Micah Maidenberg, "Fewer Products, Localized Production—Companies Seek Supply-Chain Solutions," *Wall Street Journal*, April 26, 2020, https://www.wsj.com/articles/coronavirus-disrupted-supply-chains-that-companies-are-still-fixing-11587893401.

13. Sunny Oh, "Here's Why Companies Won't Move Their Supply Chains out of China, Says Morgan Stanley," *MarketWatch,* April 29, 2020, https://www.marketwatch.com/story/heres-why-companies-wont-move-their-supply-chains-out-of-china-says-morgan-stanley-2020-04-29.

14. "Large U.S. Companies Will Continue Sourcing and Production in China," *China Global Television Network,* April 22, 2020, https://news.cgtn.com/news/2020-04-21/Survey-Large-U-S-companies-will-continue-their-business-in-China-PS6sUD7giI/index.html.

15. "A Small Town in China Makes Half of Japan's Coffins," *Economist,* May 14, 2020, https://www.economist.com/china/2020/05/14/a-small-town-in-china-makes-half-of-japans-coffins.

16. Charles Annis, "BOE Becomes World's Largest Flat-Panel Display Manufacturer in 2019 as China Continues Rise to Global Market Dominance," *Omdia* (blog), Informa Tech, June 4, 2019, https://technology.informa.com/614595/boe-becomes-worlds-largest-flat-panel-display-manufacturer-in-2019-as-china-continues-rise-to-global-market-dominance.

17. Yoko Kubota and Raffaele Huang, "China's Car-Sales Slump Extends Into Another Year," *Wall Street Journal,* January 9, 2020, https://www.wsj.com/articles/chinas-auto-sales-slump-extends-into-another-year-11578558587.

18. "USA – Flash Report, Sales Volume, 2019," MarkLines, January 4, 2020, https://www.marklines.com/en/statistics/flash_sales/salesfig_usa_2019.

19. Henk Bekker, "2019 (Full Year) Europe: Car Sales per EU and EFTA Country," Car Sales Statistics, January 16, 2020, https://www.best-selling-cars.com/europe/2019-full-year-europe-car-sales-per-eu-and-efta-country.

20. "The Changing Trends of Reshoring in the United States," Survey of Global Manufacturing (Los Gatos, Calif.: The Reshoring Institute, May 2019), https://reshoringinstitute.org/wp-content/uploads/2019/05/2019-Survey-of-Global-Mfg.pdf.

21. Yossi Sheffi, "Postponement for Flexibility," in *The Resilient Enterprise: Overcoming Vulnerability for Competitive Advantage* (Cambridge, Mass.: MIT Press, 2005), 195–208, https://mitpress.mit.edu/books/resilient-enterprise.

22. Naturally, assuming independent or negative correlation between the demand for the variants.

23. Judd Devermont and Catherine Chiang, "Innocent Bystanders: Why the U.S.-China Trade War Hurts African Economies" (Washington, D.C.:

Center for Strategic & International Studies, April 9, 2019), https://www.csis.org/analysis/innocent-bystanders-why-us-china-trade-war-hurts-african-economies.

24. "Travel 'Bubbles' Offer a Potential Way Forward," editorial, *Financial Times,* May 11, 2020, https://www.ft.com/content/d82a57d4-9086-11ea-9b25-c36e3584cda8.

25. Matina Stevis-Gridneff, "E.U. Formalizes Reopening, Barring Travelers From U.S.," *New York Times,* June 30, 2020, https://www.nytimes.com/2020/06/30/world/europe/eu-reopening-blocks-us-travelers.html.

26. "Understanding the 'China, Plus One' Strategy," *Procurement Bulletin* (blog), July 20, 2019, https://www.procurementbulletin.com/understanding-the-china-plus-one-strategy.

27. Oh, "Here's Why Companies Won't Move Their Supply Chains out of China, Says Morgan Stanley."

28. Ralf Busche, Senior Vice President, Global Supply Chain Strategy & Management, BASF Group, interview by Yossi Sheffi, June 8, 2020.

29. "Our Business," Walmart Inc., accessed August 14, 2020, https://corporate.walmart.com/our-story/our-business.

30. Liam O'Connell, "Number of Walmart Stores in the U.S. 2012-2019," Statista, April 3, 2020, https://www.statista.com/statistics/269425/total-number-of-walmart-stores-in-the-united-states-by-type.

31. "How to Rebound Stronger from COVID-19: Resilience in Manufacturing and Supply Systems" (World Economic Forum, May 1, 2020), https://www.weforum.org/whitepapers/how-to-rebound-stronger-from-covid-19-resilience-in-manufacturing-and-supply-systems.

Part 5: Of Politics and Pandemics

1. Christopher Alessi, "'All Hands Should Be on Deck' – Key Quotes from Leaders on the Fight against COVID-19," World Economic Forum, April 8, 2020, https://www.weforum.org/agenda/2020/04/covid-19-action-call-8-apr.

2. David Dayen, "Corporate Rescue: How the Fed Bailed Out the Investor Class Without Spending a Cent," *The Intercept,* May 27, 2020, https://theintercept.com/2020/05/27/federal-reserve-corporate-debt-coronavirus.

Chapter 18: The Folly of Trade Wars and Economic Nationalism

1. Bureau of Economic Analysis, "Gross Domestic Product, 2nd Quarter 2020 (Advance Estimate) and Annual Update," news release no. BEA 20–37, July 30, 2020, https://www.bea.gov/news/2020/gross-domestic-product-2nd-quarter-2020-advance-estimate-and-annual-update.

2. John Steele Gordon, "Smoot-Hawley Tariff: A Bad Law, Badly Timed," *Barron's Magazine,* April 21, 2017, https://www.barrons.com/articles/smoot-hawley-tariff-a-bad-law-badly-timed-1492833567.

3. Lynda Bryant-Work, "U.S. Growers, Ag Industry In Crosshairs Of Trump Trade War," *National Compass* (blog), July 5, 2018, https://www.nationalcompass.net/2018/07/05/u-s-growers-ag-industry-in-crosshairs-trump-trade-war.

4. Douglas A. Irwin, "From Smoot-Hawley to Reciprocal Trade Agreements: Changing the Course of U.S. Trade Policy in the 1930s," working paper, NBER Working Paper Series no. 5895 (Cambridge, Mass.: National Bureau of Economic Research, January 1997), https://doi.org/10.3386/w5895.

5. Irwin.

6. Thomas J. Bollyky and Chad P. Bown, "The Tragedy of Vaccine Nationalism," *Foreign Affairs,* October 2020.

7. United Nations, "Everyone, Everywhere Must Have Access to Eventual COVID-19 Immunization, Secretary-General Says in Video Message for Global Vaccine Summit," news release no. SG/SM/20108, June 4, 2020, https://www.un.org/press/en/2020/sgsm20108.doc.htm.

8. James Politi, "US Trade Adviser Seeks to Replace Chinese Drug Supplies," *Financial Times,* February 12, 2020, https://www.ft.com/content/73751cca-4d1a-11ea-95a0-43d18ec715f5.

9. Bollyky and Bown, "The Tragedy of Vaccine Nationalism."

10. Jason Douglas, "As Countries Bar Medical Exports, Some Suggest Bans May Backfire," *Wall Street Journal,* April 4, 2020, https://www.wsj.com/articles/as-countries-bar-medical-exports-some-suggest-bans-may-backfire-11585992600.

11. "The Raid on Remdesivir," editorial, *Wall Street Journal,* July 21, 2020, https://www.wsj.com/articles/the-raid-on-remdesivir-11595373207.

12. Mireya Solís, "The Post COVID-19 World: Economic Nationalism

Triumphant?," *Brookings* (blog), Brookings Institution, July 10, 2020, https://www.brookings.edu/blog/order-from-chaos/2020/07/10/the-post-covid-19-world-economic-nationalism-triumphant.

13. UN Conference on Trade and Development, "Global Trade Update" (Geneva: United Nations, June 2020), https://unctad.org/en/PublicationsLibrary/ditcmisc2020d2_en.pdf.

14. "Global Foreign Direct Investment Projected to Plunge 40% in 2020," United Nations Conference on Trade and Development, June 16, 2020, https://unctad.org/en/pages/newsdetails.aspx?OriginalVersionID=2396.

15. Adam Smith, *An Inquiry into the Nature and Causes of the Wealth of Nations*, 3 vols. (London: W. Strahan and T. Cadell, 1776).

16. David Ricardo, *On the Principles of Political Economy and Taxation,* 3rd ed. (London: John Murray, 1821), https://www.econlib.org/library/Ricardo/ricP.html.

17. Matt Ridley, "Third Culture," Edge, accessed August 27, 2020, https://www.edge.org/3rd_culture/serpentine07/Ridley.html.

18. "Why Trade Is Good for You," *Economist,* October 1, 1998, https://www.economist.com/special-report/1998/10/01/why-trade-is-good-for-you.

19. "A Healthy Re-Examination of Free Trade's Benefits and Shocks," *Economist,* May 4, 2019, https://www.economist.com/open-future/2018/05/04/a-healthy-re-examination-of-free-trades-benefits-and-shocks.

20. Hitesh Bhasin, "6 Reasons Competition Is Good for Business & Benefits of Competition," *Marketing91* (blog), March 9, 2018, https://www.marketing91.com/benefits-of-competition.

21. Vinny Ricciardi, "Are Cell Phones Becoming More Popular than Toilets?," *World Bank Blogs,* August 26, 2019, https://blogs.worldbank.org/opendata/are-cell-phones-becoming-more-popular-toilets.

22. Teresa Ghilarducci, "Tariffs Are Taxes: Raising Costs And Killing Jobs," *Forbes,* June 6, 2019, https://www.forbes.com/sites/teresaghilarducci/2019/06/06/tariffs-are-taxes-raising-costs-and-killing-jobs/#3353c76c60ab.

23. Ghilarducci.

24. Al Root, "How Tariffs Really Work," *Barron's,* May 11, 2019, https://www.barrons.com/articles/are-tariffs-just-another-tax-on-consumers-51557581400.

25. "Saving Global Trade," Bloomberg New Economy Conversation Series (Bloomberg Markets, July 28, 2020), https://www.bloomberg.com/news/videos/2020-07-29/bloomberg-new-economy-conversation-series-saving-global-trade-video.

26. "Saving Global Trade."

27. "Canada Retaliatory Tariffs on US Goods Come into Force," *BBC News,* July 1, 2018, https://www.bbc.com/news/world-us-canada-44635490.

28. Yun Li, "China Will Retaliate with Tariffs on $75 Billion More of US Goods and Resume Auto Tariffs," *CNBC,* August 23, 2019, https://www.cnbc.com/2019/08/23/china-to-retaliate-with-new-tariffs-on-another-75-billion-worth-of-us-goods.html.

29. Menzie Chinn and Bill Plumley, "What Is the Toll of Trade Wars on U.S. Agriculture?," *PBS NewsHour,* January 16, 2020, https://www.pbs.org/newshour/economy/making-sense/what-is-the-toll-of-trade-wars-on-u-s-agriculture.

30. Ana Swanson and Ian Austen, "Trump Reinstates Tariff on Canadian Aluminum," *New York Times,* August 6, 2020, https://www.nytimes.com/2020/08/06/business/economy/trump-canadian-aluminum-tariffs.html.

31. Nithya Nagarajan and Camron Greer, "USTR Rescinds 10% Tariff on Canadian Aluminum, Expecting Imports to 'Normalize,'" *International Trade Insights* (blog), Husch Blackwell LLP, September 16, 2020, https://www.internationaltradeinsights.com/2020/09/ustr-rescinds-10-tariff-on-canadian-aluminum-expecting-imports-to-normalize.

32. Bollyky and Bown, "The Tragedy of Vaccine Nationalism."

33. Drusilla K. Brown, Alan Deardorff, and Robert Stern, "The Effects of Multinational Production on Wages and Working Conditions in Developing Countries," in *Challenges to Globalization: Analyzing the Economics,* ed. Robert E. Baldwin and L. Alan Winters (Chicago: University of Chicago Press, 2004), 279–330, https://www.nber.org/chapters/c9541.

34. "Saving Global Trade."

35. "In Theory There Is No Difference Between Theory and Practice, While In Practice There Is," Quote Investigator, April 14, 2018, https://quoteinvestigator.com/2018/04/14/theory.

36. Joseph E. Stiglitz, "On the Wrong Side of Globalization," *The Opinionator* (blog), New York Times, March 15, 2014, https://opinionator.blogs.nytimes.com/2014/03/15/on-the-wrong-side-of-globalization.

37. Stiglitz.

38. Sylwia Bialek and Alfons J. Weichenrieder, "Do Stringent Environmental Policies Deter FDI? M&A versus Greenfield" (CESIfo Working Paper Series no. 5262, Munich: Center for Economic Studies and Info Institute, April 9, 2015), https://www.mcgill.ca/economics/files/economics/alfons_weichenrieder.pdf; Sunghoon Chung, "Environmental Regulation and Foreign Direct Investment: Evidence from South Korea," *Journal of Development Economics* 108 (May 2014): 222–236, https://doi.org/10.1016/j.jdeveco.2014.01.003.

39. Ralph E. Gomory and William J. Baumol, *Global Trade and Conflicting National Interests* (Cambridge, Mass.: MIT Press, 2001), https://mitpress.mit.edu/books/global-trade-and-conflicting-national-interests.

40. "Anticompetitive Practices," Federal Trade Commission, accessed August 27, 2020, https://www.ftc.gov/enforcement/anticompetitive-practices.

41. Friedrich List and Karl Theodor Eheberg, *Das nationale System der Politischen Oekonomie* [The National System of Political Economy] (Stuttgart: Cotta, 1841), https://oll.libertyfund.org/titles/list-das-national-system-der-politischen-oekonomie.

42. Immanuel Kant, *Perpetual Peace,* 1795, first English edition reprinted with an introduction by Nicholas Butler Murray (New York: Columbia University Press, 1939), https://www.amazon.com/Perpetual-Intro-Nicholas-Murray-Immanuel/dp/B001PAS2GI.

43. Thomas L. Friedman, *The Lexus and the Olive Tree: Understanding Globalization* (New York: Farrar, Straus and Giroux, 1999), https://us.macmillan.com/books/9781250013743.

44. Branko Milanovic, "The World Is Becoming More Equal," *Foreign Affairs,* August 28, 2020, https://www.foreignaffairs.com/articles/world/2020-08-28/world-economic-inequality.

Chapter 19: Strengthening the Medical Supply Chain

1. Bindiya Vakil, CEO, Resilinc, interview by Sheffi Yossi, June 11, 2020.

2. Austen Hufford and Mark Maremont, "Low-Quality Masks Infiltrate U.S. Coronavirus Supply," *Wall Street Journal,* May 3, 2020, https://www.wsj.com/articles/we-werent-protected-low-quality-masks-infiltrate-u-s-coronavirus-supply-11588528690.

3.   Amy Goldstein, Lena H. Sun, and Beth Reinhard, "Desperate for Medical Equipment, States Encounter a Beleaguered National Stockpile," *Washington Post,* March 28, 2020, https://www.washingtonpost.com/national/health-science/desperate-for-medical-equipment-states-encounter-a-beleaguered-national-stockpile/2020/03/28/1f4f9a0a-6f82-11ea-aa80-c2470c6b2034_story.html.

4.   "An Act Making Omnibus Consolidated and Emergency Appropriations for the Fiscal Year Ending September 30, 1999, and for Other Purposes," Pub. L. No. 105–277 (1998), https://www.congress.gov/105/plaws/publ277/PLAW-105publ277.pdf.

5.   Norimitsu Onishi and Constant Méheut, "How France Lost the Weapons to Fight a Pandemic," *New York Times,* May 17, 2020, https://www.nytimes.com/2020/05/17/world/europe/france-coronavirus.html.

6.   Yossi Sheffi, *The Resilient Enterprise: Overcoming Vulnerability for Competitive Advantage* (Cambridge, Mass.: MIT Press, 2005), https://mitpress.mit.edu/books/resilient-enterprise.

7.   Jared S. Hopkins, "Hospitals Stock Up on Covid-19 Drugs to Prepare for Second Wave in Fall," *Wall Street Journal,* July 14, 2020, https://www.wsj.com/articles/hospitals-stock-up-on-covid-19-drugs-to-prepare-for-second-wave-in-fall-11594719000.

8.   Troy Segal, "Bank Stress Test," Investopedia, August 23, 2020, https://www.investopedia.com/terms/b/bank-stress-test.asp.

9.   Onishi and Méheut, "How France Lost the Weapons to Fight a Pandemic."

10.   Hirsh Chitkara, "A Newly Proposed Bipartisan Bill Would Earmark $22 Billion to Lure Chip Manufacturers to US," *Business Insider,* June 12, 2020, https://www.businessinsider.com/chips-for-america-act-will-shift-chip-manufacturing-to-us-2020-6.

11.   Archana Chaudhary, "EU to Focus on Diversifying Crucial Supply Chains, Says Borrell," *Bloomberg,* July 14, 2020, https://www.bloomberg.com/news/articles/2020-07-14/eu-to-focus-on-diversifying-crucial-supply-chains-says-borrell.

12.   Vince Chadwick and Michael Igoe, "After the Pandemic: How Will COVID-19 Transform Global Health and Development?," *Devex,* April 13, 2020, https://www.devex.com/news/after-the-pandemic-how-will-covid-19-transform-global-health-and-development-96936.

13.   "The Face Mask Global Value Chain in the COVID-19 Outbreak: Evidence and Policy Lessons," Organisation for Economic Co-Operation and

Development, May 4, 2020, http://www.oecd.org/coronavirus/policy-responses/the-face-mask-global-value-chain-in-the-covid-19-outbreak-evidence-and-policy-lessons-a4df866d.

14.   Chris Buckley, Sui-Lee Wee, and Amy Qin, "China's Doctors, Fighting the Coronavirus, Beg for Masks," *New York Times,* February 29, 2020, https://www.nytimes.com/2020/02/14/world/asia/china-coronavirus-doctors.html.

15.   Camila Domonoske, "Automakers Might Retool To Make Ventilators," *NPR,* March 19, 2020, https://www.npr.org/sections/coronavirus-live-updates/2020/03/19/818402194/automakers-could-retool-to-make-ventilators.

16.   Robert Sherman, "Over 600 Distilleries, Big and Small, Now Making Hand Sanitizer during Coronavirus Outbreak," *Fox News,* April 9, 2020, https://www.foxnews.com/food-drink/distilleries-hand-sanitizer-coronavirus-hundreds.

17.   Melanie Evans and Austen Hufford, "Critical Component of Protective Masks in Short Supply," *Wall Street Journal,* March 7, 2020, https://www.wsj.com/articles/coronavirus-pressures-supply-chain-for-protective-masks-11583552527.

18.   Ed Edwards, "What Is Melt-Blown Extrusion and How Is It Used for Making Masks?," ThomasNet, accessed August 27, 2020, https://www.thomasnet.com/articles/machinery-tools-supplies/what-is-melt-blown-extrusion.

19.   "Polypropylene Market To Reach USD 155.57 Billion By 2026," *Globe Newswire,* August 1, 2019, http://www.globenewswire.com/news-release/2019/08/01/1895698/0/en/Polypropylene-Market-To-Reach-USD-155-57-Billion-By-2026-Reports-And-Data.html.

Chapter 20: Green Takes a Back Seat to Recovery

1.   Jean Pisani-Ferry, "Building a Post-Pandemic World Will Not Be Easy," *Project Syndicate,* April 30, 2020, https://www.project-syndicate.org/commentary/environmental-and-economic-tradeoffs-in-covid19-recovery-by-jean-pisani-ferry-2020-04.

2.   Corinne Le Quéré et al., "Temporary Reduction in Daily Global CO_2 Emissions during the COVID-19 Forced Confinement," *Nature Climate Change* 10, no. 7 (July 2020): 647–653, https://doi.org/10.1038/s41558-020-0797-x.

3.   Chris Mooney, Brady Dennis, and John Muyskens, "Global Emissions
     Plunged an Unprecedented 17 Percent during the Coronavirus
     Pandemic," *Washington Post,* May 19, 2020, https://www.washingtonpost.
     com/climate-environment/2020/05/19/greenhouse-emissions-
     coronavirus.

4.   Lauri Myllyvira, "Analysis: Coronavirus Temporarily Reduced China's
     CO_2 Emissions by a Quarter," *Carbon Brief,* February 19, 2020, https://
     www.carbonbrief.org/analysis-coronavirus-has-temporarily-reduced-
     chinas-co2-emissions-by-a-quarter.

5.   Martin Brudermüller, Climate Protection, interview by BASF, June 3,
     2019, https://www.basf.com/us/en/who-we-are/sustainability/whats-new/
     sustainability-news/2019/climate-protection-interview-with-Martin-
     Brudermueller.html.

6.   UN General Assembly, Resolution 43/53, Protection of Global Climate for
     Present and Future Generations of Mankind, A/RES/43/53 (December 6,
     1988), https://www.ipcc.ch/site/assets/uploads/2019/02/UNGA43-53.pdf.

7.   "Climate Change 2014: AR5 Synthesis Report" (Geneva:
     Intergovernmental Panel on Climate Change, 2014), https://www.ipcc.ch/
     report/ar5/syr.

8.   Chelsea Harvey, "CO_2 Emissions Reached an All-Time High in 2018,"
     Scientific American, December 6, 2018, https://www.scientificamerican.
     com/article/co2-emissions-reached-an-all-time-high-in-2018.

9.   Yossi Sheffi, "Climate Change: The Real Inconvenient Truth,"
     Management and Business Review 1 (forthcoming).

10. Melanie Curtin, "73 Percent of Millennials Are Willing to Spend More
     Money on This 1 Type of Product," *Inc.,* March 30, 2018, https://www.
     inc.com/melanie-curtin/73-percent-of-millennials-are-willing-to-spend-
     more-money-on-this-1-type-of-product.html.

11. Gregory Unruh, "No, Consumers Will Not Pay More for Green," *Forbes,*
     July 28, 2011, https://www.forbes.com/sites/csr/2011/07/28/no-consumers-
     will-not-pay-more-for-green.

12. Jonas Lehmann and Yossi Sheffi, "Consumers' (Not So) Green Purchase
     Behavior," *Journal of Marketing Development and Competitiveness* 14, no. 4
     (forthcoming).

13. Hal Bernton, "Washington State Voters Reject Carbon-Fee Initiative,"
     Seattle Times, November 6, 2018, https://www.seattletimes.com/seattle-
     news/politics/voters-rejecting-carbon-fee-in-first-day-returns.

14. Pádraig Collins, "How Not to Introduce a Carbon Tax: The Australian Experience," *Irish Times*, January 3, 2019, https://www.irishtimes.com/news/environment/how-not-to-introduce-a-carbon-tax-the-australian-experience-1.3746214.

15. "Violence Flares as Yellow Vests Mark One Year," *BBC News*, November 16, 2019, https://www.bbc.com/news/world-europe-50447733.

16. Robert P. Murphy, "Plastic Bans Are Symbolism Over Substance," *Institute for Energy Research Blog*, July 24, 2019, https://www.instituteforenergyresearch.org/regulation/plastic-bans-are-symbolism-over-substance.

17. Rob Picheta, "McDonald's New Paper Straws Aren't Recyclable — But Its Axed Plastic Ones Were," *CNN Business*, August 5, 2019, https://www.cnn.com/2019/08/05/business/mcdonalds-paper-straws-recyclable-scli-gbr-intl/index.html.

18. John Tierney, "Plastic Bags Help the Environment," *Wall Street Journal*, February 18, 2020, https://www.wsj.com/articles/plastic-bags-help-the-environment-11582048449.

19. BlackRock Inc. to BlackRock clients, "Sustainability as BlackRock's New Standard for Investing," 2020, https://www.blackrock.com/uk/individual/blackrock-client-letter.

20. Owen Walker and Attracta Mooney, "BlackRock Seeks to Regain Lost Ground in Climate Fight," *Financial Times*, January 14, 2020, https://www.ft.com/content/36282d86-36e4-11ea-a6d3-9a26f8c3cba4.

21. Attracta Mooney, "BlackRock Accused of Climate Change Hypocrisy," *Financial Times*, May 17, 2020, https://www.ft.com/content/0e489444-2783-4f6e-a006-aa8126d2ff46.

22. World Bank, "Nearly Half the World Lives on Less than $5.50 a Day," news release no. 2019/044/DEC-GPV, October 17, 2018, https://www.worldbank.org/en/news/press-release/2018/10/17/nearly-half-the-world-lives-on-less-than-550-a-day.

23. "How CEOs See Today's Coronavirus World," *Wall Street Journal*, June 11, 2020, https://www.wsj.com/articles/how-ceos-see-todays-coronavirus-world-11587720600.

24. Lisa Friedman and Keith Bradsher, "China's Emissions: More Than U.S. Plus Europe, and Still Rising," *New York Times*, January 25, 2018, https://www.nytimes.com/2018/01/25/business/china-davos-climate-change.html.

25. Karl Mathiesen, "Coal to Power India for 'Decades to Come', Says Government Planning Body," *Climate Home News,* August 28, 2017, https://www.climatechangenews.com/2017/08/28/coal-power-india-decades-come-says-government-planning-body.

26. Sushmita Patthak, "With Coronavirus Lockdown, India's Cities See Clear Blue Skies As Air Pollution Drops," *NPR,* April 10, 2020, https://www.npr.org/sections/coronavirus-live-updates/2020/04/10/831592401/with-coronavirus-lockdown-indias-cities-see-clear-blue-skies-as-air-pollution-dr.

27. Matt McGrath, "Climate Change and Coronavirus: Five Charts about the Biggest Carbon Crash," *BBC News,* May 6, 2020, https://www.bbc.com/news/science-environment-52485712.

28. "Employment Outlook 2020: Facing the Jobs Crisis," Organisation for Economic Co-Operation and Development, 2020, http://www.oecd.org/employment-outlook/#report.

29. European Commission, "Summer 2020 Economic Forecast: An Even Deeper Recession with Wider Divergences," news release no. IP/20/1269, July 7, 2020, https://ec.europa.eu/commission/presscorner/detail/en/ip_20_1269.

30. Liz Alderman and Matina Stevis-Gridneff, "The Pandemic's Economic Damage Is Growing," *New York Times,* July 7, 2020, https://www.nytimes.com/2020/07/07/business/EU-OECD-coronavirus-economic-reports.html.

31. Ursula von der Leyen, "Statement by Ursula von Der Leyen, President of the EC, on the Role of the European Green Deal in the Economic Recovery," European Commission, April 28, 2020, https://audiovisual.ec.europa.eu/en/video/I-190013.

32. von der Leyen.

33. Steven Erlanger, "Will the Coronavirus Crisis Trump the Climate Crisis?," *New York Times,* May 11, 2020, https://www.nytimes.com/2020/05/09/world/europe/will-the-coronavirus-crisis-trump-the-climate-crisis.html.

34. Ronald Bailey, "Biden's New Green New Deal Is the Same as the Old Green New Deal," *Reason,* July 16, 2020, https://reason.com/2020/07/16/bidens-new-green-new-deal-is-the-same-as-the-old-green-new-deal.

35. Erlanger, "Will the Coronavirus Crisis Trump the Climate Crisis?"

36. Bryan Brammer, "Biden: Only 9 Years Left to Save Earth from Climate Change," *Disrn* (blog), July 15, 2020, https://disrn.com/news/biden-only-9-years-left-to-save-earth-from-climate-change.

37. "Global Warming of 1.5 °C," Intergovernmental Panel on Climate Change, 2020, https://www.ipcc.ch/sr15.

38. Bailey, "Biden's Green New Deal."

39. Zeke Hausfather (@hausfath), "Climate change is a problem of degrees, not thresholds. We shouldn't give up hope if reducing emissions takes longer than we'd like. Indeed, in some ways action becomes all the more important the longer we delay, as the marginal impact of our emissions increases," Twitter, July 24, 2020, 11:47 a.m., https://twitter.com/hausfath/status/1154055387001307147.

40. Erlanger, "Will the Coronavirus Crisis Trump the Climate Crisis?"

41. Drew DeSilver, "Renewable Energy Is Growing Fast in the U.S., but Fossil Fuels Still Dominate," *Fact Tank* (blog), Pew Research Center, January 15, 2020, https://www.pewresearch.org/fact-tank/2020/01/15/renewable-energy-is-growing-fast-in-the-u-s-but-fossil-fuels-still-dominate.

42. Mary Hoff, "8 Ways to Sequester Carbon to Avoid Climate Catastrophe," *EcoWatch*, July 19, 2017, https://www.ecowatch.com/carbon-sequestration-2461971411.html.

43. Thomas L. Friedman, "Coronavirus Showed How Globalization Broke the World," *New York Times*, May 30, 2020, https://www.nytimes.com/2020/05/30/opinion/sunday/coronavirus-globalization.html.

44. Reuters, "China to Strengthen Global Cooperation in COVID-19 Vaccine Trials," *Reuters*, June 7, 2020, https://www.reuters.com/article/us-health-coronavirus-china-idUSKBN23E02Z.

45. Sam Fleming, Mehreen Khan, and Jim Brunsden, "EU Recovery Fund: How the Plan Will Work," *Financial Times*, July 21, 2020, https://www.ft.com/content/2b69c9c4-2ea4-4635-9d8a-1b67852c0322.

46. Solemn Declaration on European Union, European Council, Jun. 19, 1983, Bull. EC 6-1983.

47. Fitch Ratings, "EU Recovery Fund Is a Step Towards a More Resilient Eurozone," news release, July 23, 2020, https://www.fitchratings.com/research/sovereigns/eu-recovery-fund-is-step-towards-more-resilient-eurozone-23-07-2020.

48.   Daniel R. Coats, "Statement for the Record to the Senate Senate
       Committee on Intelligence: Worldwide Threat Assesment of The U.S.
       Intelligence Community" (Office of the Director of National Intelligence,
       January 29, 2019), https://www.dni.gov/files/ODNI/documents/2019-ATA-
       SFR---SSCI.pdf.

Chapter 21: Government and the Post-Covid-19 Economy

1.   "New Deal Programs," Living New Deal, Department of Geography at
       the University of California, Berkeley, accessed August 27, 2020, https://
       livingnewdeal.org/what-was-the-new-deal/programs.

2.   "World War II: Causes (1919–1939)" (Fairfax County (VA) Public
       Schools High School Social Studies, 2014), https://www.lcps.org/cms/lib/
       VA01000195/Centricity/Domain/10599/Causes%20of%20WWII.pdf.

3.   John B. Emerson, "The Importance of a Rules-Based International
       Order" (14th Berlin Security Conference, Berlin, November 17, 2015),
       https://de.usembassy.gov/the-importance-of-a-rules-based-international-
       order.

4.   John McCormick and Gerald F. Seib, "Coronavirus Means the Era of
       Big Government Is...Back," *Wall Street Journal,* April 26, 2020, https://
       www.wsj.com/articles/coronavirus-means-the-era-of-big-government-
       isback-11587923184.

5.   Consumer Financial Protection Bureau, "Mortgage and Housing
       Assistance during the Coronavirus National Emergency," accessed
       August 27, 2020, https://www.consumerfinance.gov/coronavirus/
       mortgage-and-housing-assistance.

6.   Erin Duffin, "Value of COVID-19 Stimulus Packages in the G20 as Share
       of GDP 2020," Statista, August 12, 2020, https://www.statista.com/
       statistics/1107572/covid-19-value-g20-stimulus-packages-share-gdp.

7.   "Rough Sleepers in London Given Hotel Rooms," *BBC News,* March 21,
       2020, https://www.bbc.com/news/uk-england-london-51987345.

8.   William Pearse, "How COVID-19 Could Change the Role of
       Government," *INOMICS (blog),* April 28, 2020, https://inomics.com/blog/
       how-covid-19-could-change-the-role-of-government-1459149.

9.   Robert P. Murphy, "The Fed and the Ratchet Effect," *Mises Daily Articles
       (blog),* Mises Institute, September 6, 2010, https://mises.org/library/fed-
       and-ratchet-effect.

10.   Zvi Horacio Hercowitz and Michel Strawczynnski, "Cyclical Ratcheting
       in Government Spending: Evidence from the OECD," *Review of*

Economics and Statistics 86, no. 1 (February 2004): 353–361, https://doi.
org/10.1162/003465304323023868.

11. "Little Public Support for Reductions in Federal Spending" (Washington,
     D.C.: Pew Research Center, April 11, 2019), https://www.pewresearch.
     org/politics/2019/04/11/little-public-support-for-reductions-in-federal-
     spending.

12. James Crabtree et al., "How the Coronavirus Pandemic Will Permanently
     Expand Government Powers," *Foreign Policy*, May 16, 2020, https://
     foreignpolicy.com/2020/05/16/future-government-powers-coronavirus-
     pandemic.

13. "Reg Stats," George Washington University Center for Regulatory
     Studies, accessed August 27, 2020, https://regulatorystudies.columbian.
     gwu.edu/reg-stats.

14. "The History of the European Union," European Union, June 16, 2016,
     https://europa.eu/european-union/about-eu/history_en.

15. Dimiter Toshkov, "55 Years of European Legislation," online
     presentation, http://www.dimiter.eu/Eurlex.html.

16. "A Crisis Like No Other, An Uncertain Recovery," *World Economic
     Outlook Update* (Washington, D.C.: Interrnational Monetary Fund, June
     2020), https://www.imf.org/en/Publications/WEO/Issues/2020/06/24/
     WEOUpdateJune2020.

17. John P. Ehrenberg et al., "Strategies Supporting the Prevention and
     Control of Neglected Tropical Diseases during and beyond the COVID-19
     Pandemic," *Infectious Diseases of Poverty* 9, no. 86 (July 10, 2020), https://
     doi.org/10.1186/s40249-020-00701-7.

18. Apoorva Mandavilli, "'The Biggest Monster' Is Spreading. And It's Not
     the Coronavirus," *New York Times*, August 3, 2020, https://www.nytimes.
     com/2020/08/03/health/coronavirus-tuberculosis-aids-malaria.html.

19. Louise Sheiner and Sage Belz, "How Will the Coronavirus Affect
     State and Local Government Budgets?," *Brookings* (blog), Brookings
     Institution, March 23, 2020, https://www.brookings.edu/blog/up-
     front/2020/03/23/how-will-the-coronavirus-affect-state-and-local-
     government-budgets.

20. UN Department of Ecnomic and Social Affairs, "COVID-19 and Sovereign
     Debt," UN/DESA Policy Brief no. 72 (New York: United Nations, May 14,
     2020), https://www.un.org/development/desa/dpad/publication/un-desa-
     policy-brief-72-covid-19-and-sovereign-debt.

21.		Chris Giles and Robin Harding, "Richest Nations Face $17tn Government Debt Burden from Coronavirus," *Financial Times*, May 24, 2020, https://www.ft.com/content/66164bbc-40c7-4d91-a318-a0b4dbe4193e.

Part 6: The Next Opportunities

1.		"How CEOs See Today's Coronavirus World," *Wall Street Journal*, June 11, 2020, https://www.wsj.com/articles/how-ceos-see-todays-coronavirus-world-11587720600.

2.		Courtney Connley, "Why Many Employees Are Hoping to Work from Home Even after the Pandemic Is Over," *CNBC*, May 4, 2020, https://www.cnbc.com/2020/05/04/why-many-employees-are-hoping-to-work-from-home-even-after-the-pandemic-is-over.html.

Chapter 22: More E-Commerce

1.		Courtney Connley, "Why Many Employees Are Hoping to Work from Home Even after the Pandemic Is Over," *CNBC*, May 4, 2020, https://www.cnbc.com/2020/05/04/why-many-employees-are-hoping-to-work-from-home-even-after-the-pandemic-is-over.html.

2.		Connley.

3.		Heather Kelly, "Small Businesses Turned to Technology to Survive the Pandemic. But It May Not Be Enough," *Washington Post*, June 22, 2020, https://www.washingtonpost.com/technology/2020/06/22/small-business-tech-pandemic.

4.		Sapna Maheshwari, "Lord & Taylor Files for Bankruptcy as Retail Collapses Pile Up," *New York Times*, August 2, 2020, https://www.nytimes.com/2020/08/02/business/Lord-and-Taylor-Bankruptcy.html.

5.		Suzanne Kapner, "Once the Innovators, Department Stores Fight to Stay Alive," *Wall Street Journal*, August 4, 2020, https://www.wsj.com/articles/once-the-innovators-department-stores-fight-to-stay-alive-11596533403.

6.		Daniela Santamariña, Abha Bhattarai, and Kevin Uhrmacher, "The Iconic Brands That Could Disappear Because of Coronavirus," *Washington Post*, May 8, 2020, https://www.washingtonpost.com/business/2020/04/29/which-iconic-brands-could-disappear-because-coronavirus.

7.		Sarah E. Wyeth, "Shakeout In Retail, Restaurant Sectors Begins With J. Crew" (New York: S&P Global Ratings, May 4, 2020), https://www.spglobal.com/ratings/en/research/articles/200504-shakeout-in-retail-restaurant-sectors-begins-with-j-crew-11472558.

8. Santamariña, Bhattarai, and Uhrmacher, "The Iconic Brands That Could Disappear."

9. "The Running List of 2020 Retail Bankruptcies," *Retail Dive,* August 17, 2020, https://www.retaildive.com/news/the-running-list-of-2020-retail-bankruptcies/571159.

10. Nicole Serino and Sudeep K. Kesh, "Credit Trends: Transportation Leads Distress Ratios As Demand Collapses Across U.S. Sectors" (New York: S&P Global Ratings, May 26, 2020), https://www.spglobal.com/ratings/en/research/articles/200526-credit-trends-transportation-leads-distress-ratios-as-demand-collapses-across-u-s-sectors-11504506.

11. "How Did Alibaba Help Retailer Lin Qingxuan Cope with the Coronavirus Outbreak?," Alibaba Cloud (blog), March 5, 2020, https://www.alibabacloud.com/blog/how-did-alibaba-help-retailer-lin-qingxuan-cope-with-the-coronavirus-outbreak_595950.

12. Martin Reeves et al., "How Chinese Companies Have Responded to Coronavirus," *Harvard Business Review,* March 10, 2020, https://hbr.org/2020/03/how-chinese-companies-have-responded-to-coronavirus.

13. Joelle Ayala, "5 ECommerce Tips to Increase Sales during COVID-19," *Happy Returns* (blog), March 27, 2020, https://retailers.happyreturns.com/blog/5-ecommerce-tips-to-increase-sales-during-covid-19.

14. Iris Ouyang, "China Cosmetics Sales Rebound in March as Coronavirus Outbreak Proves to Be a Temporary Setback," *South China Morning Post,* April 7, 2020, https://www.scmp.com/business/article/3078682/china-cosmetics-sales-rebound-march-coronavirus-outbreak-proves-be.

15. "How Did Alibaba Help Retailer Lin Qingxuan Cope with the Coronavirus Outbreak?"

16. Robin Givhan, "Fashion Was Broken Even before the Pandemic. A Reboot Could Be Just What It Needs," *Washington Post,* June 15, 2020, https://www.washingtonpost.com/lifestyle/style/fashion-retail-business-bankrupt-stores/2020/06/12/463572b0-9c56-11ea-ac72-3841fcc9b35f_story.html.

17. "Sephora Virtual Artist," Sephora, accessed August 30, 2020, https://sephoravirtualartist.com.

18. Walmart Inc., "Walmart Q1 FY21 Earnings Release," May 19, 2020, https://corporate.walmart.com/media-library/document/q1-fy21-earnings-release/_proxyDocument?id=00000172-29ed-d3ff-a3f6-bded2c350000.

19. Nathaniel Meyersohn, "Target's Digital Sales Climb 141%," *CNN*, May 20, 2020, https://www.cnn.com/2020/05/20/business/target-earnings-coronavirus/index.html.

20. Dennis Flynn, Senior Director, Supply Chain and Inventory Management, Walmart eCommerce, interview by Yossi Sheffi, June 12, 2020.

21. Adobe Analytics, "Adobe Digital Economy Index" (San Jose, Calif.: Adobe Inc., July 2020), https://www.adobe.com/content/dam/www/us/en/experience-cloud/digital-insights/pdfs/adobe_analytics-digital-economy-index-2020.pdf.

22. Gregory Magana, "Almost 70% of US Consumers Use BOPIS," *Business Insider,* February 22, 2019, https://www.businessinsider.com/us-consumers-use-buy-online-pickup-in-store-2019-2.

23. Walmart Inc., "Walmart Introduces Express Delivery," news release, April 30, 2020, https://corporate.walmart.com/newsroom/2020/04/30/walmart-introduces-express-delivery.

24. Esther Fung and Sebastian Herrera, "Amazon and Mall Operator Look at Turning Sears, J.C. Penney Stores Into Fulfillment Centers," *Wall Street Journal,* August 9, 2020, https://www.wsj.com/articles/amazon-and-giant-mall-operator-look-at-turning-sears-j-c-penney-stores-into-fulfillment-centers-11596992863.

25. Lisa D'Ambrosio and Alexis Bateman, "Grocery Shopping Habits in the US," Covid-19 Generational and Life Style Study (Cambridge, Mass.: MIT AgeLab, August 2020).

26. Tyler Clifford, "'It Was Suddenly Cyber Monday' — Etsy CEO Says Sales Spiked 79% in April," *CNBC,* May 7, 2020, https://www.cnbc.com/2020/05/07/etsy-ceo-says-sales-jumped-79percent-in-april-likens-it-to-cyber-monday.html.

27. "Etsy, Inc. (ETSY) CEO Joshua Silverman on Q1 2020 Results - Earnings Call Transcript," Seeking Alpha, May 7, 2020, https://seekingalpha.com/article/4343941-etsy-inc-etsy-ceo-joshua-silverman-on-q1-2020-results-earnings-call-transcript.

28. "Etsy, Inc. (ETSY) CEO Joshua Silverman on Q1 2020 Results - Earnings Call Transcript."

29. Teresa Rivas, "Mom and Pop Retailers Are Struggling During the Lockdowns. Big Box Giants Are Thriving," *Barron's Magazine,* May 24, 2020, https://www.barrons.com/articles/retail-giants-will-keep-gaining-ground-in-a-post-coronavirus-world-51590193284.

30. Bridget Goldschmidt, "C&S, Instacart Offer E-Commerce Solutions to Independent Grocers," *Progressive Grocer,* June 4, 2020, https://progressivegrocer.com/cs-instacart-offer-e-commerce-solutions-independent-grocers.

31. Alexandra Alter, "Bookstores Are Struggling. Is a New E-Commerce Site the Answer?," *New York Times,* June 16, 2020, https://www.nytimes.com/2020/06/16/books/bookshop-bookstores-coronavirus.html.

32. Sam Dean et al., "What a Reopened California Will Look like — and Businesses' Odds of Survival," *Los Angeles Times,* May 6, 2020, https://www.latimes.com/business/story/2020-05-06/reopening-economy-restaurants-retail-movies-sports.

33. Armando Roggio, "Facebook Shops Are an Ecommerce Game Changer," *Practical Ecommerce,* May 22, 2020, https://www.practicalecommerce.com/facebook-shops-are-an-ecommerce-game-changer.

34. Natalie Wong, "Warehouse Giant Seeing Insatiable Demand From Amazon, Walmart," *Bloomberg,* May 5, 2020, https://www.bloomberg.com/news/articles/2020-05-05/warehouse-giant-seeing-insatiable-demand-from-amazon-walmart.

35. Kate Conger and Erin Griffith, "The Results Are In for the Sharing Economy. They Are Ugly," *New York Times,* May 7, 2020, https://www.nytimes.com/2020/05/07/technology/the-results-are-in-for-the-sharing-economy-they-are-ugly.html.

36. Mike Isaac, Erin Griffith, and Adam Satariano, "Uber Buys Postmates for $2.65 Billion," *New York Times,* July 5, 2020, https://www.nytimes.com/2020/07/05/technology/uber-postmates-deal.html.

37. Lizette Chapman, "Uber Eats Ditches Seven Countries, Subsidiary Careem Cuts Staff," *Bloomberg,* May 4, 2020, https://www.bloomberg.com/news/articles/2020-05-04/uber-eats-ditches-seven-countries-where-food-delivery-lags?sref=KgV4umfb.

38. Jane Black and Brent Cunningham, "The Pandemic Is Changing How We Eat. But Not for the Better," *Washington Post,* May 7, 2020, https://www.washingtonpost.com/outlook/the-pandemic-is-changing-how-we-eat-but-not-for-the-better/2020/05/07/5e4623e6-906b-11ea-a9c0-73b93422d691_story.html.

39. Natasha Mascarenhas, "Instacart Announces New COVID-19 Policies and Plans to Hire 250,000 More Shoppers," *TechCrunch* (blog), April 23, 2020, https://social.techcrunch.com/2020/04/23/instacart-announces-new-covid-19-policies-and-plans-to-hire-250000-more-shoppers.

40. Deena M. Amato-McCoy, "Study: Consumers' Shipping Expectations Higher than Ever," *Chain Store Age*, June 27, 2017, https://chainstoreage.com/operations/study-consumers-shipping-expectations-higher-ever.

41. Heather Lalley, "Chipotle Fast Tracks Its Drive-Thrus," *Restaurant Business*, July 15, 2020, https://www.restaurantbusinessonline.com/operations/chipotle-fast-tracks-its-drive-thrus.

42. "curbFlow," curbFlow, accessed August 31, 2020, https://curbflow.com.

43. Brian Barth, "Curb Control," *Planning*, June 2019, https://www.planning.org/planning/2019/jun/curbcontrol.

Chapter 23: Remaking the City

1. Amy Gamerman, "Wealthy City Dwellers Seek Refuge From Coronavirus at Remote Ranches," *Wall Street Journal*, April 8, 2020, https://www.wsj.com/articles/wealthy-city-dwellers-seek-refuge-from-coronavirus-at-remote-ranches-11586373662.

2. Marie Patino, "Urban Living Might Just Survive Coronavirus," *Bloomberg*, June 15, 2020, https://www.bloomberg.com/graphics/2020-coronavirus-dash.

3. "Big Offices May Be in the Past, Says Barclays Boss," *BBC News*, April 29, 2020, https://www.bbc.com/news/business-52467965.

4. Uri Berliner, "Get A Comfortable Chair: Permanent Work From Home Is Coming," *NPR*, June 22, 2020, https://www.npr.org/2020/06/22/870029658/get-a-comfortable-chair-permanent-work-from-home-is-coming.

5. Lee Clifford, "Working from Home Is Going So Well That This Fortune 100 Company Is Going to Keep Doing It—Permanently," *Fortune*, May 11, 2020, https://fortune.com/2020/05/11/permanent-work-from-home-coronavirus-nationwide-fortune-100.

6. Kevin Rebong, "'Much Less Real Estate': Morgan Stanley CEO On Firm's Future," *The Real Deal*, April 17, 2020, https://therealdeal.com/2020/04/17/morgan-stanley-on-firms-future-much-less-real-estate.

7. Kim Peterson, "Companies Are Packing Workers in like Sardines," *CBS News*, March 9, 2015, https://www.cbsnews.com/news/companies-are-packing-workers-in-like-sardines.

8. Laura Bliss, "Elevators Changed Cities. Will Coronavirus Change Elevators?," *Bloomberg*, May 21, 2020, https://www.bloomberg.com/news/articles/2020-05-21/the-fate-of-elevators-in-the-post-pandemic-city.

9.   Anjelica Tan, "Americans Leave Large Cities for Suburban Areas and Rural Towns," *The Hill,* July 5, 2020, https://thehill.com/opinion/finance/505944-americans-leave-large-cities-for-suburban-areas-and-rural-towns.

10.   Marco della Cava, "San Francisco Is Losing Residents Because It's Too Expensive for Nearly Everyone," *USA Today,* October 19, 2019, https://www.usatoday.com/story/news/nation/2019/10/19/california-housing-crisis-residents-flee-san-francisco-because-costs/3985196002.

11.   Diana Olick, "Homebuilders Just Saw the Strongest June Sales since the Last Housing Boom, as Pandemic Pushes More Buyers to the Suburbs," *CNBC,* July 13, 2020, https://www.cnbc.com/2020/07/13/homebuilders-just-saw-the-strongest-june-sales-since-the-last-housing-boom.html.

12.   Michael Wilson, "The Virus Turns Midtown Into a Ghost Town, Causing an Economic Crisis," *New York Times,* July 26, 2020, https://www.nytimes.com/2020/07/26/nyregion/nyc-coronavirus-time-life-building.html.

13.   Rachel Siegel, "Hard-Hit Retailers Projected to Shutter as Many as 25,000 Stores This Year, Mostly in Malls," *Washington Post,* June 9, 2020, https://www.washingtonpost.com/business/2020/06/09/retail-store-closure-mall.

14.   Yelp Inc., "Increased Consumer Interest in May Correlates with COVID-19 Hot Spots in June, According to the Yelp Economic Average," Yelp Economic Average, June 2020, https://www.yelpeconomicaverage.com/yea-q2-2020.

15.   Liam O'Connell, "Number of Retail Stores in the U.S. 2019," Statista, July 22, 2020, https://www.statista.com/statistics/887112/brick-and-mortar-store-count-us-by-channel.

16.   Lauren Thomas, "25,000 Stores Are Predicted to Close in 2020, as the Coronavirus Pandemic Accelerates Industry Upheaval," *CNBC,* June 9, 2020, https://www.cnbc.com/2020/06/09/coresight-predicts-record-25000-retail-stores-will-close-in-2020.html.

17.   Margaret J. Krauss, "One-Way Sidewalks And Parking Lot Dining Rooms: Is This The Future?," *NPR,* May 8, 2020, https://www.npr.org/sections/coronavirus-live-updates/2020/05/08/852222980/one-way-sidewalks-and-parking-lot-dining-rooms-is-this-the-future.

18.   Justin Gillis and Heather Thompson, "Take Back the Streets From the Automobile," *New York Times,* June 20, 2020, https://www.nytimes.com/2020/06/20/opinion/pandemic-automobile-cities.html.

19.   Susanne Rust, "Bicycles Have Enjoyed a Boom during the Pandemic. Will It Last as Car Traffic Resumes?," *Los Angeles Times,* June 25, 2020, https://www.latimes.com/california/story/2020-06-25/bicycle-business-is-exploding-during-covid-19-will-it-last.

20.   Michael Laris, "Cities, Including D.C, Are Closing Streets to Make Way for Restaurants and Pedestrians," *Washington Post,* May 29, 2020, https://www.washingtonpost.com/local/trafficandcommuting/cities-are-closing-streets-to-make-way-for-restaurants-and-pedestrians/2020/05/25/1f1af634-9b73-11ea-ad09-8da7ec214672_story.html.

21.   Christopher Mims, "The Next Phase of the Retail Apocalypse: Stores Reborn as E-Commerce Warehouses," *Wall Street Journal,* July 18, 2020, https://www.wsj.com/articles/the-next-phase-of-the-retail-apocalypse-stores-reborn-as-e-commerce-warehouses-11595044859.

22.   Paul Ziobro, "FedEx, Strained by Coronavirus, Caps How Much Retailers Can Ship From Stores," *Wall Street Journal,* May 14, 2020, https://www.wsj.com/articles/fedex-strained-by-coronavirus-caps-how-much-retailers-can-ship-from-stores-11589454006.

23.   Krishna Thakker, "Raley's Opens 'Dark' Store in Response to COVID-19," *Grocery Dive,* June 22, 2020, https://www.grocerydive.com/news/raleys-opens-dark-store-in-response-to-covid-19/580228.

24.   Mims, "Stores Reborn as E-Commerce Warehouses."

Chapter 24: And the Winner Is...The Great Unknown

1.   Daniel Roberts, "Amid Coronavirus, Walmart Says It's Seeing Increased Sales of Tops — But Not Bottoms," *Yahoo Finance,* March 26, 2020, https://finance.yahoo.com/news/amid-coronavirus-walmart-says-its-seeing-increased-sales-of-tops-but-not-bottoms-202959379.html.

2.   Monica Watrous, "Hershey Preparing for a Post-Pandemic World," *Food Business News,* April 23, 2020, https://www.foodbusinessnews.net/articles/15890-hershey-preparing-for-a-post-pandemic-world?v=preview.

3.   Archie Mitchell, "Deodorant Sales Fall Due to Social Distancing but Locked down Consumers Send Ice-Cream Sales Soaring, Says Unilever," *MarketWatch,* July 23, 2020, https://www.marketwatch.com/story/deodorant-sales-fall-due-to-social-distancing-but-locked-down-consumers-send-ice-cream-sales-soaring-says-unilever-11595532255.

4.   Tom Ryan, "Will Dollar Stores Be the Biggest Post-COVID-19 Winners?," *RetailWire* (blog), June 2, 2020, https://retailwire.com/discussion/will-dollar-stores-be-the-biggest-post-covid-19-winners.

5. Raj Chetty et al., "How Did COVID-19 and Stabilization Policies Affect Spending and Employment? A New Real-Time Economic Tracker Based on Private Sector Data," working paper, NBER Working Paper Series no. 27431 (Cambridge, Mass.: National Bureau of Economic Research, June 2020), https://www.nber.org/papers/w27431.

6. LVMH Moët Hennessy Louis Vuitton, "LVMH Shows Good Resilience in the First Half of 2020," news release, July 27, 2020, https://www.lvmh.com/news-documents/press-releases/lvmh-shows-good-resilience-in-the-first-half-of-2020.

7. Maggie Fitzgerald, "U.S. Savings Rate Hits Record 33% as Coronavirus Causes Americans to Stockpile Cash, Curb Spending," *CNBC*, May 29, 2020, https://www.cnbc.com/2020/05/29/us-savings-rate-hits-record-33percent-as-coronavirus-causes-americans-to-stockpile-cash-curb-spending.html.

8. Emma Cosgrove, "Coca-Cola, Mondelez Trim SKUs as CPGs Tackle Pandemic Stresses," *Supply Chain Dive*, June 2, 2020, https://www.supplychaindive.com/news/coronavirus-supply-chains-SKUs-pandemic-Mondelez-Procter-Gamble-Coca-Cola/579017.

9. Annie Gasparro, Jacob Bunge, and Heather Haddon, "Why the American Consumer Has Fewer Choices—Maybe for Good," *Wall Street Journal*, June 27, 2020, https://www.wsj.com/articles/why-the-american-consumer-has-fewer-choicesmaybe-for-good-11593230443.

10. "Procter & Gamble Co. (PG) Q3 2020 Earnings Call Transcript," The Motley Fool, April 17, 2020, https://www.fool.com/earnings/call-transcripts/2020/04/17/procter-gamble-co-pg-q3-2020-earnings-call-transcr.aspx.

11. Gasparro, Bunge, and Haddon, "Why the American Consumer Has Fewer Choices."

12. Mary Ellen Shoup, "Mondelēz to Cut SKUs and 'significantly' Reduce Innovation Projects: 'We Are Working on Making Our Business Simpler,'" *FoodNavigator-USA*, April 30, 2020, https://www.foodnavigator-usa.com/Article/2020/04/30/Mondelez-to-reduce-SKUs-and-innovation-projects-We-are-working-on-making-our-business-simpler.

13. Jeff Gelski, "Mondelez to Reduce Number of SKUs by 25%," *Food Business News*, July 29, 2020, https://www.foodbusinessnews.net/articles/16515-mondelez-to-reduce-number-of-skus-by-25?v=preview.

14. Cathy Hart, "The Retail Accordion and Assortment Strategies: An Exploratory Study," *International Review of Retail, Distribution and Consumer Research* 9, no. 2 (1999): 111–126, https://doi.org/10.1080/095939699342598.

15. Sergei Klebnikov, "Best Buy Earnings Fall, Target Sales Soar: Here's How All The Big Retailers Fared In The First Quarter," *Forbes,* May 21, 2020, https://www.forbes.com/sites/sergeiklebnikov/2020/05/21/best-buy-earnings-tank-target-sales-soar-heres-how-all-the-big-retailers-fared-in-the-first-quarter/#382eb2245b34.

16. Mike Snider, "Despite Coronavirus Pandemic, Consumers Still Turned on by Big-Screen TVs," *USA Today,* July 20, 2020, https://www.usatoday.com/story/tech/2020/07/20/coronavirus-effect-big-tvs-have-helped-some-homes-navigate-pandemic/5432582002.

17. Tiffany Kary, "Stockpiling Germaphobes Ignite Unlikely Boom: Appliances," *Bloomberg,* May 13, 2020, https://www.bloomberg.com/news/articles/2020-05-13/deep-freezers-bread-makers-sell-out-in-coronavirus-spending-boom.

18. Briann Sozzi, "Mattress Sales Awakened by Need to Feel Cozy and Comfortable at Home during Coronavirus," *Yahoo News,* May 26, 2020, https://www.yahoo.com/now/mattress-sales-awakened-by-need-to-feel-cozy-and-comfortable-at-home-during-coronavirus-121258107.html.

19. Kate Knibbs, "Bidets Gain U.S. Popularity During The Coronavirus Crisis," *NPR,* March 22, 2020, https://www.npr.org/2020/03/22/819891957/bidets-gain-u-s-popularity-during-the-coronavirus-crisis.

20. Elizabeth Crawford, "HelloFresh, Blue Apron See Bump in Sales as Americans Turn to Meal Kits during the Pandemic," *FoodNavigator-USA,* May 5, 2020, https://www.foodnavigator-usa.com/Article/2020/05/06/HelloFresh-Blue-Apron-see-bump-in-sales-as-Americans-turn-to-meal-kits-during-the-pandemic.

Chapter 25: Flexibility for the Future

1. Jeff Kotzen and Elyssa Kotzen, J.W. Lopes and New England Country Mart, interview by Yossi Sheffi, June 12, 2020.

2. Barbara Spector, "Family Creates New Business Line during COVID-19 Pandemic," *Family Business,* August 2020, https://www.familybusinessmagazine.com/jw-lopes.

3. Kotzen and Kotzen, J.W. Lopes and New England Country Mart.

4. Eric Westervelt, "As Food Supply Chain Breaks Down, Farm-To-Door CSAs Take Off," *Weekend Edition Sunday* (NPR, May 10, 2020), https://www.npr.org/2020/05/10/852512047/as-food-supply-chain-breaks-down-farm-to-door-csas-take-off.

5. Heather Kelly, "Small Businesses Turned to Technology to Survive the Pandemic. But It May Not Be Enough," *Washington Post*, June 22, 2020, https://www.washingtonpost.com/technology/2020/06/22/small-business-tech-pandemic.

6. Dave Wheeler, Chief Operating Officer, New Balance, interview by Yossi Sheffi, May 27, 2020.

7. New Balance, "Making PPE Face Masks," news release, June 9, 2020, https://www.newbalance.com/making-ppe-face-masks.

8. "How to Rebound Stronger from COVID-19: Resilience in Manufacturing and Supply Systems" (World Economic Forum, May 1, 2020), https://www.weforum.org/whitepapers/how-to-rebound-stronger-from-covid-19-resilience-in-manufacturing-and-supply-systems.

9. "FDA Efforts to Connect Manufacturers and Health Care Entities: The FDA, Department of Veterans Affairs, National Institutes of Health, and America Makes Form a COVID-19 Response Public-Private Partnership," Food and Drug Administration, June 18, 2020, https://www.fda.gov/emergency-preparedness-and-response/coronavirus-disease-2019-covid-19/fda-efforts-connect-manufacturers-and-health-care-entities-fda-department-veterans-affairs-national.

10. Food and Drug Administration, "FDA Efforts to Connect Manufacturers and Health Care Entities."

11. World Economic Forum, "How to Rebound Stronger from COVID-19."

12. Karl Siebrecht, Co-Founder & CEO of FLEXE, interview by Yossi Sheffi, June 2, 2020.

Chapter 26: Adversity and Strength Will Build the Future

1. "Timeline: Boeing 737 Max Jetliner Crashes and Aftermath," *Chicago Tribune*, October 14, 2019, https://www.chicagotribune.com/business/ct-biz-viz-boeing-737-max-crash-timeline-04022019-story.html.

2. Clare Duffy, "Jeff Bezos Tells Shareholders to 'take a Seat' as Company Manages Covid-19," *CNN*, April 30, 2020, https://www.cnn.com/2020/04/30/tech/amazon-earnings-coronavirus/index.html.

3. Levi Sumagaysay, "Amazon Reaches 1 Million Workers amid Pandemic Hiring Frenzy," *MarketWatch*, July 20, 2020, https://www.marketwatch.com/story/amazon-reaches-1-million-workers-as-pandemic-pushes-total-up-11596136565.

4. "Amazon Global Supply Chain and Fulfillment Center Network," MWPVL International, accessed September 5, 2020, https://www.mwpvl.com/html/amazon_com.html.

5. Eric Kulisch, "Amazon Air to Expand Fleet with 12 Freighters," *FreightWaves*, June 3, 2020, https://www.freightwaves.com/news/breaking-amazon-air-to-expand-fleet-with-12-freighters.

6. "Texas Instruments Inc. (TXN) Q1 2020 Earnings Call Transcript," The Motley Fool, April 21, 2020, https://www.fool.com/earnings/call-transcripts/2020/04/22/texas-instruments-inc-txn-q1-2020-earnings-call-tr.aspx.

7. Barrett Brunsman, "P&G Ramps Up to Meet 'Strong Demand,' CFO Says," *Cincinnati Business Courier*, June 11, 2020, https://www.bizjournals.com/cincinnati/news/2020/06/11/p-g-ramps-up-to-meet-strong-demand-cfo-says.html.

8. "Facebook Inc. (FB) Q1 2020 Earnings Call Transcript," The Motley Fool, April 29, 2020, https://www.fool.com/earnings/call-transcripts/2020/04/29/facebook-inc-fb-q1-2020-earnings-call-transcript.aspx.

9. "Chipotle Mexican Grill Inc. (CMG) Q1 2020 Earnings Call Transcript," The Motley Fool, April 21, 2020, https://www.fool.com/earnings/call-transcripts/2020/04/21/chipotle-mexican-grill-inc-cmg-q1-2020-earnings-ca.aspx.

10. Heather Lalley, "Chipotle Plots Its Post-Pandemic Expansion," *Restaurant Business*, April 21, 2020, https://www.restaurantbusinessonline.com/operations/chipotle-plots-its-post-pandemic-expansion.

11. James Davies and Pearl Agyemfra, "International Approaches to Covid-19 Job Retention and Wage Subsidy Schemes," *Lewis Silkin* (blog), Lewis Silkin LLP, May 7, 2020, https://www.lewissilkin.com/en/insights/international-approaches-to-covid-19-job-retention-and-wage-subsidy-schemes.